This book is dedicated to you,
and to all working parents.

It is also and always for
L, P, and M.
I love you.

CONTENTS

3. Parental Leave and the Return to Work 75

Planning your leave • Leave length: what if . . . ? • Creating an
effective transition and coverage plan • Staying in touch while
you're out • How to use leave when you're not the primary caregiver •
How to feel in charge of your career while away • Ways to make the
return to work easier • Owning your narrative • The one-month
check-in • Celebrating new achievements

4. The First Year 101

Establishing a Point of Control • Learning to make effective
transitions to and from work • Staying and feeling connected while
on the job • Creating a new daily schedule that works—for *you* •
Navigating the important Year One milestones • Remaining visible •
Taking charge of your performance review • Setbacks—and how to
overcome them

5. From Baby to Toddler to Little Kid 121

Making the most of care transitions • Bonding with your child
through activity • Harnessing the power of repetition and ritual •
Explaining work to very small children • Confronting the screen-
time dilemma • Still owning—and updating—your story •
Considering changes at work • Staying on the right path—for *you*

6. Expanding Your Family—If, When, and How 137

Considering the pros and cons • When you still can't decide •
What to know and do when moving from one child to two—
or more • Large-family strategies useful for *all* working parents

7. School 157

Why the start of school is hard, and how to make it easier •
Educating them at home—and every day • Developing a strong
relationship with your child's teacher(s) • Homework • After-school
activities • Talking with your manager and colleagues about school

PART TWO

Resources—and Smart Ways to Use Them

Making the Most of What You've Got When
Combining Career and Family

PART FOUR

Staying Well and Whole

Taking Good Care of Your Family—and Yourself—
While You're Hard at Work

PART FIVE

Your Family, Your Way

Special Tips—and Extra Encouragement—for Winning at
Workparenting in Any Family Structure

Conclusion: A New Template, All Our Own 505

Appendix: The Workparent Leader 509

Sensible advice for:
• Becoming a more workparent-friendly organization
• Setting up a working-parents network in your community
  or organization
• Managing workparents, day-to-day

A NOTE ON LANGUAGE

Workparent is an inclusive book. It recognizes that working parents come in all forms: male and female; biological and adoptive; single and partnered; gay and straight; from all regions, backgrounds, and beliefs; in every profession; and parenting children of different ages. Throughout, I've done my best to keep things editorially simple while using language that embraces that full, wonderful spectrum.

If you're an adult who holds responsibility for raising a child, you're the *parent*. Your spouse, life mate, or coparent is referred to as your *partner*. Parents, babies, children, managers, coworkers, and working-parent supporters appear alternately as *hes*, *shes*, and *theys*. The words *boss* and *manager* represent any workplace authority figure even if that person is a partner, investor, counterparty, or customer instead of a traditional boss. The language around sexual orientation and identity is still evolving; I've used the respectful abbreviation *LGBTQIA+* here. The term *foster parent* should be read to include traditional and interim foster parents, legal guardians, and kinship caregivers.

Throughout the book, you'll notice that the word *workparent* appears frequently and interchangeably with *working mother* or *father*. Workparent is the new, positive label for all of us who are working hard to earn a living and build our careers while raising children we love. It captures the beautiful and complex reality that each of us lives, day-to-day—as one whole, complete person performing two distinct and important roles.

I hope that as you read, you see yourself in these pages—and feel a welcome, respected, and essential part of the workparent community.

You Can Do This

Finding Success and Satisfaction as
a Working Mother or Father

You're a working parent or planning to become one. And you're feeling daunted, conflicted, exhausted—or all three—by what you're going through, or by what lies ahead.

How could you not? It's already hard to lead a healthy, full life *and* succeed on the job, much less build a long-term career. When you then also become a mother or father, and are raising children you love more than anything, it stretches you to extraordinary new limits: personal and professional, practical and emotional. It's *normal* to be overwhelmed.

But what if things could be different? Think what it would be like to have more confidence in your ability to combine work and family—and a clear, realistic view of how to do so over the next eighteen years. Imagine that instead of all this working-parent guilt and stress, you felt more capable, more calm. Picture your many working-parent questions being met with simple, straightforward answers, and having a thoughtful, experienced group of working mothers and fathers right beside you all along this route, ready to give advice and encouragement. Well, each of those things is possible—and they're what *Workparent* is all about.

This book is your guide to combining career and children. It covers what you need to know and do to be the professional, parent, and person you want to be from the day you find out you're expecting until the day your child leaves home.

In these pages, you'll get advice for handling practical challenges like planning your leave, finding great childcare, managing your packed calendar, advocating for advancement, getting the right kind of flexibility, even getting a healthful family dinner on the table after a long day of work. We'll also look at effective ways for navigating more-personal and -nuanced challenges, like dealing with difficult feelings and less-than-supportive coworkers; truly connecting with your kids when you do have time with them; or fitting parenting together with your professional ambitions (even when those two things seem fundamentally at odds). Whatever profession you're in or type of family you have, *Workparent* will help you move from enduring working parenthood to taking charge of it, and in your own, authentic way.

Does that sound too aspirational? Unrealistic, even? If that's what you're thinking, I welcome your skepticism. In fact, I used to share it.

Back when I worked as a corporate-careers and -leadership expert, the talented men and women I supported regularly confided in me: not only about their professional ambitions and on-the-job wins, stresses, and stumbles—but also about the tough time they were having working while raising kids. After my management seminars, participants would come up and ask how to squeeze child-related responsibilities onto their packed to-do lists. Normally poised, articulate professionals came to me panicked when they found out they were expecting but didn't know how to tell the boss. Once, during last-minute prep for an important meeting, the executive I was helping rehearse his pitch suddenly went quiet. His son had been sick, he said, and it was impossible to focus.

Of course, just like every other professional in my field, I'd been aware of the "work/life" issue for years. But because of my particular specialty and seat—doing one-on-one coaching for professionals who were really beginning to hit their stride in their careers, and doing that work as a behind-the-scenes insider in each organization—I had a up-close, nonretouched view of the problem, a view that few other people have. I saw all the annual performance reviews *and* spent hours with people trying to figure out how to do well at work while being loving, on-the-job parents. I'd finish up a "who should get promoted" discussion with senior leaders and then go straight into a coaching session with someone eager for promotion but worried that it meant even more time away from the kids. Managers told me about their high expectations for their people, and those same people told me about their lack of sleep and hunt for decent childcare.

Work/life? No—this wasn't an abstraction I was dealing with, or an issue that would fit neatly inside a single euphemistic label, and my coachees weren't numbers on a page. They were real individual human beings who, behind closed doors, talked with me about feeling tired, uncertain, and alone, who described loving their work and their kids at the same time but getting ground down trying to do right by both. The more I listened, the more my coachees revealed. Many told me they felt guilty or helpless—like bad parents *and* professional failures. (The words *bad* and *fail* came up a lot.) Sometimes it felt as if I were standing at a busy intersection with career pressures and expectations whizzing by in one direction, and personal goals, feelings, and family needs running just as fast in the other. I had a full view of both lanes, but I didn't know how to play traffic cop or prevent the inevitable accidents. And accidents there were—of many kinds. I saw immensely talented parents change jobs or even leave their careers outright in a bid for relief. Others stayed the course, but gradually lost their confidence, energy, and mojo.

I tried to help, but nothing from my years of organizational-psychology practice or leadership-development work, or even from my MBA degree, had ever really prepared me to teach people how to bring together self, career, and children. And as I gradually realized, I could executive-coach someone until the cows came home but if that person *also* had six-month-old twins that weren't sleeping, or was having trouble finding decent daycare, my impact was going to be limited.

Nor could I find any practical advice, or answers. Despite searching mountains' worth of career and psychology literature, I couldn't find anything under the category of "sustainable work success, with kids."

When I had my own first child the problem became acute and personal. Back at work after leave, I struggled to find a feasible schedule. Each day felt like a test of speed, agility, and endurance as I raced between client meetings and care changeovers, coaching sessions and diaper changes. So much was unclear: How was I supposed to tell my boss's boss that I was focused on promotion even though I'd just had a baby (and could anyone out there reassure me that that was even OK to begin with)? What was the right amount to spend on childcare while my husband and I were saving to buy our first home? Were there ways to manage the stress of a more-than-full-time job and a tiny person who needed me? When working long hours, how could I still be a present, loving parent?

Remember: *I was the careers and leadership expert.* Helping people find the most-effective ways to do their jobs was my stock in trade, but I was coming up empty handed for my clients and for myself. Not only did I not know how to help the moms and dads I worked with alleviate the constant sense of guilt so many of them walked around with— but I also had no clue how to tell my colleagues I needed to leave the office early when my little one spiked a fever. Talk about humbling!

I couldn't imagine facing eighteen more years of similar pressure— and figured *somebody* had answers. So I did what came most naturally to me, as a career coach, business journalist, and concerned parent: I started asking questions.

One by one, I approached friends, mentors, and trusted colleagues who had kids and seemed "together." I told them that I needed some personal help (true), and that I wanted to know what habits, life hacks, or guiding principles made having a busy career and kids not just doable, but thrive-able. *What's your best advice on working parenthood? How can I manage myself, my career, and my family simultaneously? What do you wish you had known from the get-go about combining career and kids?* Starting small, I quickly expanded the circle and grew bolder, asking senior people I worked with, people I met at professional conferences, friends of friends of friends, folks next to me in line at the supermarket . . . in fact, nearly every working parent I met, because what I heard was surprising, and incredibly motivating.

First, every single parent I spoke to—male and female, biological and adoptive, gay and straight, in every profession, level, and industry, whatever their beliefs and wherever they lived—felt that they, too, were grappling with the problem. Whether I was talking to someone in a fancy glass-walled office or at the neighborhood playground, these questions created a kind of instant fellowship; I immediately felt less alone. Second, while no parent saw him- or herself as an expert, each was happy to share stories and experiences and able to offer a few powerful kernels of advice. I realized there were tons of techniques and solutions out there, ripe for the picking. And the parents who seemed the most comfortable in their dual roles were not, as I had cynically suspected, the ones with the deepest resources. In fact, they were an incredibly diverse group, in every way but one.

What these parents had in common was an *outlook*. Regardless of what working parenthood threw at them, they looked ahead and moved forward. They thought things through and made decisions in the context of their whole lives, without labeling themselves as "bad" or apologizing, to anyone. Whether by choice or experience, they had developed a certain *here-I-am*-ness, a special kind of working-parent resilience. And each saw him- or herself as a whole, complete person, even while performing two distinct and important roles. I wanted to use all their smart, nuts-and-bolts ways of handling working parenthood, and I wanted to *be* that kind of working parent myself.

Shortly after starting this research, I began dispensing the advice I'd gathered to my clients in a specially distilled, highly concentrated form with my own human-capital and coaching expertise whisked in. For a new parent fretting about finding a good childcare provider, I'd deliver a best-insights-from-other-parents briefing—combined with the most powerful interviewing and assessment techniques I'd picked up over many years of doing talent assessments myself and some you-can-do-this type encouragement. I offered "back from parental leave" tutorials to anyone who wanted them; essentially, the smartest things I'd heard from other veteran parents on the topic, along with the practical guidance I'd give any leader transitioning into a new role. For parents who found themselves at that *I can't take this anymore* breaking point (ever been there? I have), I'd gently help them pick apart their calendar and commitments until it all seemed manageable again.

To my delight, these sessions worked. Mothers and fathers who had come to see me glum about their prospects for ever finding any kind of flexibility would call a few months later to happily tell me that they had figured out a viable schedule and sold their boss on the new arrangement. Parents who had worried how to announce they were leaving work for the school play reported back that, using the special working-parent verbal jujitsu moves I'd given them, it wasn't so awkward after all. Others reported that yes, they had accepted the big new job or promotion—but that using the techniques we had reviewed together, they felt as confident in their parenting as ever. Word began to spread. Men and women I'd never met before started reaching out for my advice, and what had started as an off-the-edge-of-my-desk project gained momentum. I began writing about working parenthood for *Harvard Business Review*, decided to refocus my career, and founded the specialist coaching and training firm I run today.

In the past several years, I've had the privilege of speaking with hundreds of parents around the world, as researcher, adviser, and fellow working parent. They've included mothers and fathers from different cultures, professions, family structures, and beliefs; parenting children of different ages; in Manhattan, Mexico, Mumbai, and places in between; who've shifted careers and dealt with setbacks of different kinds; who work every conceivable schedule and are raising children with unique needs. In other words, they represent the full range and reality of who we are as modern working parents.

This guide consists of their advice and encouragement, blended with my own expertise in career development, my insider's know-how as to the ways managers and organizations approach people-management and people decisions, and my own day-to-day experiences as a parent, living every inch of this problem, just like you. I deliver it to you as I would to my in-person clients: as your coach, with the sole agenda of helping you achieve *success* and *satisfaction* as a working parent, however you define them. That means I'll teach, push, challenge, and encourage you every step of the way until you get there, and we can both feel confident that you will.

As we go, you'll find very few statistics or references to academic research, and you won't see any quotations from prominent workplace or parenting experts. That's because in our work together *you're* at the center of things. You know the details of your family and career and workplace and relationships and preferences better than anyone else, and you make the choices. *You're* the expert, and that's how we'll treat you. That might be disconcerting at first, but you'll quickly become more comfortable making your own, personal decisions without the need for any third-party validation. You'll become better able to work and to parent at the same time and in your own unique, authentic way. Building your skills, and confidence, and sense of being in the driver's seat, all at the same time: that's what good coaching does, and what you'll find in the pages ahead.

A New Role—and Frame of Mind

While this book will help you chart your course through working parenthood, my hope is that it will also allow you to experience yourself in a new way: as a *workparent*—a whole, complete person capable and deserving of success in both spheres of your life and at the same time. That new way of thinking will be invaluable in this role—one which may be new for you, and in reality is new for *every* working mother and father. Here's why.

When you think "working parent," you may think of your parents or grandparents and how despite working hard to earn a living, they sat down to dinner with you every night. Or you may think of the more-senior leaders in your organization who *somehow* seemed to make working parenthood work despite serious professional pressures. Your mind may even drift back to TV shows you watched growing up, in which the parent characters were apparently able to balance the personal and the professional without undue strain. With those images in mind, you're left believing that *good parents always eat with their kids* or that *combining career and kids is possible if I work hard enough* or similar.

But your life is likely very different, in many ways. In those TV shows, maybe one parent worked and the other focused on the home front. Today that's true for only 25 percent of American working families; the rest are dual-career or single-parent families. Perhaps your parents or other family members spent the bulk of their working years with a single employer, but statistically speaking, you'll probably be in your current role for only four years—and you may therefore be feeling pressure to network and manage your LinkedIn profile during what would otherwise be family time. Remember also: if your mentors and career role models had kids prior to 2007, they didn't have to work and parent amid the always-on expectations and 24-7 pressures created by the smartphone. In other words, the expectations you're holding yourself to likely don't match your current reality. Maybe when you were little, your parents worked extraordinarily hard and the family budget was tight, but Mom probably didn't have to panic as much as you do about her job getting outsourced or becoming technologically obsolete, and Dad didn't have to spend every evening and vacation glued to a little screen. Being a working parent doesn't just *feel* harder than thirty years ago, or than your image of it tells you it should be. It actually *is* harder.

At the same time, *no one and nothing has emerged to help working parents cope.* That's something that every working mother and father is aware of, but it's recently become more widely acknowledged and understood. Throughout 2020, the global pandemic shone a huge glaring spotlight on the fact that working parents carry an extraordinarily heavy load, and that even "in extremis," we're left to find solutions on our own. Maybe you are one of the "lucky" parents who has good working-parent leave, and flexibility, and benefits, and convenient, high-quality, subsidized childcare. Even if you have those wonderful supports, though, they won't help you turn away from your phone during dinner, or get that dinner on the table after a twelve-hour shift, or help you get through your performance review, or handle the conversations you have with your hard-driving boss about the hours you're working. They're not going to print out the worksheets your eight-year-old needs for school, or help you finish up reading all your colleagues' messages after your kids go to bed, either. Let's hope, for so many important reasons, that an emergency situation like Covid-19 never comes around again. But let's also use what's happened to help us finally acknowledge that we're in a whole new game here. We're facing a very large problem, and there's no more pretending that it doesn't exist. We need a fresh and comprehensive set of approaches for taming it—throughout our society and in our organizations, certainly, but on a personal level as well, and starting with our own frame of mind. It's that personal piece that *Workparent* addresses—and the new tools, confidence, and full-selfness that you'll begin building, starting from chapter 1.

How to Use This Book

This book is structured to reflect workparenting as you'll actually experience it, and to give you the techniques, energy, and emotional support that will be most helpful in real time.

In part 1, "Workparenting, Phase by Phase," you'll get the advice, perspective, and encouragement you need starting before your child's arrival and continuing through the teenage years. In part 2, we'll cover how to maximize your most important workparent resources along the way: your support network, time, and money. Then, we'll turn our attentions to how you can achieve the success you want to, both at work and at home. Part 3 will help you fine-tune your plan for getting where you want to go as a working mom or dad. Whatever your goals are, in part 4, we'll explore how to take the best care of yourself and your family as you pursue them. Finally, in part 5, we'll go over extra tips and tools for bridging your work and unique family—for bringing together yourself, your career, and your life with the people you love.

Read this book in the way that fits how you think, and that fits your current life. You may prefer to go through it cover to cover; use it as a reference to dip into when you need specific support; or decide to skim around, hopscotching between chapters to get insights on the particular issues most important to you while developing a better sense of workparenting as a whole. If you're currently expecting, or thinking about starting a family, you'll want to start at chapter 1, in which we cover some holistic, good-for-every-working-parent advice. But if your daughter starts school next week or your son is already a teenager, it may make more sense to turn directly to chapters 7 and 8, on school and the teenage years, and then circle back to chapter 1 when you have more time. Follow your smarts and intuition: you know what you need. The overall goal here is to get good information and support on a timely basis, while building the important feeling that *I'm wise to this game, and I've got this.*

Whatever your approach, I encourage you to read with a pen and paper (or the electronic equivalent) in hand, with a view toward action, and with an open mind. In each chapter, I'll guide you through some important self-reflection, challenge your thinking, and encourage you to commit to next steps. We're going to cover a lot of new ideas here, so it will be helpful to have your reactions down on paper, and over time, reassuring to refer back to your own notes. Of course, just because you've jotted an idea down doesn't mean you're shackled to it, or that you have to run with everything you find here, and certainly not all at the same time. Your working-parent life is constantly changing, and some techniques you'll use, put down, and then pick up again later—and that's fine.

Note that throughout the book I make no assumptions as to whether or not you have a partner, what your family structure looks like, or what kind of community you're part of. *You're* my client. That said, you may very well be workparenting alongside a life partner or coparent, who might also be a working parent, and you may feel as if many of the choices and approaches we cover here need to be taken as "two for the road." If that's the case, the advice and information you find in chapter 22, "The Two-Career Couple," and in chapter 23, "Sole or Almost-Sole Earner," will be important for you. You and your partner may even decide to work your way through this book together, discussing each bit as you go. If so, simply read all my references to "you" as plural, instead of singular.

Regardless of the details of your family life, I do suggest talking about what you learn here, and how you may want to apply it, with other people. Work through the book with a good friend or another family member. Pull in what you've read here during get-togethers with the other moms and dads at work, or in the parents' group in your neighborhood, or at the preschool. Start a conversation, get those other parents' advice and coaching, and—most important—feel part of the powerful workparent community: connected, supported, strong.

Just One Rule

As your coach, I'm going to be gentle yet relentless in encouraging you to *try out* and *consider* many new approaches to working parenthood. We'll open up the aperture together, and then I'll trust you to pick from the techniques and tools you find here, focusing in on the ones most relevant and useful, and adapting them to fit. I'll use every shred of my coaching experience to help you succeed, but what I won't do is throw down a ton of "have tos," absolutes, and directives. Except one, right now, which is this: **no judgments, ever**.

I want you to stop listening to evaluations and critiques about how you're combining career and family, whether they come from colleagues, the media, social media, your mother-in-law, or anywhere else. Being a working mother or father is hard enough already without catching that kind of flak. Just as important: stop finding fault with yourself, too. Beating yourself up because you just had a difficult daycare drop-off or because you ordered pizza for your family's dinner again is totally self-defeating. Every ounce of attention and energy you spend on self-criticism only makes it *that* much harder to perform at your best or be fully available to your children.

Tune out the noise and naysayers. Treat yourself with the same firm kindness you'd use with your own child. Learn from your setbacks without lingering on them. Remind yourself that this is your life, your family, and your career—*yours*—and that there are no "right" solutions or decisions beyond the ones that work for you.

You're giving working parenthood everything you've got. With that focus and determination, and trusting your own genuine, deep-down sense of the professional, parent, and person you want to be, you're in the perfect place to move forward.

Ready? Then let's turn the page together—and get started.

PART ONE

Workparenting, Phase by Phase

How to Navigate the Demands of Career and Parenthood with Confidence and Calm over the Next Eighteen Years

1

While You're Expecting

Setting Yourself Up for Working-Parent
Success—from the Very Start

The pregnancy test was positive, or you just got a call from your doctor or the agency. Knowing you're going to be a parent is incredible: joyous and exciting in a way that nothing in your life has ever been before. But beneath that excitement lurk uncomfortable questions: *What does parenthood mean for my career? How do I find childcare? How will my boss react? Can I afford this? Where am I even supposed to* begin? Reeling—in a good way—from the news and in the face of so many unknowns, your instinct may be to start *doing* right away: calling HR for the parental-leave paperwork, for example, just to get that reassuring sense that you're in control and making progress.

As strong as that urge may be, *pause.* You don't have to go into action mode immediately, and you don't need to have the next eighteen years (or even weeks) figured out yet, either. You're 100 percent right to want to be proactive, and that instinct will help foster your working-parent success over the long haul. Right now, though, your true priority is to think about what the transition to working parenthood really means so that you can approach it calmly, effectively, and on your own terms. With that perspective and self-assurance, you'll be in a much better position to take the first practical step and share the good news at work. Then, once you've gone public, you'll still have plenty of time

Not expecting yet?

Maybe you're trying to start a family. Or maybe you're years away from having kids but are curious or apprehensive about how this whole job-plus-family thing works. If so, welcome—you've come to just the right place. This book will pull back the curtain and let you get a real-deal look at how workparenting can work—in general, and in the context of your own life and career.

Read through this chapter, paying special attention to the section on understanding your Workparent Template. Then, if you have certain specific questions or concerns (*Can I get promoted while being an on-the-job parent? How will I get enough sleep? Is working-parent guilt inevitable?*) skip ahead to the relevant chapters for insights. Think of yourself as planning a trip: you're glancing through the guidebook ahead of time, looking for some practical tips and making this new country you're headed to feel less foreign, less scary. And because you've started early, you've got plenty of time.

to tackle what you need to during this important get-ready phase. The "first *think*, next *tell*, then *do*" approach will help make the next several months more focused and less stressful—and ensure that you become the happiest, most confident working mother or father you can be right from Day One.

First: *Think*

You wouldn't kick off a major project at work, start a new degree program, take a new job, or make any other big life move without first doing some *active anticipation*: deliberately thinking through what you're really taking on, reflecting on how things will change, acknowledging your nerves, and focusing on how you want it all to go and what you want to get out of it. The same should hold true here.

As soon as you find out you're expecting, carve out some quiet, uninterrupted time to consider the transition you're about to make. Start small: go someplace you can think well and without interruptions, whether that's the local coffee shop or your backyard, and spend some time imagining how life will be different, personally and professionally, when your child arrives. What's exciting about those changes? What are your biggest questions? Fears? How do you see yourself adapting? Be honest with yourself. It's OK to admit that *I'm excited for . . .* but *I'm worried that . . .* or *I have no clue about . . .* It's also OK to realize that there are certain aspects of your life or career that you really don't want to change. If you feel foolish, or selfish, try to gently push such judgments aside. "See" your emotions without labeling them. Whatever comes to mind, no matter how overwhelming or awkward, remember that thousands of other workparents have had the same thoughts and concerns, and that getting them out in the open—just for yourself—will help you find the best ways forward.

As you do this exercise, you may find yourself energized, or fearful, or with more questions than when you started, or potentially even drawing a great big blank. As you mull things over, and particularly if you feel worried or stuck, two powerful tools can help anchor your thinking and keep you moving in a positive, productive direction.

Tool 1: The five key truths about the transition to working parenthood

Whatever your background, family structure, line of work, income, or any other details of your personal or professional life, the transition to working parenthood will invariably mean five things. They're nothing to be scared of: in fact, getting your head around these essential truths will help make what you're facing feel more familiar and doable.

- **You're starting a new job.** Working parenthood is a different role than you've had in the past, and it comes with its own set of responsibilities and expectations. As with *any* new job, it's likely to be overwhelming at first and require a ton of learning and adjustments. But just as you've weathered other big professional and personal transitions, you're going to get through this one, too.

- **What's allowed you to succeed in other jobs is going to allow you to succeed now, as a working parent.** When you've done well at work in the past, it's likely been because of a special personal characteristic or set of skills that come as second nature. Maybe you're a numbers geek, or have an incredible ability to motivate other people, or you're really creative, or the most organized person around. *Those professional super-powers will be your working-parent superpowers, also.* If you've always been a good organizer, for example, you'll find yourself using that gift to manage your calendars and to-dos clearly and efficiently—key for the success of any working-parent family.

• **If you know where you're headed as a working mother or father, it will be easier to get there.** If you can create a mental picture of where you want to be professionally, personally, and as a parent years from now, it will make the responsibilities of working parenthood feel much more feasible and comfortable today. With a specific and positive outcome in mind—an outcome that *you* have chosen—all the smaller, daily decisions you face will become more straightforward, and you'll have the satisfaction of knowing that all the hard work you're putting in right now is serving an important purpose. With a sense of momentum toward that goal, you'll also feel more energetic and motivated. If, for example, you know that you want to

  – *Save enough for retirement, while being the kind of family that has dinner together most nights,*

  – *Lead this division, and one day this firm, while remaining the central adult in my children's lives,*

  – *Keep doing great creative work while raising my kids to become happy, self-sufficient, economically independent adults who remain connected to our family's faith and heritage,*

then you'll feel much more on-your-front-foot and "together" than if you simply try to improvise your way through the next several years, enduring whatever stresses and strains come at you and making pressured, on-the-spot decisions. Don't worry if you don't have a "success picture" in mind just yet. It will naturally begin to crystallize over the next few weeks as you adjust to the news, and as you work through the following few chapters while preparing for your child's arrival.

- **You're the boss.** *You* have final say on the baby's care arrangements. In the face of a big career decision, it's up to *you* to determine what's best for you and your family. After a long day of work, *you* decide how to walk through that door and greet the kids. There are many aspects of life you don't have control over, but *no one* today, tomorrow, or in the arc of time will ever be more engaged in or have more authority over how you combine your career and parenting than you do.

- **You'll find success in the process.** Careers change rapidly, children develop, and—particularly as you become a mother or father—you're changing and developing in a lot of ways, too. Becoming an effective and happy working parent isn't like throwing a single dart and hitting the bull's-eye. It means learning and adapting as you go, and constantly discovering effective new techniques and solutions that work for yourself, your career, and your family.

Tool 2: Understanding your Workparent Template

Your *Workparent Template* is a collage-like collection of all the experiences you've had, observations you've made, and advice you've heard about working parenthood throughout the course of your life. Over time, these impressions and inputs have solidified into your own unique, personal view as to what working parenthood really means and how it works.

If your own father pulled long hours to support the family but was always there for you when you needed him, your template may include a deep belief that *parents can work hard and love their kids*. On the other hand, if Dad worked long hours while you were small, was difficult to reach, missed a lot of weekends and holidays, and was grouchy and preoccupied when he was around, you may associate being a working parent with being strained, or out of touch. Of course, your template isn't formed only in childhood; it's constantly evolving, even today. If many of the parents in your current organization work reduced schedules, for example, you might have absorbed the idea that *flex work is feasible in this profession*, or that the same arrangement your colleagues have settled into will be the right one for you.

None of these beliefs are good or bad, per se; your template isn't inherently right or wrong. It is, however, *yours*, and when you become a working mother or father, it's essential to be conscious of what it looks like and of how, in ways large and small, it might influence your feelings—and thus your choices and actions—now and in the future. When you can see your template fully and clearly, you get to control *it* rather than letting it control *you*.

To understand your own template, think carefully about how it was created, and about the people and forces that shaped it. Those will include:

- Your parents and other childhood caregivers

- Your education and early-career experiences

- The coworkers and mentors you've had over time

- The unwritten expectations and norms of your industry and organization

- Your partner—and partner's family

- Your friends and broader social community

- Your faith, cultural values, and/or belief system(s)

- The media: how you've seen working parents and the "working-parent problem" portrayed in movies, the news, or online

- Social media: the debates, opinions, and consensus found in your chosen virtual community

As you look down this list, think about what examples, attitudes, and beliefs about workparenting—both explicit and implicit—you've absorbed from each one. Did the grandma you adored tell you that all decent people eat dinner with their children every night? Did that

Your own working parents, your template

" My father's advice was 'work hard and care more.' He got over more hurdles than anyone I know, starting a business when he couldn't afford it and then creating a successful buying group when everyone told him he was crazy to compete with big-box stores. For me, his advice transcends business. It allows the phrase *hardworking dad* to have meaning."

—*Vito, home-appliance store owner, father of three*

" During my first year in medical school I went to this 'Women in Medicine' dinner, and two different physicians on the panel told us that there was no way we could have families and succeed in this profession. That advice just didn't ring true. My mother was an ophthalmologist. She worked long hours and was one of the only mothers in our town who didn't drive carpool, but she was always there for us. My dad also worked full-time and was very involved with our family. Working and raising kids is part of my DNA."

—*Elizabeth, physician, mother of three*

" I watched my grandmother—who had adopted me—work twelve-hour days, and listened to her stories about getting into the workforce, gaining responsibility, finding her own success. Not every bill was paid perfectly on time, but they all got paid, and she earned enough money to send me and my sister to a private parochial school. She drilled it into me: work and have that independence—and allow yourself the pleasures of family."

—*Kelly Ann, airport operations, mother of one*

" On the door to my mom's home office, she hung a sign that said 'Don't interrupt me unless you're bleeding.' I always found that reassuring: she worked hard, but was available for me and my brother whenever we needed her, and she had a sense of humor about it all. When my brother went off to college and told his roommates about that sign, they acted as if it was grounds for calling Child Protective Services. It just depends on what you're used to."

—*Tom, nonprofit CEO, father of one*

terrific mentor at your first job talk about how in-home childcare was the "only" option? Throughout those tough years in school and during your early professional training, did the instructors keep emphasizing that your personal life was going to have to take a back seat to your career if you wanted any chance of success? As you go, it will be helpful to sketch out your template. Table 1-1 provides an easy space to do so. (Note: throughout the book, you'll get simple "frames" like this one for organizing and capturing your thoughts. If you prefer to keep your notes in a separate format, or on your phone, etc., then go with it. Do what works. The value here is in your reflections, not the worksheet itself. Whatever you do write down, though, hang on to it. We'll be doing many similar exercises, and it will be helpful to have all your insights easily accessible and together in a single Workparent folder.)

Once you've thought through all the individual pieces of your template, step back and take a look at the whole, scanning for themes and through lines. As you do so, your template's contours will begin to emerge. For example, you may realize that you're quite confident about working parenthood in the long term, but freaked out about how to find decent childcare for an infant, or that you've had excellent workparent role models in your personal life, but none in your industry. Whatever the case, that generalized anxiety you felt about working parenthood will suddenly have a shape and focal points. Because it does, you'll have a clearer sense of your best action steps—whether that's doing more research on childcare options or connecting with other working parents in your field. As you call out your fears and blind spots, they start to lose their power over you.

Be aware that this exercise may be difficult, for various reasons. Most Workparent Templates are complex and a little contradictory. Thinking yours through may involve sorting through some baggage that you might well prefer to leave circling the carousel over in Emotional Baggage Claim. But the more *aware* you are of your assumptions and beliefs around working parenthood, and why you hold them, the more conscious, efficient, and happy a course you'll be able to chart for yourself in these critical months to come.

TABLE 1-1

Mapping Out Your Workparent Template

	Upsides/role models/positive examples/motivators	Questions/concerns/ gray areas	Negative experiences/ limiting beliefs
Family			
Education; early career			
Industry, role, organization			
Community			
Belief systems			
Media, online			

Next: *Tell*

Announcing the news

Once you've had the chance to step back and take in the big picture, to get your head around the working-parent transition and begin understanding and taking control of your working-parent views, your next move—pivoting to a very practical one, now—will be to share your news with the people at work. As you get ready to do so, you'll likely feel keyed up, apprehensive, and awkward. This is your public debut as a workparent, and while you don't know exactly what words to use, you want them to be *right*. Fortunately, there is an effective formula for what to say—and how, when, and to whom.

- **Pick your timing carefully.** As tempting as it may be to blurt out the news early, hold off until you've gotten the practical assurances you want from your healthcare provider or adoption or placement agency. If you're part of a two-career couple, be certain to share the news at the same time. You don't want your news reaching your colleagues through the grapevine. And remember: once you share the information that you're expecting, you can never unshare it. If in doubt, wait a bit.

- **Start with your boss.** Your boss evaluates you, goes to bat for you at pay and promotion time, and has a big say in how your career moves ahead. She's also the one who can allow you to tack on a few weeks of vacation to parental leave or approve your work-from-home request. For practical reasons and as a sign of respect, you need to communicate with her first.

- **Find some peace and quiet.** Try not to have the conversation as a major deadline looms, in a "fishbowl" environment, or in any other context where either of you is likely to be distracted, interrupted, or watched. Instead, pick a slower day, and get a dedicated call or book the quieter conference room down the hall. If you work in a high-traffic zone or an open-plan space, ask to speak outside the building or over coffee.

WHILE YOU'RE EXPECTING **25**

If the due date is uncertain

As an adoptive or foster parent, you may not be aware of precisely when you'll be welcoming a new child, or may be concerned about plans changing. If so, you may choose to let the folks at work know that you've committed to expanding your family, while explaining that the precise due date is uncertain. Many prospective parents take this route once they're far enough along in the process that the future placement begins to feel real.

In the case that broader communication doesn't feel right for you, consider letting your manager (and potentially a few additional trusted colleagues or team members) in on your news, but asking them to keep it under wraps. This quieter approach lets you get your manager's overall personal and professional support, allows you to meet any obligations you have to provide advanced notice before taking leave, gives you time to have important discussions around how leave will work, and lets you preview the flexibility you'll need when you get that all-important phone call. At the same time, it allows you to avoid being peppered with questions from nosy coworkers, or having to explain a sudden change in plans. If you do *not* wish to speak with your manager, but need an employer reference letter as part of the placement process, or are required by company policy to give a certain amount of notice before taking parental leave, or both, ask for your HR representative's help on a confidential basis.

Throughout the process, continue engaging with the staff at your adoptive or foster agency. They've seen many families through this journey from start to finish, and can provide specific support, or even connect you with other parents who have been in the same situation. At the end of the day, though, trust yourself. No one knows more than you do about your career, work relationships, or feelings. Plan ahead for a smooth and happy arrival, but trust your gut sense on how to do so.

- **Get right to it.** Don't start off with a flurry of small talk or embed the news in a conversation about this year's marketing budget. The sooner you get to the point, the better.

- **Work from a script.** Rehearse what you're going to say, and keep your comments direct, upbeat, and brief. Remember that you're sharing information, but not asking permission, or apologizing. A good baseline speech is: "[Manager name], thanks for meeting with me. I'm here to share some exciting personal news: [your partner's name, if relevant] and I are expecting a baby in June, and we couldn't be happier. I'm certain that as I tell you this, you'll have many questions—about my plans for leave, or how we'll cover my work while I'm out. I'm one hundred percent committed to my job and to our team's success, and know that in the coming months we'll find the right answers together. For now, I just wanted you to know." Note: the only points you have to get across are that you're *expecting*, *collaborative*, and *committed*. All other details and decisions, including the dates of your parental leave, should be ironed out later.

- **Remember that you're both human.** You may get flustered or even emotional while speaking—lots of parents, both men and women, do. (You're announcing a *person*, after all!) Your manager may also be visibly taken aback, or unexpectedly lunge out of his chair to hug you when he hears the word *baby*. All of those reactions are normal, and it's OK to acknowledge them by saying something like, "As you can tell, I'm a little nervous," or "I can see you're surprised by the news." In general, the more genuine and relatable you are, the easier and more effective the conversation will be.

> "I'm a private person, and the idea of telling my colleagues, 'Hey, I'm having a kid' didn't come naturally. I didn't expect a bad reaction, exactly, but this is a high-growth, hard-work kind of environment, and I worried that people would think I wasn't as committed anymore, or willing to put in the hours.
>
> It took me four weeks to find the right spot—there was just never a right time. One day after a big meeting, I finally mentioned it, very casually. The guys I work for were so happy for me, and both immediately started giving me parenting advice."
>
> —*Josh, business development manager, father of one*

- **Figure out immediate next steps.** It's fine to keep this meeting brief, but before you wrap up, make sure to agree on how and when 1) you'll tell the rest of your team the news, 2) who will alert the higher-ups (if relevant), and 3) your timeline for regrouping on any parental-leave plans.

- **End on a good note.** However the conversation goes, closing out with a statement like "I appreciate your support," "I'm looking forward to working through this effectively together in the months ahead," or even a simple "Thanks for speaking with me" will build goodwill—and let you showcase the positive, proactive approach you'll be bringing to working parenthood from now on.

As the meeting ends, you'll likely feel relieved—and exhausted. No matter how receptive your boss and overall workplace are, it takes a lot of mental energy to have this conversation. Be sure to take a break

Telling clients, customers, or investors instead of a boss

How do you tell the investors that just seeded your startup that you're pregnant, or the patients that rely on you for specialty care that you'll be away for three months on paternity leave? Four strategies can help.
1. **Make your announcement a little later.** This minimizes the time your clients have to be worried or distracted by the news.
2. **Have a solid, detailed plan in place.** Don't treat this as an open-ended discussion or problem-solving conversation. Share exactly how things will work over the next several months, and be ready to address any questions and concerns. For example, "While I'm gone, Dr. Thacker will be able to see you for your follow-up appointments. I'll make sure she's up to speed."
3. **Refer to future partnership—and future outcomes.** Telling your key buyer that "I'll be back well before product launch," or your tax-preparation clients that "I'll be handling your filing this year, as usual," will help diffuse uncertainty and stress.
4. **Set the tone.** Present the fact that you're becoming a parent in a straightforward, undramatic way. Your counterparties will take their cues—and confidence—from you.

afterward and to give yourself some credit. You've just brought your parenting self into the professional world for the very first time and in the best possible way.

When others aren't expecting it

Maybe you work at a startup, and none of the other members of the team has kids yet. Or you're welcoming a child as a single parent, an LGBTQIA+ mother or father, earlier or later in life than typically expected, or into an already-larger-than-average family. For many different reasons, your news may catch your colleagues by surprise, and that surprise may make things feel tricky or awkward.

You don't own your coworkers' feelings, and it's not your responsibility to educate anybody on the realities and diversity of modern family life. But if you do anticipate that your announcement may catch coworkers off guard, there's a graceful way to take charge of the situation: by preempting it. Simply add one brief additional section into your announcement script: "I realize that this news may come as a surprise. You may not have known that [becoming a parent/welcoming an additional child] was part of my immediate plans. But I'm sure you appreciate that, just like any other [mother or father], I'm thrilled. I also know that I can rely on your understanding and support in the months to come, and that means a lot to me."

A statement like this lets you take control of the situation—and in a pleasant, professional way. It acknowledges your listeners' feelings, and generously allows them a moment to collect themselves and step into the right headspace to process your news. It also sets up a great big blinking neon arrow pointing them toward the appropriate, supportive reaction. If anyone still seems to be at a loss for words, suggest taking a break ("I can see you're digesting what I've just told you! Why don't we regroup tomorrow?") and then steer clear until they've had a chance to get their act together.

How to handle questions and detractors

It's normal to be nervous about breaking your news, but expect that the majority of reactions will be positive. Most of the people you encounter in the course of your professional life have either been in the

Pregnancy and parenting discrimination

Your boss didn't take the news that you were expecting well at all, that jerk down the hall keeps making comments, or to your surprise and dismay you're let go while expecting. Are you the victim of parenting discrimination?

Maybe—and maybe not. While the term *discrimination* is often used casually or descriptively, it has a narrow, well-defined legal meaning: one that isn't intuitive, may not map to your sense of what's right and wrong, and can vary from one jurisdiction to the next. In other words, colleagues may say or do things that you find objectionable or unfair but that, technically speaking, are within the law. And getting an employer to accept responsibility for—much less, correct—wrongdoing can be a very difficult task. Between the time involved, any legal fees, and the potential collateral damage to your reputation and career, a discrimination claim can be very expensive, in all senses of the word—even if you're in the right.

If you do find yourself on the receiving end of what you feel are inappropriate comments or treatment, try some firm self-advocacy first. A simple and calm "I'd appreciate it if you would stop making those types of jokes" may be all it takes to jolt an errant colleague into better behavior. If the problem is bigger or persists, consider connecting with your company's human resources team. Be aware, though, that the HR function ultimately exists to protect the company's long-term interests, not your own.

If you do experience what feels like discriminatory behavior, be sure to document it in detail: keep a log of exactly what comments were made; what actions taken, by whom, on what date, and in what context; when you met with HR reps; how they responded; etc. And make certain to keep hard copies of any relevant emails or other communications. If at any point you decide to pursue a formal claim against the organization, that detailed history and paper trail will be the very first thing any employment attorney or nondiscrimination authority will want to see.

Bigger picture: whether the treatment you're getting is truly discriminatory or merely out of line, remember that there are plenty of managers and organizations out there who treat working parents with respect. It may not be your first choice, or easy to do, but you can always vote with your feet.

> " When I announced I was expecting my first, the CEO of one of my
> portfolio companies said, 'I've never worked for a pregnant boss
> before.' I told him, 'Well then, I guess we'll *both* be learning new things!'"
>
> —*Anne, private equity executive, mother of two*

position you're in now or have hopes of being in it one day. You may
even be surprised on the upside: that gruff senior manager may be
delighted to find out that a member of the team is expecting, or you
may find yourself on the receiving end of an almost annoying number
of unsolicited hugs and effusive congratulations.

While *most* of your colleagues will respond well, not *all* will, and
you'll feel better and steadier if you know up front exactly what types
of questions and detractors you may have to deal with and how to respond to them effectively without getting knocked off your game. The
big silver lining here—and yes, there is one—is rehearsal and practice:
the more deftly you can handle these less-than-fun conversations now,
the more it will build your confidence and capability for handling
other equally delicate workparenting conversations later on.

Less-than-supportive coworkers, professional contacts, and—for that
matter—friends and family members will usually fall into one of four
categories:

- **Investigators** barrage you with questions about every aspect of
  the impending arrival and your future career plans. Where are
  you delivering? Are you really coming back after leave? These
  folks see your business as their own.

- **Naysayers** relish informing you of the many downsides and
  perils of working parenthood. They'll declare that being a
  good parent in your industry/role/function is impossible . . . or
  point out what a hassle it will be for the team to have you on
  leave during busy season.

- **Zero-filters** blurt out questions or advice that's both unsolicited and overly personal. They'll want to know if the baby was

Facing loss at work

When you're facing the heartbreak and sense of helplessness that can come from a miscarriage, or an adoption that doesn't go through, the idea of sharing that news at work may be overwhelming.

If your colleagues weren't aware that you were expecting, you have the option of saying nothing, and of retaining full privacy during this difficult time. On the other hand, telling your manager, HR staffer, or a few trusted coworkers may help you secure time off from work (in the form of sick or personal days, or short-term disability), needed for physical and emotional recovery. If you do share your news, chances are high that you'll get more understanding and sympathy than you expected. While losses like these often go undiscussed, they're common. Many of your coworkers have been in similar situations themselves and will most likely be warmly supportive.

Whatever route you take, at no point should you ever feel pressure to answer coworkers' questions or share any details you don't wish to. This is a personal matter, and a simple "I appreciate your support, but I prefer not to discuss it further" is all the response needed.

planned, if you met the egg donor in person, or if you're still hoping to get promoted this year.

- **Nonreactors** pretend they haven't heard you. They'll greet your news with poker faces and keep putting meetings and deadlines onto your calendar regardless of your child's due date.

As frustrating as dealing with any of these folks can be, a few simple approaches can help keep them at bay while preserving your calm and dignity.

- **Decide up front what information to share and what to keep private.** Under intense questioning from the Investigator, you may find yourself having to make a spot decision on whether to share the baby's gender or that your wife went through IVF. Set your intentions, and stick to them.

- **Don't take it personally.** In their own graceless, misguided way, Investigators may be trying to signal warmth; the Naysayer may think he's being helpful in warning you of the potential difficulties; and the Nonreactor may be trying to keep herself tears-free at work while battling infertility; etc. Give each the benefit of the doubt.

- **Have effective responses at the ready.** Don't get caught groping for words—or left fuming in the hallway in the aftermath of a negative encounter. To shut down an awkward conversation without coming across as abrasive, say:

  - "These are all great questions, and I'm sure I'll figure each one out as I go."

  - "Thanks so much for your interest and support. I tend to be quite private about these matters, though."

  - "Yes, working parents certainly do have a lot to think about!"

  - "You're right—it won't be easy. But I'm fortunate to have great support at work and at home, and I'm confident things will move in a good direction."

  - "As you know, the baby's due June 15, so we'll either need to do the meeting earlier or determine a way to make it go well in my absence."

  - "Thanks so much for your interest and input—I'll take that on board. Back on the budget projections, though . . ."

If you can deliver these lines firmly, confidently, and with a smile, most colleagues will get the hint.

Then: *Do*

There are several important things to do before your child's arrival to ensure that you become a successful and satisfied working parent, both short and long term—and once your news is out, you can get moving. Together, these items may feel like a strain on your already full to-do list, but go one deliberate step at a time, and you'll be able to cover all you need to.

What to begin planning for . . .

As soon as your news is out at work, start:

- Imagining day-to-day life as a working parent. The more aware of and comfortable you are with the nitty-gritty details and realities of working parenthood, the easier your transition will be. Knowing what's coming will keep you calmer, and it will allow you to make better up-front decisions around childcare and other practical matters. One great tactic for gaining these useful and detailed insights is *shadowing*: ask other recent-vintage working parents you know if they can walk you through their daily schedules in full detail, or—better yet—if you can actually, physically tag along with them through their morning and evening routines so you can see what's in store. As you watch a friend or colleague navigate the childcare handover, the commute, and dinner prep, take detailed notes—and imagine how you'll handle the same yourself when the time comes.

- Thinking through your childcare plan. Once you've gotten that "typical day" view, consider the type of childcare that will be right for you. While it may feel too early to be planning out— much less looking for—childcare, it isn't. Finding care you're comfortable with is *the* single most important factor to becoming a successful, satisfied workparent during your child's early years, and the more thoughtful and unhurried you can make this process, the better. (Not sure where to begin? Don't worry. In chapter 2, you'll find a step-by-step guide to finding care that works for your family, career, budget, and feelings.)

- Getting your "life documents" together. Get a will drafted, put a financial power-of-attorney order in place, establish a just-in-case guardianship plan, and take out sufficient life insurance. Thinking about ever needing any of these supports is sure to leave you a (temporary) emotional wreck, but were the

> " I'm the only female firefighter at our station, but most of my colleagues are dads, and balancing work and kids is a topic of daily conversation. It's *welcomed*. One of the guys I worked with and his wife were expecting at the same time, and we would compare notes. Later on, if I came into work shattered from being up late with the baby, my colleagues all understood. We all share parenting tips, talk about how our kids are doing in school. It's lovely."
>
> —*Kylei, firefighter, mother of one*

worst to happen (God forbid), you would absolutely want your family to have these protections in place. This paperwork can take forever, and it's the absolute last thing you'll want to deal with when taking care of a new baby, so it's good to get the ball rolling now.

- Building a financial cushion. The next year is going to bring a number of bulky, one-off expenses: you'll have to pay for things like a childcare-center deposit or au pair agency fee on top of the costs of healthcare, baby gear, the move to a new apartment. To soften the impact, see if you can set aside your annual tax refund, start saving some amount of money from each paycheck, or ask friends and family to consider giving cash instead of baby gifts. Think through what nice-to-haves you're paying for now that could be cut back or traded in to give you more budgetary breathing room later. (If you cut back your monthly payments by driving a less-fancy car, that money can help pay for the *real* luxury of a backup daycare service.) Tactically, you may want to create a special Workparent Reserve bank account as a practical and psychological protection against extra expenses. Whatever extra slack—and just as important, *feelings* of slack—you can create in your finances now will help you avoid that much extra stress later on.

Once you've tackled these bigger-picture, long-lead items, it's time to turn your attentions to:

- Creating a circle of working-parent mentors. You're going to need a *lot* of advice, support, and encouragement in the months ahead, and now's the time to begin enlisting the people who can provide it. This doesn't need to be a formal or stressful process. Just seek out fellow working mothers and fathers you know or work with, and who seem to have their acts together, and ask if they'll be willing to talk for twenty minutes. Solicit a diverse group, and don't be shy. One of the happy surprises of working parenthood is that people you barely know will be delighted you've asked for their ideas and will be eager to share their hard-won wisdom. If your organization has a working-parents employee network, sign up for that now, also. The goal here isn't just practical; connecting with other working parents will give you a comforting, motivating sense of belonging and fellowship.

- Getting familiar with your organization's working-parent benefits, as relevant. Look at your company's benefits intranet page or the employee handbook or ask an HR rep for information on any working-parent programs you have access to. Be ready to *dig deep*—to be an investigative reporter. Even organizations that pay up to give their employees fantastic family benefits can be lousy at communicating them. It's perfectly common to have to go to eight different places on your company's intranet to learn about five different family benefits. Hunting down and reviewing benefits literature is no joyride, but don't be deterred, because ignoring the supports and savings that might be available to you is essentially the same as tossing your paychecks into the shredder. If there *is* an emergency backup care plan, a special system for setting aside pretax dollars for childcare expenses, lactation facilities, a flexible-work option, a back-from-leave mentoring program, or any other parent-friendly benefit, now's the time to get smart on it.

- Planning your leave. This involves educating yourself on the type and amount of leave available and developing a high-level plan for what will happen while you're out. (For a detailed

Working-parent employee networks

If you work in a mid- or larger-sized organization, you may have the opportunity to join an internal working-parents employee network (sometimes referred to as an "affinity network" or "employee resource group"—or "ERG," for short). This group may be:

- Highly organized and offer specific services, like a formal mentoring program and parenting seminars
- A completely informal, volunteer-led effort that lets moms and dads meet over a monthly brown-bag lunch in the break room
- Technologically based: a messaging channel that allows working parents to swap tips, support, and childcare leads

Whatever the case, the group can be a tremendous benefit: an easy, free way to connect with other parents living and breathing the same professional experience that you are; to get extra advice, tips, and encouragement; and to stave off any sense of loneliness or isolation, particularly as you start your workparent journey. So sign up for distributions, go on the website, and try attending an event or two, and if you find these things helpful, stick with them. But if the group isn't welcoming, or seems to focus on working-parent problems instead of solutions, save yourself the time. You're busy, and an ERG is an opportunity, not an obligation.

If your organization doesn't yet have a workparenting group, consider spearheading one yourself: invite the other parents you know—and the parents *they* know—throughout the organization to meet up at a specific time to share tips and tricks for a common workparent challenge, like time management or the childcare search. Don't worry about getting official organizational sanction to do so. Be open about your activities, but know that you're well within your rights to gather with fellow employees to discuss things that will ultimately help the organization. (If you're ever challenged, or told you lack the authority needed to start an ERG, point out that your efforts can help make the organization *more inclusive*.)

Even if you work solo, freelance, or in a very small company, you can still create a group. Just tap members of your own network, or start one as part of another organization, like a trade group, neighborhood association, alumni club, or faith community. Regardless of backdrop or format, if you keep the invites inclusive and the conversation can-do, the group will likely gain traction.

explanation of how to plan, take, and return from leave, turn to chapter 3.)

Throughout the *entire* time you're expecting, make certain to continue:

- **Delivering workplace wins.** With so much excitement and so much going on during this period, it can be easy to let your eye wander a bit off the professional ball—to not contribute as actively, energetically, or creatively as you could. Yet doing a terrific job *now* is the best way to gain flexibility and understanding *later*. If your boss sees you as a fantastic contributor, he's much more likely to accommodate that flex-work request, and not blink when you're unavailable on the day the baby's sick. Keep doing good work, keep going the extra mile—and keep letting other people know about it.

- **Paying attention to your professional brand.** It's fine—in fact, it's a *good* thing—to refer to your upcoming arrival, and to express excitement about becoming a parent. But remember: you're there to do a job, and if colleagues feel that you're more focused on nursery decor or choice of stroller than on your work, that doesn't put you in the best light.

- **Using future-framed statements.** Examples would be ones that begin with "As soon as I'm back from leave," "Next year," "Once we've completed the product launch," etc., which will send subtle but powerful cues to your boss and colleagues that you're focused, committed, and around for the long term.

. . . and what can wait

Dealing with insurance documentation and creating a written parental-leave coverage plan may feel like milestone, Code Red tasks, or ones you'll want to bang out early. In reality though, they're straightforward, and if you've already managed to announce your impending arrival with confidence, collaborated well with your boss on your general leave plans, and are doing a terrific job, they're really just paperwork and can be handled quickly. Unless you're a biological mom having health issues or otherwise expecting an early arrival, don't spend too much time on this stuff until a few months before your due date. If you're concerned about timing, ask your manager or HR rep if there's an organizational guideline on when to check these items off your list.

Most important: *defer any and all decisions on changes to your schedule, hours, or responsibilities* until you're already a parent, or better yet until you're back at work after leave. You just won't have all the information—practical or personal—needed to make fundamental career- and income-related decisions until then, and you may come to regret any professional stakes you drive into the ground this early. Think ahead, but keep all your options open.

Focusing forward

Expecting a new child is a profound, exciting thing: you're waiting to meet a person who for the rest of your life will be at the center of it. It's only natural to want to use this time to do things that channel that wonderful sense of anticipation: looking at the ultrasound pictures, getting the nursery set up, planning the baby shower, or enjoying some last-hurrah outings with friends. And with everything you've got going on right now—practically, emotionally, and perhaps physically, too—your return from leave and actual debut as a working parent may seem abstract, or really far away.

The efforts you put into working parenthood now, though, will have huge upsides later on. The more you understand how you've been wired to think about working parenthood, the more deliberate, conscious, and authentic your choices around it will be. The more insight you have on what's ahead, the less stressful it will become. The more confident you feel talking with your manager and colleagues now, the easier working-parent conversations with them are likely to be later. By paying attention to working parenthood *before* it actually starts, you give your family—and yourself—an important gift for the future.

2

Care

Everything You Need in Order to Put Together—and Start Using—a Day-to-Day Childcare Arrangement You Trust

Finding good-quality childcare isn't the *only* hurdle to becoming a successful and satisfied working parent, but it is the most important, particularly in these early days. And unlike in the wonderful, classic film *Mary Poppins*, in which the ideal caregiver floats magically down from the sky, your search for it will likely take meaningful time and effort. A perfect care arrangement will be hard to find—if such a thing even exists—and while you're looking for it, you'll need to focus on things like costs, daycare licensing requirements, the looming end of parental leave, and your backup care plan, which of course no character in the movies ever seems to have to consider. If you're like the vast majority of parents, you'll also have to grapple with complicated feelings when actually starting care: worry, sadness, or both.

Don't let yourself get too tangled up emotionally, though—or worse, become immobilized because you're not sure what practical steps to take. If you start thinking about childcare early on, approach finding care as a *process* (just like so many others you've capably handled both on and off the job), and pay good attention to your own needs and instincts as you go, you'll be in a good position to find—and start using—safe, trustworthy, nurturing care that works for your career, your emotional well-being, and for the entire family.

When to Start Looking

If you've recently found out that you're expecting and are wondering when to gear up your childcare search, the answer is: **right now—or as soon as possible**. That might strike you as strange or alarmist: *Why start looking at daycare centers today, when the baby's arrival is still six months off? There will be plenty of time for this later!* Be aware, though, that simply determining the right *type* of care can involve real introspection and trade-offs, and that finding and locking in the care arrangement itself can then take weeks, a few months, or more. When you're handling a project whose end result is this critical, you want to be certain to give it, and yourself, as much lead time as you can.

Still not convinced? Then think in purely practical terms. The best daycare centers—the ones you'll want to have your child in—often have months-long waiting lists, so unless you sign up early, you might not get a spot when you need it. And if you don't have good care in place by the time you return to work, you'll be in the deeply uncomfortable position of either having to leave the baby with caregivers you're not completely confident in or having to do frantic, last-minute negotiations for additional time off, which your employer may not grant or which may result in a hit to your wallet. And sure, you *could* defer thinking about care until you're on leave . . . but do you *really* want to be starting at square one when you're exhausted, adjusting to the demands of parenthood, and recovering from the baby's arrival?

To give the process the attention it's due, to maximize your chances of finding terrific care, and to keep your blood pressure within normal range, start early.

What Kind of Care?

The first step toward finding great childcare is determining which *type*. If you've already made a decision about what kind of care is right for

What if you can't agree?

You say daycare. Your partner insists on a nanny. How to break the stalemate—and move forward?

- **Go bigger picture.** What's right for your family, as a whole? Which option best fits your overall careers, care needs, budget? Which care type will be best at lowering your stress?
- **Ask yourselves: Who bears more of the practical brunt of this choice?** Does it really make sense to push the daycare option if it's your partner, and not you, who will be doing all the drop-offs and pickups?
- **Talk through the underlying issue(s).** Maybe your partner worries that an in-home caregiver will become a "parent re-placement." Or maybe, exhausted and postpartum, you're not relishing the idea of a having a supermodel-esque twenty-year-old au pair from Sweden living in your spare room. Don't laugh here. Remember, you're parents, but you're also people, and you're going to be sensitive in all kinds of idiosyncratic, unex-pected ways. Acknowledge your own feelings, and give your part-ner safe harbor to talk about his or her concerns as well.
- **Give it six months.** No arrangement has to be forever. Disagree, but commit for now—and commit to the possibility of revisiting.

you, skip ahead to the next section, "Finding, Assessing, Choosing, and Hiring a Care Provider." If, however, you want to better understand your various options, or if you need help in narrowing them down, read over the following descriptions of each common type of care and then review table 2-1 for the benefits, considerations, and cost compo-nents of each. Note that what follows here is a *lot* of information—deliberately and carefully presented in a neutral way. You're not being nudged toward any particular solution or care type: you'll read and, as you do, have your own thoughts and reactions.

- **Daycare** is group-based childcare provided at a dedicated cen-ter or facility (also sometimes called a "nursery" or "crèche"). A daycare center may be managed independently, be part of a chain, be offered through your employer or a government program, or be run by a local place of worship or community organization. Any daycare center you consider should have a current, government-issued operating license in good standing.

- **Home-based daycare** involves having your child—and, potentially, a small group of other children—looked after by an individual caregiver inside that caregiver's own home, perhaps with the support of one or two assistants. As with any larger center, these caregivers should have valid, state-issued operating licenses.

- A **nanny** or **babysitter**—the terms are interchangeable— provides dedicated one-on-one care for your child inside your own home. You may hire a nanny independently, or through a placement agency or service. In either case, you are responsible for managing her work and for mutually agreeing on hours, terms, and responsibilities. A nanny may work full- or part-time, and in certain circumstances you may be able to split the caregiver's services with another family in what's known as a "nanny share" arrangement.

- An **au pair** is a young person (usually female, although there are so-called "bro pairs") from abroad who lives in your home and provides a set number of childcare hours per week in exchange for room, board, and a modest stipend. While the term *au pair* is often used informally to describe any young, live-in sitter or caregiver, within the United States, the Au Pair program is an official, government-sanctioned cultural-exchange program complete with its own category of work visa. Under that program, au pair placement may be done only through specially licensed agencies, and strict guidelines around au pair living conditions, salary, and work hours are in place to ensure a positive, safe experience for both caregivers and families. Note that while program details and visa requirements vary from country to country, the "red thread" running through the au pair experience is that it is *at its core a cultural-exchange program* (not a low-cost route to round-the-clock childcare).

- A **family caregiver** is one of your, or your partner's, close relatives—a grandparent, aunt, cousin, etc.—who looks after your child either in your home or in theirs. Think of this option as "a nanny from inside the family." This relative may be willing to work for free or lower-than-average childcare rates, or of course may ask for the same pay as any other professional caregiver.

- **Staggered care** describes an arrangement in which you, your partner, and/or other family caregivers take turns working and providing childcare. For example, you may work overnight shifts, and care for your children in the morning, while your partner works days but takes over at home in the evenings.

- **Hybrid care** refers to any blended, multipart combination of the solutions above. The flexibility and customization of a hybrid arrangement can be mission-critical if you're coping with long or irregular work hours, frequent business travel, single parenthood, a two-career partnership, or are looking to stretch your childcare budget. For example, in a hybrid arrangement, you might:

  - Have your child attend daycare from 8 a.m. to 6 p.m. Monday through Thursday, and then have a family caregiver cover Fridays

  - Use a full-time daycare and *also* hire a babysitter to help cover those weekends spent working

  - Take care of the baby in the mornings, have your partner do so in the evenings, and use paid care to cover the midday stretch between your respective shifts

The number of specific hybrid solutions is endless, but their general purpose is always the same: to let you tailor a complete childcare arrangement to fit both your needs and your wallet.

If you've reviewed all the options and are still finding it hard to choose, think over your most likely childcare-need pain points, and how each option still on the table might help solve them. (If you regularly

TABLE 2-1

Childcare Options at a Glance

Out-of-home options

Care type	Advantages	Barriers and considerations	Typical cost components*	How to ensure quality
Daycare center	• Quality assurance: state-licensed facilities will have strict caregiver-to-child ratios, proper safety equipment, etc. • Reliability: even if one professional at the center is off work, or leaves, it won't disrupt your care routine • Socialization: provides your child exposure to multiple other adults and children • Clarity and consistency: the center's policies, schedule, etc., should be provided to parents and closely followed • Convenience/connection: if the center is on-site or near your workplace, you may be able to drop in and see your child during the workday • Care can "grow" with your child, evolving from infant/baby care into a preschool environment	• Logistics: requires getting your child to and from the center each day, with any required gear (bottles, expressed milk, spare clothes, etc.) • Even with a small caregiver-to-child ratio, less individual attention than in-home care • Can't use when your child is sick • If there's turnover among daycare workers, your child may not develop long-term bonds with individual caregivers	• Up-front fee/deposit • Monthly fee based on days per week and/or hours per day of use • Late-pickup fees, often determined by the minute	• State licensure • Your own review of the center's policies and procedures • Tour of the center • Discussion/interview with center director • Reference checks with both current and past parents • Unscheduled visits

Home-based daycare	• Potentially, a "best of both worlds" option: warmth, consistency, and close attention of an in-home setting with the socialization and quality control of a larger center	• Logistics: same as daycare center • Fewer "eyes on the baby" than in a larger center • Requires an extremely high level of trust; your child is with one provider—on the provider's turf • A solo provider creates "all eggs, one basket" risk • May not be able to use when your child is sick • Does the provider's vacation/break schedule match yours (and if not, can you work around it)?	• Weekly or monthly fee as negotiated with provider • Overtime or late charges as agreed • At your discretion, an annual/holiday bonus payment	• State licensure • Tour of the home • Interview with care provider • Reference checks with current and past parents

In-home options

Nanny or babysitter	• Ease and convenience of in-home care • Ensures 1:1 attention • Flexibility: nanny may be able to cover if you're working long hours, traveling, or have a nonstandard schedule	• You become responsible for direction and quality of the nanny's work • No "second set of eyes" on what's happening while you're at work • Privacy issues: a nonfamily member has full and complete access to your home	• Hourly rate, or weekly salary based on a set number of hours • Overtime, as agreed • Annual/holiday bonus payment	• Interview process • Background and reference check • Unannounced drop-ins • If written into your contract: a 2–3 week probationary period at start of work

(continued)

TABLE 2-1 (continued)

Care type	Advantages	Barriers and considerations	Typical cost components*	How to ensure quality
Nanny or babysitter (continued)	• Possibility of long-term relationship with caring, trusted, parent-like figure • Caregiver also typically provides light housekeeping and home-management services (accepting packages, keeping sink free of dishes, etc.)	• Distraction potential: if you work at home, having a small child and an additional adult around may strain your work focus • All eggs in one basket: if caregiver is ill, decides to leave, or doesn't work out, you're (temporarily) left without care	• If sourced through a service, up-front placement fee • Costs associated with any other benefits provided—e.g., a monthly parking pass or the cost of food if you agree on an "open kitchen" policy	
Au pair	• Ease and convenience of in-home care; because au pair lives in the home, may also be able to provide morning, evening, or weekend support • 1:1 attention • Superb way to expose your child to another culture and/or language • Depending on ages of your children, may fill a dual role of "trusted caregiver and big sister" • Possibility of long-term relationship with past au pair(s) living overseas • Potentially a good component in a hybrid arrangement	• Need to offer room and board • Hours limited; cannot provide overnight care • Certain turnover • Au pair may have limited previous professional and/or childcare experience • Cultural and language differences may make the relationship more challenging • Less day-to-day control and oversight than a center • Distraction potential • All eggs in one basket	• Up-front placement fee paid to au pair agency • Weekly stipend • Cost of room and board	• Agency performs up-front interviews as well as background and reference checks • Your own interview • Unannounced drop-ins

Family caregiver	• Care delivered by a loving, trusted member of your family • 1:1 attention • Superb way to expose your child to another generation and/or broader family relationships • Potentially, lower- or no-cost option	• Family dynamics • Potential resistance to direction or feedback; a "this is how I do things" approach • If caregiver is older, certain physical activities may be limited • Distraction potential • All eggs in one basket	• As agreed with family member/caregiver	• Your own knowledge and experience with the family member/caregiver
Staggered care	• Your child spends 100%, or close to 100%, of his or her time with a parent or other trusted caregiver • Lowest-cost solution; depending on schedule, you may be able to avoid the need for any paid care at all	• Only possible if schedules allow; best for hourly work, shift work, and self-employment situations, when you can set your own hours • Limits the amount of time that can be spent as a whole family unit	• While there are little to no direct costs, important to consider indirect ones: Will working certain shifts or times of day change pay, or overtime eligibility?	• Limited need for quality assurance—child is with a parent or other trusted caregiver at all times

Blended solutions

Hybrid care	• A multiprong, multicaregiver solution that "fits your family": your work hours, personal preferences, logistical needs, and budget	• Greater complexity in scheduling, logistics, communications, etc. • More than one caregiving solution may mean increased expenses • Likelihood of ongoing change/flux in caregivers and practical arrangements	• Depends on solutions chosen	• Combination of methods above

*Note that actual costs for each type of care will vary widely. A company-sponsored daycare program may be significantly cheaper than other options—but more expensive than the one at the local community center, for example, and local market rates for in-home care can vary widely by geography. Try to get information from other parents you trust, or see if you can glean any information from parenting groups on social media as to standard pay practices in your area. Childcare isn't the right place to drive a hard bargain, but you do want to be as smart as you can on the costs.

The right care arrangement is the one that works for you

" Mondays and Tuesdays, our nanny comes. Wednesdays and Thursdays, she goes to the nursery. Fridays, I'm at home. On the days I have to do drop-off and pickup, it means getting into the office a little later, and leaving a little early. Sometimes I work on my flex day, or past 8 p.m."

—*Sarah, law partner, mother of one*

" My husband works from 5:00 a.m. to 1:30 p.m., Monday through Friday, so he's home for the kids in the afternoons after school, and on weekends. And my mother-in-law lived with us for thirteen years, which was a huge help. We wanted the kids to have a parent or relative taking care of them."

—*Jennifer, retail store manager, mother of three*

" We're comfortable using daycare. Our son seems happy, and we think it's good for him."

—*Eduardo, online retail company cofounder, father of one*

have to work late nights, for example, would an in-home provider make more sense than daycare—or is a hybrid arrangement what you really need?)

If you're still stuck, take a step back and ask yourself if general nervousness or anxiety about care is really the issue. If so, now's the time to connect with other working parents who are happy with their own arrangements, and there are plenty of them. The additional color and anecdotes they share with you can help bring each option alive and should make the emotional part of decision-making easier. Remember also that while your goal is to find good-quality childcare, this doesn't have to be a "forever choice." You can always decide to make adjustments or even switch caregiving types entirely down the road as your career and family needs change.

Daycare licensing

To get—and maintain—an operating license, any daycare facility, whether a large center or small in-home operation, must demonstrate that it is meeting certain standards of safety and cleanliness, that it maintains an appropriate staff-to-child ratio, and that all daycare workers are properly screened and trained, among other hurdles. Licensing rules are typically extensive, although they vary by geography. For details on specific requirements in your area, check your local government's childcare-licensing website.

While an up-to-date license does not guarantee that you'll like a particular center, or that it will be a good all-around fit for your family, it does provide important assurance that the center is monitored as a secure and developmentally appropriate environment for small children. *Always* check licensing status for any center where you plan to leave your child, including on an emergency-backup or short-term basis. If any center is unlicensed, has had safety violations, or has had its license suspended or revoked, look elsewhere for care solutions.

Virtual care

During the Covid-19 pandemic, many working parents began leaning on an all-new and improvised form of care: the *virtual sitter*—a relative, friend, or paid caregiver who, while unable to come to your home, is able to distract, entertain, supervise, and engage with your child, all over videoconference.

In the right circumstances, virtual care can be a wonderful help. A grandparent can read your five-year-old a story, keeping her happily busy and out of your way while you get work done in the next room. Or a teenage sitter can help get your older child through his math homework, freeing you up as algebra tutor so you can get on that conference call. It's an effective, small-scale, stopgap measure for children old enough to engage by screen.

What a virtual sitter can never do, of course, is ensure safety. Your five-year-old may love having Grandma read to her, but you still need to be there, watchful, and available.

Finding, Assessing, Choosing, and Hiring a Care Provider

As soon as you've settled on the right type of care, you can start the hunt for a specific provider. At this thoughts-into-action transition point, many new parents begin feeling overwhelmed or options-constrained. You're facing a big task! The best way to tame it, to make sure you turn up the very best caregiving options possible, and to keep yourself together along the way is to see and to treat the search as a *process*, or series of discrete, doable steps. Work the steps carefully and thoroughly, and they'll lead you to the best possible result.

Step 1: Determine your target start date

Perhaps the very first question any potential care provider will ask is, "When are you looking to start?" To make these conversations productive you'll want to have a firm answer. Having a clear deadline will also help keep you focused and on point throughout what may feel like a lengthy, nonlinear journey.

Give *very* careful attention, though, as to what date that should be. If, as many parents do, you decide to begin care just a few days before returning to work, you risk putting yourself in a terrible pinch. You and your caregiver may not have enough time for that important "get

---

Considering a caregiver who's different than you are

To provide terrific care, your caregiver doesn't need to look, talk, or act like you or have the same personality. In fact, caregivers' differences can become a terrific benefit. That calm, reassuring nanny could complement your type A approach, and exposure to the various characters at the daycare center may help bring out your baby's own. And the au pair? She's going to jump-start your child's understanding and appreciation of other cultures—which is essential in our ever-more-diverse and -globalized world. As long as you're confident that your prospective caregivers can provide a secure, stable, and nurturing day-to-day experience for your child, don't worry so much about those dissimilarities.

to know you" phase that's essential to building trust and confidence, and if for any reason the arrangement doesn't work out, you just won't have enough time to find a plan B. And realistically, if leaving the baby at daycare is a brand-new experience on Day One back at work, it's going to be disconcerting, if not downright scary.

If at all possible, plan to start care a minimum of two weeks before you really need it, and even more if you can. That may sound like overkill, but those "buffer weeks" will let you go back to work significantly more comfortable about your care arrangements. Starting care doesn't have to mean starting it full-time or cutting into your precious parental leave; you may choose to leave the baby at daycare for mornings only, or ask the new nanny to come just a few hours each afternoon. Yes, you will have to pay for that extra care you use, but that money will be the best investment you ever make in the baby's safety, your own career, and your overall peace of mind.

Step 2: Get organized

Throughout the search process, you're going to be deluged with details and information: daycare-center literature, the center director's callback number, the notes you took during each parent tour, and so on. Without a structured system for capturing and managing all of it, it will be hard to keep sight of your many to-dos and very difficult to accurately compare one caregiving option to the next. Whether it's a spreadsheet or a set of file folders, having an organizational system will save you time, help you make better decisions, and let you feel more in charge.

Step 3: Create a simple job spec

You've already determined what general type of care you're looking for, but in order to find options that fully meet your needs, it's helpful to drill down further. If you've settled on daycare as the best way forward, for example, you may decide that you want *a family-run daycare center no more than a five-minute drive from your house* or *a larger daycare center with an active toddler program that's open until 7 p.m.* If you've decided on in-home care, you may choose to look for a bilingual caregiver, or one who can work occasional weekends, or who's already taken care

> " We interviewed a *lot* of potential caregivers—and very different ones, both women and men. We realized what we fundamentally wanted was someone with a big heart and a moral compass. Those two things had to be there."
>
> —*Brian, real estate agent, father of two*

of twins. You don't have to get fancy or too detailed here, and there's no right or wrong criteria; your spec can be a sentence or less, and it should be completely personal to you. But having it will help accelerate the care search—you'll be ready to make quick decisions on which caregiving options to take a closer look at and which to take a pass on.

As you develop your spec, **keep your standards high**. Under pressure to find care, it's all too easy to move into *I'll take the best I can get* mode or to favor decisions that just make this process *end*, already. "Good enough" is not what you're searching for here—this is your child, and you want the absolute best care you can find. To stay in the right frame, start whatever one-sentence spec you put together with the phrase, "A highly responsible, completely trustworthy, terrific caregiver who . . ." That *I'm not settling* mindset will help you stay on the right path.

Step 4: Start tapping your network—and other sources—for leads and referrals

Looking for care is a volume game—just like a job search, or dating. The more initial options you turn up, the more likely you are to find "the one." Cast your net as wide as possible. Go broad!

Sources for good care-option referrals include:

- Your friends, family, and coworkers

- The working-parents network group in your organization

- Your child's healthcare provider's office (check the bulletin board in the reception area; there may be notices from families seeking to outplace their own caregivers, or from local daycare organizations)

- Your alumni group, trade organization, or civic or faith community

- A local parents' group on social media

- The "help wanted/positions wanted" section of a local newspaper (as hopelessly old school as this option may sound, many community publications do have active, well-used employment pages)

- Your state's official list of licensed childcare facilities

- A childcare agency or placement service

If you need an outreach script, it's this: "Starting in September, I'm going to need excellent childcare for my [infant son or daughter]. I'm focused on finding a terrific, trustworthy, [insert your spec description, here], and I'd be grateful for any leads you may have. Please feel free to forward this to members of your network. If you do have any referrals, I can be reached at [email or phone]." Be certain to keep careful track of all responses.

Step 5: Start making calls

With a list of initial options in hand, your next step is to get in touch with each one by phone (note: *not* by text, email, social media, or other,

> Our state keeps a database of all the licensed facilities in the area, and I started there. I did a ton of online research, went to a lot of open houses, and had clear criteria: a center that was communicative with parents, took a collaborative approach, and that carefully tracked the kids' developmental milestones. Of course, I also wanted a place my son would be happy. Your mommy- or daddy-sense goes off quickly on that one. When he didn't want to leave at pickup time, I knew it was a good sign.
>
> What ultimately made the difference was being willing to commute a little further. For an extra twenty minutes in the car each morning, we were able to find the right spot."
>
> —*Kendra, marketing project manager, mother of one*

more-efficient means). Ostensibly, you're calling the daycare center to schedule a tour or the nanny candidate to check her availability to come for an in-person interview. But these calls aren't just about scheduling: they have an important evaluative purpose. They're what any experienced headhunter or recruiter would call an *initial screen*—a quick-hit, first-round interview process that lets you eliminate less-than-stellar candidates quickly. As you make your calls, pay careful attention: Did the person who answered the phone at the daycare center sound unfriendly, or keep you on hold? Did the prospective in-home caregiver have an unintelligible outgoing voicemail message or sound chilly or "blah" when you spoke? You're looking for *warm, can-do,* and *responsive* here—if that's not the vibe you're getting, move on.

Step 6: Do formal tours and interviews

Once a caregiver or center has passed your initial phone test, it's time for a closer look and an in-person evaluation. To get the best information and to keep your process moving along, think about doing these visits and meetings in two successive phases. (If any prospective care provider pushes back on the idea of a second get-together, take that as a serious, red-flag warning.)

In **Round 1**, your goal is to get a generalized sense of the center or caregiver's capabilities, personality, and competence. You're looking for answers to the questions, "Is this someplace and/or someone I would feel reasonably confident entrusting my child with? Would she be happy and well taken care of?" While you may find yourself very tempted to approach this round in checklist fashion—racing through dozens of specific, must-ask questions—it's much more effective to keep your questions few and probing, to make the candidate do most of the talking, and to spend the majority of your time in careful, thoughtful observation. Use your eyes, ears, and parental instincts, focusing on the holistic picture. How does the prospective nanny talk about her work, and particularly her past charges? Does the center feel orderly and cheerful? How does the staff appear to interact with the children? To develop that all-important gut sense as to whether or not this caregiver might be right for you, try asking the questions in table 2-2.

TABLE 2-2

Childcare Provider Round 1 Assessment Questions

Question	What it really lets you assess
Tell me about yourself/the center OR Walk me through your past work experiences OR Can you please describe the center's philosophy, organization, and curriculum	• What information does this care provider choose to lead with? What's important to them? How do they see themselves? • How do they think? Express themselves? Organize information? • Might this be a good general fit?
What does a typical day of care look like? What about a week?	• To what degree will this care be structured and routine-driven versus more free-form? • Are daily experiences varied to provide children with stimulation, particularly as they get older?
How do you usually communicate with parents?	• How would this provider see their relationship with me? • If I have questions or if issues come up, how will we begin to resolve them? • Are there likely to be day-to-day surprises here?
When have you been proudest of your/the center's work? AND/OR What's been the toughest situation you've handled?	• How reflective is this provider about their work? • How forthcoming are they?
Who would your center or approach *not* be a good fit for?	• To what degree is this provider committed to finding a genuinely strong fit versus being in sales mode? • What isn't this provider set up to handle?
What types of relationships do you maintain with children and families once they've "aged out" of care with you?	• Do they see this as a job, a relationship, or both? • What should I be probing during later reference-check calls?

With the insights and impressions from Round 1, you'll be able to choose which centers or caregivers to respectfully take a pass on, and which to investigate further.

If Round 1 answered the question "Can this caregiver generally do a good job?" the goal of **Round 2** is to discern whether or not the caregiver can do a *consistently good job in the context of your unique family and*

Tips for acing the interview

To be sure you're getting the most complete and accurate picture of any prospective care provider, use the same interview-and-assessment techniques that the savviest headhunters and recruiters do.

- **Don't talk, listen.** If you're speaking more than 25 percent of the time during any tour or interview, it's too much. Get the caregiver talking instead.
- **Ask open-ended questions.** That means ones that can't be responded to with a simple yes or no. Questions that start with *describe, tell me about, to what degree, what's your view on,* or *how would you handle things if* will elicit richer and more-telling information.
- **Probe further.** Never settle for simple, pat answers—dig: "How so?" "In what ways?" "What happened then?"
- **Ask for another.** Most interviewees are smart enough to have a few positive, canned anecdotes at the ready. To get the *real* story on how the daycare center handles discipline, say, "That's a great example—I'd love to hear a few more."
- **Drill down on transitions and changes.** Why did the daycare center close its second location across town? Why did the nanny change jobs then? You want to know how the caregiver handles setbacks and tough decisions.
- **Preview your reference checks.** Tell the interviewee: "As part of this interview process, I'll be speaking to [each of your past employers/other parents who have had children at this center]. What will they tell me that we haven't covered here today?" If she's withholding key information, this should prompt her to come clean.
- **Make it clear that you'll be on the job.** Mention that you'll be popping by the daycare center often—or that friends and relatives will often come by the house unannounced. Any caregiver who's uncomfortable with being closely monitored will likely self-select out of the process.
- **Leave plenty of time for questions.** What the caregivers ask *you* is just as important as what you ask *them.* Any interviewee should have two to three good questions that convey warmth and interest in your family.

career, now and over time. That means stress-testing the impressions you've already developed, covering any particular issues important to you, and projecting forward. In this round, make certain to ask about:

- Major developmental milestones (solid foods, walking, talking, etc.), and how the daily routine or schedule will change with each

- How the center or caregiver deals with differences of opinion, or follows through on directions they disagree with

- How emotions and discipline are handled; how your child will be comforted or redirected when upset or misbehaving

- The support of, or flexibility to accommodate, a certain diet, twins/multiples, other caregivers in a hybrid-care arrangement, your particular family structure, a bilingual child, or other specific concerns and needs

- Potential caregiving interruptions—e.g., dates the center will be closed, its sick-child policy, an in-home caregiver's vacation requests, the prospective nanny's plans for making her commute work in bad weather, and so on

- The details of health, welfare, and emergency plans. Does the nanny have her CPR certificate? Does the center monitor the

> " We hired one nanny who constantly called out sick, and we had to let her go six months later. It was only when I got serious about what I needed and about my expectations that the stars aligned. I put my specific criteria for a caregiver down on paper—we wanted someone who would cook our kids healthy meals, for example—and I decided to trust my instincts.
>
> When our current nanny came to interview, the first thing she did was ask to wash her hands. Throughout our conversation, she spoke so highly and warmly of the other families she had worked for. When my kids interrupted her, she was gentle and patient. I knew right away that it was a good fit. She's been with us for four years."
>
> —*Leigh, human resources leader, mother of three*

children's temperatures each morning? Where are the children evacuated to if the building's fire alarm goes off?

- Hours, scheduling, and flexibility on each

- Fees, including overtime, late-pickup charges, and any other extras

Step 7: Repeat steps 4, 5, and 6, as needed

If the stars align, you'll find a terrific caregiver among the very first few you speak with. Most likely, however, they won't align—and you'll need to continue chasing down new leads and generating and assessing new options. If so, don't see it as a setback, but simply as a natural part of your very thorough and thoughtful process. Keep your eyes on the prize here: good care isn't only wonderful for your child, it's helpful to your career, to your relationship with your partner, to your own peace of mind. Try to see this "more and more" part of the search as comforting, allowing you to do increasingly sophisticated and discerning evaluations, to do more-careful comparisons, and to develop a stronger gut sense for what good-quality care looks like.

Step 8: Narrow the field to two or three finalists—and perform thorough background and reference checks on each

A **background check** lets you ensure that "what you see is what you get" with any potential caregiver. For a licensed daycare provider, this means going to your local government website, double-checking that the center's license is valid and up-to-date and that recent inspections have not turned up any meaningful violations. For an individual caregiver, this means verifying her identity, credentials, and work experience; confirming that she has no criminal past or record of civil judgments and that her credit history is unconcerning. If you choose to be very thorough, you may evaluate her use of social media. (We're all free to be ourselves online, but do you really want to hire a nanny who posts vulgar, biased, or otherwise offensive material?) Note that you will need the caregiver's permission and personal information, such as date of birth or passport number, to perform some of these checks, and that they can be complex and time consuming. You may prefer to hire a professional background-checking firm to do the work for you for a moderate fee.

Reference checking means speaking to the prospective caregiver's past clients or employers about their experiences. It can't be said often, strongly, or loudly enough: *a caregiver's past performance is the best and most reliable predictor of that caregiver's future work for you.* When you know how a daycare center or nanny has partnered with other families, it provides you with powerful insights on what your own experience is likely to be. While every daycare center or nanny should be able to provide a few stock references, it's a good idea to ask for more, and better yet, to speak with people who aren't on that list, if you can identify and access them. That way, you're more likely to get the real-deal, unvarnished view on the prospective caregiver as opposed to a sanitized, scripted message. Bring a careful eye as to just who you're speaking with; as paranoid as it sounds, you want to make certain that you're really speaking to past clients and employers—not to the caregiver's friends or family members posing as such. On those reference-checking calls, make sure that all basic information, such as dates of employment, line up with exactly what the caregiver provided you. Ask about general impressions and experience; greatest strengths; any weaknesses, disagreements, or disappointments. Ask how likely, on a scale of 1 to 10, the reference giver would be to use the same care if it were possible to go back in time and do things all over again. The Childcare Concerns Framework (table 2-4, later in this chapter) will help you figure out the right response to any issues surfaced during these calls.

As laborious or bureaucratic as background- and reference-checking can be, *never* give these steps short shrift. They are your power tools for finding good care and for keeping your child happy and safe. One way or another you're going to get important insights through this phase. If you do get concerning feedback through these processes, avoid creating "explanations" or feeling surprised or betrayed. You've simply and smartly dodged a bullet, and it's time to move on.

Step 9: Make your decision

Deep breath, now! Trust your instincts and all of the research and leg-work you've done. You're the parent, and no one is going to have bet-ter insight and a better feel for the right decision here than you will.

Step 10: Formalize it

Whether you choose to enroll your child in daycare or hire an in-home care provider, it's a smart idea to get the terms of your arrangement down on paper and agreed to before care begins. You want to make sure that you and your caregiver are—quite literally—working off the same page, and reduce the likelihood of disagreements later on. (You won't be surprised by the center's late-pickup charges or find yourself negotiating paid leave with your nanny if it's all there in black and white to begin with.) Larger daycare centers should provide their own standard form, but for home-based arrangements you may need to cre-ate a simple contract document yourself. Whichever the case, be sure it covers:

- The precise scope of caregiving responsibilities

- Hours, including overtime or late-pickup policies, etc.

- Fees/salary, overtime rates, and any additional benefits or costs (e.g., for an in-home care provider, a gas allowance or "open kitchen" policy)

- Vacation and holidays: the number of days off, paid and unpaid, when they can and can't be taken, and with how much notice

- Safety-related dos and don'ts (for example, that the sitter should always keep the front door locked or stairs gated)

- What happens when either your caregiver or child is sick

- The notice period if either of you chooses to end the arrangement

Never agree to or sign any caregiving contract holding you to a cer-tain period of time in care, or to unusual or excessive fees for ending

Paying for it

Good childcare is hard to find—and typically very expensive when you do. To confront those costs, start by checking if, based on residency and income, you're eligible for any child-related tax credits and if it's possible for your employer to put a portion of your pretax salary into a dependent-care flexible spending account. Any "found money" from these two sources can go a long way toward easing the strain on your wallet, regardless of what kind of care you've settled on. Second, consider if there are any out-of-the-box ways of limiting your total overall childcare outlay. Maybe you could share a nanny's services with another family—or put the baby in part-time daycare and have a family member cover the other hours. Third—and yes, this may be an uncomfortable step—look to your existing family budget for any other areas where you can cut back. For in-depth advice and a holistic system for managing your working-parent finances, turn to chapter 11, "Money."

As you stare at your monthly bill thinking *how is it humanly possible that I'm paying this much*, remember: there's no greater investment to be made than in your child's day-to-day care—and soon, this too shall pass. In a few years, the kids will be in school and care costs will go down dramatically.

it: if you need to, you should be able to end care quickly and without undue cost.

What You May Be Thinking and Feeling While Waiting for Care to Start

With your caregiving start date confirmed, you may—rather than heaving the huge sigh of relief you expected to—find yourself anxious, and battling a raft of worries about the arrangements you've just taken such pains to set up. Feelings like these are completely, 100 percent normal. In fact, being so deeply concerned about your child's care and safety is a *good* thing: it's evidence that you're a diligent and loving parent. But it's important not to let yourself get derailed, either practically or psychologically, by these concerns.

Creating your Emergency Contacts Sheet

Before starting care—of *any* kind—be certain to put together a workparent-appropriate Emergency Contacts Sheet, which should hang in a prominent place inside your home, and be provided both electronically and by hard copy to everyone involved in your child's care. You'll find a sample Emergency Contacts Sheet at the end of chapter 19, "Health—Yours and Theirs."

To help take the temperature down a notch, try using the technique of *realistic reframing*, which simply means identifying (or admitting) the specific concerns or worries you're grappling with and then, in mental dialogue with yourself, beginning to diffuse them.

Let's say, for example, that the plan is to have your son start in daycare on April 15. It's April 1 now, and you're up nights thinking about what's ahead. Your reframing conversation might look something like what is shown in table 2-3.

Pushing back like this on your tensions and fears won't completely make them go away—but it will help soften them and put things in better perspective. If your anxiety level is high enough that you find yourself unable to do this type of reframing solo, ask your partner, a relative, a good friend, or a trusted colleague to talk it through. You've found good care for your child, and it's OK to also seek out some care and support for yourself.

The First Few Days and Weeks

A few approaches can make the actual transition into your care arrangements calmer and easier for everyone.

- If at all possible, keep the first day of care free from any other personal or work obligations.

- Treat Week One as a phase-in, rather than a hard start. Have the nanny come or plan to leave the baby at the daycare for just

TABLE 2-3

Reframing Your Worries About Starting Care

Common worry	Realistic reframing
I don't really know the people who run the daycare! They could be uncaring or negligent or worse. This could end up like one of those horror stories you see on TV.	No, I don't really know these people. But they work in an accredited, well-regarded childcare center, and I've done extensive reference-checking with other parents, who all had good things to say about the place. All my careful research indicates that the baby will be in good hands.
How do I know this childcare situation will even work out? It could go wrong . . . and I'll be right back at square one.	Even with all of the interviewing, researching, and background-checking I've done, this childcare arrangement could turn out not to be the right choice. And if so, I'll make a change. That change won't be easy or fun, but I'll do it as an on-the-job parent who's always committed to what's best for my child.
The diapers, the feedings, the spit-up— this is the precious stuff, and my responsibility. Why should a stranger do it?	Small children need a *lot* of care. There will be plenty of diapers, feedings, naps, etc., ahead, and it will be a nice thing to have some help. And big picture: having good caregivers allows me to continue with my career. Plus, this isn't a competition . . . there's no electronic scoreboard anywhere tracking how many diapers I've changed versus anyone else.
How can I possibly leave him? I'm going to collapse/cry when I do. And then I'll not only be upset but embarrassed.	Leaving him will be emotional, and when human beings get emotional, it's normal and healthy for us to express it. Any tears will only go to show how attached to him I am, and any caregiver worth her salt has seen parents get upset like this before. On that first day, I will remind myself that I'm going to be back to pick him up in just a few hours.
He's going to end up loving his caregiver(s) more than he loves me.	My position as this child's [mother or father] is unassailable. I will *always* be the central figure in his life. And if he *also* feels bonded and connected to his caregivers, that's a good thing. I don't want to leave him with adults he only feels so-so about! The more he feels his caregiver is loving, trustworthy, and part of his life, the healthier it is—for everyone.

> " If you told me that I would hire someone to live in my house and look after my kids on the basis of a thirty-minute Skype interview, I would have said, 'Are you *insane*?' But the au pair agency checks all the candidates, and you develop a clear sense of what you're looking for in terms of personality and experience—what will work in your home. Before our first au pair arrived, my wife and I sat down and wrote a twenty-page guide to living in our house, how we do things, and what we expect. That process forced us to think about how we take care of our kids, and why. It actually made us better parents."
>
> —*Ethan, professor, father of two*

one to two hours to begin with, and then on each successive day, lengthen that time.

- Set aside the first thirty minutes of the first day of care as orientation. At the daycare, make certain you know where to put all baby gear and extra clothing, spend time looking around the classroom, read what's up on the bulletin board by the front entrance, and introduce yourself to the other care providers. Or show the nanny or au pair around the house—where the sterilizing equipment is kept, how the washer/dryer works—and then go over baby's nap schedule. Your goals here are 1) to increase your familiarity with the caregiver, and the caregiver's with you; 2) to make sure everyone has the logistical information they need to make the next few days and weeks go smoothly; and 3) to begin gaining comfort and familiarity with your new routine.

- As soon as the time you've set aside for orientation is over, *get out of the way*. Don't hover or linger by the door, which will only make the transition harder. Step back and let your caregiver do her job. If you're still a little nervous, it's fine to stay close by: take yourself to the coffee shop around the corner from the daycare, or if nanny and baby are in the living room, head to your home office upstairs.

- Throughout the first two weeks, leave ample time at the beginning and end of each care day for the additional orientation,

Becoming the boss

Hiring an in-home caregiver—whether a full-time nanny, a family member, an occasional sitter, or any other type of provider—comes with important obligations. Depending on the type of care and where you live, you may need to adhere to strict rules on hours and overtime, offer an adequate number of sick and vacation days, become responsible for your caregiver's tax withholding and reporting, and ensure adequate insurance coverage. To make sure you're doing all the right things, it's a good idea to consult your childcare placement agency, if relevant, personal accountant or tax preparer, family attorney, and insurance broker (will your homeowner's policy cover it if your babysitter sprains her ankle on your front stoop?), and to get help from a "nanny payroll" service that can manage payments and tax filings for a reasonable fee.

Equally important is your personal, managerial, and moral obligation to ensure a safe, respectful, healthy, and fair work environment. That means providing clear and reasonable feedback, ensuring adequate breaks and mealtimes, and developing a good overall rapport. Under no circumstances is it ever acceptable to treat your caregiver with disrespect or create an environment that involves any type of harassment (physical, psychological, or verbal). If ever in doubt, ask yourself, "Would I be comfortable being treated this way at my own job?" Big picture, remind yourself that your caregiver is a critical member of your Village, and just like you, a hardworking professional and human being. Do right by her.

questions, observations, and information-sharing that will help get you off to a good start. You're learning to work together, and it's natural, say, for daycare providers to have questions about whether the baby usually flips herself over and sleeps on her stomach, or for the au pair to need a tutorial on how to fold the stroller so that it fits into the car.

Expect that everything will go well as you go through this critical introductory period and that you, your child, and the caregiver will quickly settle into a stable, satisfying routine. Just to be certain things are on a good keel, though, and to give yourself some extra reassurance, plan to do a few "spot checks" throughout these first few weeks. If daycare pickup is usually at 5:30 p.m., show up once or twice around 4:00, explaining that your "meeting ended early"—or circle back home twenty minutes after you leave so that you can peer in on the nanny, while picking up some important object that you oh-so-strategically forgot. If you do see something amiss during these unexpected visits, that will be important information, and if you see something seriously amiss, you'll be able to take immediate action. Most likely, though, you'll find a happy scene—your caregivers showing the baby a toy, giving a bottle, or busy with other work while she naps—and the experience will help cement your faith and trust that the care arrangements you've put in place are the right ones.

Communicating with Your Caregiver(s)

Developing an open, trusting, friendly relationship with your child's caregiver(s) is essential. In fact, many fellow working parents will tell you—only half-jokingly—that their partnership with the caregiver is just as important as the one with their actual life partner. And as in any close collaboration between two people, the glue that holds everything together is positive, open, and regular communication. To make sure you're speaking effectively—and speaking enough—with your caregiver:

- Agree on the rules of the road. Have an informal agreement on when, why, and how to be in touch and share information. Will you debrief at the end of each day? Set aside a solid fifteen minutes each Friday to catch up on what happened during the week? Expect a text message if the baby seems unusually fussy? There's no need for an elaborate protocol here, just a mutual understanding on how communication can and should happen.

- Plan to set aside adequate time for daily handovers. Mornings and evenings can be extremely rushed, but be sure to carve out a few dedicated minutes for each caregiving transition and during that time to give your caregivers your full attention. If you have an in-home caregiver, she'll need a few minutes to get her coat off and wash her hands upon arrival. At a center, you'll need to spend a few moments to get your child settled in. During the evening transition, those "extra" minutes will be useful for learning important details about what happened throughout the day—like if the baby woke up early from her long nap, or seemed hungry again shortly after a big feed. Just as important, they will provide opportunities to develop a friendly, positive rapport.

- Be direct, honest, and open—but pick your spots. If your son has seemed overtired after daycare recently, ask his caregivers to ensure he gets a longer nap. If you prefer that the nanny not host playdates during flu season, say so. But if she folds the baby's undershirts differently than you do, *just let it go.* You're striving to manage an overall environment of safe, responsible, happy care—and some of your caregiver's actions or habits, even if they rub you just a tiny bit the wrong way, aren't worth your time or the relationship cost of getting into.

- Ask nicely. Depending on the culture of your industry or workplace, you may be used to direct—even curt—communications and requests. Your boss may often say, in so many words, "Make this happen! Get it done!" But this isn't your workplace, and your caregiver's feelings about her work, and about you, truly matter, and a softer approach is called for. "Can I ask you a favor . . ." "Would you mind . . ." "When you get a free minute, would you . . ." "It would be great if . . ." are more gentle ways to start asking for what you need. You don't have to tiptoe around or sugarcoat things; just ensure that your caregiver feels respected.

- Solicit her opinions and advice. Nothing fosters the two-way-street nature of this relationship better than asking for your caregiver's perspective and expertise. Does she think it's time to drop the 10 a.m. feeds? What's the best way to handle teething? Now that the baby's sitting up unsupported, does your caregiver imagine she'll be crawling soon? If you ask questions like these, you'll not only get new information but be signaling that you see this relationship as a collaborative partnership.

If You Need to Make a Change

Maybe you've gone from a full-time to a part-time schedule, and your care needs and budget have shifted. Or maybe you're developing a gut sense that the care arrangements you've just started aren't working out. Either way, you may find yourself feeling anxious, guilty, and uncertain about what exactly to do next. Here's how to take charge of the situation and make the right moves.

If your needs have changed, start by determining exactly what your new arrangement will look like, as well as your desired timing—e.g., *we'll need to ramp down to three days a week at daycare by mid-October*. Once you have that clarity, an honest conversation with your care provider is in order. If you started care recently, this may feel like a difficult conversation: you're essentially initiating the classic "it's not you, it's me" breakup. To make things easier, lay out the facts clearly and calmly (your job has changed; your partner has decided to stay home); assure your caregiver that your decision is not in any way a reflection of your feelings about her work; make it clear that you will follow the terms of your contract, whether that includes a notice period or severance payment; and offer to do whatever's needed to ensure a good transition. That might mean serving as a reference for the daycare center or helping your in-home caregiver secure a new full-time spot with another local family.

If you have concerns about your current care arrangement, trust those parental instincts, but try to put a finger on exactly what the issue is; the clearer you are on the problem, the more easily the solution

Do I need a nanny cam?

A nanny cam is a generic term for any video-surveillance system that allows you to monitor your in-home caregiver's interactions and behavior with your child. If you feel you need one, ask yourself if you're looking for an extra layer of reassurance—or if what you really need is a new nanny.

> At drop-off that first day, the center was a completely different place than when we had toured. There were more children in the infant room. One of the caregivers was seven months pregnant and struggling to keep up. An older baby started commando-crawling toward my son while he was on his play mat. It wasn't what we had signed up for, but I *had* to go to work.
>
> My mom had come with me to do the drop-off, and as we were turning to go she said, 'Let's get him out of here.' We never went back. I don't know what I would have done if she wasn't there.
>
> We quickly found another arrangement that's worked well."
>
> —*Danielle, fashion wholesale executive, mother of two*

When the care arrangement is going well

If daycare is working out just the way you'd hoped or you see the nanny as part of the family now, it's a wonderful, reassuring feeling—and important for your caregiver(s) to know. Say so—and be direct: "It's been two months now, and from our perspective things are going great. We're impressed by all the great work you've done, and appreciate the care you're providing [child's name]. We couldn't have hoped for better." Consider backing up your comments with a small amount of cash or a gift card, presented as "an additional way of expressing our thanks." If daycare center rules prohibit gifts, bring flowers or write a nice note. If you use in-home care, frame a picture of your sitter with the baby, and display it among other family photos in a prominent place in the house; it will send a warm, wonderful, inclusive message about how you see the relationship progressing. Caregivers will naturally feel happier, more loyal, and more motivated when they know that you value their contributions.

will follow. To help sort things out, try using the Childcare Concerns Framework (see table 2-4).

If your concerns fall into the Green category, provide your caregiver some honest, direct feedback ("It's important to me to get to work on time, and to do that, I need for you to be here each morning by eight"), and monitor the situation. If they're in the Yellow zone, you

TABLE 2-4

Childcare Concerns Framework

Concern level	Green	Yellow	Red
Caregiver issue or behavior	• Stylistic or personality differences • Occasional lateness • Small mistakes or miscommunications	• Pushback on original contract terms—e.g., requests for additional time off or changes to fees • Occasional unresponsiveness • Occasional distractedness—e.g., cell phone use while on the job • Uneven levels of warmth/enthusiasm • Failure to perform needed tasks (e.g., does not keep baby on requested schedule) • Resisting or debating directions; insistence on doing things "my way"	• Compromising your child's safety • Overall lack of warmth or enthusiasm • Habitual distractedness—e.g., regular cell use or social-media activity while on the job • Failure to communicate in a timely, thorough way • Sudden changes in or erratic behavior • Pushback on basic requests • Loss of caregiving license • Evidence of drug or alcohol use • Absenteeism • Lying • Theft

may want to make additional observations, see if the problem is one-time-only or represents a pattern, and/or weigh the single concern against what might otherwise be very good care. If you are in the Yellow zone, though, set a time limit. Too much Yellow will get very stressful for you, and any persistent Yellow issue should be considered a Red. All behaviors in the Red category mean that you need to end the caregiving arrangement as soon as possible.

If you do need to end your care arrangement because of any quality or safety issues:

- Pick a notification date, and do not permit the caregiver to have any access whatsoever to your child, belongings, home, or billing information after that point. If you had an in-home caregiver, change the locks and alert the neighbors. If the caregiver had access to any of your accounts or technology, such as your Wi-Fi, freeze the account and/or change the relevant passwords.

- Deliver the news in person, in a neutral, public location and with your partner, a friend, or someone else present. While the likelihood of any legal follow-up or contract dispute is limited, you'll want witnesses as to how the arrangement ended. And while the chances of any in-person altercation are remote, it will nonetheless be comforting to know that you've got help immediately available.

- Say what you need to directly and unambiguously ("today is your last day with us"), but do not feel that you need to provide an explanation or reason. Keep the conversation brief.

As disheartening and emotional as it is to have to exit a disappointing care arrangement, do not let yourself get too flummoxed by it. Bad caregivers exist; but *most* are committed and trustworthy, and you *will* find a care arrangement that works. In the meantime, remind yourself: you've just done exactly what a committed, on-the-job, protective parent should.

Emergency and Backup Care

Your daughter spikes a fever and can't go to daycare. Your mother-in-law, who usually watches the baby, was just called up for jury duty. The au pair gets homesick and quits. Life happens, and even the best and most reliable care arrangements will at some point fall through. To

> My husband, my mother, my mother-in-law, and I round-robin: whenever one of the kids is sick and can't go to daycare, we take turns covering."
>
> —*Tracy, nurse manager, mother of two*

ensure your child's care and safety—not to mention your own ability to deliver at work—backup care isn't an afterthought, it's an absolute must. When your caregiving plan A otherwise erodes, you need to have plans B and C in your pocket and ready to go. And to stay safely out of the dreaded Childcare Emergency Zone, those plans can't be hypothetical or unrehearsed.

To start preparing for hiccups in your regular care arrangements, consider which of the six most common backup care options are available to you, and which you'll prefer to use.

- A friend, family member, or neighbor. Whoever it is agrees to take the baby on an occasional basis.

- An emergency backup care program offered through your company or organization. A backup care program can be an excellent, last-minute source of high-quality care. Depending on the arrangement or service, care may be offered in a qualified daycare center, or a screened, vetted daycare worker may be dispatched to your home. Corporate programs typically offer participating employees a set number of days of backup care with a minimal copay.

- A qualified babysitting agency with a dedicated backup service. If you live in a larger urban area, you should be able to find a high-quality babysitting agency capable of providing backup sitter support. (Note: be careful about relying on "childcare marketplace" type websites; consider seeking out a reputable agency that screens, background-checks, vets, and refers appropriate sitters, and that trains them on how to handle such one-off, just-in-time jobs.) In this instance, you contract directly with the agency and full costs come out of your own pocket. Those costs may include an up-front agency fee, a subscription, hourly rates, and extra charges for short-turnaround requests.

- Taking your child to work. Depending on the structure, location, and nature of your job, as well as on your organization's culture, this may be a natural, easy option . . . or a complete nonstarter.

- Having your partner sub in. Or he or she could take turns doing so with you.

- Acting as caregiver yourself. This might involve working remotely or taking the day off.

As you read over this list, the most viable—and desirable—options should quickly jump out. If your in-laws live in the neighborhood, they might be your first line of defense, or if the college-age sitter you use on weekends has a flexible schedule, she may be an option, too. Whatever the case, settle on what options you'll use, in what circumstances, and in what order. As you do so, play around with possible scenarios: the one-day emergency because your regular caregiver is under the weather versus the three-week gap you'll have to fill when the au pair quits.

Then, get tactical! Emergency backup care *ideas and intentions* don't work—only *plans and preparations* do. Play the entire situation through, imagining the rough spots and what will make them easier to deal with. If you'll be using corporate backup care, for example, make certain you're registered for it through your company's benefits system, that the service's number is programmed into your phone, that you've done at least one visit to the center itself so that you know how long it takes to drive there, that you've met the staff, and that you're familiar with the setup. Whatever your plans, always keep an emergency-care go-bag filled with an ample, twenty-four-hour supply of feeding, diapering, and clothing essentials in the front hall closet, ready for use. In other words, never let yourself be left caught and panic-stricken, wondering how to make things come together last minute and scrambling for information on the corporate backup program you only vaguely know about—get ahead of those emergencies. Always be ready to switch, as seamlessly and stress free as possible, into a well-thought-out plan B.

Even with careful preparations, backup care days are likely to be stressful, or at least, not your best. When they happen, focus on essentials and try to cut yourself a break. The baby's safety is completely nonnegotiable, but if he needs to spend a day at a new daycare center, or if your toddler is over at Grandma's house being fed more ice cream and watching more TV than you would ever normally allow, it's OK. Even if you do miss a few work obligations, it's not the end of the world—you're a parent, and things happen. Soon enough, you'll all be back in your regular, happy routine.

Trusted Caregivers, Happy Child

As you wait to become a parent, and then when you see your child for the very first time, you may find yourself overwhelmed by deep, almost animal feelings of protectiveness: this tiny new human being is the most precious thing in the world to you, and there's nothing you wouldn't do to keep him well and safe. And when you're in this natural, normal, and healthy "protect the tiger cub" mode, the idea of leaving your child with a caregiver—*any* caregiver—can feel incongruous.

But finding and starting care isn't a contradiction to good parenting: *it's an essential part of it.* The more caring, trustworthy adults that surround the baby, the more he'll thrive, both now and as he grows. The more comfort and trust you have in those caregivers, the more calm and centered you'll be. And the more calm and centered you are, the more you'll be able to deliver at work, take care of the family for the short and long term, and—ultimately—be the parent you want to be.

3

Parental Leave and the Return to Work

Managing the Great Big Initial Transitions—and
Coming Out Safely on the Other Side

You're counting down the days until your leave but encoun-
tering more practical decisions, awkward conversations, and
I don't know what to do moments than you'd prefer. Or you're
on leave . . . and having serious trouble facing that first day back. Or
you've already returned to work but feel as if you're riding a practical and emotional roller coaster, and getting queasy. Transitions are
inherently tough, and becoming a working parent means managing
through several big ones in quick succession. The right information
and approaches can make things easier, practically and personally,
and can give you the confidence you need to start working parenthood
strong.

Planning Your Leave

Figuring out the details of your parental leave should, in an ideal
world, be completely straightforward and take about five minutes. For
the majority of expectant mothers and fathers, though, it turns into a

Attention, American moms and dads

In the United States, the Family and Medical Leave Act of 1993, commonly known as "FMLA," allows many (not all) parents to take twelve weeks of unpaid, job-protected time away from work in connection with the birth or arrival of a new child as well as to care for a newborn, newly adopted, or newly arrived foster child. During that time, parents get to continue in their same health-insurance plan and on the same terms.

Both mothers and fathers can use FMLA, but it does not apply to private-sector organizations with fewer than fifty employees, to people who have worked for their company or business for less than twelve months or have worked fewer than 1,250 hours in the twelve-month period immediately preceding the leave, or to contractors or freelancers. If you've just joined that great startup as employee number forty-six, or if you work full-time for an organization but on a nonemployee basis, you're not technically FMLA-eligible. Other special provisions of the law apply to military personnel, seasonal workers, and geographically dispersed companies.

The US Department of Labor website explains FMLA in full and should answer all your questions: https://www.dol.gov/agencies/whd/fmla/faq.

longer and often very confusing process. Why? Because the amount of time you take is often determined by a combination of complex national leave laws; local laws, which can vary widely and change frequently; and employer policies, which can appear cut-and-dried but are often riddled with "ifs" and exceptions (some organizations will deny you paid leave if you've worked there for less than a year, for example). Your employment status can be a significant factor also: if you're an entrepreneur, a small-business employee, a part-timer, or a freelancer, of if you are paid by the hour or are working outside your country of citizenship, you may be held to a different set of rules—or not eligible for the leave you expected. And of course, even if you are *technically* eligible for a certain leave, there's your company's culture and unwritten rules to think of, as well as your own sense of what's best and workable for your family and career. When you're eagerly

What should I expect from HR?

Your company's human resources team should be able to do a thorough, timely, and complete job helping you get ready for leave: pointing you to the right benefits plans, providing timelines of when (and what) paperwork needs to be done, and answering any specific questions on leave policies or logistics. They may also be helpful in preparing you for working parenthood, longer term; be sure to scour the benefits website and ask your HR rep if there are any parent-to-parent mentoring programs, return-from-leave checklists, or other resources for navigating that all-important first year back. Expect your HR interactions to be positive ones.

Understand, though, that HR's function is to deliver and oversee company policy in an equal and fair way across the employee population—not to negotiate special side deals for individual workers. Push your HR rep for an exception to the standard parental-leave policy, and you put her in a very difficult position: saying yes to you means creating a new organizational precedent. If HR says no, or appears rigid and rules-obsessed, don't take it personally—most likely, the reps are acting in good faith and trying to ensure consistency and fairness.

looking forward to your child's arrival and suddenly finding yourself confronting this kind of bureaucracy, fine print, and need for subjective decisions, it can be jarring, but if you know where to look for information and know all the right questions to ask, you'll be best able to get this sorted out as quickly as possible.

Unless you're already rock-solid certain of what you're eligible for, start by taking an hour or so simply to educate yourself. Double-check both national and local government websites for the most up-to-date guidelines and any pending changes on parental leave, and then check your company's employee handbook or intranet for the same. Go straight to the source: do *not* rely on parenting blogs, news articles, or coworkers for hard data. Given the complexity and constant flux in leave laws and policy, and the many factors influencing how those rules may apply to you, there is a real possibility that you may be given inaccurate, incomplete, or out-of-date information.

Once you've got a grasp of the legal and policy basics, do some "soft research" by checking in with a few trusted colleagues, as well as with friends in the industry or at similar organizations. Ask for any extra detail and color on how they were able to negotiate, use, or extend their leaves, and what in retrospect they would have done or tried to do differently. Were they allowed to work from home the last week before their due date? Add on accrued personal days? Does your organization offer long leaves on paper but frown on people who actually take them? Your goal here is to round out the hard facts with full and detailed context—and to make yourself as savvy a consumer of parental leave as possible. (Think of approaching leave the same way you would buying a car: with a lot of up-front research yielding the best outcome.) Only after you've done all your research and benchmarking will you be ready to have an informed conversation with your manager or human resources representative to make sure you're on the same page, to clear up any gray areas, and to nail down your specific plans.

First-leaver advantage

If you're the first man or woman in your organization to take parental leave, the lack of policy and precedent can be disconcerting, and yet wonderfully liberating. You're free to negotiate for the time you really need—and potentially help other families in the future.

Before making your ask, inform yourself about standard leave policies in your function or industry—and at your organization's competitors. Then think through how to frame your request in terms that will resonate with the boss: asking for x weeks of leave "so that I can set up a good care arrangement and come back to work fully ready to contribute during busy season," or mentioning that "offering y amount of parental leave would make us a leader in the industry," will likely be more effective than simply asking for the time. The conversation will go best when you're seen as reasonable, well informed, and a team player focused on the organization's needs as well as on your own.

Be sure to come away from this information-gathering process with answers to *all* of the following questions:

- How much time am I eligible to take? What happens if, for medical or other reasons, I need or wish to extend that time?

- Do I have to take this time all at one go? Can I break it up and take it in chunks?

- How is the start of my leave determined? Is it the day the baby's born, my last day in the office or workplace, or a specific day I agree on with my manager?

- If I'm a biological mother, and placed on medical disability or bed rest before the birth, how will that affect my leave and pay?

- Can I extend my leave period by adding on vacation time, personal days, or any other accrued time off? Are there any other "unofficial" ways to get more time?

- How much will I get paid, and by whom (the company, the government, an insurer)?

- If my leave is paid, can I take extra time unpaid? If so, how much?

- How will parental leave affect any aspects of my pay beyond my base salary (e.g., overtime, vacation allowance, bonus, stock grants, vesting of any incentive compensation, tuition reimbursements, accrual toward retirement benefits, etc.)?

- How do health and all other benefits (wellness programs, ongoing education, etc.) carry over throughout my leave?

- What am I guaranteed upon my return to work? The same job? A similar job? What defines "same" or "similar"?

- How will my leave be taken into account at performance-appraisal time? (Note: this is a trick question. Parental status or leaves should never be factored into your job evaluations.)

Using your judgment—and getting creative

My second daughter was born twelve days after I started my new job. Our company has a great leave policy, but it felt strange to show up and then disappear for three months. Plus we had our nanny helping to take care of our older daughter, and my mother-in-law was in town to help for several weeks, all in a small New York City apartment.

I ended up taking a week off after the birth, another week a few months later around the Thanksgiving holiday, and then some additional time at year end. Stretching it out like that let me get up to speed in the new job, and also allowed me to be there when my family needed me, including when my wife transitioned back to work."

—*Basil, P&L director, father of two*

After each of our kids was born, I took leave and then my husband—he's an engineer—used his accrued vacation and sick days to take a month, also. No one at his organization had ever done that, but we had planned ahead. He had been banking his days off for years, and he stood firm.

If you're considering an unusual leave arrangement and find yourself thinking, 'There's no way that will work,' push yourself, and push the people you work with, too. Ask, 'Why *not*?'"

—*Laura, chief marketing officer, mother of two*

- What's the procedure for documenting my leave? Who should I connect with about the paperwork, or if I have additional questions?

If you're at all confused, push a little. Don't be afraid to nudge the HR person for additional detail on how nonsequential leave periods can be timed, or to point out to your manager that *other* mothers and fathers at your organization have beefed up their leaves by using vacation days. Good decisions and good self-advocacy start with good information, and you're well within your rights to ask for complete clarity on something so important. Be certain to do any of this questioning and pushing in a polite, constructive way, however. You don't want to come across as whiny, or entitled. Remember: how you operate as a working parent is an important part of your professional brand.

Leave Length: What If I'm . . . ?

Once you've determined the actual length of your leave, you'll want to address your own questions and concerns about how to make that amount of time work best for you. In this section, we'll look at each of the most common leave-length dilemmas, and at sensible ways to approach them. We'll start with longer time frames and work our way down to short leaves, or no leave. Focus *only* on the sections that apply to you and your particular situation. If you get a whole year's worth of paid leave, then yes, it will be appalling to think about people who get none—and if you get little leave, it's going to be tough to read about people who have more leave than they actually want. Leave equity is an important, and emotional, issue. But for right now, focus on how to do right by *you*.

. . . not sure I can/should take all the time I'm technically entitled to?

Many parents wish they could take longer leaves than they can, but it's also possible to find yourself grappling with the opposite problem: you may be able to take a solid stretch of time away from work—with pay, even—but worry if taking it all is going to be the right thing to do. Maybe you work in a client-intensive business, and are concerned about neglecting the terrific relationships you hustled so hard to build. Maybe you just joined a fast-moving startup and worry about being "out of sight and out of mind" for too long, or you love what you do and are eager to get back to it. For any number of practical or psychological reasons you might—as taboo as it can feel to say—want to take *less* time than allowed.

If you find yourself in this position, and perhaps feeling a little lonely or guilty, try to widen the lens. Leave is an essential, one-time-only opportunity to bond with your new child. Every single minute of it is precious, and to enjoy it, you're going to need to tolerate some inherent if short-term discomfort at turning your attentions away from work.

> When my son was born, I took as much time as I was allowed. It wasn't even a decision; there was no question that I was going to be there as much as I could for my partner and the baby. Nothing else mattered. There were other doctors who could cover. The hospital would cope.
>
> People can make whatever comments they want. Have a thick skin, and refuse to take what they say on board. It's your *right* to take this time."
>
> —*Jon, physician, father of one*

Think of this time as practice for what's to come: if you don't develop some experience and "muscle memory" in prioritizing family now, it's going to be very hard to do so later. That said, you also have a family to support, a career to maintain, ambitions for the future, and your own happiness and well-being to think of, and any one of those factors can point you toward an earlier return. In other words, look at this as a whole-life, deeply personal, and head-of-family decision, as opposed to a moralistic or purely black-and-white one. Do what's right for you, personally, as opposed to managing toward the "shoulds."

Think about middle-ground solutions too: perhaps you could take a "partial leave" by working a reduced schedule, or take all the time you can but find creative ways to engage with those important clients while you do. Or consider splitting the difference: if you're wavering between six and twelve weeks off, for example, commit to nine. As you mull things over, remember that leave is a benefit, not a rigid, all-or-nothing obligation.

. . . planning to take a long leave, of six months or more?

A long leave can be a wonderful benefit for any working parent. The ample, unhurried time allows you to recover from the arrival, adjust to being a mom or dad, find childcare that suits your needs, and fully bond with your baby.

This wonderful opportunity also comes with its own set of challenges. After many months away from work, it's easy to feel "out of it" or to start losing professional confidence. Even with a supportive manager

> I took a full year's leave, which was amazing. Most of my work was for big clients, who colleagues could help look after while I was away. I stayed in touch, though: coming back for office events, department lunches, keeping up-to-date on one big project.
>
> Shortly before I went on leave I had also relocated to a different city and office, so it was the same firm but a whole new environment. When I got back from leave, I took care to go out to drinks after work, to socialize—to get to know people I work with. Initially, I dreaded the return—but I got into things quickly, and was glad that I did.
>
> Looking back, the whole key was in being flexible."
>
> —*Sarah, law partner, mother of one*

and colleagues, you may fall victim to an "out of sight, out of mind" situation during a reorganization or when it comes to professional opportunities and staffing. The business dynamics and leadership may have shifted while you were out. In fact, it may feel more as if you're starting a new job than coming "back" at all. And if you've settled happily into the role of full-time caregiver, returning to work after an extended leave may be even tougher than coming back from a short one.

If you *are* planning six months or more away from work, here's what to expect—and do—to ensure a smoother reentry.

Throughout leave:

- Have a monthly call with your manager(s) to discuss new projects, priorities, and changes within the team. You'll stay up to date and on the radar screen, and keep up your rapport.

- Continue attending high-visibility, high-information events, like team off-sites, strategy-planning meetings, town halls, the holiday party, the annual promotion lunch, and so on.

- Focus on maintaining your professional mindset and confidence—whether that's by keeping up with colleagues, reading the trade news, doing some professionally related volunteer work (mentoring calls, for example), or—as basic as it sounds—occasionally getting dressed in your work clothes.

Upon return, expect:

- **Changes in your workplace.** Budgets tighten, strategies shift, managers and customers come and go, technology changes. That big research project may have ended, or the whole department may be in retrenchment mode, again. Most organizations and teams are constantly evolving. Anticipate differences, be ready to adapt to them and to signal that you're fully on board with the current direction and plan.

- **Questions—direct or implicit—about your level of commitment.** Are you really glad to be back? Planning to stay? Willing to pull the hours you used to? Right or wrong, colleagues may assume that your choice to take a longer leave was a sign of diminished ambition. As always: own your narrative.

- **A much faster or slower ramp-up than you anticipated.** You may be hit with a huge backlog of work—or spend the first several weeks twiddling your thumbs, waiting for the next big project. Don't worry; three months from now, things will be back at their usual pace.

- **Unthinking comments from coworkers** about your "year off" or about the huge efforts put in to cover for you. Ignore the first; respond to the second graciously—by saying that you appreciate the leave that you, and all other parents at the organization, are eligible for, and that you're delighted to be back on the job.

Throughout the transition back, make sure to:

- **Stay conscious of your professional brand.** Pick five to seven adjectives that capture the impact and impression you want to make as you start back at work. Being clear that you want to be seen as *articulate, judicious, responsive, hardworking,* or *a mentor* will help you shape your behavior toward those things, and let you have the impact you want.

- **Rekindle your network.** Use the first few months back to do deliberate, organized outreach to key stakeholders—in the organization and outside. You are who you know.

- Deliver quick wins. Nothing will give you as much back-to-work energy and confidence, and send a more positive message to your coworkers, as a few early, demonstrable achievements.

- Be seen going the extra mile, at least occasionally. Start early, work late, raise your hand for the tough assignment, or go above and beyond to help a colleague. Show that your head—and heart—are in the work.

. . . worried that my leave will be too short?

Let's say you've got x weeks, and try as you might there's no way to find, negotiate, or cobble together any more. You've heard stories about how quickly leave time flies and how hard the return to work can be when your child is still so small. You're getting increasingly anxious. What to do?

Your best course of action here is to try to *maximize* your leave—by, as much as possible, returning it to its intended consequence, which is to allow you to care for and bond with the baby. Same amount of time, more impact and satisfaction from it.

Practically speaking, that means:

- Locking down your care arrangements early. If you've got twelve weeks of leave and ten of those are spent in a frenzied search for daycare, the time will feel very short. But if you've already toured multiple centers and have an assured spot at one you like, you'll get much more, and more-relaxed, time with the baby.

- Extricating yourself from work as fully as you can. Make sure your while-I'm-out coverage plan covers every contingency, and cut off contact with your office or workplace while away.

- Providing your Village clear, unambiguous direction on how to support you during this time. Can the grandparents lend a hand by making meals? Do you really want all those visitors? Either you set the agenda—or you risk spending much of your leave time dealing with someone else's.

- Setting personal boundaries. Because this may be the first time in your adult life you've had twelve underscheduled weeks at home, you may feel tempted or duty-bound to put the time to "productive" purpose: to get the living room repainted or clean out the garage. Those things can wait. For now, your full-time job is to adjust to and enjoy being a parent.

- Prioritizing self-care. The eventual return to work will feel much easier if, throughout your leave, you've set aside time to rest (as much as possible), exercise, and do whatever else gets you into a good physical and mental frame.

For advice on finding childcare, building your Village, and building your own energy and resilience, turn to chapters 2, 9, and 20.

. . . not eligible for paid leave—or any leave—at all?

There's no two ways around it: if you're an expectant mother or father and don't have any paid leave, or *any* parental leave at all, coming to you, then you're in a tough spot. Your goal now is to try to maximize any flexibility and benefits you *do* have to create at least some small amount of "effective leave." To do so:

- Check if you can bank any vacation days, personal days, comp time, or extra hours worked for use when the baby arrives.

- Ask, bargain, sell, and negotiate—even if the winds of corporate policy are blowing against you and you think the answer will be no. Maybe your boss will advocate for you, or someone higher up will be sympathetic and willing to make an exception. If you're a contractor or freelancer, see if you can get your key clients to agree on a set number of weeks away while projects are paused and/or contracts are kept intact.

- Double-check your local parental-leave policies. Particularly in the United States, state and municipal laws are changing. You may be eligible for local government benefits if not employer-provided ones.

- Get creative on ways to save, and generate, cash to cover any time you do get off.

- Enlist as much help and support as you can from friends, family, neighbors, and other members of your community.

- Start searching for care options early.

Creating an Effective Transition and Coverage Plan

Once you've nailed down your leave timing, you'll need to figure out how your work will be covered while you're away. If you'll be gone for a month or less, this should be fairly easy; the handover can be very similar to any you would do before going on a vacation. If your leave will be longer, your plan will have to be more thought-through and formal, and you'll want to invest in getting the folks covering for you up to speed. That may sound like a lot of work, but if you know the important dos and don'ts, you'll be able to create an effective coverage and transition plan without having it become a job unto itself.

When developing your "while I'm out" proposal, you should:

- **Be the instigator.** Your boss may have ultimate accountability for everything that happens in the department, but your job is your job. You need to offer up potential solutions and get the conversation rolling.

- **Go broad.** Think top-to-bottom about your responsibilities, and don't leave the unseen or "housekeeping" parts of your job uncovered.

- **Get it down on paper.** Transition conversations will simply go better when you have something in front of you to refer to. You want to be working—quite literally—off the same page as your boss and team.

- **Keep it simple and future-focused.** Think of your plan as an answer to the question, "How will we ensure success in the coming months?" And put it in a quick-gulp format: a one-page table with columns marked *project* (or *client*, *shift*, *product*, etc.) *owner*, *key actions*, *deliverables and target outcomes*, and *key things to know*, works well, and can easily be tacked up on your boss's wall.

- Include notes on how you want to be contacted, for what, and when. Should you be kept in the loop when the litigation settles, when quarterly numbers are released, or if your main supplier misses the delivery window? By email, phone, messaging app? Include this information to save yourself time and confusion, and to avoid uncomfortable "why didn't you tell me" moments later on.

- Socialize it. Once you've agreed on the plan with your boss, discuss it with all relevant coworkers. If you work extensively with partners outside the organization, make them aware of your high-level plans, too. If you work in corporate public relations, for example, you may want your key contact at the digital agency to be in the loop. In general, the more buy-in you have and the more questions you preempt, the smoother your leave will go.

- See it as a personal marketing opportunity. Aside from job interviews and your annual review, you don't get a lot of chances to discuss the totality of what you do and your full value to the organization. Think carefully about how you come across, and make sure your transition plan speaks to your value and impact.

And conversely, you shouldn't:

- Make it feel too bureaucratic. You're human, and so is your boss—and the quality and tone of your conversations will be much more important and effective in driving your overall experience than whatever appears on page 8 of a written plan.

- Expect too much of one person. An overburdened coworker may not do the work to your preferred standards and may deeply resent having to carry so much extra load. There's potential risk here, too: if the person you've handed everything off to leaves the organization, you'll be left in the lurch. Spread responsibilities out among various colleagues, if you can.

- **Make the mistake of thinking that "in writing" means "will absolutely be honored."** The fact that your transition plan is on paper doesn't make it a legal agreement—and realistically, workplace budgets, strategies, and staffing levels can change. Expect the document you create to be used as a guideline, not as gospel.

- **Ignore the return to work.** Your transition plan needs to cover *two* transitions: your departure and your return. Way too many parents make the mistake of focusing heavily on the former and ignoring the latter, shortchanging themselves badly in the process. Identify who will cover while you're gone, but also be certain to agree on exactly how (and just as crucially, *when*) they'll pass the work—or customers, P&L, extra shifts, or juicy career opportunities—over when you get back.

Staying in Touch While You're Out

If you decide to stay fully on top of work and in touch with your colleagues while you're away, you risk turning this precious time with the baby into an effective work-from-home arrangement, which defeats the entire purpose. On the other hand, if you turn all of your attentions homeward, you risk feeling professionally out of touch, and of having the transitions to parenthood and then back to work feel even more abrupt. If you can think of leave as a timeline or continuum, though (instead of as a zero-sum, "do I engage, or don't I?" choice), you'll be able to strike the right personal and practical balance.

 Don't worry about being out of touch. If you were doing great work and making an impact before you left, they won't forget you."
—*Lauren, consumer-insights specialist, mother of two*

However long your leave is, think of it as having four phases:

- **Phase 1:** During the first third of your leave, focus on yourself and your family, and give yourself permission to completely check out from work. Put your smartphone away and let the emails go. Use this time to recover from the arrival, if you need to, and to be an all-in mom or dad.

- **Phase 2:** During the middle portion of leave, keep tabs on work, but in a limited way, and *quietly*. Check messages without responding to them, monitor what's in the shared drive without making edits, or get informal updates from a few trusted co-workers. You'll stay up to date on everything happening on the job, but your time will remain your own. Easier said than done, of course: your professional instinct will be to jump back in feet first at the slightest sign of trouble on any project, or in an effort to make certain things are done right. A month or two into parenting, you may also be craving the reassurance of work—that feeling of competence and authority. Beware, though, that as soon as you get back into the fray, it will be impossible to get yourself out. Once your colleagues see that you're responding to messages, you'll be deluged with them.

- **Phase 3:** In your last few weeks or months away, begin responding to messages, have a transition-in meeting with your manager, schedule upcoming shifts or important meetings, sketch out key priorities, and do whatever else you need to for an organized, effective, good-momentum return. But be careful: to avoid being pulled back in too early, set a firm daily or weekly time limit on this work.

- **Phase 4:** At the very end of leave, return to phase 1, and put every ounce of your attention back at home. With all the pieces in place for a good start back at work, you can immerse yourself in parenting, savor every minute, and know that you're using every last second of your leave to its fullest.

How to Think About—and Use—Leave When You're Not the Primary Caregiver

If your partner is pregnant, and/or if the plan is for him or her to take the lead on childcare, you may find yourself harboring secret—or not-so-secret—apprehensions about going on leave yourself. What are you supposed to be *doing* while both of you are home? Do you *really* want to be around all day when your partner is this exhausted, or is post-partum, or is feeding the baby and you can't help anyway? Wouldn't it just be better if you stayed at work? These concerns are all standard, and you're right to listen to your instincts on how much time to spend at home. That being said, you have an important mission here, and with the right moves, you can become an unsung hero in this story.

Think of yourself as having three critical functions while on leave:

- As **defender**, you'll help draw the boundaries needed such that your primary-caregiving partner can either rest and focus on the baby, or put his or her energies into the return to work. You'll make certain that the stream of well-intentioned relatives, neighbors, and other would-be visitors doesn't become too overwhelming, and if your partner is also a working parent, you'll encourage him or her not to spend too much time on work emails and not to get pulled back into the job too early. Playing this kind of defense now will pay off later, when things are on the best possible keel at home.

- As **fixer**, you'll take charge of the practical details that can become overwhelming with a new child around: organizing all the insurance paperwork, restocking the diaper supply, making the pediatrician appointments, and so on. No, this work won't be glamorous—but your professional skills are invaluable here, and taking operational charge during this time will set your family off on a strong, stable footing and let your partner find more of a day-to-day caregiving groove.

- As **coach**, you'll help your partner through his or her own transition to parenthood and/or working parenthood, providing regular reality checks, reassurance, and praise.

If your apprehensions are deep enough that you're leaning toward not taking *any* of the leave you're entitled to, step back and think: you're a role model now, whether you like it or not. The aspiring parents at work may never admit it, but they're watching you like a hawk to see if parenting is possible in your field or organization. Do you really want the next person to think "See? I shouldn't/don't need to/can't take parental leave" because of your own behavior? Taking your leave—and talking positively about it—is your best way to lay good groundwork for other moms and dads in the future.

How to Feel in Charge of Your Career While Away

You're going to be busy while on leave—*very* busy. Between diaper changes, feedings, health appointments, finalization of your care arrangements, and ongoing lack of sleep, what initially looked like a good long stretch of "time off" may slip by in an exhausting, frenetic blur. It's essential right now that you pump the brakes on any type-A tendency toward feeling as if you need to be accomplishing anything, or moving forward in your career. Give your regular ambition a sabbatical: your

Parental leave as a reset

Throughout your working life, you have very few opportunities to do any kind of meaningful professional reset: to alter your portfolio of responsibilities, to project a new personal "brand," or to work differently than before. Resetting is most feasible when you change jobs, get a meaningful promotion, move roles internally—and on the heels of your parental leave.

While you're out, give careful consideration to what projects or responsibilities you want to avoid, or assertively raise your hand for, on the way back in. Think through how you want colleagues to perceive you, post leave. If you've always been *the hardest worker* in the office, for example, perhaps now you become *the most efficient*. Maybe a certain type of work or project has been your signature, and now you want to pivot. Whatever those changes might be, don't squander this natural opportunity to try to make them.

child is precious, leave is short, and you'll have plenty of opportunities to shine professionally in the coming months and years.

If being on leave has left you with some career-related anxiety, however, or if you feel that it's taking you uncomfortably far out of the game, try using these easy ways to help tamp down that worry, reassert control over your professional life, and regain your sense of accomplished self, all without eroding your precious time away.

- **Update your résumé.** Creating a complete summary of all your professional achievements is the swiftest, most powerful way to build—or retain—professional confidence.

- **Gussy up your LinkedIn profile.** Add any recent projects completed, clients won, recognitions received, and any meaningful extracurricular activities or volunteer work.

- **Join any local networking events run by your industry or trade group.** An hour or two spent in circulation can help you feel like your professional self again and serve as a sort of mini–dress rehearsal for the return to work later.

- **Refresh your network.** Reconnect with past managers, mentors, peers, or recruiters you haven't had contact with recently. In-person meetings may be too much to handle right now, but a brief email update or social-media connection can do the trick.

- **Ensure all your professional certifications are fully up-to-date.** Also identify a few professional-education opportunities—attending that conference, getting that advanced certification—you want to pursue over the coming few years.

- **Read up on emerging trends in your field.** Get smart on emerging technologies, pending legislation, and what your competitors are up to.

- **Identify any low-time-investment, high-professional-visibility opportunities.** These would be pursued over the coming year or two. Think about speaking at a professional conference, writing an article for a trade magazine, or raising your hand for an organization-wide committee or project that will give you more face time with colleagues outside your regular circle. You don't need to take any action right now; just draw confidence from the fact that—as always—you're actively thinking about your career and planning a few steps ahead.

Go Back on a Thursday—and Other Ways to Make the Return to Work Easier

Whether you've been away from work for a week or a year, and whether it's your first child or fifth, the return from parental leave can be hard—both practically and emotionally. As your leave time winds down, you'll likely begin slipping into a dark and gloomy mental space: wondering whether the care arrangements you've worked so hard to put in place are really the right ones, if it's even possible to get morning feedings finished before 6:30 a.m., how you're *ever* going to make it through that first day—and so many more days just like it—without the baby, if your career is really worth it, and so on. Every one of these thoughts and feelings is completely normal, very common, and should be taken as reassuring, wonderful proof of how bonded you are to your child.

Nonetheless, that first day back is looming and daunting, and you'll want to navigate it as best you can. Here's how to make reentry easier.

- Rehearse it. A few days before returning, hold an "as if" day: get up, get dressed, have breakfast, get the baby ready, do the caregiving handover, and make the trip in to work. (When you get there, simply turn around and go home.) This run-through will reveal any potential logistical snags—drop-off takes longer than you thought, for example—and provide a no-stakes chance to work around them. Then, on your first real day back you'll be out of improvisation mode and have some good *I know what I'm doing* confidence.

- Get as much help as you can. Ask the grandparents to come stay so they can act as on-site emergency childcare—and cheerleaders. See if your neighbor will look in on the baby and his caregiver and keep you posted. Or take a tag-team approach:

Phaseback programs

A "phaseback program" allows you to work flexibly, on a reduced schedule, or both, for a defined period of time upon your return from parental leave. As the name implies, phaseback is designed to make the transition back to work gentler and easier, and allow you a gradual ramp-up. These programs are now commonly found within many large companies and are increasingly offered at smaller organizations. Managers and organizations see and use phaseback as a low-cost way to support recent returnees and keep attrition rates down.

Practically speaking, the extra flexibility phaseback offers may be exactly what you need if you've had a shorter parental leave, are nursing, are still struggling to set up the right care arrangement, or are finding the transition back to work difficult. And if you want to try out flexible work before committing to a longer-term arrangement, phaseback is a great way to do so. Exercise caution, though, because one size does not fit all. After a long leave, you may be eager to get back into the regular routine of work, but the particular pressures of your job may actually make it harder to work part-time rather than full-, or remotely rather than in person. And there can be practical considerations, too: working from home with an infant isn't easy in a small apartment. Think of phaseback as an option, and rely on your own instincts to determine whether or not to take it.

If your organization doesn't yet offer a phaseback program, don't be shy about trying to negotiate one. Keep your requests reasonable, limited, and time-bound, and frame them as a way for your boss and organization to keep you—and keep you productive—for the long term.

have your partner take your first day back at work off, and vice versa. Those extra layers of support and backup will go a long way toward minimizing your stress.

- **Go back on a Thursday.** Head back to work on a Monday and you'll face an unbroken five-day stretch away from your child. Return on a Thursday and that first week back becomes far less menacing. You'll have two good days to get into your new routine—and then, before you know it, get to enjoy a weekend with your family.

>   Each time was easier intellectually—I knew what to expect—
> although the same emotionally.
>
> Here's my advice: take one day at a time and remind yourself that
> you do not need to make any decisions right away. You're in control,
> and if after a little while, you feel it's not working, you can try chang-
> ing things up. Your goal is to get yourself into a new routine, and to
> feeling that you're contributing."
>
> —*Andrea, regulatory relations leader, mother of five*

- **Tell people you're returning a day later than you actually are.** If
  your coworkers don't realize you're back yet, they can't deluge
  you with questions, tasks, and to-dos. A silent return buys you
  a brief window of unhurried, unpressured time to get your
  bearings.

- **Have a contact list.** Think of your workplace allies and supporters, including colleagues you like; customers or clients who
  particularly appreciate your work; trusted mentors; and other
  recent-vintage working parents. During your first few days
  back, call or stop by to speak with them. Their tangible enthusiasm ("You're back! Good to see you!") will give you a jolt of
  energy.

- **Book in your next vacation.** Returning to work without any
  kind of break on the horizon is a recipe for feeling overwhelmed and beaten down, and fast. But if you can savor the
  thought that in just a few short months you'll spend a whole
  week with the baby enjoying your sister's beach condo, or relaxing at home as a family over the New Year's holiday, that early
  time back will be easier to face, and go by much more quickly.

Owning Your Narrative

Once back on the job, you may be tempted to get straight to work—
and keep your head down. And that's understandable: when you're

Thanking your parental-leave cover(s)

When you get back to work, don't forget to express sincere, direct thanks to the person or people who covered for you while you were out. Sure, maybe they were hired and paid just for that purpose—or maybe they "owed" you after you carried the ball during their own leave last year. Nevertheless, recognizing their efforts is a gracious, leader-like thing to do, and it can help build your long-term professional capital. You don't need to get fancy: a short, sincere thank-you email with a cc to that person's boss will do the trick.

handling such a huge transition and eager to finish up as early as you can each day, you won't feel like spending those twenty minutes messaging your colleagues about weekend plans or wasting time in aimless chitchat around the water cooler. Don't make the mistake of undercommunicating, though, or of assuming your colleagues have an accurate take on your thoughts and actions. If your colleagues don't know your real story, they may make assumptions: silence may be interpreted as lack of commitment, for example, or your boss may automatically think that as a brand-new parent you're more interested in flexibility than promotion. It's essential to take control of your story right now, and to leave the impression you want. Doing so means getting "out there," deliberately connecting with coworkers, and talking about yourself as a working parent—which may feel deeply awkward. Even if you're an extrovert and a communications natural, this is an interaction you've probably never prepped for or gotten any hand-holding on.

To make your working-parent message easier and more effective, think of yourself as putting it inside a frame defined on four sides by your *priorities*, *next steps*, *commitment*, and *enthusiasm*. Let's say it's Day One back from parental leave, and you've got colleagues dropping by your desk to say hello. Say something like, "It's good to see you and great to be back! I'm spending the next couple of days getting up to speed on the product specifications so we're ready for the design meeting on Tuesday. I'm looking forward to getting approval on the

> ❝ Two months after my first son was born, I was back working at
> the Met. I was glad to be there, but I struggled a bit with my
> identity. Everyone was so supportive, though: the costume crew kept
> telling me, 'You look great!' I wish I hadn't let my worries get to me so
> much. After a few weeks, I knew it was going to be OK."
>
> —*Blythe, opera singer, mother of two*

new prototypes." That will work vastly better than a simple, "It's good
to see you"—or silence. The first statement brings your listener(s) into
your full professional and personal plan and showcases your dedication to the team. You've minimized the chance of misunderstandings,
taken control over perception and messaging, and kept things positive and authentic. (This same four-part framing technique works in
many different situations; throughout the book, we'll explore how you
can use it to your advantage both in your day-to-day and high-stakes
workparenting conversations.)

If you need to advocate for yourself, correct a potential misimpres-
sion, or make a specific ask during the return-to-work period, be direct, and try using if-I-were-you language: "You may be wondering if
I'm still interested in taking on more, given the twins' arrival. But I
want you to know that I'm still ready, willing, and able to become as-
sistant principal this fall." And if you're feeling blue or experiencing
a sense of loss at the return to work, it's OK to admit it in a moderate,
balanced way, saying something like, "It's not easy to be away from my
little guy, but it's good to be back with the team." You're being authentic, but positive—and every colleague with a heart will understand.

The One-Month Check-In

During your first several weeks back at work you'll feel as if you're
learning to ride a bike: you'll be wobbly, you'll have to make constant
adjustments, and there will be a lot of stops and starts. You may suddenly get emotional (or even teary), or find that the manufacturing
contract you had whipped into shape before your leave now needs to

> ❝ Be thoughtful about what you pick back up. The organization has been surviving without you, and this can be an opportunity to transition over work that someone else is capable of handling. Don't feel guilty about that, either. You're just giving other people an opportunity."
>
> —*Katherine, chief of staff to the COO, mother of two*

be renegotiated. While the reentry phase can be rough, don't assume that one difficult day means you're doomed, try not to come to any sweeping long-term conclusions about workparenting, and above all, resist the urge to take your emotional temperature too often. Your goal now is just to move ahead, one day at a time. In doing so, you'll gradually find your footing.

After the first month or so, though, it can be very helpful to do a review and reset: to step back, look at how things are going, and consider any new approaches or tweaks that can make your workparenting life easier, better, and more satisfying. Reflect by yourself first, and then check in with the other key players: your partner, caregivers, mentors, and boss. You're not looking for praise, or for a letter grade, but for new life hacks and sensible actions. After thinking through the daily routine with your partner, for example, you may agree that taking turns getting up fifteen minutes earlier each day could relieve a lot of the early-morning frenzy, or after reflecting on the professional routine you've got in place you may decide to take on some overtime hours again.

For the people closest to you, of course, you can keep these take-stock-and-recalibrate conversations completely informal. If you choose to speak with a boss or higher-up, though, you may want to be a little more scripted: "I'm four weeks back from leave, and while it's certainly been a transition, I feel I've managed to get a good handle on things. Given our work together, though, I wanted to check in, ensure you feel the same, and see if there are any additional adjustments I should make, particularly as we get the store ready for the holiday sales." Putting it like this reminds your boss to recognize and appreciate the work and thought you've put into your transition, and—particularly if he's a working father himself—may prompt some good, authentic advice. Be careful to keep the conversation positive, and not to ask about your boss's *concerns*, *observations*, or *feedback*. This isn't a performance evaluation—it's about process improvement, with some appropriate self-marketing thrown in.

Celebrating New Achievements

Up until this point in your life and career, you've thought of "achievements" as big, objectively desirable, easily measurable milestones: you've completed your degree, lived abroad, landed a great job, bought a house, run a marathon, or been promoted. Now, as a brand-new working parent, it can feel like a victory to get to work on time and without spit-up stains all over your clothes, or just to stay awake on the job after a long night up with the baby. For most motivated, committed professionals, this is a major, humbling adjustment. You may feel even less professionally powerful and competent than you did at the very beginning of your career, and be wondering if, when, and how you'll ever get back to the top of your game.

As hard as it is, be patient with the process of becoming a workparent, and try to see what you're doing now as a major milestone achievement all its own. You're still every bit as hardworking and high-performing, but for right now your successes are of a different sort. And soon you'll be racking up the kinds of achievements that *only* a working parent can: you'll get that deep satisfaction that comes from nailing a huge new contract—and a few hours later walking through the door to see your smiling baby; or of putting that first check into his education-savings account. Becoming a positive, proactive workparent is a stand-up, affirmative choice. You've started the new job well, you've got a lot to be proud of already—and will have much more throughout Year One.

4

The First Year

Mastering—and Enjoying—Your New Normal

You've weathered those big initial transitions and the first few weeks back on the job. Well done! Take confidence in what you've already achieved: you've done what seemed scary or downright impossible just a few months ago.

Because you have, you're now ready to make a few important additional adjustments that will let you better fit the self-career-and-kids puzzle pieces together throughout Year One and beyond. These new approaches—personal, practical, and professional—will help you move from *getting through* working parenthood to *owning* it. As each week passes, and as your new ways of working and of thinking take root, you'll feel more settled in your dual role and more satisfied in it, too.

Personal Adjustments

Workparenting means working both *more* and *differently* than you have before. To reach that new bar, and to do so sustainably, **you need to operate from a position of personal strength**. The more in-charge, confident, and fulfilled you feel, the better you'll be able to handle everything your workparent day throws at you. Three techniques can help get you into the right mental and emotional frame.

1. Establishing a Point of Control

Balancing a demanding career and caring for children you love can be, particularly early on, a hectic, messy undertaking, and it's likely that at some point in these first few weeks back at work, some very well-intentioned colleague or mentor encouraged you to "embrace the chaos," "forget about perfect," or similar. That may be good general advice, but realistically, you're not going to do your very best work or be a centered and attentive parent when gripped by feelings of frenzy and mess. Sure, life is complex and busy—but retaining a sense of competence and "togetherness" is essential to delivering what you want to in both spheres. One small, simple trick can help stoke those feelings throughout these first several months of workparenting, and thereafter: you can create a Point of Control (POC).

Your POC is a single, small part of your life that you have complete authority over, that you can engage with easily and often, and that provides a disproportionate boost to your overall sense of well-being. It may involve a place, action, object, habit, or some combination, and it doesn't have to relate to either your kids or your job. It's really all about you, and how your mind and personality work. Your POC might be:

- Keeping the car in excellent working order, with the trunk free of dirt and debris

- Doing the same short exercise routine each morning, even on weekends or when you're traveling for work

- Organizing your closet so that your pants and shirts are lined up tidily and by color

> " I jumped back into work pretty quickly after my children were born, but I also started getting up early a few mornings a week to just read—to see what's happening in the news, to stay alert and aware to the world around me. It lets me start my day feeling on top of things, and inspired."
>
> —*Lindsay, childcare agency founder, mother of two*

- Making yourself a really good cup of coffee each morning with your special espresso maker and the imported coffee beans you splurge on

- Meditating or praying

Amidst the go-go-go of working parenthood, your POC allows you to think, *I've got things well in hand*. It lets you feel like an in-control *person* regardless of your circumstances.

To find your own POC, just spend a few days observing small routines or things that you take pleasure in and that bring you "back to center" without too much time or effort. Your specific POC may change over time, but at any given moment, pick just one. Having more than one becomes its own burden, rather than providing what it should—some psychological lift, fresh energy, and (after just a short window of engagement) the ability to step back into the working-parent fray on your front foot.

2. Learning to make effective transitions to and from work

With a classic five-day-per-week at-work schedule, you're going to make five hundred total home-to-work and work-to-home transitions over the coming year. If you're working remotely, and have your laptop set up near the baby's room, you'll make thousands more. Each of those moves from professional mode to parenting mode (and vice versa) is an opportunity to feel in control of your dual roles, to leave a good impression with your colleagues, to express warmth and love to your son or daughter. On the other hand, they add up to five hundred chances to feel torn in two, to appear harried and gruff to your child and colleagues, to run late, to forget your phone at work, to misplace your notes from that VC, and to be left anguished and wondering if this working-parent thing is inherently painful or just plain impossible. Crossing the workparent boundary line may feel like a small, inconsequential act, but at no other moment do the two spheres of your life crash into each other with such force, and leave you feeling the impact. And let's face it: five hundred is a *lot*. The better you are at making these moves, the stronger you'll feel, and the better your first year—and the ones after it—will go.

To make your transitions smoother and easier:

- Set your intentions. Think about who you really are and want to be perceived as. If you're clear that you want your colleagues to think of you as *upbeat, personable, high-energy,* and *smart,* and that you want to be a *warm, patient, nurturing,* and *attentive* parent, it's going to be a lot easier to project, and actually *be,* those things from the first moment you walk through that (real or virtual) door.

- Fuel up. When you're low-energy and low-blood-sugar—and who isn't at those natural workday transition points (early morning, midday, early evening)?—it's virtually impossible to be at your best. Yes, perhaps before you had kids you were able to pull out an amazing performance on coffee and adrenaline, but you're in a much more demanding game now. Put something in the tank before arriving at or starting work, and grab a snack on the way home or before coming out of your home office if you need to. Make sure you're as *physically* ready as possible to be a great professional and parent.

- Create a checklist. Checklists are powerful tools for staying on track and preventing unforced errors when you're in high-stakes situations (which is why every airplane pilot in the world uses one, both at takeoff and landing). To avoid making the small mistakes and oversights that can leave you scrambling and anxious—like forgetting to restock the diaper bag before leaving for work or forgetting to check in with your line manager at the end of the day—keep a "Don't forget . . ." list taped to the doorframe or easily accessible on your smartphone.

- Let it go. As hard as it is, try to release the worries of the workday, at least temporarily, as you pivot homeward, and likewise set aside your parenting concerns as work begins. When your child hasn't been with you for nine hours, you don't want to spend those first few minutes with her furrowing your brow and obsessing about that big project being over budget, nor do

> Before work, I listen to business news, read my messages, get ready for the day. The temptation is high to work on the train on the way home as well, but instead I listen to music or an audiobook— something that gets me more mentally ready for time with my kids.
>
> As soon as I get home, I change clothes, partly because I don't want ketchup or magic marker on my blazers, but really because when it's my time to play with the kids, having on my own play clothes helps me be more present."
>
> —*Caitlin, account executive, mother of two*

you want to join that all-important meeting still mulling over how to tell the caregiver that no, she can't have another paid week off. In other words, make certain that your brain and your heart are in the same place as your body.

- **Add a ritual.** If you find it hard to "shake off" your worries and concerns from one sphere as you move into the other, make your transition more marked, more deliberate. Always get off the subway a stop early and use the walk to clear your head, for example, or imagine your bulging to-do list as a file that you can close down, as on a computer, or make it a habit to touch the family photo you keep on your desk when it's time to knock off work and become full-on Mom or Dad.

- **Do a final pause.** Before you walk through that door, take a moment to regroup. Linger in the office lobby or sit alone in your car for a minute, or close your eyes and take a few deep breaths after shutting your laptop. That last extra bit of time will help you move between worlds in a deliberate, authentic way.

3. Staying and feeling connected while on the job

While you're hard at work, you may miss the baby like crazy—and miss being in the role of nurturing parent. That holds true even if you work at home and are just a few paces down the hall. But to stay connected both to your child and to your "parenting self," should you ask the nanny to do regular video chats, immediately look at all the photos the daycare center sends, or keep popping between your home office and the nursery? Or should you put your head down and dead-sprint to the end of the day so you can get back to parenting mode just a few minutes earlier? Neither approach may be feasible or fully satisfying.

Instead, acknowledge that even while working you have a normal and healthy emotional need to see your child and to *still be a parent*. The Mom or Dad part of you doesn't have to be abandoned or denied while you're on the job—it can still be, and needs to be, recognized and nourished. The trick is to achieve that in ways that don't make work harder, practically or emotionally, and that don't in any way affect your professional brand.

Think about making your staying-connected mantra *regular and sufficient, but never distracting*. In practice, that might mean setting aside five or ten minutes around lunchtime each day to videoconference with your caregiver and the baby, or letting yourself scroll through pictures and videos you took last weekend while you're in line for lunch or your afternoon coffee. If you work remotely, maybe you have a policy of spending fifteen minutes each morning and afternoon on "parent break." Whatever those habits are, make them *just* robust enough that you feel an emotional connection, without letting them take up so much time or headspace that they interfere with work. If you're always looking at pictures, it will be hard to focus, and if your coworkers notice that you're never in your home office when they call, which they will, you may get judged for it, or worse. Find your middle ground.

Practical Adjustments

The demands workparenting places on you in Year One are intense and constantly evolving. You may have to take a whole new approach to your schedule, and to getting your work done—while continuously changing your game at home, as the baby grows. Working from your new, greater position of personal strength and confidence, though, you'll be ready to tackle and tame these toughest logistics.

Creating a new daily schedule that works—for *you*

Hard facts: as a working mother or father you're going to be *doing* much more than you used to, and suddenly the time you have to do all your work *in* is banded and defined by your child's caregiving arrangement. If you used to keep plugging until you'd returned every single email, now—even if your inbox is crammed full—you've got to wrap up before the daycare center closes or the caregiver needs to leave. And in the midst of this newly jam-packed day, of course, you'll also want to find some blocks of satisfying, unhurried time with the baby.

Those three variables can feel contradictory: How can you possibly *do* more in *fewer* hours and still manage to carve out dedicated Mom or Dad time? It's not an easy or intuitive task, but even in the absence of a flexible working arrangement, most working parents lean on one of three general scheduling solutions: the Split Day, the Shifted Schedule, or the Alternating On/Off Approach. Each one is described briefly below and in more detail in table 4-1, "Workparent Sample Timetables."

- In a **Split Day**, you take your standard workday in two separate stretches: the first and longer one during the hours you have

Need a little more time with baby?

If so, then remember: those moments don't have to be part of a formal flexibility plan or even be officially sanctioned. Simply knock off work an hour earlier now and then so that you can give your daughter her bath; or book an "important meeting" on your calendar and join her at the baby music class; or take an occasional vacation, personal, or sick day to spend as a full-time parent; and if your business-trip flight lands at 2:00 p.m., give yourself permission to head straight home instead of back to the office. This kind of small-scale, selective, self-granted flexibility on the job isn't enough to affect your performance, and your colleagues likely won't even take notice. Chances are, they're all doing the same themselves.

TABLE 4-1

Workparent Sample Timetables

	Pre-kids schedule	Workparent schedules		
		1. Split Day	*2. Shifted Schedule*	*3. Alternating On/Off Approach*
Morning	• Sleep • Breakfast, get ready for work • Gym, email catch-up, etc. • Commute	• Up early with baby; feed, dress, prep for the day • Get self ready for work • Commute/caregiving handover	• Up before baby • Early arrival at work • WORK for a few hours before colleagues arrive and standard day starts	• Up early with baby; feed, dress, prep for the day • Get self ready for work • Commute/caregiving handover
Core workday	• WORK • Catch up with colleagues • Think ahead to new projects • Use free moments as breaks, or to attend to "life admin"	• WORK: complete what's needed before the "hard stop" of evening caregiving handover • Free moments used for life admin	• WORK: complete what's needed before the "hard stop" of evening caregiving handover	• WORK: complete what's needed before the "hard stop" of evening caregiving handover
Early evening	• WORK, if needed • Get organized for next day • Commute	• Commute/caregiving handover • Dinner, bath, bonding time with baby • Jump back online to see what I've missed at work in last 90 minutes	• Commute/caregiving handover • Dinner, bath, bonding time with baby • Jump back online to see what I've missed at work in last 90 minutes; respond as needed	"On" day • WORK: get more done so I can have tomorrow evening free "Off" Day • Commute/caregiving handover • Dinner, bath, bonding time with baby
Later evening	• Friends/family/hobbies • Life admin • Free time	• WORK: Complete what I didn't get to during the day • Life admin • Free time	• Life admin • Free time	• Life admin • Free time

care, and the second in the evening, after a period of bonding with and focus on the baby. Same wood, just chopped into two pieces.

- With a **Shifted Schedule**, you keep your workday in one piece, but move it to a different part of the twenty-four-hour clock. Instead of starting at nine and stopping at five, you may start at seven and stop at three, for example. Ever known someone who always gets into work crazy early? They're likely using a Shifted Schedule.

- The **Alternating On/Off Approach** will be familiar to anyone who's ever participated in organized sports. In this scheduling solution, you toggle back and forth between "easy" and "hard" workdays, getting done all the work you need to but still keeping regular, dedicated time focused on personal matters. Sprint, and then recover.

Notice that each one of these scheduling approaches lets you do the same *amount* of work, but at different times than you used to. Each also allows you to spend a dedicated chunk of time at home, with the baby, while additionally offering some free time to spend alone with your partner or on essential "life admin" tasks. What they also have in common is compression: there's enough time to get it all done, but there's no lollygagging, no fluff.

The scheduling strategy that's right for you will depend on many different personal factors, including what you do, the degree of autonomy and control you have over your work schedule, your commute, if you have a partner or caregiver who can cover those early mornings

> " After my son and daughter were born I spent four years at home, and just recently went back full-time.
> For me, what works is getting in really early, and then leaving earlier to pick up the kids. I just prefer to do things in continuous blocks like that. After that work block is done, I can fully focus on my family."
>
> —*Wendy, technology product marketer, mother of two*

Pumping at work

Expressing milk at work will require the correct equipment, including a breast pump, storage containers, and an insulated bag for transportation. Breast pads and a change of clothes will be useful to have on hand in case of unexpected stains or leaks. You'll also need an appropriate space to pump in; that means somewhere clean and private (i.e., with zero visibility to the rest of your workspace and a door that locks). Before heading back to work, speak to your human resources or benefits team, to fellow nursing-mom colleagues, and to your healthcare provider or lactation specialist for information and advice, and if you encounter pushback or hurdles of *any* kind—for example, your manager is unsupportive or your organization doesn't provide you an adequate space to pump in—remember that this is your right. Be ready to be your own advocate.

That said, be ready for some adjustments and challenges, too—ones that you'll have to take the lead on working through. When traveling or "in the field" for work, you'll have to find places to pump, figure out how to transport your expressed milk, have a backup pump ready in case your regular one malfunctions, and so forth. Think through your day-to-day and month-to-month work calendar, and try to play the more challenging scenarios through. If you can "see" the curveball logistics coming, it will be much easier to make lactation work.

Realize also that while lactation is your right, *it is not an obligation.* If you prefer to formula-feed after your return to work, then go right ahead. If that sentence surprises you, or sounds blasphemous, let's pause and step back for a second here. *You* are this child's mother, and *you* get to make the decisions here, based on the totality and complexity of your working-mom life. No one else gets to tell you what to do, and the people who try (whether they be media, breast-feeding advocates, healthcare providers, parenting "experts," or well-meaning friends) are extremely unlikely to show up at your workplace with sterilized bottles or to cover for you at the meeting you would otherwise miss. If what's running through your mind is "but breast milk is best!" remind yourself that what's really best for your child is to have a mom who doesn't feel overwhelmed or guilty. Whatever decision you make is the right one—as long as *you're* the one making it, with full knowledge and context as to what will work best, holistically, for you, your career, and your family.

or late evenings, whether you're an early bird or a night owl, your boss's outlook and habits, and so on. And you may well find that the best solution for you is a combination—working some Split Days, some Shifted, and some On/Off.

Whatever your new routine:

- **Know your nonnegotiables.** If your plan involves leaving work every day by 6 p.m. to make it to daycare pickup, *always* be at the elevators or logged off by 5:55, and if colleagues attempt to waylay you, be firm in your response that, "I'll get back to you on that at 7:30, once the baby's down." The firmer the boundaries you set early on, the better trained your colleagues will become and the easier that schedule will be for you to keep.

- **Pick either mornings or evenings to spend a dedicated, focused stretch of time with the baby.** Carving out a meaningful block of time with your child at both the beginning *and* end of the day will be tough in most pressured, demanding, modern workplaces. So prioritize one of the day's brackets: plan to wake up extra early each morning to enjoy a full hour with your child before the day begins, or start work a little earlier, but treat the dinner-bath-bed ritual as sacred. Whichever works for you, you'll have the satisfaction of unhurried, meaningful bonding time every single day.

- **Educate people on your new system.** Don't let coworkers assume that because you're disengaging earlier than you used to that you're working *less*. Explain your new approach to your

> I used to work from 9:00 a.m. to 9:00 p.m., and then run at night, training for marathons. My new rule is to be home by 8:00 so I can be there for our son's bath and bedtime. For a few months, I stopped exercising, until I realized *wait, this is important to me.* Now I get up earlier and can get in a run before my wife leaves for work. You keep adjusting, and figure things out."
>
> —Eduardo, *online retail company cofounder, father of one*

boss, and if you work in the evenings or other "off" times, make others aware of it: send a few 9 p.m. emails, or during the team meeting, mention "while I was reviewing the documents this weekend . . ." As always: own your story.

Navigating the important Year One milestones

Throughout your baby's first year, those developmental milestones—rolling over, sitting up, using a pincer grip—will keep on coming, and each one will be exciting. A few will also require new workparent strategies and routines.

- **Reacting and interacting.** At around the two-to-three-month mark, your baby will start to smile, coo, babble, watch faces, and otherwise respond—adorably so—to you and the other people around him. Near his first birthday, he'll be able to say "Mama" or "Dada." With each communicative leap he makes, you'll fall even further in love—which will make leaving, or turning your attentions to work, even harder. To help soften any sense of loss:

  - Keep the time you do spend in parenting mode as unhurried and uninterrupted as possible. Whenever you can, turn off your devices and savor every one of his new gestures and sounds. (Yes, it's important to be responsive, but your colleagues' emails can wait for thirty minutes.)

  - Think ahead. Remind yourself that there will be plenty more smiles or new words waiting for you tonight—and tomorrow, and this weekend.

  - Focus on your "why." You're working to give him a stable home, a good education, and a bright future, and meeting those needs is a powerful expression of love.

- **Stranger anxiety.** Somewhere between the ages of six and fifteen months, your child will develop a deep apprehension about new people and—important for working mothers and fathers—about transitions of all kinds. At this age, *any* shift between caregivers, even between you and your partner, can be upsetting. The baby may start clinging to you at drop-off or fuss and cry when you return. Do *not* be surprised or upset. It's not that he doesn't love you, or a sign that your care arrangement isn't working: it's just a natural developmental phase. Until it passes, allow more time for day-to-day caregiving transitions and make them as gradual and gentle as possible. Instead of swooping in to pick him up as soon as you're in the door, for example, get down on the floor a few feet away, smile, speak softly, sing a favorite song, and let him take his time to crawl on over. When transitions are kept unpressured, calm, and reassuring, your child's anxiety will dissipate—and yours will too.

- **Mobility.** When he's about eight months old, your child will start getting around on his own: first by crawling and then by cruising, walking, and climbing. He'll quickly gain all the mobility of an adult and then of a professional mountaineer, but with absolutely none of the judgment. At this point, it's a good idea to:

  - Do a top-to-bottom review of your childcare setup from a physical-safety perspective. Thorough childproofing is a must at home, but you'll also want similar safeguards anyplace your child may spend time as part of your secondary or emergency care plans. If your sister-in-law is your emergency backup sitter, for example, the stairs at her house should be secured.

  - Update your Emergency Contacts Sheet to include your child's dental-care provider, the closest walk-in urgent-care center, and Poison Control. Provide every person involved in his care with a fresh copy.

  - Follow up on previous conversations with your caregiver(s) about when and why to contact you at work: if bumps, scrapes, bruises, or tumbles merit a call, let them know.

– Get as much help and support as you can. Besides the period of extreme sleep deprivation you went through when your child was a newborn, this twelve-to-eighteen-month period is likely to be the most physically exhausting of working parenthood. After long, intense days on the job, you'll spend evenings and weekends literally running after your child, and it will deplete your energy quickly. Now isn't the time to be a hero. If it's possible to get extra assistance of any kind either at work or at home, take it.

Note: even if you're working from home or on a reduced schedule, as a working parent you will almost certainly miss some of your baby's "firsts." When you do, don't beat yourself up. Celebrate the fact that he's rolling over, playing peekaboo, walking, or talking now—just the

No comparing: previous generations

As you settle into working parenthood, you may start comparing yourself with working parents you know from prior generations—your parents, in-laws, or older mentors and colleagues. *My mom worked full-time,* you may think, *and raised us three kids just fine.* Older folks may also make pointed comments evaluating your working-parent efforts versus their own. "Why are you spending so much money on takeout food?" "Back when I became a parent, nobody worked remotely." "Your father had a big career, but he still got home every day at six."

Well, maybe. But many of these former working parents got to work eight hours a day, while the standard today is more like ten . . . if you're lucky. And those senior colleagues didn't need to change jobs every few years the way most of us do now, or have to avoid having their jobs outsourced while they were raising babies. And remember that *nobody* workparenting prior to 2007 did so amid the always-on, 24-7 pressures created by smartphones. The simple fact is: working parenthood doesn't just *feel* different than it was twenty-five years ago, it actually *is,* and any comparisons between today and "back then" or between yourself and your parents is unfair, unsettling, and unproductive. So don't go there: focus on yourself and what you're doing well in the here and now instead.

way he should—and that you'll have the joy of seeing so yourself when you get home.

Professional Adjustments

So much has changed. And because it has, your playbook for being recognized and achieving success at work needs to change also. Here are the professional tweaks you need to make to stay on track on the job while being the parent you want to be.

Remaining visible—and visibly engaged

Throughout your first year of parenthood, you're likely to be absent from work much more, and at different times, than you've ever been before. Even if you have the best support system in the world, between parental leave, doctor's visits, daycare drop-offs, any care snafus, and the desire to just be around your child more, you won't—physically or hours-wise—be around as much on the job. That doesn't mean you're working or producing any less. In fact, with the urgency and efficiency that working parenthood brings, you may be getting *more* done than ever. To the colleagues around you, though, it won't necessarily appear that way. They may not understand that your early departure for daycare pickup is going to be followed by long hours spent in front of your laptop this evening, and they may get the incorrect idea that you're "focusing on other things." That assumption may feel, and be, unfair—but it's not good for you or your career, either.

> I'll tell my colleagues that I can't do a 4:30 meeting because I need to leave the office at 5:00 to make daycare pickup. Most get it—but on the flip side of that understanding is what I call *over*standing: people not asking me to do work, or overpraising every little task. It's well intentioned, but they're projecting a view of how much I can handle and how much I'm available as a single mother with a baby. I try not to get defensive. I'll say, 'Listen, it's 2:00 p.m., and I'm here till 5:00. This is my *job*.'"
>
> —*CJ, government lawyer, mother of one*

You want to correct that erroneous impression, to take steps that raise your visibility and gently signal to your colleagues that while, yes, you are a parent now, your contributions and commitment are the same as ever. That includes small but high-impact moves like:

- Speaking early on during meetings, and making your voice heard on important conference calls

- Still going to work outings and events, like the regular Thursday after-work drinks, at least occasionally, and even if you have to get a babysitter to cover at home

- Taking the long way around the office to get to the coffee machine, stopping to chat with a few colleagues as you go

- Occasionally starting work earlier than your colleagues, or staying later

- Sending emails and updates during those hours when you are working hard but others aren't

- Taking care, if working remotely, to leave "markers" of your work—e.g., participating more actively in a messaging channel

In other words, figure out how to stay top of sight and top of mind. And then, with zero guilt, go focus on your family.

Taking charge of your performance review

Leave and parental status shouldn't color your performance evaluation or annual review one iota: you should be evaluated on the work you *did* in a given year, not on what you didn't. Unfortunately, that's not always the way it works, because most organizations' review systems—even the ones that are carefully, thoughtfully designed—just aren't set up to accommodate the realities of leave, of phaseback, or of parenting in general. All too often, they're rigidly based around specific metrics (like sales per year), run according to strict rules ("you must have eight or more peer raters"), and generate zero-sum outcomes (like numerical scores or forced rankings) that then determine your pay, promotion eligibility, and future. Of course, you may be in a smaller

Changing ambitions

It's possible to find your career motivations shifting now—perhaps significantly, and in surprising directions. If you've always been a go-getter, you may feel like slowing down a bit. Or the reverse: you may suddenly develop goals, grit, and determination you never knew you had. These changes aren't unusual, may not be permanent, and aren't any cause for alarm. You're simply—and smartly—recalibrating your professional outlook and approach in the face of a major life change and in the context of wanting to be the very best parent you can.

Honor your workparent instincts, but in a tempered way. If you cut your hours back now, for example, do so in small increments, or in a way that lets you ramp them up again next year. If you feel more driven at work, try raising your hand for a few new responsibilities before making any larger career switch. If you are considering larger-scale changes, consult chapter 15, "Flexibility," or chapter 12, "Getting Ahead." Whatever the case, trust your gut, think holistically, and remember: you're in the workparenting game for the long term.

or more informal organization that doesn't have a formal review system but that relies instead on subjective manager assessments. In that context, you're vulnerable to the opinions and biases of any less-than-supportive boss. And even if you have the most supportive manager in the world, she may have easily forgotten about all the great work you did earlier this year, before your leave, or fail to "see" all the work you're doing during off hours. In other words, the way in which you're evaluated probably just isn't set up to factor in the reality that you've been on leave for four months or working differently now—and this can have serious career consequences. It's too easy for you to get shortchanged, even if no one around you has ill intentions. With that in mind, and if you have even a remote concern about how this first post-leave review will go, don't leave things to chance: take charge.

Before the review process begins, ask your manager or HR contact how your evaluation will be handled. You're not insinuating anything, or on a witch hunt; just seeking to understand. Maybe there's a special formula the organization uses to annualize the billable hours you've worked, or maybe instead of eight peer raters you need only five. If so, good to know. If not, be ready to suggest other fair solutions to "equalizing" your review: perhaps you could be evaluated on your last four full quarters of sales numbers instead of on the past twelve months, or maybe in addition to your manager's write-up, you can draft a personal performance statement that can be put in your permanent file. Share any apprehensions, but in a constructive, positive way: you simply want your performance evaluated fairly and accurately. You may not get the precise reassurances you're looking for, but the more—and more effectively—you advocate for yourself, the better. If you're required to write a self-review or summary of your own achievements, don't shy away from leave but don't overemphasize it, either. Point out how smooth and seamless your transition was—and then call out key wins you've delivered since you've been back.

Setbacks—and how to overcome them

Even with rock-solid professional strategies in place, and with months of working-parent experience, you will discover that things still can—and will—go wrong. Setbacks happen. Childcare arrangements fall apart . . . someone on your team quits and you're left covering the workload . . . the whole family gets a stomach bug during busy season . . . you're put on an important, career-making project that means six weeks of missing out on the baby's bedtime. It's the rare working parent who reaches the end of Year One unscathed by these or similar events. And when you're still adjusting to working parenthood, any extra bends in the road can be very hard to steer through. You may be left feeling overwhelmed, or distracted at work, or with dampened ambition, or wondering if you need to scale back or change jobs. Whatever the setback, it's essential that you not let it damage your confidence and feelings too much, or let it hurt your career and performance. When you do have to confront reversals of any kind, here's how to regroup, summon your best professional self, and move on.

- **Get practical.** When you're under pressure, it's easy to focus on your feelings and reactions to that pressure instead of on solving the problem that's actually causing it. It *is* infuriating and unfair that the nanny quit, or you've just had more work dumped on you. It's normal to be upset and angry in these situations. But right now your mission is to find a new care arrangement, or to delegate more, or to advocate for the work to be reassigned or reconfigured somehow, or all three. Compartmentalize: focus on what you need to *do* now, in real time, to address the problem.

- **Get some support.** Now is the time to tap your working-parent mentors and peers for practical advice and encouragement. Their straight talk, empathy, and perspective can help get you through this. And consider telling your boss as well, even if you have a more formal relationship and the setback is a personal one. Telling him "Our nanny quit, and in the next few weeks, I'm going to be focused on finding a permanent childcare solution in addition to delivering at work" isn't oversharing or a complaint: it's an important FYI.

- **Take a very short- and very long-term view—simultaneously.** Don't think about the next six months of long hours. Just concentrate on getting through the pile of work you have *today*—and remind yourself that a few years from now, today's fiasco will be a distant memory.

- **Depersonalize it.** Avoid slipping into the terrible trap of seeing any setback as some kind of personal failure, a "sign" that you should quit your job, or as cosmic feedback about your long-term prospects as a working parent. It's none of those: sometimes, junk just happens.

A new identity

Your *identity* is who you are. It's what, at your very core and in a completely honest way, you feel yourself to be. You may be *Dan's son, Andrea's daughter, an athlete, an introvert, a committed vegetarian, of Italian descent, a university graduate, religious, a soldier, an artist, a tech expert*—and much more likely, some unique combination. Whether you acquired those characteristics through chance or hard work, they feel natural, comfortable, and right.

During the first few months, being a working mother or father isn't likely to feel natural, comfortable, or right—or even like an identity at all. It may seem more like a job, a contradiction, or an act: like something you're doing, forcing together, or faking your way through as opposed to something you *are*.

Gradually, very gradually, over the course of Year One, that will change. You'll start taking work-to-home transitions in stride. A brand-new workparent will seek out your advice, and you'll be able to provide him with good tips and warm reassurance. You'll notice that you're able to strike up a quick rapport with coworkers or customers by mentioning that, just like them, you also have a son or daughter . . . and it will feel oddly natural to talk about your family, even in a professional setting. With each additional day of experience, you'll step further into your new, dual role. You'll realize that other people see you as an all-in, capable, working parent now, and that—bit by bit— you've become one.

5

From Baby to Toddler to Little Kid

Strategies for Adapting at Work and at Home as Your Child Grows and Develops

Sure, the first year of working parenthood was a huge adjustment—but these *next* several years are likely bringing change on a scale and of a speed you've rarely had to deal with before. All of a sudden the baby's walking . . . and talking. Then she's three, and demanding to know why you have to leave her to go to work each morning and why she can't have the iPad again. Or with everything that's happening at home, the new schedule you just went to great lengths to negotiate with your boss isn't meeting your needs anymore. It may feel as if *every* time you find a good working-parent groove, things shift and you have to find all-new ways to cope. You're constantly flexing, and reinventing—and fortunately a few simple, powerful, consistent strategies will help you do so. During this time of constant change, here are ways to stay on your front foot, both at home and on the job.

Making the Most of Care Transitions

During the first year of working parenthood, your beginning- and end-of-workday caregiving transitions were critical but fairly straightforward. Conversations with your care provider centered mostly on timing and logistics: on feeding and napping schedules, for example. But as your child grows, his needs change and become significantly more complex. Eating and sleeping are still important, but so are his emotional development, socialization with other children, physical abilities, and growing readiness for the eventual start of full-time school. With so much in flux, the partnership you have with your caregivers becomes ever more important, and important to get right. Good communication is essential now, and in this relationship, morning and evening handoffs are your main connection points. As you enter Year Two, it can be helpful to rethink how to use these daily check-ins.

- **Broaden the frame.** Begin talking about a larger range of topics—and ask your caregiver more, and more-differentiated, questions, too. How is your child interacting with other children—and who is he making friends with? What activities does he enjoy most? When left to his own devices, what toys or activities does he gravitate toward? Were there any surprises, particularly happy moments, or disappointments throughout his day? How does he express joy, or frustration? Have your caregivers noticed any new behavioral patterns? Abilities? Fears? The extra texture and insight you get will let you feel more on top of your child's development as it occurs—which, while you're working so many hours each day, will be deeply reassuring. To be clear: you don't have to turn every conversation with the sitter into an interrogation. A few extra minutes each morning and evening will let you cover everything you need.

- **Make it a two-way street.** Offer your own updates and observations, too. If your child has been having more tantrums at home, let your caregiver know. When you're heading into busy season and will be working very long hours, or if your partner is changing jobs, share that context as well. Your care provider may have insights on why the tantrums are happening and how to defuse them, or can provide extra attention and reassurance.

- Observe—and be open to learning. Don't be shy about spending extra time quietly watching your nanny or daycare providers in action: how they comfort your child when he's upset, for example, or encourage him when he's frustrated, or what games they use to stimulate his activity and thinking. Remember, your caregivers likely have much more practical experience in child development than you do. The changes and new behaviors that are baffling for you may be old hat to them, and they can teach you some wonderful new tricks.

- Maintain a unified front. Babies are oblivious to how you interact with your caregiver, but even a two- or three-year-old can sense when there's a difference of opinion, if interactions are rushed, or if your relationship is strained. Take care to greet your caregivers warmly, and don't override the decisions they've made or directions they've given your child throughout the day. If you have any difficult questions or issues to resolve, do so out of your child's earshot. Your relationship with your caregiver should be a constructive partnership—and your child should feel that too.

A visible schedule

Your child may be too young to tell or understand time, but be certain to talk with him about daily plans, particularly if your work or caregiving schedule is complex or varies. Starting each morning understanding the basic "pegs" of his day—who will be dropping him off, whether he'll be doing the extra hour at daycare, who will be putting him to bed, etc.—lets him feel safe and secure. One easy tactic to help here is to make the daily schedule "readable."

Hang up a cork or magnet board at his eye level in some visible, high-traffic area of the house, and each morning tack up pictures, in chronological order, of what he'll do and who will take care of him during the day: A photo of Mom (who will take him to daycare), followed by an image of the daycare building, then a picture of the sitter who will pick him up, and so on. He'll be proud of being able to decipher the schedule by himself, and you'll feel better when you've made his day understandable and familiar.

Bonding with Your Child Through Activity

At some point during the toddler phase, the moments of reconnection you have with your child after each workday will become frustrating and emotionally fraught. This is due to a fundamental difference in how adults and children are wired, and how you each want that precious time together each evening to begin.

While adults relate to and show affection for each other by talking and asking questions, children can't. Get home after work, eagerly ask your three-year-old, "How was your day?" and you'll most likely get a blank stare, an "I don't know"—or be completely ignored. When you've been looking forward to seeing her all day and stopped work early to be able to hang out with her before her bedtime, that lukewarm response can be disappointing—and feel like a rejection. But it's nothing personal: at this very young age, your child simply doesn't have the ability to sort and categorize her experiences the same way you do, or to capture her feelings in words.

What will work to make those pivot points easier and more rewarding for both of you is action: *doing* things together, instead of talking. As soon as you arrive at the daycare center, get down on the floor and join in whatever game she's playing. Or when you arrive home, pull out a puzzle or toy to enjoy together, put on some of her favorite music and ask her to dance, or encourage her to act along in her play

> " Every morning when I get up, I create an 'invitation to play.' I set up a game or a toy in an interesting way that I know will engage him—something creative but not complicated. This morning it was a little cave made out of blocks with a couple of his animal figures inside.
>
> When he wakes up, he runs to find what I've left for him. If I'm still at home, we can have fun with it together. If I have to leave early for the salon, he'll show me what he's doing over FaceTime. It's our little ritual, and it's a win-win-win. He's excited and looks forward to it, my wife gets thirty extra minutes to chill out and wake up, and I get to interact with him, even if I'm not there."
>
> —*Devin, hairdresser, father of one*

kitchen while you're cooking dinner. Better yet, let her lead; simply ask, "What should we play?"—and then follow along with what she chooses. Unhurried, engaged in an activity she has chosen, and without any pressure to go back and forth in adult-style conversation, your child will feel much more at ease, those transition moments will go more smoothly—and talk will quickly follow.

When you're carrying around a lot of work stress or feeling harried by a nonstop schedule, this "action first" technique can be easy to forget or tempting to skip. When you're under pressure, and as you're nearing home or the preschool, remind yourself, *Hugs first, then play, then talk.* What feels counterintuitive or like an extra step now will solidify into habit quickly—and those precious end-of-day reunions will become reliably happy, for both you and your child.

Harnessing the Power of Repetition and Ritual

While transition moments are critical, so is the *rest* of the limited time you spend together. Whatever your work schedule, those mornings, evenings, and weekends can feel very short, and you'll want to make them as enjoyable and high-impact as possible. Your key technique for getting there is R&R: *repetition and ritual.*

Watch any episode of a TV show made for little kids, or read any children's book that's part of a series, and you'll notice that it's remarkably similar to the next one. Characters always wear the same outfits, plots always unfold in the same way, and the theme song plays at exactly the same time. The writers and producers all know that predictability helps *anchor* children—that it makes them look forward to watching the program or having the book read aloud and that they will enjoy it when they do. For your small child, the world is a brand-new and complex place, and when he can see patterns in it or accurately spot what's coming next, it gives him a sense of security, mastery, and delight. For you, repetition is dull. For your toddler, repetition is wonderful and reassuring.

So borrow this technique—and create rituals of your own. The ones that will work best are ones that feel natural, that can happen frequently, that involve both you and your child, and above all, that are easy to do.

Chores

Now's the time to start enlisting your child's help by asking her to do basic self-care and household chores. That doesn't mean expecting your toddler to do all her own laundry or to de-ice the car, but she can easily handle small, simple tasks like putting her dirty clothes in the laundry basket, tidying up toys and games, bringing napkins to the table at dinnertime, or helping to wipe the kitchen counter after a spill. Doing so will build her sense of capability and self-esteem, and get her ready to take on larger responsibilities—like homework, or laundry—later on. Don't fall into the "it's faster if I just do it for her" trap, or wait to assign chores when she's bigger and more capable. The more your kids understand early on that *their* help is valuable, too, the easier it will be to run your working-parent household.

If your son knows you'll pick him up and hug him in the same way when you come through the door each evening, he'll look forward to it—and be thrilled when it happens. Sing that favorite song together each day on the way home from daycare, begin each Saturday morning with the same breakfast, and tuck him into bed in a consistent way each evening. With little effort, you can weave small but deliberate threads of routine like this throughout the time you have with your child—and make those hours more satisfying, comforting, and happy for both of you.

Explaining Work to Very Small Children

When your child is very young, work can feel—to him—like a mysterious competitor for your time and attention. *Why does Mommy leave every morning? Why can't Daddy put away the computer or stay home and play?* Without decent answers to those questions, your daily commitment to work can be read as abandonment, and the tears, emotions, bargaining, and flat-out tantrums that can result may leave you feeling helpless and guilty.

Talking with your child about work—regularly, honestly, and directly—won't be a perfect solution, but it can help. When she understands *why* you're going to work, and that you have to, it can allay a lot of

The daily goodbye

Whether you're leaving for a day at work, doing daycare drop-off, or just headed into your home office, be sure to mark your leave, and keep those goodbyes loving, reassuring—and brief. An extended farewell only provides more time for your child to be upset, and if she observes that knee-grabbing hysterics prompt you to hang around for a while, she'll likely continue. Tell her in a firm but tender way that you know she's sad, but that her trusted caregiver is with her, and that you'll be there later in the day to pick her up or to put her to bed. And then *go*.

If she's routinely distraught at your departure for work, check with her caregiver(s) as to how long the sadness typically lasts. Most children recover from daily separations quickly; she may be happily playing again less than a minute after you've gone. Consider a "goodbye ritual" also—like a certain type of hug, or a favorite song. If she knows that Mommy or Daddy *never* leaves without giving her a high five at the doorway, but *always* leaves right after, it will limit the drama and help protect everyone's feelings.

difficult feelings. Over time, it will also allow her to feel more secure in your affections, to take interest and pride in what you do, and to begin to understand work as an important part of your life and ultimately of her own.

To help your very small child understand your job and its demands:

- Keep things as simple as possible. Use the kinds of plain terms, descriptions, and examples your child can easily grasp. If you work in a hospital, you "help sick people get better," or if you're a chef, you "make good food for people to eat." If you work in a professional setting that's harder to explain, describe it in terms of relationships and feelings; try saying that you have to "go to the office and work because people there depend on me," or "will be upset if our team isn't together," or similar. Lean on words and concepts familiar to small children, like *helping, building,* or *making.* Terms like *clients, projects, deadlines,* or *responsibilities* will be mostly unintelligible.

- **Let your child see where you work.** Show her your workstation, the copier, the supply closet, the break room. If your work requires a uniform or special equipment, show her the changing area or where those tools are kept. Plan your visit for a weekend, or other quiet day when you can avoid noise and distraction and focus solely on your child's experience and questions.

- **Be open about your "why."** It's OK to tell your child that you like your job—and there's no need to shy away from the economics. Statements like "I really like building new houses for people to live in" or "working lets me earn the money to take good care of you and Daddy and baby Oliver" are direct, reassuring—and the truth.

- **Keep it positive.** Yes, your boss may be difficult, the hours long, and the work occasionally tedious, but those aren't problems your toddler can in any way solve or relate to. And from her perspective, it will be upsetting to think that you're leaving her each day for something you don't enjoy or take interest in.

- **Talk about her job, too.** The demands of your real, adult work may be hard for your daughter to get her head around, but the overall idea of "working" comes naturally to and fascinates most kids. If you have to catch up with work-related reading on a Saturday, set her up with paper and crayons and ask if she'll "work" alongside you. During playtime, be willing to play the role of sick animal to her veterinarian, or of customer to her shopkeeper—and compliment her for the effort she's putting into these make-believe jobs. When work is positioned as

> " It's a two-way street: I try to involve my kids in my life as much as I want to be involved in theirs. My youngest is three, and too young to understand what I do yet, but if I need to make a home repair, I take him to the hardware store to get what we need. I'm showing him how the adult world, and adult mind, works."
>
> —*Brant, chief information officer, father of seven*

> My son's only four and a half, but he understands. I work steady midnights, which means 10:00 p.m. to 6:00 a.m. When I tuck him into bed, he'll say, 'Bye Mommy—have a good night at work!' This year I did a special visit to his pre-K classroom, wearing my uniform, and talked to the kids about safety. He was ecstatic—and so proud of his mom."
>
> —*Evelyn, police officer, mother of one*

something that *everyone* does and that's important, interesting, admired, and praiseworthy, it will go a long way to helping tears and guilt go away.

Confronting the Screen-Time Dilemma

Between ages one and five, your child will become increasingly more physically active, more interactive, and more vocal. You'll be more tired, and it will be harder to get work done when he's around—to find the quiet time you need on a Sunday to square off all the details on an important project before a Monday deadline, for example. This is when you'll likely start having anxiety about screen time. Should you give your three-year-old the iPad and enjoy twenty more minutes of badly needed sleep? Allow him to watch TV while you're emailing with your boss? Use the latest Disney film as a sitter when you're working remotely, and without a caregiver? Or should you believe the experts who say that *any* amount of screen exposure is terrible for small, developing brains? Most working mothers and fathers do all four—and end up feeling all kinds of wrong.

Instead, try to find a moderate, realistic approach that works for the entire family—and that acknowledges the pressure points of your career and daily schedule and the circumstances we're all in. We're living in a stressful modern reality here, and allowing a toddler to watch a single fifteen-minute show each morning makes eminent sense if it lets you get showered, dressed, and ready and helps get the whole family out the door to daycare on time. Likewise, when

Bonjour, Monsieur iPad!

To make that screen a little less appealing to your young child *and* make you feel a little more virtuous when you offer it, only allow him to watch shows and movies in a foreign language. Explain that Mr. iPad doesn't know, or has forgotten how to speak, your native language, and queue up all of your child's regular favorite programs in another one. Either your little one quickly loses interest and finds something else to do, or he's exposed to a new language. Either way: you win.

you have to take an important conference call during your vacation, there's no harm in queuing up one of your child's favorite movies so you can speak professionally and undisturbed. Landing that big new project may depend on it. It's likely you watched some amount of TV growing up, and it didn't derail you, did it? On the other hand, if you find yourself using screens as go-to babysitters or depending on them for hours each day (if you're *abusing* them rather than *using* them), then it's probably time to cut back or reconsider.

If you are going to allow use of the iPad or TV:

- Contract it. Have a clear set of rules for yourself about how much screen time you'll permit and when. Maybe you decide that the iPad's OK when you get urgent work calls after hours and your partner's not around to help. Or maybe you create a firm two-hour-per-week aggregate limit and use the time flexibly as a way to catch a breather amid your nonstop schedule. Whatever you choose, make the rules specific and transparent and stick to them. To ensure consistency, make sure that all caregivers, family members, and your child's Third Parents are fully aware of them too.

- Plan it. Preselect age-appropriate and educational games, movies, or shows so they're ready to go when needed. Don't get caught hunting for an appropriate movie or waiting on a slow download at professionally critical moments.

- Time it. If you're allowing thirty minutes of TV, announce it—
  and then set an egg timer, or put an easy-to-read clock near the
  screen. When time is up, it's up: no surprises, no tears, and no
  "just five more minutes, Daddy!" type negotiations.

- Hide it. Eliminate temptation by keeping screens out of sight
  when not in use. Put the iPad and remote controls in a drawer,
  out of your toddler's reach and mind. When devices are away,
  you'll be more likely to use and savor the limited time you have
  with your child, too.

Still Owning—and Updating—Your Story

When you became a working parent, you carefully crafted a message
for your manager, colleagues, and clients. You told them about your
ambition—and new needs—in a compelling, authentic way. Now, a
few years later, you may have a new boss, or new responsibilities; the
organization's strategy or budget may have shifted; or the schedule
you're keeping as the parent of a four-year-old may be much different
from the one you kept when he was a baby. You may have been promoted, or risk being passed over for promotion if you don't raise your
hand. Things change, people can forget, and even the best and most
thoughtful manager or coworkers can't read your mind. Throughout
these first several years, therefore, it's imperative to stay in control of
your story. Fortunately, there are several natural openings in which
you can create the overall workparent narrative you want.

- Performance reviews. Feedback conversations are the right
  environment in which to reassert—and reset—your high-level
  expectations and needs. *Never* go into an annual review without knowing what key workparent points and messages you
  want to get across. If you've been handling an unreasonably
  high workload despite a reduced schedule, for example,
  or if you've gotten into a solid working-parent routine and are
  ready for new challenges, bring those things up with
  your manager now along with proposed next steps and
  solutions.

- Day-to-day communications. Leaving to take your child to a healthcare appointment? Be sure to let your colleagues know using the *priorities, next steps, commitment, enthusiasm* framing tool we first covered in chapter 3. Saying, "I'm leaving for my son's doctor's office now, and will be back at work by 3:00, when I'll finish updating the storyboards so we can have a fresh version for approval tomorrow. Looking forward to getting this into production!" will bring people into your plans, alleviate their concerns, showcase your dedication—and minimize the risk of misunderstandings.

When you're on the phone

C'mon, we've *all* been there: had work conversations interrupted by our small children, and felt mildly embarrassed or unprofessional as a result. While those break-ins are inevitable—little kids simply aren't capable of understanding work boundaries or phone or videoconferencing etiquette, no matter how often they're explained—they don't have to leave you apologizing or distracted.

If you do need to take a call when your little one is around:

- Alert the person you're speaking to. "My five-year-old is home with me; you may hear or see her in the background" is all it takes. What's not surprising isn't embarrassing.
- Make technology your friend: know how to mute the phone quickly, install a slidable tab over your laptop's camera, or download a professional-looking backdrop onto your videoconferencing platform (most green-screen-type backdrops will pick up only one face).
- Have a "diversion object" ready: an interesting toy or gadget, or a small piece of candy, that can reliably distract and quiet your child.

When you do get interrupted—which you will—resist the natural instinct to be terse with your child or to start explaining yourself, both of which will make you sound frazzled or not-so-nice and only draw more attention to what you're trying to downplay. If you need to, ask for a quick break to get your child's needs sorted out. And don't be surprised if the person on the other end of the line laughs, or sympathizes: they've been there, too.

- **Outside events, executive recruiters, and social media.** If you haven't circulated at a networking event or industry conference, bent a headhunter's ear about your recent achievements, updated your LinkedIn profile, or otherwise sent signals to the broader professional community about your commitment and achievements within the past six months, do so now—and then set a calendar reminder to do so again on an every-three-months basis. You've worked way too hard to develop your professional brand and your reputation in the field to let it go stale through benign neglect. Careers are made by doing brilliant work—and then by making that work well known. Regardless of how busy working parenthood gets, it's in your best interests to keep your contacts and profile fresh.

Considering Changes at Work

Even if you were one of the rare mothers or fathers who raced eagerly back to work after parental leave, there will be moments during your first five years of working parenthood when you find yourself mulling over and revisiting your professional choices. You may start thinking about going part-time, changing jobs or careers—or taking a professional break. With so many pressures at work and at home and with your kids growing and changing so rapidly, it's completely normal to worry about what you're missing at home, to seek relief from the strain, and to want more slack in the system. The risk you face, though, is in making these kinds of professional choices reactively or hastily—in leaping toward what appears on the surface to be a good solution yet might not ultimately be the right one for you. Before deciding:

- **Take a vacation, and any other time off you're due.** The burnout you're feeling may ease up, at least partially, during a well-deserved break, or you may gain a different perspective on how you're handling the pressures of parenting and work. With some rest, and distance from the day-to-day grind, you'll be in a much better frame of mind to chart any new course forward.

- Find quiet, unhurried time and space to think things through. It will be impossible to come to good conclusions when you're exhausted, multitasking, or interacting with a cranky toddler. You don't need weeks of uninterrupted contemplation on a mountaintop someplace, but do try to get out of the office and catch a short break from your regular routine. Even an hour by yourself at the local coffee shop will let you better consider your needs and options.

- Speak to colleagues and mentors. What workparents do you know—and trust—who have been through this challenging "baby into little kid" period and come out the other side? Their encouragement can be invaluable, and they may be able to steer you toward solutions you didn't think of.

- Get creative. Perhaps practicing corporate law while parenting a toddler feels impossible, at least right now. But could you stay with your firm in another practice group with better hours? Take an in-house staff position for a year? Work for a client on secondment for six months? Whatever your role or circumstances, cast your net wide and think broadly about potential solutions.

No comparing: other parents

It's normal to look around at how other workparents are managing things, and it's healthy to seek out their differing perspectives, encouragement, and advice. What *isn't* productive is to start benchmarking or evaluating yourself against other moms and dads. *How did she get promoted on a part-time arrangement? Should we have our second child now, like everyone else? How do they seem so "together" with twins and big careers, when I feel tired and overwhelmed all the time?* The simple answer is: their careers, ambitions, personalities, parenting styles, and budgets are different than yours, and comparisons serve no real purpose. Find support, solutions, and inspiration among your workparent community, but stay focused on what works for *you*.

> ❝ When the kids are this little, and you're in a tough phase, it feels like it lasts forever. Potty training will drive you cuckoo. I tortured myself about it—but then the phase passes.
>
> The work you put in now will pay off when the kids are older, because you've given them a model for managing life and navigating independence. If you make big changes to optimize for this one brief time in your family's life, you may limit your options later. Picture your kids when they're twenty-five years old, and the good ways they'll describe you to their friends, or partner. Play the long game.❞
>
> —*Karen, macro trends expert, mother of two*

- **Take a longer-term view.** This patch of working parenthood—when change is the most rapid, your kids need you so much, and your career may be accelerating—can be tremendously difficult, but it's *finite*. A few months from now, the big deadline may have passed, your child will be able to do a bit more for herself, and things will invariably get a little easier. And five years from now, or twenty, you may be very grateful that you persisted with your career in the way that you did.

If you've considered your situation calmly and holistically and you're still interested in a change to your career or schedule, turn to chapter 15 for advice on negotiating and using flexible working arrangements and/or to chapter 17, which covers breaks, sabbaticals, and other time off.

Staying on the Right Path—for *You*

When you're working a demanding job and parenting small children with ever-changing needs, it can be easy to let your own friendships go unattended, put hobbies and interests on hold, let exercise or spiritual practices fall by the wayside, and constantly be in go mode, without any time for reflection. And when that happens, you may start losing sight of something vitally important: yourself.

> " In our office we work 9:00 to 5:00, but we also see every production, and have networking events three or four nights per week, and there's a lot of travel to conferences and trade shows. The job demands a lot, but I'm passionate about the work, and my coworkers are a tight-knit group who have each other's backs. My son is five, and that's what I hope to show him: that this wasn't just a job, a paycheck—that I loved what I did, and was contributing."
>
> —*Allison, Broadway marketer, mother of one*

As hectic as things are during this baby-to-little-kid period, try to stay involved with the activities and people that were important to you before you were a parent. If you've always been close with your college buddies and were an avid runner before your child was born, organize the next get-together—and then lace up those shoes and hit the trail, at least occasionally. Take the time to think through your professional goals, also—and think how you can move closer to them. Keep up with your mentors, and keep asking for their advice.

And along the way, cut yourself some slack. It's OK to have allowed your toddler an episode—or more—of her favorite TV program, to have lost your cool during her third tantrum of the weekend, to work different hours than you used to, or to be craving unpressured time alone. Your children are always changing, but you are too—and the more you can keep yourself on a good path, the steadier and more confident a working parent you'll be, both now and in the years to come.

6

Expanding Your Family—If, When, and How

Deciding to Have A(nother) Child, and Ways
to Handle It if You Do

It seems like a monumental decision because it *is* one. You're
thinking about welcoming a new human being into the family and
all the responsibility that entails. You're also considering how an
additional child would affect all the various aspects of your workparent life—your workload, your finances, your emotions, your ability to
get ahead on the job, and the time you'd have to spend with your oldest,
to name just a few. It's also a private deliberation, it can feel pressured,
and much of what you're mulling over may seem unique to your own
situation.

Rather than having you spend any more time stewing, though, or
feeling conflicted or alone, let's try out a new approach to thinking
things through—one that gives you a bit of a break. Let's imagine that
instead of having to hash through the whole matter solo, you could
put two smart colleagues to work *for* you. In the first part of this chapter, as your diligent teammates Pro and Con debate each of your concerns about growing (or not growing) your working-parent family, sit
back and reflect on which of their points you find the most resonant
and persuasive. When they're done, we'll get practical, covering

> ## If you don't have kids yet . . .
>
> . . . good for you for thinking and planning ahead! Use this chapter as a first step in considering this important decision, and then turn to other parts of the book for more working-parent insights that can help you decide whether and when.

specific ways to ensure workparent success if you do decide to welcome another child.

To be clear: there are no "right" answers here, but with the confidence of knowing that you've approached everything thoughtfully, thoroughly, and with eyes wide open, it will be easier to move toward the best answer for *you*.

Considering the Pros and Cons

The decision as to whether and when to expand your family may feel so bulky, multistranded, and tangled up that it seems more like a plate of spaghetti than a regular life choice. In reality, though, your questions and apprehensions most likely fall into three discrete categories:

- Professional considerations: how having another child might be feasible in your current role, or affect your short- and longer-term career prospects

- Cultural and societal pressures: what you "should," or feel you should, do based on the standards and expectations of your community, or of society at large

- Personal concerns: what's right for your family, for you as a mother or father, and for yourself, as an individual human being

We will—with Pro and Con doing the heavy lifting, of course— address each set in turn. Warning: there won't be any conclusions drawn here. Pro and Con will simply shine light on both sides of each issue during their active, honest debate.

Professional considerations

Because professional considerations can often feel the most unyielding and beyond your own control, let's unpack them first. Read through the Pro and Con back and forth, and as you go, mark it up. Circle the questions and concerns that feel most relevant to you, and note which arguments strike a chord and which make the most intuitive sense. Then add in other questions and concerns you have that aren't covered here, and use same the Pro/Con approach to work them through.

I just started here. I need to wait at least twelve to eighteen months before having a baby.

- **PRO:** You only get one chance to make a first impression. What you do, how well you do it, and how you spend your time now send important long-term signals about your work ethic, potential, and commitment. Plus, professional transitions—and parental ones—are tough, to put it mildly. The very last thing you want is to be in "ramp up" mode at work *and* have a new baby at the same time.

- **CON:** "Need to"? Says who? There's nothing in your contract or employee handbook to that effect—and for good reason: it would be illegal! Besides, you know as well as anyone that it's possible to do a terrific job while expecting, and with a small child at home. And what looms so large for you is much less of an event to your boss and colleagues. *You* have to take care of your new son or daughter for eighteen years; your boss and colleagues get you back right after parental leave ends. Might they be surprised when you announce you're expecting? Sure. But news flash: people have kids—it happens. And besides, this is your life and your family we're talking about: Are you really going to put off having a baby for the sole purpose of abiding by some imaginary rule?

My organization's parental-leave benefit is only available to employees with *x* length of service, which I don't have yet.

- **PRO:** Workparenting is hard enough; it would be foolish to deprive yourself of such a substantive benefit just to have a child a little earlier. Don't shoot yourself in the foot. Wait.

- **CON:** Whether you're planning on having a child biologically or any other way, it's not going to happen overnight. Chances are high that you *will* be eligible by the time the baby actually arrives. If not: try negotiating. More and more organizations are improving their leave policies; perhaps yours will too.

It's an unspoken rule that in this profession you don't expand your family until you're a certain age/title level/done with training/licensed/tenured/etc.

- **PRO:** And likely for good reasons. The demands and rigor of this earlier part of your career are high, and adding children into the mix may bring you to a personal and/or professional breaking point. You don't want to jeopardize your progress thus far by adding in an extra challenge right now. Think about it this way: What you're really doing now is *investing* in your future career. Kids can come later, if you still want them. Play the long game: defer.

- **CON:** Unspoken, because it isn't actually a rule—a *pattern*, maybe, but not an actual directive. It's also highly likely that that pattern was set many years ago, when the world, and the group of people doing this job, was very different than today. Besides, you're not managing to the good of a whole profession—you're managing your own career and life. You know yourself, your budget, your Village, and what you want for your future. If it feels right and feasible to have a child, then it is.

I don't want to wait too long, but expanding our family will be much easier after the next promotion/big project is over/ relocation/raise/IPO is completed/etc.

- **PRO:** Workparenting is hard—financially, professionally, personally, practically, and in every other way. If you can choose between adding to your family now, when things might be harder, and later, when they might be significantly easier, then the choice is clear. There's never a "perfect time" to have a child, but you still need to make smart choices.

- **CON:** Be *very* careful with "over the next career rainbow" thinking. There's always another rainbow—and you could easily defer expanding your family for years, or even decades, based on that logic. Besides, you can't predict the future; you may change jobs, or that promotion may never happen, or the IPO market may dry up. And then how will you feel knowing you've delayed your life choices for nothing?

The senior people here are all "big family types" *OR* have small families or no kids because they are maniacally focused on their careers . . . and if I don't follow suit, I'm limiting my long-term prospects.

- **PRO:** Looking closely at the careers, lives, and choices of the senior leaders in your organization is a powerful thing to do. It lets you answer the question, "What works here? What's valued? What flies, culturally?" Of course, you could work against the cultural grain of your company or organization and still succeed—but that's going to be tough.

- **CON:** There's no single model of success, particularly for working parents. If you don't see your own desires for a larger/smaller family reflected in the senior ranks, then look further: maybe there are other great role models at *other* organizations. Take a critical eye to the generation gap, also: your organization's senior leaders may have made certain career choices years ago to get where they are today. That doesn't mean *you* have to make those same choices in our current environment. Bigger picture: Are you *really* willing to hand over effective authority for your family planning to a job and organization you may be part of for only a few more years? Does your work *really* get that kind of say over your life?

What other professional concerns are top of mind for you? Try taking a Pro and Con position on each. How does your thinking on each issue change as you do so? Do you still feel uncertain or ambivalent about the "if and when" decisions from a holistic professional perspective? That's completely normal: the intersection of your life and career is simply too important and nuanced to allow for the luxury of absolute, black-and-white thinking. What ideally became *very* clear as you read, though, is that for every career and workplace "must" or "must not" about expanding your family, there's a sensible—and often very powerful—opposing argument. You're not straitjacketed by other people's views, or by "the system." There's no one single or best way to manage your family, and no one else is holding the trump card, here. Whatever your professional situation, and with full command over all the underlying issues, you should feel comfortable deciding if and when.

Cultural and societal pressures

Now let's turn our attention to the expectations and *shoulds* you may be working with as a member of your broader community. That community may be ethnic, religious, regional, educational, familial, or economic. Or it may be defined by an activity, a lifestyle, or a social-media group, or be drawn along any other lines. Most likely, you're the member of more than one kind of community, and each has provided you messages—direct, subtle, and conflicting—about the "correct" size of your family and when it's right to have kids. Just as you did with the prior Pro/Con debate, make this your own: circle the arguments and issues you're grappling with, jot down any notes, and think about any other concerns and questions not listed here that may also be affecting you.

The norm within my community is to have a larger family than I do now/smaller family than I want.

- **PRO:** Being part of this community is important to you. It's part of your identity—it's who you *are*. And in many ways, the concept of family is at the community's core. Why would you buck centuries of tradition/choose to be an outlier? Besides, norms exist because they *work*. If the standard is having a larger/smaller family, it's because there's a lot of proof that it's the right way to go.

- **CON:** The norms within your community—whatever kind of community it is—may have been created in a completely different era, and before the dawn of workparenting as we know it. They may originate in a time before the eighty-hour workweek, the dual-career couple, or current technology. You need to make decisions that work for you, in the here and now—not for others, for the sake of tradition, or to avoid judgments or raised eyebrows. It doesn't matter what your peer group is doing or how your choices look or feel to others. You don't actually *need* their approval. Realistically, not all members of your community are following the norms, anyway. You may not be plain-vanilla average, but you're probably not as much of an outlier as you think.

We should have a second because one child isn't a real family/it's not good to be a single child.

- **PRO:** The "two parents, two or more kids" model has endured for a reason. And when parents are working long hours, sibling relationships can become very important. Your child's "family" isn't just his or her parents.

- **CON:** Whoa—let's hold up on the moral and pseudoscientific judgments for a minute! Family isn't a number, it's a *relationship*. And if you're looking for conclusive evidence about whether or not it's a good thing to be an only child, you're going to be looking for a very long time. More important: think what a wonderful, powerful thing being an only-child workparent family can be—even when your time and resources are limited, they're concentrated on *one* child. That means less worry about the daycare bill, the bigger rent, or the small amount of time you have to spend at home in the evenings. Having "just one" solves a whole lot of the most pressing workparent problems, letting you engage both with your career and your child in a satisfying way.

All my friends have, or are having, their second/third/more. Now's the time.

- **PRO:** There's a lot of positive power in being in the same "life phase" as your friends and colleagues. And likely, your peers are grappling with the same workparent issues you are. If *they* can handle a second/third, *you* can.

- **CON:** Put your blinders on and run your own race. This is your life, not anyone else's—and *you're* the one who's on the hook for raising your kids. If it's the right decision, and right time, you'll make it.

What other societal, familial, or community pressures are you dealing with? Have a Pro/Con debate on each.

Did reading this over feel mildly uncomfortable? It's good if it did. We're discussing issues not usually discussed—and certainly not in a professional context. You want to get all those *shoulds* and *have tos* out on the table, if just for yourself, and see how they map to the realities of your working life and to your true desires and *want tos*. Whether or not you decide to expand your family, this type of candor, and reflective thinking, will help you make your ultimate choice(s) with deeper confidence and in a more genuine, authentic way.

Personal concerns

Finally now, and having worked over some of the professional and community issues, let's turn our attention to the most important decision factor of all: *yourself*. Repeat the same read/write/react process, now addressing your own thoughts, worries, and other feelings.

I've always imagined having two/three/more.

- **PRO:** You need to be true to yourself, your own feelings, and your life plan. Jobs come and go; family is forever. Create the one you want.

- **CON:** That imagination occurred *before* you were dealing with the stresses and strains of workparenting. What you held in your mind's eye years ago is less important than what you want and know will work today, in your current circumstances.

I want another.

- **PRO:** Then do it! See above.

- **CON:** It's fine to want another—in fact, it's wonderful that you do. Just be careful that what you "want" isn't only the joyous bit but also the practical reality. You want another child—but do you also want the sleepless nights, the daycare bill, the emotional strain, the worry that childcare may be taking you away from the career success you really want? You have to buy the whole package in order to make this work.

I don't want another.

- **PRO:** Then don't. Full stop. It's hard enough to workparent when you're overjoyed to be a parent. When you're ambivalent or reluctant, it's all kinds of no good.

- **CON:** Do you *really* not want one? Or are you saying that because you're in a rough patch—the baby's not sleeping, you're having a hard time back from leave, you caught a snarky comment from a coworker about flex time, or you're dealing with a bigger workparent setback? Decisions like this are best made from a neutral state of mind. Wait a while before you come to a firm conclusion.

We're financially stretched as it is.

- **PRO:** Adding another is only going to stretch you further, and it may lead to some difficult compromises, stress, and real long-term impact. You're wise to keep financial issues top of mind.

- **CON:** Workparenting expenses usually go down after the first few years, and there may be ways to make things easier. Turn to chapter 11, "Money," for guidance on managing your workparent finances, and to understand the phases of workparenting expense.

I have no idea how we'll make it work/find childcare/handle the increased load/manage to keep ourselves together and not completely lose it.

- **PRO:** You're a smart person, and if you have "no idea," that's a sign it may be too difficult or too much to take on. Workparenting isn't the Olympics; there's no medal to be won here, and it's not a test of strength or endurance. Do what's feasible.

- **CON:** Try talking to other workparents for their ideas and solutions. Other people have done this, and if you choose to, you can too.

I was so busy at work that I missed out on a lot in these early years. Having a second/third/etc. would give me the chance to really enjoy and savor that baby phase—and be the mom or dad I want to.

- **PRO:** That sense of loss can be devastating. If you want to have another child, and it's doable for you, then go ahead—and enjoy that baby and small-child phase to the fullest.

- **CON:** You're talking about adding a *human being* to the family. That's a commitment and choice that goes well beyond the little-kid phase. What about focusing more time and attention on your existing children and savoring the phase they're in now—instead of having more? Besides, if you do have another, how can you be certain that the problem won't repeat itself?

We had trouble having our first child; we don't want to wait to start what may be a long process to have our second.

- **PRO:** You know your situation, and between your own judgment and the advice and guidance of your doctors, adoption agency, etc., you'll determine the right path forward. Welcoming a child can be a long and involved process.

- **CON:** Before you get on the adding-to-the-family path, just be certain that you're ready. Becoming a parent may take a very long time—or go much faster than you think.

We're definitely having another, but planning to do so in *x* amount of time, because we've read that the optimal timing difference between siblings is *y*.

- **PRO:** The decision *when* to have another child is just as important as *if*. Manage toward what you think will work best.

- **CON:** Happy, well-adjusted families and sibling relationships come in all forms and packages. And the supposed experts opining on the "right" amount of time between siblings aren't talking about how your career might be affected by all this—nor are they talking about your specific family.

What other personal questions or apprehensions do you have? Repeat the Pro/Con process for each.

Whew. You've just done a lot of tough analysis and introspection—it's productive, but likely exhausting. If you find yourself battling tears, or a cortisol spike, or both, that's normal. Once you've had the chance to catch your breath, though, go back and do a quick scan of your notes and reactions to all three segments. How did your overall thinking change, if at all, as you worked them through? Which Pro or Con argument was new, or felt right, or wrong, or like a relief? Were there any themes across all three categories—do you tend to follow conventional wisdom in each area, for instance, or worry about expanding your family too early or too late (whatever that means to you)?

Whether this exercise has led you to a firm conclusion or not, and whatever your personal observations, the good news is that you've just thought through the "do I have another child" decision from a *holistic working-parent perspective*—and in a genuine, authentic way. If you need to keep thinking things through, you also have a balanced method—the Pro/Con approach—for doing so.

When You Still Can't Decide

If you've been sitting with the decision for some time, and have gone through all of the Pros and Cons and *still* feel indecisive, two additional techniques may help you part the clouds.

Technique #1 is *Play It Through*. Play It Through is simply an organized way to imagine the future impact of any current action or decision. To use it, grab a sheet of paper, and down the left side mark off rows, labeled with various time increments: three months, six months, one year, two years, three, five, ten, fifteen (yes, that far out). Across the top of the page create columns marked *Professional, Financial, Familial, Personal, Emotional*. You're now left with a grid and, as you fill it out, a forecast: a tangible, vivid view of how your decision will likely pan out. (Note that the columns can appear in any order you wish, and you can

How to deflect awkward questions at work

"Aren't you going to give little Susie a brother or sister?" "You haven't closed up shop yet, have you?" "When are we going to hear some good news?" Unfortunately, awkward, direct, and overly personal questions about plans to add to your family don't just come from nosy friends and tipsy relatives—they come from bosses and colleagues too.

While it's satisfying to imagine delivering a biting retort, you want to be very careful about your personal brand, and about coming across as harsh or defensive. The trick is to shut these colleagues down, while remaining professional, polite, and upbeat. Have a go-to line that fits the bill and feels comfortable. Responses like . . .

- "I'm not certain how your question relates to our work together" or
- "I just feel so fortunate to have the wonderful family I do" or
- "What? Sorry, I'm focused on the budget numbers; we've got to get these back to the finance team ASAP"

. . . should work, particularly when delivered in a firm, pleasant way.

If you find yourself stewing over rude questions you've gotten, remember: your interrogator may not have meant to be offensive, and the last thing you need is to waste emotional energy on the matter. Let yourself be frustrated for a few minutes—and then move past it.

add/tweak any labels you like. If you prefer to skip the paper entirely and simply do this as a "mind's eye" exercise, that's fine, also—whatever works best for you and helps foster your active and honest thinking.) As best as you can imagine today, how *will* you be feeling about a new addition to the family two years from now, or five? If you decide to add another child to your family, what would the financial picture look like six months from now, or one year, or ten? Do the near-term professional consequences you're so worried about now loom so large later on? Does your fifteen-years-from-now self regret any personal time lost or professional opportunities missed as a result of having a larger (or smaller) family? You're not a fortune-teller, and Play It Through isn't a crystal ball. But you *do* know yourself, and the process of unspooling your decision into the future like this should prompt a stronger and genuine feeling about it today, one way or the other.

If it doesn't, try Technique #2: wait. Give yourself a three-month hiatus from the draining task of wrestling with this huge choice, and focus your mental and emotional energies back on your work, yourself, and your current family. That doesn't mean punting the decision, or ignoring it, but simply allowing yourself a defined period of time in which to gather more data and let your personal tank refill a bit before picking it back up again. After all, things may be quite different three months from now. Maybe you change jobs or get a new boss, or that promotion and the raise that comes with it change both your schedule and your financial picture. Or maybe the baby's sleep problems begin to resolve themselves and the *I have no idea how we would manage with two* feeling that's been haunting you starts to fade . . . or the hunch that you don't want to have another child grows. When the three months are up, and if you need to, work your way back through the earlier parts of this chapter. Fresh eyes and three months' worth of additional workparenting experience should help advance your thinking.

What to Know and Do When Moving from One Child to Two—or More

The single biggest working-parent transition you'll ever make is from zero kids to one. No other workparent change will ever come close.

Infertility and the busy professional

Infertility treatment can involve a significant time commitment as well as personal and emotional strain. If you do need to be away from work for tests and procedures, or the experience is affecting how you "show up" for work, you may want or need to alert your manager to what's going on. However, if for personal reasons you don't want to discuss your desire to grow your family, you can always present the matter as a "medical issue" or "health concern" that requires expert attention. That happens to be the truth, and it lets you discuss a private and potentially highly emotional topic in more-neutral, safer-feeling terms. Your manager should not ask for more detail; if he or she does, simply say that you're uncomfortable discussing the specifics. If you get any real blowback, talk to HR about how to handle your need for treatment—and for privacy.

On this particular path to parenthood, be aware that you may begin to experience feelings of powerlessness, or reduced competence. As a hardworking, can-do, experienced professional, you're used to tackling complex tasks and projects, working them through, and reaching success. But now, despite your intentions and efforts, outcomes aren't within your direct control—and the fact that they aren't can feel strange and demoralizing. To feel better and to regain that sense of personal empowerment, you may find yourself tempted to double down at work. Many prospective parents find themselves cycling through periods of complete focus on the job and phases in which more time and energy is invested into fertility options and treatment.

Whether you fall into these common patterns or not, self-care is essential. You're working hard *and* taking on a huge and logistically, physically, and emotionally complex task. Get all of the rest, help, and personal support you can along the way.

And if you've already successfully cleared that doozy of a hurdle personally and professionally, then expanding your family further—whether from one child to two, two to three, or more—shouldn't worry or frighten you. Have confidence in yourself. You know what you're doing.

That said, certain things *will* be different the second time around, and you don't want to make the all-too-common mistake of thinking, *I've already done this, so I'm good to go.* You'll almost certainly need to apply some patches and upgrades to the overall workparenting operating system you've worked so hard to get into place, in order to "scale it up" for your larger family. That will involve some thought and doing, but it's not a bad thing. Think of it as an opportunity to refresh and reset—to tinker with what hasn't worked so well, and to take things to the next level.

To reset effectively and with a minimum of hassle, think through each of the important pivot points below. Each will be well familiar to you from your first working-parent transition; what you're effectively doing here is another, "lite" version of that first big shift. If you need to do a deeper dive in any of these areas—a wholesale change-up of your childcare situation, for example—refer back to the relevant prior chapters, which will help you do so.

Parental leave

With Child #1, parental leave was about bonding with the baby, learning to become a parent, and getting ready to return to work. With Child #2, you *still* need to focus on those three things—but you'll *also* have to manage your older child's transition to big brother or sister, *and* find ways to best use this wonderful window of time to bond with him or her. At the same time, because your work colleagues see you as an old hand at workparenting now, they may treat this leave more casually than your first—looping you into work communications, for example, or expecting your real-time engagement and inputs as things unfold at the office. In other words: parental leave may be more packed and busy than you anticipated or experienced before.

Your move: In order to fully enjoy and get the most from your leave, do some up-front thinking on 1) how you want to maximize your time with each of the children, alone and together, 2) how you can carve out some personal R&R, however brief, and 3) how to set expectations with your colleagues regarding how much you'll be available and when.

> 66 It felt strange to tell people at work that I was expecting my sec-
> ond child when I had been on maternity leave so recently. I wor-
> ried that people would make comments, or judge—but everyone was
> supportive. I realized that those concerns, and any awkwardness, were
> on me."
>
> —*Sarah, acceleration-capital fund COO and senior director,
> strategic analysis, mother of two*

Childcare

With the arrival of Child #2, your childcare needs may change, for
practical, emotional, or budget reasons. In-home care may be less
costly than a double daycare bill, for example . . . or with more going
on at home, the family caregiver you've relied on until now may not
be up to the task . . . or if school and daycare pickups will have to happen simultaneously, you may need to make special arrangements.

Your move: Think through your day-by-day schedule, how your new
arrival will affect it, and the care your family will need. As you did
when first considering care options, be certain to factor in what you'll
need during busy season, if working overtime, during work travel, and
so on. And don't be surprised if no single care option feels sufficient.
With more than one child, you may find that a hybrid arrangement
is needed.

Your budget and spending

New care setup. Bigger car. Fewer overtime hours. Double the diapers.
The addition of Child #2—or #3, or #4—may change your family's
spending in any number of ways.

Your move: Run the numbers and have a plan. Don't wait until the arrival to figure out where that extra money will come from. For extra
help, turn to chapter 11.

The amount and type of support you need from your Village

As you grow your family, you'll want to grow the amount and type of help and support you're getting at work and at home, too. Are there new workparent mentors who can help advise you through the next few months? An app to help manage your more complex grocery-shopping plans? You'll want all the help you can get.

Your move: Using the 8-C tool found in chapter 9, go category by category through all the different types of workparenting help and support. Identify any new resources available to you, and figure out how to use existing ones more, or to greater effect. That may involve asking for more, spending more, or getting creative.

Daily scheduling, particularly morning and evening routines

If getting up, fed, dressed, ready, and out the door usually takes an hour with one child, it may take ninety minutes with two. Which, in turn, may affect when you get into work, and thus when you leave, and therefore your nighttime routine, and how much sleep you get—and on and on.

Your move: Whatever your current schedule, bring fresh eyes to it, and play with the pieces until you've created a new one that supports the changes in your family. As you work, remember that the question isn't *how do I survive the day* but *how do I get through the day effectively,*

> We had twins, so suddenly moved from one child to three. One key difference was how we approached our time at home in the evenings. With one child you want to be attentive and focused, but if something important is going on at work and you need to sneak a quick look at your messages, it's easier to. With three, there's no multitasking—they take your full attention."
>
> —*Nicole, management consultant, mother of three*

and *is this sustainable?* You may need to make larger and more fundamental changes to when and where you work to answer it.

Time together and time off

You don't have much downtime as it is—and as you add to your family,
that precious amount may get squeezed even further.

Your move: Think about how your Village resources can help you preserve the time you need to step back, to rest, and to spend on things
you enjoy doing, with or without your partner. With two or more
children, you'll deserve—and need—it.

Large-Family Strategies Useful for *All* Working Parents

Whether you have one child or four, the home- and life-management
techniques common within large workparent families can help make
things more feasible and satisfying for you and your family, too.

- Raise your expectations. Even small children can handle certain self-care and household tasks themselves, and older kids
  are eminently capable of helping to take care of the younger
  ones. Give each child "stretch assignments"—whether that's
  putting on their own socks or watching over a younger sibling
  while you make dinner. The kids will gain a sense of personal
  agency and can-do spirit, and your overall workload will decrease, if just a little. *Everyone* should be contributing, and to
  their true capability.

- Learn how to use time in very small bites. Those fifteen minutes between meetings will let you finish off the presentation.
  The five minutes in line at the supermarket will let you return
  a phone call. During the few moments after you send that work
  message, you can throw in another load of laundry. Learn how
  to use even the smallest windows of opportunity.

- Make it a habit to connect with each child, one-to-one. As your
  family grows, it's natural to play "zone defense"—to treat the

> " It would be easy to allow 100 percent of my time to be taken up by work and by the baby's needs. I have to be conscious of carving out enough time for my older one, particularly now that school is getting more serious. I want to stay on top of how he's doing academically, and with his friends—to really *be* there for him."
>
> —*Danielle, fashion wholesale executive, mother of two*

> " It doesn't have to be a big-deal kind of outing. We might go to the hardware store or get a frozen yogurt, or go into the yard and water the plants—but I deliberately spend time with each of my daughters, alone. I'm raising a pack of lionesses here, and even if I'm at work all day, I want to connect with each one."
>
> —*Robert, learning specialist, father of three*

kids as a group, rather than as discrete individuals. Zone play is effective, and usually needed. But don't let it, or your drive for speed and efficiency in household matters, prevent you from spending time with each child alone. Whether it's a brief weekly outing with each of your two kids or a monthly "parent date" with each one of your seven, take some relaxed, dedicated, private time with each of your children on a regular basis.

- **Let it go.** Whatever perfectionist tendencies you have, do yourself a favor and try to release them. Your hospital-bed-corners approach toward life may have served you well, prekids, but it will be impossible to sustain now as a working parent, particularly one leading a larger family. Maybe the beds aren't made, or you didn't spend the two extra hours editing that report for work and making it extra good. So what? Does it really matter? Focus on real essentials, and let smaller details go.

You Decide

By this point in your career and life, you've become adept at both making and defending your own decisions. Every time you've interviewed for a new job, you've had to convince the interviewer that your past career choices were well-timed and thoughtful. In important work meetings, you've learned how to showcase your good judgment. When your boss or a client has questioned "why you did it this way," you've always had a solid answer. You know how to think things through, come to the right answers, and present a compelling argument.

And then you confront this choice, and it's unlike any you've ever made so far. It's huge, and complicated, and private, and permanent, and despite what you're told, there's no real playbook for making it, and it can seem fraught on all sides. *And you don't need to explain it, or follow a linear process in making it, or get anyone's approval, either.* It's a hard choice, but it's your choice—and the only thing you need to make it is your own conviction that it's right.

7

School

Giving Your Children the Best Possible Education
While You're Hard at Work

Beyond the kids' physical health and safety, nothing is as important to you as their education: it's their potential, their minds, their *future*. But when your five-year-old is having a difficult time adjusting to the school routine, your eight-year-old needs help with a science project, you've just had a critical client meeting scheduled at the same time as your parent-teacher conference, and the test that determines who gets into the accelerated math group is next month, too, it puts you in a real bind. You've already got two important jobs, and staying on top of your child's education means taking on a third.

When you can pinpoint what makes the start of school so hard, though, it can help make the transition a little smoother. And with some specific workparent tactics and approaches, you'll be better able to handle all of those details and logistics while focusing on the piece that really matters: your child's overall academic development and long-term success in school. To learn more, read on.

Why the Start of School Is So Hard—and How to Make It Easier

When your child enters school for the very first time, the small, happy, trusted, stable workparent triangle you've created between you, your child, and your caregiver(s) is suddenly broken open. A huge new cast of characters takes the stage: teachers, school administrators, the school-bus driver, sports coaches, new friends, the new friends' parents, the new friends' siblings, and so on. As exciting as "big kid" school is, it also means that academic pressures begin to set in, and for the very first time, you find yourself thinking not just about your child's safety and happiness, but about his performance, abilities, and future. Adding to the challenge, many of the practical working-parent solutions you've used up until now and the daily routines you've so carefully honed over the past few years—the pickup time and backup care plans, the way you've stayed connected to your child while busy at work, even the way you spend your mornings and evenings together—may have to be revisited. The changes are many, meaningful, and disconcerting, and it can be a jolt to realize that something so profoundly positive, and that you're so deeply committed to—your child's education—is throwing you off your game.

All that said, here are several ways for you to get *ahead* of the schooling challenge, to defuse some of that tension, and to make the move to school easier and happier, for the whole family. These techniques

> " I work with a lot of my clients in the mornings, evenings, on weekends, which meant that before my daughter started school, I got to spend weekdays with her. I took her to all her playdates, and we went to 'mommy and me' classes. I *loved* that time together.
>
> Then she started school, and all of a sudden, it was gone, and that was awful. I had all these strange emotions: that I should be working more to provide for her—even though that made no sense, and nobody had said anything like that to me.
>
> I realized I had to make some concessions in my schedule and carve out time, just for her. Tuesdays and Wednesdays are Daddy-daughter time. But the biggest change is that I've made that time more intentional. I'll take her to her tae kwon do class, and then we'll practice the forms together. I'll take her to her favorite pizza place, and while we're having dinner, focus 100 percent on her."
>
> —*Justin, fitness educator, father of two*

work both in that very first year and in all of the back-to-school seasons that follow.

- **Provide a positive preview.** Whether the start of school is smooth or strained will depend, in large part, on how your child *feels* about it—which will depend in turn on the cues you send. If your child's first year in school, or fifth, goes undiscussed, it remains mysterious and scary, but if you refer to it excitedly, read your child stories set in happy classrooms, assure her that you'll be carving out extra time from work to be with her in those first few days, and even do an informal school visit together, the whole transition will lose some of its sting. Set the tone, up front.

- **Get the family calendar under control.** The start of school means an exponential increase in both the amount and complexity of the working-parent logistics you have to deal with. If you haven't yet developed an organized, integrated, single-view family calendar and established times for regular review of it with your partner and/or other caregivers, do so now. Then, as soon as the school calendar is available, ensure that all of those dates are loaded in, with special events and exceptions—like Curriculum Night or the earlier pickup time on the Fridays before holiday breaks—clearly flagged. (For more specifics on managing the family calendar and competing priorities, look ahead to chapter 10, "Time.")

- **Make—and protect—time for the transition.** Try to find as much give as possible in deadlines, travel, shifts, and work responsibilities for the two weeks before and after Day One of school. For those critical first few days, mark drop-off and pickup times as "booked" on your work calendar if you can; even if you're not physically there, you'll want to be available. (Expect to do the same at the end of year as well, when class events and parent obligations usually peak.) Plan on letting other personal and community obligations go during this period.

- **Rehearse.** Before school starts, hold a "dry-run day" to practice the morning getting-ready routine, the lunch-box prep, and the dual commute. What makes transitions feel so destabilizing is their unknowns; the more natural the daily routine feels, the easier it will be for your kids to learn and for you to work without worry.

- **Create a key-people list.** As you learn the names of your child's teachers, friends, fellow class parents, the school librarian, lunch attendant, and so forth, write them down on a single consolidated list. When you're pulling long hours at work, you'll feel much more informed and in-charge knowing exactly who your child is interacting with—and being supervised by. It will make conversation with your child easier, too. Asking your son if he finished the tie-dye project in Mr. Delgado's art class, for instance, will prompt a much better conversation than simply asking "How was your day?"

- **Partner with other parents.** With babies and toddlers, it's very difficult to pass off childcare responsibilities. But during the school years you can—and should—develop a trusted circle of fellow parents who can help with pickups or carpools, when you have to work late or there's a school cancellation because of terrible weather. Don't worry if you don't have a team in place yet: this group will emerge organically, as you connect with like-minded mothers and fathers in your child's class throughout the year, and gradually you'll feel more comfortable asking for and offering specific help.

- **Acknowledge your own emotions.** Starting school is a big deal for your child, and let's be honest: it's a big deal for you, too. As you approach Day One you may find yourself buffeted by multiple, contradictory feelings. That sense of relief (*I'm glad she's becoming more independent . . . and we don't have to pay for daycare anymore!*) may be accompanied by disbelief (*My baby's starting school?*), loss (*How has the time gone so fast—and did I miss too much of it while I was working?*), or self-doubt (*Will she* *do well even if I'm not home every afternoon to check her home-work?*). Each of these feelings is completely normal, and you'll likely find that all the other mothers and fathers in the class, whatever their work commitments, are thinking and feeling various versions of the same. Those concerns should begin to dissipate as your child settles into the school routine, as the whole family adapts to the new rhythm, and as you get to watch—and enjoy—her new experiences and achievements.

Fostering Learning—and Success in School

Even if you're to-the-wall at work, you can still be your family's chief learning officer and nurture the kids' academic achievement.

Educating them at home—and every day

Most formal, structured learning happens in a school setting . . . but don't make the mistake of thinking that *school* and *education* are the same thing, or that the development of your child's intellect is some-how inherently better handled by school professionals. You're *always* your child's most important teacher, and you don't need a blackboard, flash cards, worksheets, or an advanced degree to be a first-rate edu-cator, either: you can foster your child's learning naturally—day to day and at an any age—with a few simple techniques.

- **Read—together and apart.** A primary driver of your child's success in school is how much he reads and how much he en-joys it. Read aloud, let your child read alone, and let him see you enjoying your own reading material, also. For great ideas on age-appropriate books, ask for your school's reading list or check out your local library.

- **Step up your vocabulary.** Use newer, more-complex words and phrases. Go a few grade levels ahead. If you child doesn't know a new word, explain it, use it in a sentence—and then be sure to use it again several times over the next several days to "ce-ment" its use.

Fostering academic success: what *really* works

In 2014, Professors Keith Robinson, of the University of Texas, and Angel L. Harris, of Duke University, published *The Broken Compass*, a large, first-of-its-kind research study analyzing the impact of more than sixty different types of parental involvement on long-term student performance as objectively measured by grades and test scores. The study looked at more than three decades' worth of data, and across a large, diverse set of students and families. The study sought to answer the question, What really works, in terms of parental involvement in children's education?

The key takeaway: many common forms of parental involvement have negligible impact on educational achievement. In fact, some common forms of involvement—like hovering over homework assignments—are actually correlated with reduced academic outcomes.

So what will, for the most part, work? Reading to your child; making it clear that you expect him or her to go to college/university; talking about what happened during his or her day at school; and requesting that the school assign your child specific teachers all show the most-consistent benefits to children's achievement outcomes.

Bottom line: don't worry if your work responsibilities make certain kinds of engagement in your child's schooling difficult, or if you don't have hours to spend on school volunteer activities. Keep your focus, and your family conversations, centered on the value and long-term importance of education, and on enjoying learning for its own sake.

- Ask "why" and "how" questions. Encourage the kind of independent, logical, multistep thinking that will be required on standardized tests, later on in school, and in adult life by asking such questions as, "Why do you think fire trucks are red?" "Why did the bear give away the apple at the end of the story?" "How would you solve this problem?"

- Count it. The more time your child spends thinking about numbers, the more easily she'll latch onto important math concepts, and daily life brings ample opportunity to think numerically. Ask your child, "How many cookies do we have here?"

When she answers "five," respond by asking, "So if I give one each to you and your sister, how many would we have left?" Addition and subtraction—pain free.

- **Encourage interests and expertise.** Your child may be obsessed by ceramics, swimming, outer space . . . or all three. Support her as she learns to enjoy research, sustained interest, and the sense of pride that comes with knowledge and mastery of a subject.

- **Get out there.** Use weekends, vacations, and spare time to visit museums, libraries, historical sites—many of which offer free entry or reduced rates for children and families, and may offer special online access, tours, or programming.

- **Amp up the screen time.** Don't give more of it, of course, but choose more-educational options. The science-oriented show

---

Homeschooling

" My wife is a trained educator, and we homeschool—but we also try to help them learn new things all the time. I've always excelled at math, and I'll try to find ways to work numbers into things the kids are passionate about. Vacations, we avoid crowds and costs and take them places they can see something new. We want everything to be a learning experience."

—*Robert, learning specialist, father of three*

" Our work allows us to spend part of each year living abroad and homeschooling. In a way, we had that working-while-overseeing-school Covid-19 experience before it happened. A few things have helped us make it work.

First, we keep the hours limited. Home is usually a respite for kids—and if they have to work too long and too much, school begins to feel like a punishment. Second, we set expectations for the kids that they have a job to do here—just the way we have jobs, too. And third, because we've realized we can't teach them everything under the sun, we focus on what we want to leave them with—on our family's values, how we want them to approach things."

—*Shelly, communications firm founder, mother of three*

can keep the kids just as engaged and happy as their favorite cartoon program.

Developing a strong relationship with your child's teacher(s)

Teachers and school administrators are your key allies as a working parent. They educate—and evaluate—your child, they provide important insight into his ongoing development and needs, and they serve as parent-like figures for hundreds of hours each year. Besides you, they're the most prominent figures in your child's education—and future. It's critical to develop strong relationships with them, and to do so early on.

Plan to communicate openly and directly, especially when changes in routine or other events at home may affect your child's behavior or performance at school, and expect that some, if not all, of that communication will be by phone or email rather than in person. Tell the school office that you'll be away on business next week, in case your first-grader acts out. Flag it when your son is struggling with his foreign-language homework—and ask about the best ways to support him. Let the science teacher know your daughter loved the chemistry experiment. Write a thank-you note, copying school administrators, to the math teacher who stayed after class to tutor the kids on long division. You may not get much, if any, response—remember, each teacher works with dozens of parents—but rest assured, your message and approach will be noticed. And just as you would with any important customer or senior person at work, plan to keep those communications regular. You don't want to be a nag or a pest, but you do want to stay top-of-mind. Bring the old client-coverage rule in here: if you've gone three weeks or more without being in contact, find a reason to get in touch.

To strike the right tone when dealing with school professionals, think of each one as you would a trusted coworker: someone who you appreciate and depend on, and whose constructive comments you take graciously, offering your own in a spirit of respect, trust, and good humor. Teachers are highly trained and extremely hardworking professionals. They're also humans—and often working parents themselves. They'll notice and appreciate your warmth and collaboration, and likely respond in kind.

The committed professional's guide to parent-teacher conferences

Your parent-teacher conference may feel like a performance review, but it isn't. It's a collaboration—a place from which to refine your educational game plan.

As you listen to the teacher:

- Remember that *every child, yours included*, has ways he or she can develop. Be open to what you hear. Take the attitude that both you and the teacher are working toward your child's long-term good.
- Listen and absorb without reacting. Periodically paraphrase to make certain you're understanding exactly what the teacher has said. For instance: "She seems happy in the classroom, but is shy around new peers?"
- Compare notes: when a development area is discussed, tell the teacher whether it's a surprise or consistent with what you observe at home.
- Grasp the context: Is this a completely normal challenge for most six-year-olds and likely to resolve itself without intervention, or should you be consulting a specialist? To ensure clarity, ask the teacher whether the issue she's flagging falls under the category of *observation*, *concern*, or *problem*.
- Turn the teacher into a coach, and consultant: have her tell you which activities or approaches you could use to support your child in these areas while she's at home.

As you leave the meeting and afterward, be certain to focus on the totality of what you heard—not just the constructive or developmental areas, but the *whole*. Shyness and phonics may be concerns, but if your daughter works hard, has made friends, and has adjusted beautifully to school, then *that* should be your primary take-away.

> We divide and conquer, and coordinate. I'll go to Curriculum Night, and then my husband will go to parent-teacher in person while I videoconference in on his phone. The teacher sees my face and knows she has my full attention. That way, we both get to be present, and the teachers know we're both involved."

—*Keywanda, senior timekeeper, mother of two*

Homework

Take-home assignments were originally intended as a way to teach kids responsibility and to reinforce lessons taught at school. Unfortunately, homework can all too often morph into an overwhelming, time-consuming exercise that ends past bedtime, in power struggles and tears. What should be a simple algebra worksheet can leave you feeling torn: *of course* you want your child to succeed academically, practice resilience, and feel comfortable tackling new challenges—but when you've got so little time to spend together each evening, the last thing you want to do is spend it carping at your child to finish her assignment, or checking it for errors. So:

- Figure out an organizational system that works. Review your calendars together at the start of the week so that you and your child both know what's coming as far as homework, quizzes, and tests; set up special baskets to hold uncompleted assignments and library books to be returned; and have your child lead "backpack check" each evening. Think like your work self: get the whole team involved in making the system work as smoothly and time-efficiently as possible, and in improving it when it doesn't. When setting up your routine or organizational system, think what's age-appropriate and will work for your child. Your daughter won't be able to file her papers into special folders if she can't yet read the labels, and a color-coded system may work better if she's visually oriented, anyway. But do find your system: if you can keep things calm and shave even ten minutes off the evening ritual, that's a lot of emotion and relationship value saved—and an hour more a week to spend reading with the kids.

- Emphasize that homework is your child's, rather than a family, responsibility. Encourage your kids to start their assignments earlier in the day and involve any other caregivers in reinforcing that message. Even if you plan to review your son's Spanish conjugations, let him know that you're there to help when he's truly stuck, not to remind, nag, proofread, or otherwise serve

> ❝ We set the expectation early on that homework was the kids' responsibility. Sure, if they need help or for us to check something, we will. But in general, evenings should be family time."
>
> *—Jeff, investor, father of two*

as unpaid labor. As he grows, help him think ahead about bigger projects, particularly ones that involve research or special materials. As the science fair approaches, for example, ask "What's your plan?" for making the papier-mâché volcano rather than leading the project yourself.

- **Hold a family study hall each evening.** Make it a family ritual to have daily, silent, dedicated work time around the dining table together. The kids do their homework, while you catch up on office emails or reading. Pick a reasonable length of time—ten minutes for a young child, ninety for a teenager, for example—and set a timer on your phone to go off when time's up. When it does, the whole family gets to enjoy downtime or a relaxing activity like watching a favorite TV program together. Not only will you set an example, your kids will learn how to focus better, to work more efficiently, and to use the "sprint and recover" approach when tackling a large workload—all skills that will make them more successful and happier in school and in their futures. You'll also have established a clear boundary between work and play, which is vital and healthy for all of you.

After-school activities—and ways to think about them

After-school activities can supplement your child's education in wonderful ways, help you "stretch" care arrangements, and bring an element of fun into the relentless homework-and-testing cycle of modern education. If your daughter loves field hockey, if it lets her blow off steam, if it fosters her discipline and perseverance, and if it keeps her busy until 5:30, when you can pick her up, well, then everybody wins.

Play and playdates

You've reached professional success because of your focus, prioritization, and action-oriented mindset. In the work world, these get you ahead . . . but try not to bring too much of that same outlook and approach into your kids' education. A key part of your child's learning comes through play—which, unlike work, is inherently undirected and not focused on any particular outcome.

Consider blocking off a certain amount of time per day and/or afternoons per week for your child to spend in completely unstructured activity, and be sure to keep materials that encourage open-ended, creative use—like building blocks, art supplies, and dress-up costumes—around the house. And organize regular playdates, if you can: learning how to navigate relationships and get along one-on-one with others is a critical part of your child's development. An afternoon spent building—and knocking down—Lego towers or playing hide-and-seek in the yard with a friend is just as educational and valuable as time spent in the classroom.

Taken too far, however, after-school activities can put terrible pressure on any working-parent family. Overscheduling exhausts children, making it hard for them to perform academically or, for that matter, to behave well at home. Certain sports and lessons can become jaw-droppingly expensive, and the commitment required for others can seriously encroach on the narrow windows of evening and weekend time you would otherwise get to spend with your child.

Here's how to keep perspective, ensure that extracurricular activities remain a positive, and make the choices that are right for you.

- Avoid using activities to plug an emotional hole. It can be easy, if you feel guilty about working long hours, to "compensate" by stretching to pay for expensive ballet lessons or by spending all weekend, every weekend, focused on your child's chess tournaments. And, particularly if your professional life is a very demanding one, you may try to convince yourself that success on the stage or playing field now will make your child's later life much easier. (She won't ever have the financial struggles you've had if she becomes an Olympic athlete, right?) Those instincts show the depth of your commitment as a parent; you want the best for your kids, after all. But overpaying, overscheduling, and overextending will only make working parenthood harder, and very likely reduce the benefits those same activities are supposed to bring. Besides, your kids may prefer spending those hours doing low-key, at-home activities instead, or in dedicated one-on-one time with you.

- **Stay neutral and balanced.** For each potential extracurricular activity, carefully consider its pluses and minuses. If it helps your child academically or socially and doesn't require huge expense or time investment, great. If it makes scheduling and logistics easier, even better. But beware activities that leave you feeling like you've got yet *another* job to do.

- **Go slow.** For anyone used to pushing themselves at work—and to thinking in terms of sales quotas, time-to-market, performance reviews, and the like—it can be tempting to take a "more is more" approach, cram in as many extracurricular activities as possible, and do each one to the max (to join the competitive football team, for example, instead of the local league). But your child is still growing; she doesn't have an adult's focus, energy, or drive, and her livelihood—fortunately—doesn't depend on her performance on this field just yet, either. Think about setting reasonable limits—e.g., one after-school activity per week or one sport per season—and let your kid say no if she wants to. Remind yourself that you can always sign up next semester, or as she grows and her interests change.

- **Reinforce the lessons.** Help your children "see" and apply what they're learning in extracurricular activities in other areas of their lives: to use the good sportsmanship they've learned at tennis in social situations, for example, or to use the same kind of can-do spirit they picked up at Scouts in geometry class.

Making the Time—and Being There

Your job pulls in one direction, parenting in another, and school commitments in a third. Here's how to be where you're needed, when you can't be in three places at once.

Talking with your manager and colleagues about school commitments

Even if you've grown confident discussing care arrangements or visits to your child's health provider, talking with your manager and colleagues about school-related issues can feel different—and harder. "I need to take my sick child to the doctor" may seem like an easier, more defensible message than "I need to meet Mia's teachers" or "I'll be offline this afternoon for the school play/bake sale"—which seem more elective.

Instead of worrying or being defensive, try explaining the *why*, not just the *when*, of time away from work, and think about using the same *priorities, next steps, commitment, enthusiasm* framing tool you've used in other workparent conversations. For example, rather than telling your boss and colleagues that you'll be "out of the office tomorrow afternoon," explain that "I won't be available from 1:00 to 3:00 because of a meeting with Mia's teachers. Her math scores have been suffering, and we need to figure out the game plan for next year. I'll be back online by 6:00 p.m., and I look forward to going over the budget draft at tomorrow's meeting." The second statement will be more comfortable to share, will make it easier for colleagues to understand, sympathize, and ally themselves with you—and will do a better job of telegraphing your commitment.

Volunteering

Even with a very flexible job, it's unlikely you can make it to every school performance, library fundraiser, and field trip, even if you wanted to. So here's what you can do instead.

In the first week of school, tell your child's teachers and/or the school's volunteer coordinators that you're eager to put in your fair share of sweat equity—but that you will be doing it all in one go. You'll

Interacting with nonworking parents

In many school communities, there's a subtle—or not-so-subtle—tension between working and nonworking parents. People make assumptions and judgments about individuals in the other group, and it may even feel as if there are two opposing "camps." Do *not* be influenced by or play into this dynamic! Who cares if other parents have made different choices? And anyway, from a practical perspective, nonworking parents can be some of your best allies and informers—keeping a watchful eye on playground dynamics at pickup, sharing information on school happenings, and just generally being your eyes and ears on-site. There is simply no value to be had in an adversarial, "us versus them" stance. Do what you can to close the divide, create good relationships, and be an example for others around you—including the kids.

> At first, I wanted to be involved with the school in a way that would let me use my skill set. Now, I only take on projects that I can do *with* the kids. I want to be smart about getting as much time with them as I can."
>
> —*Michelle, marketing director, mother of three*

schedule a personal or vacation day well in advance and use it entirely for school volunteerism. Maybe you'll be the "reading helper" in your daughter's class in the morning, walk the school's neighborhood safety patrol in the afternoon, and take the minutes during the school fundraising-committee meeting at 5:00 p.m. When the day is over, you'll enjoy knowing that your yearly contribution has been made in full—and efficiently. That "I'm not doing enough" guilt will go away, and you'll be able to focus back on family and career.

If your child's school requires you to contribute supplies or materials as well as time—if you're on the hook to bring in the class snack once a month, for example, or to provide decorations for the end-of-term class parties—keep it a "one and done" hassle. Go to your local discount retailer, buy that huge crate of generic-brand granola bars (or paper plates, or art supplies), and have them in the basement ready to go when you need them. No more adds to the to-do list or frantic night-before trips to the convenience store; you have better things to do with your money and time.

How to be present—and what to do when you can't

As someone completely committed to your child's education, you'll likely feel it essential to *be there*, in all senses of that term, throughout his school experience. But when you've got a crazy schedule, are at work, have limited flexibility, or—most likely—all three, then showing up, even virtually, can be tough. When your job or pay depends on your hours, full concentration, or physical presence—if you're a nurse, pilot, or retail salesperson, for example—it may be impossible. Even amid nonstop work pressures, however, a few specific strategies can help you feel and be more present.

First, make the windows of time you *do* give to anything education-related regular, even if brief. If you can't do drop-off every day, fine, but perhaps you can do a "Daddy drop-off day" once every other week. If it's impossible to make it home before homework is done on a regular basis, don't kick yourself about it, but do have a daily five-minute video call to help on that hardest math problem. That consistency, and not sheer hours or physical presence, will let you feel on top of things, and help your child feel your complete commitment.

> I've tried to train the school to give parents more lead time on school plays and other big events, because if I know about it two months out I can sometimes schedule around it. If I can't, I'll tell my daughters, 'Dad loves his job, and Mom loves hers. The *nature* of our jobs means we can't always be there. But I'll ask so-and-so to take a video of your concert, and I can't wait to watch.' Instead of over-apologizing, I just explain. And I don't wear guilt as a badge of pride, because no one gets advantaged from that."
>
> —*Rick, airline pilot, father of three*

Second, think about digging down into the average, day-to-day parts of your child's education. When you've got very limited time, it's natural to focus on special school events like the class play, holiday concert, parent-teacher conference, or arrival of his report card. Those are important showcases and milestones, and they carry a big psychological premium, but they *don't* provide insight on the times when he isn't performing, celebrating something, or being evaluated. Neither do they give you the chance to show that even though you work hard, you care about what school really looks and feels like. So think about taking a "school day": a vacation or personal day (or two) per year spent fully focused on the school routine. Do drop-off, have coffee with another parent from the class afterward and compare notes on how the year is going, host a playdate, attend the sports practice, drive the carpool, supervise homework, let him test you on those tricky spelling words— and just generally be around with no agenda except supporting and observing. In a short period of time, you'll get new insights into his life, get to spend a very different kind of time together, and develop better perspective on his classes, friends, and teachers—on the whole-enchilada school experience.

Third, and very practically, don't be afraid to go high-tech, particularly when you're in a scheduling jam. Until recently, most of us felt real pressure to make it to parent-teacher conferences in person, and of course it's great if you can, but the one beautiful legacy of the 2020 pandemic is that none of us needs to pretend that the world will fall apart if we go virtual. If the only parent-teacher slot available is for 3:00 p.m. on a Thursday, a time when you can't make it in person, alert the teacher that you see this conversation as all-important but that you'll need to do it via videoconferencing. If you sense hesitation, remind the teacher that you're in a role—like hers—that means having to show up in person and during set hours. Similarly, when a work obligation keeps you away from the year-end concert, ask a friendly fellow parent to take and send you videos, and then make it your first order of business to watch the videos together with your child, and with great fanfare, as soon as you get home. Those scenarios may not feel ideal. (Would your own mom have "phoned it in" to parent-teacher? Probably not.) But we're living a twenty-first-century reality here, and the cellphone shots of the slides from Curriculum Night will give you all the important information you need.

Taming the Logistics

Along with the challenges of education and learning, school brings a whole new set of practical matters to contend with. Here are the most important—and how to handle them.

Safety

When your child was a baby and started a new care arrangement, you worried about safety. Could you trust the other adult(s) to take good care of him? Would you know when something was wrong? Those same apprehensions will likely come back now—different, but magnified. School brings new people, places, and situations into her life, and you may feel that you have much less control than you had before. But there are ways to help ensure your children's security, and to mitigate those concerns.

Whatever your child's age, means of transport to and from school, and overall care arrangement, make it a habit to:

- **Regularly review—and rehearse—core safety rules.** Make certain your child knows the safety guidelines and habits appropriate for his age, whether that's "don't talk to strangers," "never get in a car with someone you don't know," "always buckle up on the school bus," or "don't answer the door until I get home." And don't leave these simply as platitudes or concepts—practice them. Have your child playact saying "No!" to the talkative stranger, for example.

- **Identify "safe" adults.** Emphasize that there will never be any negative consequence for alerting you or these trusted grown-ups to safety issues or concerns.

- **Ensure she knows phone numbers.** Your child should know where you and/or your partner can be reached during the day, your home address, and the name of her school. (At the same time, explain that she should not share that information with others.)

- **Ensure she knows how to use the phone.** Rehearse phone usage on both cell phones and landlines. (Listening for a dial tone or dialing a long-distance prefix before the memorized number won't be intuitive for a child raised in the cell-phone era.) If there's any chance that she will get your voicemail or connected to one of your coworkers when she calls, make sure that she knows what to do next—e.g., to call your partner instead or to say it's urgent and ask to speak with you.

- **Remain alert during transition times.** The school years mean more transitions than you may have had to deal with before. Your child will be moving—a lot—from place to place. There's school drop-off, dismissal, the bus to swimming practice, and then the carpool ride home. If you can, keep an eye on the phone when you know your child is on the move in case you need to help rearrange pickups, playdates, or transportation. If work responsibilities mean you can't be available at certain times—if, for instance, you're on a plane, arguing a case in court, waiting tables, or giving a presentation—make sure your partner is on top of things, ask a trusted colleague to watch your cell, or reach out to your Parent Team for backup.

- **Plan and practice for unsupervised time.** If your child will spend any portion of the day unsupervised, be clear and specific on safety rules and protocols (e.g., no detours on the walk home, no using the stove). Do one or more "dry runs" of the unsupervised part of the day, and discuss what your child should do if he feels unsafe or finds himself in an unknown situation—if no one meets the school bus, for example, or if he starts getting messages from an unknown number. Finally, practice any backups, like ringing a neighbor's door for help.

- **Get technology on your side.** Older kids may have smartphones, but there are many easy-to-use, inexpensive, emergency-call-only flip phones made for younger ones. For the smallest children, you may want to consider one of the small GPS tracking devices that clip inside a jacket or backpack and let you track their real-time location.

Handling school-related emergencies

When you became a workparent and created a holistic care plan, you carefully established one or more backups. Now, with school-age children, you need to refresh that plan: to adapt it so that it will let you cover those random holidays when schools are out, sick days, sudden closures, and other unexpected events that may interrupt your regular routine. Three things can help:

- **Expanding your network of support.** The elderly relative who couldn't handle the physical demands of a baby a few years ago may be perfectly capable of looking after a feverish six-year-old or driving over to the school to do a last-minute pickup. Or perhaps that occasional evening babysitter with the flexible schedule can jump in as needed.

- **Collaborating with other parents.** Most families are in the same boat as you are, so see if you can create informal arrangements to cover each other on a rotating basis.

- **Getting ready at work.** If you have to leave work suddenly, who can step in and get the job done? Can you "bank" extra hours—or favors—on the job now to create more flexibility when you need it down the line? Now that he's older, is there any way your child can spend the day with you at work—and if that's a plan, do you have enough books or toys or iPad movies at the ready to keep him busy for eight hours?

There's no single right answer here, but you do want to make sure that you've done all of the up-front legwork you can. As you do this advance thinking, new solutions will likely emerge—and you'll feel more in control knowing you have options.

For more ideas and support for handling sick-child emergencies, turn to chapter 19, "Health—Yours and Theirs."

When school's out—but work isn't

All working mothers and fathers have to cope with time when school stops but work doesn't. If you can afford backup babysitters or summer camps to help fill in the bigger gaps, that's great—but those extras require significant resources, and even then, you'll be left with "stub" days to solve for. Regardless of your circumstances, school breaks will require more of your time and attention . . . and mean that you need to get a little working-parent creative. To make good plans for school breaks:

- **Look ahead, start early, and stay organized.** Most school calendars are set long before the school year actually starts, which allows you to get an important jump on planning for the times school will be out. As early as possible, start sketching day-by-day plans for holiday breaks and week-by-week plans for summer. As you go, make sure you're capturing all options, information, and next steps in a single, central place.

- **Explore your options.** Check in with other parents at your school to see what their plans are, and ask the school or teachers what other working-parent families commonly do. Does the school have a summer extension program? If your organization has an emergency backup care program, does it cover summers and/or older children? What's available at your local community center, church, or temple, or at other local community or civic groups, like the Girl or Boy Scouts? Many similar organizations offer cost-controlled summer programs, and financial help may be available. Go broad.

- **Consider costs.** In addition to evaluating the price of each individual activity (e.g., day camp versus a week at Grandma's versus a short-term babysitter), you'll also want to add up the totals and see the full cost for the entire summer or holiday break. Don't forget to include "hidden" expenses—like new gear for the sports camp, or the train ticket to Grandma's—in your calculations.

- **Explore a collaboration with other parents.** You may be able to form a "vacation pool" with other working mothers or fathers, whereby each one of you takes turns watching the kids on pre-planned, scheduled days off from work.

- **Look for help that's also out of school.** If your younger kids are on break, older kids will be too. Ask your network about teenagers and twentysomethings who might be willing and able to babysit at moderate cost (particularly if shared with other parents).

- **Don't put more pressure on yourself than you have to.** Your child doesn't need to be in an academic-enrichment program or advanced tennis classes every week of the summer, and it's not a big deal if you can't get a spot at, or afford, the "right" performing-arts camp, either. Slower, unstructured time with a sitter or relative, or in another low-key setting where the kids have to make their own fun, is just fine—and a healthy antidote to all the homework and testing that comes throughout the school year.

Once you have a plan in place, document it carefully, and on a day-by-day basis. And remember to communicate the plan—particularly a complex one—to caregivers, to backups, and to your kids. The more everyone knows what's coming, the more comfortable everyone will be.

The working-parent-friendly school

You may or may not get to choose where your child goes to school, and you can't control how that school is managed. But if you are considering various schooling options, or if as a volunteer or concerned parent you're trying to make your school more working-parent friendly, here's what to think about and push for:

- A single, consolidated, institutional and/or class calendar with key dates, holidays, and parent commitments marked out well in advance.

- On-site after-school extension programs or activities that help you "stretch" the school day to better map to work hours.

- Clear policies regarding scheduling problems and emergencies. For example, if you're late for pickup, the school should have a consistent way to keep your child safe until you arrive.

- A strategy for big-picture emergencies—including those that involve lengthy school closures.

- Consistent, comprehensive use of technology both to communicate important information like grades and attendance and to handle details of dismissals, to submit health forms, to get notification of bus delays, and the like.

- Clearly defined, age-appropriate, and limited amounts of homework. Kids should be able to "own" their assignments, and the homework philosophy should be available via clear, thoughtful, written policy.

- Teachers and administrators who are available—at least some of the time—during workparent-feasible hours. For example, a certain number of parent-teacher conference slots should be available before 9:00 a.m. and after 5:00 p.m., teachers should be willing and able to respond to emails, and there should be clear windows during which you can reasonably meet or speak with school professionals.

- An active, informal network of fellow working parents. Ask another parent you trust for color or see if you can attend a PTA meeting or review the minutes. (If parent-to-parent discussion is all about new volleyball uniforms and doesn't touch on after-school care, that will give you an important clue.)

- Regular insight on day-to-day activities and curriculum. It's hard to feel connected—either to your child or to the educational process—when you're not often physically at school. Weekly emails and photos showing "what we're studying" can provide important information for working parents and serve as a jumping-off point for conversation with your son or daughter.

Focusing on what really matters

With all of its deadlines, complexity, evaluations, and social pressures, school can be a daunting experience, for kids and for their working parents. Amid all the noise, it can be helpful to remember the two key outcomes you—and every parent—are really shooting for: *independence* and *opportunity*. You want your son or daughter to develop into a competent, responsible adult capable of managing in a complex world. And you want him or her to find the maximum possible number of open doors in terms of college and later in terms of career. But you don't need to ensure that your child has a bump-and-bruise-free experience at school in order to get there. It's OK—desirable, even—for your child to struggle with long division or have an argument on the playground, or for you to miss a few sports games. They're the experiences every child needs in order to become resilient, independent, and ultimately successful in his or her own right. And remember: school won't be the only place your child gets an education. Like all parents, you will teach your child the greatest lessons: the importance of hard work, the value of commitments to family, and the satisfaction that comes from a tough, complex job well done.

8

The Almost-Teen and Teenage Years

Twenty-One Essential Tips for Workparenting as the Kids Get Older and Move Toward Independence

During their almost-teen and teenage years, your kids are going to have to deal with changing bodies, hormone levels, and moods; friendship issues, including peer pressure of various kinds; competition in the classroom, on the sports field, and elsewhere; social media; learning to drive; exposure to drinking, smoking, drugs, and sex; academic stress; high-stakes standardized testing; the college or university application process; and the necessity of starting to chart their own independent life course and direction, including separation from you, as they mature and get ready for adulthood. That's *a lot* for them to handle—and parentally speaking it would be a lot for you, too, even if you *weren't* working. But you are, and your career is also likely reaching its crescendo: your responsibility and earnings levels are at or near their peak, the professional and financial stakes may be higher than ever, and it's very possible that you have even less time for the kids than you did when they were small.

Having been a working parent now for a decade-plus, you needn't do a wholesale self-reinvention. Yet in order to keep workparenting as effectively, authentically, and confidently as possible throughout this phase, what you *do* need are straightforward, honest answers to your most pressing questions. So that's precisely what we'll do in this chapter: look at each of those big, nagging concerns in turn—and at twenty-one specific ways for you to allay them.

Since my kid entered the teenage years, I feel as if we're constantly in opposition—and given how little time we have together, it's killing me. How can I keep the tone of our relationship more positive?

1. Beware the Great Inversion! When you first became a working mother or father, one of your greatest challenges was figuring out how to be, and talk about, your "parenting self" at work. Now, you've likely got the reverse problem: you may be bringing home way too much of your professional skills and self. Think back on the past year or so, and ask yourself if you have:

   – Treated family dinner like a workplace report-out

   – Given the kids performance-review-style feedback on their academic results

   – Provided here's-how-you-do-it style directives on their friendships and social concerns

   – Used words like *manage* or *efficient* when discussing weekend plans

   – Ever spoken to the kids the same way you might talk to underperforming employees

   If you have, then you're caught in this common trap. There's nothing wrong with your workplace habits and skills; they've served you very well over time. But applied in the context of a parent-child relationship, and during this particularly sensitive, high-change, high-emotions period, they're going to create friction. If you can resist the temptation to keep your work

> " Parenting teenagers is kind of like mentoring, but these aren't coworkers; it's hard to not invest all of your emotions along with advice. And they have an emotional life that's very different than the ones you and I had at that age. For us, home was a refuge away from social pressures. Now, with social media, that stuff follows your kids right to the couch. One of them can be having a perfectly calm evening, and all of a sudden, they're in turmoil because of what one of their friends just posted, or didn't. It helps to be tuned to those pressures."
>
> —*Jeremy, human resources executive, father of three*

hat on at home, or can think of yourself as being a *mentor* to your teen in addition to a *leader* or *boss*, a lot of that adversarial tension will begin to dissolve.

How can I keep my kids safe when I'm hard at work all day, and not around to play police officer?

2. **Make safety a constant drumbeat.** If you're incessantly nagging your teenager to clean up her room, practice the clarinet, and only wear unripped T-shirts, among dozens of other things, the message that *I care first and foremost about your security* can easily get lost. But when *most* of your instructions and requests center on the idea of staying safe, your teen is more likely to hear you, and to take those messages seriously. Keep personal security the number-one topic: weave it into big-picture talks and regular daily conversations, too. "Do you have a safe way to get home from Brian's house?" is a better question than "How will you get home?" Make it clear that safety is *always* top of mind—and most important.

3. **Appoint safe-harbor adults.** If your son can't always reach you while you're at the office, or if he's reluctant to open up to you about how his friends have started vaping, it's useful to have a few specific, trusted, designated adults that he can reach out to instead. Those might include your Third Parents, aunts or

uncles, family friends, even a former caregiver. Assure him that while those aren't secret or off-the-record conversations, they'll never result in judgment or punishment. You simply want him to have reliable adult guidance, whatever he's facing, and whether you're busy with work or not.

4. **Agree on a protocol for moving from A to B.** The beauty of daycare was that your child spent the day in a single, fixed, secured location. But adolescents roam, and it's when they're on the move that safety issues tend to crop up. So agree on the rules of the road: that your daughter will always text when she gets safely home from school, let you know before heading to a friend's, or ask permission before using the car. It won't cramp her style too much, and that mutual understanding will let you keep tabs while you're working and step in as needed.

5. **Have a secret language.** While he's surrounded by his peers and you're on the job, your teenager may have a hard time telling you—either on the phone or by message—whether or not he made the soccer team, or that he needs a ride home because the people he's with have been drinking. Establish a few private signals—slightly unusual words, a tune he can hum, specific emojis—that let him convey messages like *Success!, I'm upset, I can't speak freely right now,* and *Get me out of here* without having to tell you so directly.

6. **Give safety some spice.** Few teens will see the overall topic of safety as interesting—unless they're getting an immediate personal benefit from it, it's exciting or entertaining, or it becomes a bragging right. So encourage them to get summer jobs as lifeguards, go on that overnight wilderness course, get certified at the rock-climbing gym, apprentice to a paramedic as part of their school's Careers Day, or even just watch that TV show about search-and-rescue operations. The edgier and more personal safety is—the *cooler* it is—the more likely your teen will be to embrace it.

What are the best ways to stay *connected* to my teenager, when I have to spend so much time on the job?

7. First, rethink what you mean by connection. If you define *connecting* as spending large blocks of time together, speaking freely about your lives and feelings, and being perfectly, mutually understood, then you may have a very hard time achieving it. Your work pressures, plus your teen's own schedule and current emotional wiring, may make that style of bonding close to impossible. Try to think of *connection* as something different now: as simply being together, without interruptions or conflict. That may mean throwing a ball around in the backyard, with no real agenda, or sitting side by side on the couch, after homework is finished and work emails returned, watching TV. The point is to be there—and be there for your child.

8. Observe your kids in their native territory. How does your son behave when he's around his peers? What are the other kids on the debate team talking about? Listening to? Even if your work schedule only lets you do so occasionally, try to get some windows of time just to watch your son in context and to understand his day-to-day life away from you. When he does talk to you about his friend's problems, or about the debate-team dynamics, you'll be much better able to have the conversation.

9. Don't react; pause, then paraphrase. If you have only forty-five minutes to spend with your daughter in the evening between when you get home from work and she starts her calculus problem sets, that's not a lot of time. And if, during that brief window, you respond to whatever she tells you judgmentally or by snapping, she's unlikely to talk to you at all. If, however, you can listen to whatever she has to say and then nod, wait a beat, take it in, and then repeat what you heard ("So your friend is planning to go to the concert, without asking her parents?"), then she's more likely to keep on sharing information.

10. At least once a year, go somewhere. You don't have to travel to an exotic foreign city, but if you can take a road trip together

> " Chastise and fuss less. If they think they're going to get in trou-
> ble, they won't talk."
>
> —*TJ, marketing and branding firm founder, mother of one*

to a relative's house a few hours away, or go camping overnight
in the local state park, that one-to-one, in-depth time will
be more valuable and truly connective than weeks' worth of
rushed mornings, homework-laden evenings, or after-school
phone calls. If overnight travel is out, take a day trip.

11. **Turn off—and turn it off.** Set at least a short weekly blackout
period during which you don't make or allow social plans, and
commit to turning off the home Wi-Fi and disregarding to-dos
and deadlines. It's impossible to truly relate to your teen, or for
your teen to relate to you, when you're online, surrounded by
others, multitasking, or attempting to be "productive." Make and
preserve the downtime you need for real connection to occur.

**How can I help my kids get ready for their "next steps" and
adulthood without dropping the ball on my own career?**

12. **Open up.** When the kids were little, you learned to set aside
your work concerns when you came through the door each
evening; you weren't going to talk to your then-toddler about
budget overruns. But don't shield the kids so much from
your work now; talk more about your own work relationships,
stresses, and deadlines, and how you navigate them. Offer the
kids a realistic if curated glimpse of what you're dealing with,
and help them imagine themselves in the same position.

13. **Ramp up the chores, and make them "zone jobs" instead of
discrete tasks.** Ask your daughter to take top-to-bottom responsibility for the dog, instead of just filling the water dish
each morning or handling a single vet's visit. Tell your son it's

> " Never act resentful of your work. When the kids are younger, you don't want them to resent you being taken away, and as they get older, you want them to understand that you're doing something you enjoy. My daughter's fourteen now, and I talk with her about the excitement of designing a show, and show her pictures of what we created."
>
> —*Shawn, lighting designer, father of one*

his role to get dinner on the table each Sunday evening, as opposed to "helping out" in the kitchen. Make their household contributions look and feel more like the actual adult jobs that you'll want them to flourish in.

14. **Encourage them to get jobs.** This means real, paying ones, not of the résumé-padding, "internship" kind. A few weeks spent watching the neighbor's kids, in customer service, waitressing, doing some kind of manual labor, or any other real, fee-earning job will stoke more maturity and readiness for the real adult world than any class at school or lecture from you.

How can I handle the logistics of the ongoing education process, while still delivering at work?

15. **Forewarn your colleagues.** Your coworkers won't have a good sense for the timeline and actual requirements of the college- or university-admissions shuffle unless you tell them. And conversely, if you don't tell them, your obvious distraction or repeated, unexplained absences from the office may begin to grate on them. Give your manager, colleagues, and other important counterparties a heads-up, still using the four-part framing strategy you learned back in chapter 3: "Over the next six months, I'll have various commitments related to Charlie's university-admissions process. I'll be handling all those during

post-production, and they'll be over before the show pre-
mieres. Six months to airtime!"

16. Appoint a project manager: your child. It's going to be tough
to take on all of the logistics and planning yourself, on top of
your day job. And if you do, you're effectively denying your
son or daughter the opportunity to own and to learn from
this first major step toward adult life. Instead, tell your
child that while you're ready and able to help where needed,
he's in charge and—if he wants to leave home like all of
his friends—he's responsible for seeing this process
through.

17. Use the same collaboration tools you do at work. Don't waste
time nagging your daughter to show you the latest version of
her application essay, or the timeline she's put together for
campus visits: set up a shared drive, agree to save everything
onto it, and have full, immediate insight as to what's being
done, how well, and when. Yes, your daughter will hate
this—but real-time digital collaboration is how the world
works.

18. Frontload, where possible. You and your child may have
to handle a huge number of tasks in a short period of time,
including campus visits, interviews, tests, applications, and
financial-aid forms. Where you can, get a jump on the process:
visit campuses a year ahead, fill out aid forms as soon as possible, start writing the essays the summer before, and so on. The
more you can accordion out all the to-dos, the less overwhelming they'll be, and the less of a dent they'll put in your family
life and career.

**The strain of workparenting a teen is getting to me. Are there
ways to make it easier, personally?**

19. Resist the natural inclination to see your child's every move,
statement, or emotional outburst as performance feedback on

> " Being an early-childhood teacher is wonderful work, but by the time I get home, I'm tired. Sometimes in the evenings, my daughter—she's eleven—will vent at us or act out a little, which is normal, and she knows she can do it because we're her parents, and love her. When that happens and I've had a tough day, though, I'll think, *I'm a person, too!*
>
> I try to make things easier by reading up about the phase she's in—trying to understand her more. I do my best to listen, without judging. And I take care of myself. I'm an eight-hours-of-sleep-per-night kind of person, and I meditate for at least five minutes each morning, ideally longer."
>
> —*Amy, pre-K teacher, mother of one*

your parenting. After so much experience in the workforce, you've grown accustomed to constant evaluation; used to reading the tea leaves of senior leaders' comments, behavior, and body language; and hypersensitized to the political climate around you. But this is a different environment, and a different relationship: not every one of your kid's choices, glances, or snits "means" something; it's not necessarily caused by anything you did; and it's not a referendum on your capabilities or commitment as a mother or father. Don't overthink the regular ups and downs of teenage behavior.

20. Remember self-care. As a brand-new working parent, you may have been more conscious of the need to make your own health and welfare a priority—to squeeze in trips to the gym between daycare drop-off and arrival at work, for example. When you're fifteen years into workparenting, though, and your child's end-of-year exam period is looming, it can be easy to ignore your own needs or to let your self-care regimen slide. Try to find some regular, routine time for exercise, hobbies, friends, time alone, and anything else that replenishes your energy.

No, it's not because you're working

If your child got a D grade in trigonometry, has been grappling with social issues or bullying at school, or just put a dent in the car, don't do what so many working parents do automatically, which is think, *This wouldn't be happening if I weren't working, and were around more to prevent it.*

Adolescence is a fraught, complex time, and every single teenager makes mistakes. There's just no proof that children of hardworking, committed professionals fare worse than their peers. Look around at the other kids you know: plenty, if not *all*, of the ones with full-time parents at home have goofed up or are facing some challenges, too. It's not because you're hard at work.

No comparing: other children

Don't compare yourself to other working parents—and likewise avoid comparing your kids to other children. Parenting doesn't work like the performance-review cycle at the office, where members of the organization are evaluated against each other, or stack-ranked. Even if your older child is getting all As, or your colleague's son is a champion tennis player, it does you no good to fixate on it, or worse, to call out those differences in front of your kid. Even if you feel your comments are harmless, teenagers inevitably hear comparison as disapproval, and the perceived negative feedback can damage your relationship and keep your kid from opening up to you. Also try not to compare your kids and their lives to what *you* were like or doing at their age. They probably won't listen, and it may backfire, creating resentment rather than motivation. Focus in on your child's unique talents, and encourage her to turn in her own best efforts, whatever they result in.

**The kids are so big now! How did that happen . . . and have
I made a terrible mistake and missed out on really parenting
them during all these years at work?**

21. No, you haven't—and try to avoid letting the looming end
     of full-time workparenting become too much of a trigger for
     revisionist thinking, for regret, or for remorse. That "where
     did the time go" feeling hits *every* mother or father with kids
     this age, not just the ones who have invested in their careers.
     Think back on why you went down this road in the first place:
     you didn't decide to work *despite* the kids, but *for* them. The
     example you've set for them on combining career and family
     is just what they'll need in their own futures. And no matter
     how long you have left before they move on to the next phase
     in their lives, you can still make a conscious effort to set more
     time aside to be with and enjoy them. Even when you do be-
     come an empty nester, you will forever and always be a work-
     ing parent.

PART TWO

Resources—and Smart Ways to Use Them

Making the Most of What You've Got When Combining Career and Family

n chapters 1 through 8, you got guidance on the workparent phase you're in today, and insights on what's to come. Here in part 2, we're going to pivot and take a good, close look at each of your three most important workparent resources—on what you have at your disposal to navigate each phase of workparenting *with*. When you hear the word *resources*, it's normal to be concerned, or feel constrained, but don't waste any time beating yourself up or feeling defeated about how much support you have or don't have, or how packed your schedule is, or how much you have in the bank. In the next three chapters, we'll cover workparent-specific ways to manage and maximize your Village, Time, and Money so you can be more of the working parent you want to be.

9

If "It Takes a Village," Then You're the Mayor

How to Build and Maintain Your Workparent Support Team

You've gotten where you are today through hard work and a willingness to take on more. But when you become a working parent, and as your child grows and your career progresses, the demands—and the hours, and the stakes, and the sheer range of what you're responsible for—ramp up sharply. You can't go this alone: you need help, of many different kinds, and fast.

Even if you do buy into the old wisdom that "it takes a village to raise a child," though, where these hypothetical Villagers are supposed to *come* from is another story. (Somehow, you didn't find them all waiting eagerly in the living room on the day you brought the baby home.) How do you actually go about finding and recruiting people who can lend you a hand, at home and at work? What assistance can they provide *you*, and not just your child? And how are you supposed to manage and stay in touch with your resources and helpers when you're so crazy busy?

In this chapter, we'll take the big, ambiguous task of "building a Village" and break it down into its component parts. By starting with some gentle personal reflection, and then using some new commonsense tools and approaches, you'll be able to piece together a larger, more complete, and more effective network of allies and support.

Are You a Do-It-Myselfer?

If the idea of asking for assistance makes you cringe a little, you're not alone. Most of us have been conditioned to regard requiring aid as taboo, or a sign of weakness. In today's culture even the simple phrase *he needs help* has become code for someone dealing with a major life challenge.

Of course, really owning all of your work and responsibilities is a positive thing. But if you bring too much of an it's-all-on-me approach to working parenthood, you're in for a very hard time. You've never had as diverse, vast, and high-consequence a set of to-dos before, and

---

Give and take

Much of the support you'll need and can get as a workparent will come at no charge. Many of your parent-contemporaries, at work and outside of it, will be more than happy to provide advice on how to ask for that promotion when you're just back from leave or to offer encouragement when you're hunting for the right daycare provider— and to do so without strings attached. They're parents, too, they've been through the same ordeal themselves, and most will be willing to "pay it forward"—within reason—when and where they can. Likewise, bosses and mentors are often flattered when asked for their working-parent coaching and advice; most relish the role of expert and enjoy seeing themselves as mentors. And family members may be thrilled to get their hands on the kids: particularly for older or retired relatives, helping nurture and care for a small child can provide a deep sense of joy and purpose.

That isn't to say that helpers shouldn't be rewarded for their efforts. If you've been on the receiving end of a favor—if your neighbor watched the baby on the morning the nanny was late, for example— it's essential to respond in kind; offer to look at her son's first professional résumé, for example. And as always, of course, graciousness rules: a thank-you phone call or email is always in order.

Attention, expectant parents

If you're already building out your Village before the baby comes, good on you! As you do that important work, though, *don't* make the all-too-common rookie mistake of pinning too much on any one of your prospective Villagers. Sure, maybe your own mother has offered to "help" and "be there" for you—but what does that mean exactly? Is she willing to babysit occasionally, be your backup care provider, or take on more? Does "more" include staying up nights when the baby has colic, or helping with household chores when you need it? If so, how often—and is that offer realistic if she's still working full-time herself? Is she *really* going to be able to manage hours of physically demanding babycare given her own age and health issues?

You get the point here. It's better to be realistic-to-the-point-of-pessimistic and go big and broad when building your Village rather than make assumptions, over-rely on anyone, and set yourself up for scrambling and frustration later on.

no matter how much effort or how many hours you put in, it's going to be virtually impossible to handle everything solo. Even if you did, you wouldn't be awarded any gold stars, and there's no Supreme All-Knowing Working-Parent Evaluation Committee anywhere, waiting to offer its cosmic approval. You're in a fundamentally different game than you've been in before: to be able to deliver the performance you want to at work, and to be a caring and attentive parent at home, you're going to need some assistance, and there's nothing wrong with getting it. Think about the situation in leadership or even in sports terms: you can't run a great organization or play well without building a strong team.

If, as you read this, your reaction is, *Bring it—I'll take every shred of working-parent support I can get*, then skip ahead to the next section, where we'll start sketching out your (expanded) Village's blueprints and then begin construction. If you're still a little uneasy with the overall idea of help, though, or if you're convinced you've already enlisted all the support you can, or if you're curious whether you do in fact suffer from a touch of Do-It-Myselfism, let's get to the bottom of things right here and now.

Take five minutes and complete the quick self-assessment in table 9-1, scanning the statements and then marking yes or no next to each.

For questions 3, 6, 7, 9, 10, 12, and 13, give yourself one point for each "Y" you circled. For questions 1, 2, 4, 5, 8, and 11, count each "N" answer as one point.

TABLE 9-1

The Workparent Do-It-Myselfism Assessment

1. In the past year I've attended a group meet-up, event, or gathering specifically for working parents.	Y	N
2. During my most recent working-parent transition (e.g., return from leave, start of school or caregiving arrangement, promotion or job change, etc.), I spoke to one or more people outside my "chain of command" who had recently been through something similar.	Y	N
3. Since becoming a parent, my use of technology has remained consistent. I still rely on all of my same favorite tools, apps, and sites.	Y	N
4. I know exactly what my organization offers in terms of family-friendly benefits, and am familiar with the "ins and outs" of using them.	Y	N
5. When the demands of working parenthood start wearing me down, or when I catch flak about my dual responsibilities, I know where to turn for advice and encouragement.	Y	N
6. There are certain tasks I just don't ask my partner, or my child's caregivers, to do. They won't do them as well as or in the same way that I do.	Y	N
7. I'd like to take more time for myself, but that just isn't possible with a busy career and young children.	Y	N
8. The foot traffic through our home—e.g., the number, frequency, and type of visitors—has changed since I became a parent.	Y	N
9. If I were on a work trip and my airplane was trapped in an hours-long holding pattern, significantly delaying my return and leaving me absolutely no way to call home, I would be worried.	Y	N
10. My own parents worked hard while they were raising us kids, and they didn't bellyache about it, or take much help, either.	Y	N
11. I've got a plan for augmenting my regular childcare arrangement when I face major deadlines and during my workplace busy season.	Y	N
12. Sure, I'd love more help with housework, childcare, transportation, or meal prep, but that's not money I can or should spend.	Y	N
13. I'm the baby's mother/father. This is my *job*.	Y	N

> Being a professional is all about efficiency. But a working parent? It's all about redundancy. If my son spikes a fever and has to get picked up from school, and I'm in the classroom teaching, and my wife is at her office forty miles away, someone we trust still needs to pick him up. You have to think in layers."
>
> —*Ethan, professor, father of two*

If your total score was 3 or more, it's an indication that you have a tendency toward working-parent Do-It-Myself thinking and behavior. There are times when you could feasibly reach out for help and assistance but, for whatever reason, don't. If you scored a 5 or higher, you've got a definite habit of going it alone when support may be available. If your score was 7 or above, you've got a confirmed case of Do-It-Myselfism.

So should you beat the stuffing out of yourself about this, and add it to the long list of your self-perceived workparent flaws? Of *course* not. Relying on your own work and efforts isn't a personal shortcoming. Quite the opposite: it can be a big personal asset, it comes from a good place, and God only knows that the world could use more people with your roll-up-the-sleeves attitude. But to make working parenthood feasible, both short and long term, and to make it personally sustainable (to avoid time crunches, logistical disasters, exhaustion, burnout, and worse), you're going to need to rein in those Do-It-Myselfer tendencies a little.

The good news is that there's likely more support available to you than you realize. To ensure that you fulfill your promise as both a talented professional and loving parent, we'll now go about finding it.

The 8-C Method for Assessing—and Expanding—Your Village

In chapter 2, you developed a plan for your child's day-to-day care. And good on you for doing so, because without the right frontline caregiving arrangement, working parenthood becomes impossible. Even

Making the ask

Your Villagers aren't clairvoyant. If you want assistance that's truly useful—and that comes on time, as needed—you're going to have to provide some direction. In other words, you're going to have to *ask*.

To get the support you're seeking and keep relationships with your Villagers strong, make your requests as direct, specific, and positive as you can.

- "Is there any way you could throw the laundry into the machine for me this afternoon? That would be such an enormous help!"
- "Can I take ten minutes of your time to talk about work-from-home options? Your perspective would really be valuable here."
- "If you can handle daycare pickup on Thursday, I can stay late and finish the proposal, which means I'll be free and can pick up the slack at home this weekend."

When your supporters know what to do, and get a sense of the impact their efforts can have, they'll be much more likely to deliver what you really need.

if you've beautifully constructed that one critical corner of your Village, though, it's essential to look at the *whole*: to get a full view of the settlement as it stands, and then to create a complete, deliberate, 360-degree picture of what you can build it into.

A simple and effective way of doing so is the 8-C method, which lets you look, in an organized, clear, brisk fashion, at where your overall foundation of support is strong and where it has cracks and gaps. It also lets you quickly identify prospective new Villagers and Village resources and the types of help they might provide you. Those insights form the basis of your Village-building action plan.

In 8-C, each *C* stands for a source, or overall category, of assistance. While most of that support comes from people, some comes in other, nonhuman forms. To use 8-C for yourself, start by glancing through table 9-2 to understand what each *C* represents.

Once you've done an initial read, go back over the list again, this time more slowly and deliberately, beginning to think about who or what might fit into each of the categories for you. *What managers,*

TABLE 9-2

The 8 Cs

Category of support	Potential Village members or resources
Career	All of your managers, mentors, and sponsors—both in your current role and from past jobs.
Colleagues	Any coworkers who have "been there" as working parents themselves. These may be close work friends, or other members of your team or group who are roughly in the same life phase and at a similar level of seniority. They may also be people you don't know well, who work in a completely different area of the organization, or who are more senior or junior than you. The key criteria are that 1) they're approachable and 2) they seem to "have it together."
Corporate/ organizational	Company-sponsored benefits, programs, and policies—formal and informal—that can help you during your parental leave, throughout your return to work, and over the longer term. Examples would include both the emergency backup care program as well as the ad-hoc dads' group that occasionally meets over sandwiches. Note: finding these resources may involve doing some active reconnaissance, such as speaking to HR, looking at the employee handbook, scouring the organization's intranet, asking colleagues—or all four.
Care	Childcare providers or household help of any kind, whether paid or volunteer. That includes the daycare center; your mother-in-law, if she's offered to watch the kids on the days you run late from work; the weekend sitter; etc.
Computer/ technological	Programs, apps, sites, or systems that help you manage day-to-day work-plus-home logistics, or that connect you to other workparents.
Clinical/wellness	Your child's healthcare provider, the staff in that provider's office, and any other adviser you look to regarding your own and your family's overall wellness. That might include your own doctor, a nutritionist, the leader of your weekly exercise class, and so forth.
Couple	Your partner, or anyone else you consider to be a true coparent.
Community	Other people who are a part of the fabric of your regular life, including: <ul><li>Neighbors</li><li>Fellow members of outside organizations—such as your alumni club, volunteer organization, or faith community</li><li>Expert-services providers—for example, your tax preparer</li><li>Members of your professional network</li><li>Extended family</li><li>Friends</li></ul>

Thinking about the Village as a whole

" I have three biological kids, the oldest of whom is in college now. I'm also an interim caregiver, which means that I take care of babies who need a home immediately after birth, or while their biological parents are making the decision on adoption.

As a foster parent, I have to make sure that all the people who are lending me a hand—whether that's relatives, friends, or paid sitters—are officially listed as 'resources' with the agency. Any parent can use that idea, though: just put together a list of all the people you can get help from. There's no reason that the people on that list have to fit a certain model. You don't have to have an old-fashioned, 'three generations of a happy family, all working together under one roof to raise the baby' kind of picture. Families are formed in all different ways, and so are support networks."

—*Catherine, gym owner, mother of three*

" My boys both have unique needs, and I've created what I call our Family Team to help meet them. That includes doctors, therapists, teachers, family members, even my own team leader at work. When I start working with any one of them, I'll say, 'Congratulations—you're part of our team!' I talk openly about the role I think they can play in ensuring our family's success.

When my older one was diagnosed, I didn't have that network in place. I quickly realized that I needed to humble myself: to surrender to the fact that I needed help, and to be willing to receive it. Telling myself, 'I cannot do it all' felt so empowering."

—*Jenny, research technical leader, mother of two*

mentors, and sponsors might help me think through handling my career now that I'm a dad? Who can I rope in to do some occasional weekend babysitting? Can the nurse practitioner at our daughter's doctor's office help me figure out how to manage the tantrums she has each night before bed? Think expansively: Can the trainer at your gym help you come up with a five-minute workout routine that will help you feel more energized each morning? And don't rush. You may even want to put the list away for a few days and let fresh ideas come to you while you're going about

> 66 My schedule changes, and I'm not always at home when it's time for homework. Sometimes my son will send me a picture of what he's working on, and I can help by phone. Sometimes I can't, and our neighbor—she's eighteen—will pitch in, or tutor him. Think about everyone who can help you."
>
> —*Jinelis, hotel front-desk manager, mother of one*

other business. With some time, and as you consider each category, options should begin jumping out. Maybe your ex-boss can provide some advice on navigating your company's promotion process when you're on a flexible work arrangement, or maybe an app can help streamline the family calendar.

You'll also naturally home in on the *C*s you're missing—the types of support you don't or won't have access to—or on ways in which your Village falls short. You may even find yourself mentally protesting a bit, thinking, *Sure, having corporate help is all well and good for people at big companies, but I'm self-employed,* or, *But we just moved here for Jonathan's job, and there aren't many people we feel comfortable asking for favors.* That's normal: your Village will inherently be different to other parents', and it's certain to be better-populated in certain areas and much sparser in others. Very few parents—even those lucky enough to have tons of resources—feel that their Village is as fully staffed as they want. What you're doing here is taking realistic stock, and then figuring out how to *maximize.* You're plotting how to make the most of the resources you do have while, as carefully and thoroughly as possible, hunting around for more.

When you've done some good thinking and can grab an hour or so free, jot down all of your ideas. To stay organized and keep yourself honest, place those notes in a blank 8-C grid. Keep working as broadly and out-of-the-box as you can, covering each category in turn. As you go, avoid self-censure (no, that senior colleague you admire might not have the time to speak with you about how she manages the big job and life with twins, but it's not going to hurt you to ask).

What you might be feeling when family help isn't an option

If you've suffered the loss of a family member or are estranged from your family of origin, or if relatives can't help now that they themselves need care, you may be left grappling with some complex, painful emotions. The intense sense that *I miss Mom* may now be deepened and magnified by the feeling that *I wish she could help when I need her the most*. There should be a special word for this kind of absence, and grief.

As small a comfort as it may be, try connecting with other working parents who have experienced the same. Being able to speak openly with, and feel understood by, others in the same situation may provide some small measure of relief. Remind yourself, too, that the job you're doing as a working parent is one that *every* member of your family—whatever your relationship with them, and whether they're still with you or not—would, or should, be proud of.

When you've finished, your list may look something like table 9-3. Step back a little, and reread with fresh eyes everything you've got down on the page. As you do, you'll likely be struck by:

- The fact that there are more *types* of support out there than you may originally have assumed, whether relating to childcare, career advice, time and cost savings, personal motivation, or other needs.

- A feeling that you're not alone: there are other people who can be "in this" with you.

- Relief that you now have specific and/or additional allies to reach out to when you do need help or find yourself in a work-parenting jam.

- A glimmer of pride in the strategy you've just created for making the career-plus-child picture come together: you've just stepped into the role of Village mayor. This is *your* town now.

TABLE 9-3

Sample 8-C Chart

Category of support	Potential Village members or resources—and how each can help
Career	• The team lead from that huge project I was on last year. She's smart about how to use time. • My assigned mentor back in my first job. He's funny, blunt—and has three kids. How does he handle weekend work? • The executive recruiter who placed me here. Get her insights on other working parents building their careers.
Colleagues	• The other father on my team, whose baby was born three months before mine. • Mary over in marketing—who always seems to have her act together even with an intense job and three teenagers. • The bulletin board in the cafeteria where other parents put up notices about babysitters and gently used baby gear.
Corporate/ organizational	• The dependent-care account—talk to payroll about putting aside pretax money for childcare expenses. • Look at what my health plan covers in terms of stress management. (Discount gym membership? Therapy?) • Those personal-finance seminars the benefits team runs every year. • IT. Can help me upgrade my work-from-home setup.
Care	• Daycare, when we start it. Ask the center director for any advice on transitioning back to work. • That housekeeping service we used once last year. Pricy, but maybe they can come once a month for heavy cleaning. • Jonathan's aunt—who's retired and eager to babysit. See if we can make it a regular weekly commitment.
Computer/ technological	• Start keeping a shared grocery list, and put household supplies on automatic reorder. • Join the neighborhood parents' group on social media.
Clinical/ wellness	• Ask Dr. Pagioli about how to get the baby onto a better sleep schedule. • See if gym staff can recommend stretches or moves that will help with back pain from constantly sitting and lifting the baby.
Couple	• Coordinate our calendars to make logistics easier. Start taking turns on daycare drop-off. • Pep talks . . . we both could use more support and encouragement. • Sign up for emergency backup care through Jonathan's work.
Community	• The new-parents group at our temple. • Our tax preparer. (Can I start taking a home-office deduction and use some of the extra cash for a house cleaner?) • Cousin Maya. She may be willing to take on some occasional babysitting jobs during her school vacations.

> " It's important to find working-parent support on the job. Work is one of the most important communities you have, and nobody's going to understand your day-to-day the way a colleague will.
>
> Hopefully you don't work in an environment where it's only permissible to talk shop, but rather one where you can be open about the realities of being a working parent. Even inside the stuffiest organization, though, you can still pick up on little cues and clues. Maybe you hear one of your coworkers on the phone with the daycare center, or someone's got a picture of their kids at their desk. Then, just ask—tell them you're looking for a daycare yourself, and could use their advice. Most people find that vulnerability refreshing."
>
> —*Basil, P&L director, father of two*

With your 8-C notes in front of you, you also have a tactical Village-building plan. Instead of feeling the pain of not having enough help, you can start to work the problem. Begin following up on each individual to-do: signing up for the parenting group, getting in touch with the IT help desk, calling your cousin about babysitting, and so on. If you've been suffering from Do-It-Myselfism, this part of the process, where you actually start enlisting help, is the antidote. And if you've been uncertain, practically speaking, of how to go about securing additional support, having this concrete list of action items should feel really, really good.

Take care to keep your 8-C brainstorm notes in the same folder as your other workparent exercises, and someplace where you can pull them out easily and often. Building your Village will take some time, and you'll want to make additions and renovations in the months and years ahead—as your child grows, your career develops, and your needs evolve.

Third Parents

Within that larger overall group of villagers, you'll want to handpick a select few to serve in a special role as your child's Third Parents.

> " In general, I'm not a big fan of my cell phone. When I'm home I keep it on the nightstand and focus on the kids. But I do use it to stay in touch with my kids' teachers, and on top of their assignments, and I've got alarms on there telling me when it's time to do everything from go to lunch to leave work to take my son to soccer practice. Your phone has a lot of potential to help you, if you use it well."
>
> —*Keywanda, senior timekeeper, mother of two*

Third Parents are your fully trusted, when-needed parent stand-ins—your parent proxies. They're the individuals who, in emergencies or when you're not around, you have complete confidence entrusting your children with, both practically and emotionally. You know they'll act effectively in your stead and with the same level of care and judgment. If you can't make the school play because you're trapped at work, a Third Parent is a person you would feel comfortable asking to attend and applaud in your place. If you have to take your older child to the emergency room for stitches, a Third Parent is the one you'll ask to pick the younger one up from daycare and babysit for a few hours until you get home. These trusted villagers aren't daily caregivers—in fact, you may only seek their help a couple of times per year, if that. They're more like understudies: they may rarely get called on stage, but knowing they're in the wings releases you from a whole lot of *what-if* stress.

After doing your 8-C exercise and identifying your full bench of potential Village recruits, take some additional time to think through who could become your Third Parents. If very good friends or immediate family members live nearby, bingo—they're your natural options. Third Parents may also be colleagues or neighbors, and over time a paid caregiver may even take on this more intimate, family-like role.

Once you've settled on a few Third Parents—and a few is all you need—you'll want to explicitly enlist their help. To simultaneously convey the seriousness of what you're asking and to avoid making the role sound burdensome, try using a script like this: "Bill, as you know we

> " My daughter was sick, I was home taking care of her, breaking news came out, and I had to cover the story. I called my step-mom, who's retired, and said, 'I need two hours.' She came right over, and I was able to get it done.
>
> It's really helpful to have that roster of close friends or other people who can help you—a list of who to reach out to, and in what order. It's much easier than starting from scratch in an emergency."
>
> —*Melissa, journalist, mother of one*

consider you to be a wonderful friend to both of us. We trust you with everything, including now the baby. It would give us a lot of comfort to be able to list you as a secondary contact at the daycare, and more generally to know that you might be willing to temporarily step in to make certain Jordan is safe and well cared for if our family were ever facing a real emergency. We know how incredibly busy you are at work and with your own family, and we'll never abuse your time." If Bill is a dear friend and the request is framed like this, he's likely to say yes.

To make any Third Parent's job easier, and to put your own mind further at rest, think about what he or she would need, tactically speaking, in order to come in on cue. Depending on your child's age, that might include:

- A "backup bag" containing all the regular contents of an overnight or diaper bag, *plus* a complete Emergency Contacts Sheet, a copy of your child's health-insurance card, and a spare key to the house

- A copy of your detailed family schedule, or access to the one you keep electronically

- Instructions for reaching you when you're unreachable at work (e.g., "If I'm on a sales call, call my supervisor, tell her it's urgent, and ask her to track me down")

- Formal authorization allowing the Third Parent to pick your child up from school or daycare

- Any special medical information or directions: like a list of allergies or instructions on how to use the inhaler

- Enough toys, games, and educational movies that your child can stay distracted and occupied for at least several hours

- A small amount of cash or a prefilled debit card that can be used for taxis, pharmacy purchases, or last-minute takeout meals

In all likelihood, most of these logistical preparations will never be needed and that bag will rarely be opened, but both you and your Third Parents will feel more relaxed and in-charge knowing you're ready for any contingency.

Communicating with the Village

As soon as you become a working parent, engaging in *proactive communication*—that is, communicating when you haven't been asked to do so, or don't technically need to—typically drops down to the bottom of your to-do list. Gone are the days of regularly reaching out to colleagues, friends, family members—or even clients—just to say a cheerful hello and shoot the breeze. Under so much time pressure and with so much going on at work and at home, you do things when you need to do them, or when they become urgent, and that includes getting in touch. Unfortunately, the "I'll call you when I need you" approach, while highly time-efficient, can erode Villager goodwill quickly. If every phone call or message from you starts with "Do you have time . . ." or "Could you . . ." then even your biggest supporters may get a little frustrated.

Be deliberate in your villager communications and balanced in your messaging. For each "ask," think about having at least one inessential topic of conversation. Do a regular mental review of who you've connected with, when, and for what, and make sure you're mixing it up—call the aunt who babysits for you to share some piece of family gossip, or stop by to make a joke with that one caregiver at daycare, for example, rather than only asking for a report on your child's day.

Village relationships—*all* relationships—are like bank accounts: you can't make withdrawals unless you make deposits.

On a micro, time-saving level, make sure you know exactly how to reach each of your Village resources. If the family-benefits page is hopelessly buried on the company intranet somewhere, for example (which in most organizations it is), find a friendly face in HR to tap for the information. Have "uh-oh" messaging distribution lists ready so that if your child suddenly gets sick on the way to daycare and you can't make the meeting, or you're trapped at work and can't get to daycare before closing, you can quickly reach the people you need to. Fiddle around with the phone prompts at your child's doctor's office until you find the one that moves you past the hold music. The less time and effort you spend on nuts-and-bolts Village management, the easier things will be, and the more bandwidth you'll have for other priorities.

Adapting Your Support Network over Time

As your child continues to grow and your career moves ahead, your support needs will naturally change, and you'll want to update your Village to meet them. If you did 8-C a few years ago and not since, then you're doing yourself a disservice—you're not growing and tweaking your support network as it naturally needs to be grown and tweaked over time. Think about setting aside a defined time for a regular 8-C review; at a minimum, don't let a year pass by without doing one. Managing your 8-C is like doing your annual tax filing or getting a medical checkup: it gives you a complete, timely picture of your Village's health and total working-parent support assets, lets you keep those assets current, and provides you important reassurance that you're managing your overall workparent life most effectively.

That review process needn't be exhaustive. Just scan your old 8-C notes with an eye to what recent life changes may prompt you to edit your Village a little. For example, you may decide that you need some new on-the-job mentors who have already weathered the toddler years, or that you don't need so much babysitting support now that the kids are older. A few life events will almost certainly trigger larger and

Sympathy versus real support

You need to feel heard, and understood. We *all* do. When connectedness tips over into commiseration, however, the value of any professional peer-to-peer or mentoring relationship plummets. Yes, in the moment, it can be wonderful to talk with another, sympathetic parent about your boss's hostility to flexible work arrangements, about your sense of internal conflict at raising your hand for promotion while your son is still so small, or about the tough lot of working parents in general. But if you keep seeking emotional relief in the problem-discussion zone, you risk getting stuck there.

Whether you're face to face with a workplace mentor, or even just chatting with other working parents online, try to focus the dialogue on next steps, action, alternative ways of thinking, and specific ways to feel better. What's their advice on how to pitch your boss on a shifted schedule? What are new ways to get more comfortable with the trade-offs that new schedule might bring? Don't use workplace supporters to affirm or air negative feelings—see them as catalysts and coaches.

more fundamental Village updates: If you move, change jobs, expand your family, have a change in your family structure, or if the kids start or change schools, for example, it will be key to take a fresh look at your support needs. If you've moved jobs, you'll want to understand what's on offer at your new organization in terms of backup care and to connect with a few other working mothers and fathers who can explain "how things work here." When your child starts school, you'll want to create an informal team of fellow parents who you can coordinate with on pickups, school activities, and so on. And when the kids become teenagers, you'll want to consider enlisting a few additional adults who can help ensure their safety.

For more advice on how to keep your family well cared for and your career on track during these particular change points, turn to chapter 7, "School"; chapter 8, "The Almost-Teen and Teenage Years"; and chapter 13, "Transitions."

Strong Village, Strong Working Parent

Hard work, making things happen, taking personal responsibility—they're who you are at your core.

Over these eighteen years, though, success at work, satisfaction at home, and even your child's well-being hinge, in very large measure, on your seeking help, and on the direct involvement of other people. Support from friends, colleagues, and your partner makes the transition back to work after parental leave less daunting. Good counsel from working-parent mentors can move you in positive directions on and off the job. The grocery-list app will let you spend just a little more of your scarce time on what really matters. And most important, the more loving, trusted adults you can surround your children with—caregivers, neighbors, family, and friends—the more secure and happy your children will be. You're more dependent, and depending on more people, than ever before—but for all the right reasons, and in exactly the ways you should.

10

Time

Managing Your Priorities, Calendar, and Commitments

Whether you've thought about it relatively little in the past, or whether you're a calendar-organization obsessive, working parenthood forces you to think longer and harder than ever before about time management. From Day One straight through the teenage phase, you've got more to accomplish each day than time to accomplish it *in*. The relentlessness and urgency can easily leave you feeling harried and depleted. If that's the case, your colleagues and kids have probably noticed.

While all of the usual techniques for handling busyness and a high workload—working longer hours, sleeping less, multitasking, reorganizing your time-keeping system—may help a tiny bit in the short term, they're not going to have the big-picture impact you *really* want, which is to move you away from feeling and being so endlessly crazy-busy.

Realistically, as a working mother or father you'll always have a lot to do. But you don't have to resign yourself to feeling quite *this* stretched and stressed—or to having either of those two things become part of your identity, or professional brand. With a small number of working-parent-specific tools in hand, you can grab the "not enough time" problem by its roots, start pruning that endless to-do list, and feel more in control over how much you're doing and when.

Sorting Out What's *Really* Important

Your real challenge isn't to run harder and faster, it's to winnow your overall priorities *down*. With a sharper, more specific sense of *what I should be doing* and—just as important—*what I can let go of*, fully or partially, you'll be able to start reclaiming your time, taking more charge of your calendar, and developing confidence that you're putting your energies and hustle toward the right things. To help you do so, let's start by defining *priority* in the workparent context—and then walk through a quick, effective process for examining and determining your own.

Before you had kids, *priority* meant *something important*, or *that took precedence over other, less important things*—but now, as we've seen, you have to be much more specific and more stringent. To determine if something fits on your true working-parent priority list, ask yourself the following five questions.

1. **Does this task or activity represent a "highest and best" use of my time as a working mother or father?** Does it affect my ability to earn a living or keep the kids healthy and safe? Will this somehow enhance my career, my life, my family? Or is this something I'm doing automatically, because I feel I should; because I've always done it, to meet somebody else's expectations; or because it's simply fallen into my lap?

2. **Is this something that *only* I can do?** Does it really require my skills or presence? Could somebody else do it in my stead and nearly as well, or with the same impact?

3. **Will this feel important, or be beneficial to me, my career, and my family, five years from today?** What will this add up to, or accrue toward? Am I doing it just because it's easier not to find an immediate workaround, or because it feels good in this moment?

4. **Does this task or activity have special meaning to me?** Does it align with my values as a professional, parent, person? My vision for my family? My career legacy? The future? Does it make me feel more energetic and alive?

5. Does it benefit or sustain other parts of my life? If I do this one task at work, for example, will it have positive "spillover" effects at home, with the kids, or for me as a person?

Granted, we're setting an extraordinarily high bar for *priority* here—but that's the entire point! To get through the next decade-plus with your career, family relationships, and nerves intact, you'll need to become *very* discerning in separating true priorities from the merely important, and those importants from the nice-to-haves and the shoulds.

Try this method of stress-testing your own priorities by putting three or four of today's most urgent tasks through the five-question gauntlet. Be merciless: pretend that you're a flinty senior manager willing to make tough decisions on behalf of a lean and mean organization (that organization being *you*).

Most likely, one or two of your priority items will come out the other side completely whole and unscathed, while the others will feel at least slightly less important. For example, you may realize that the seemingly small act of putting your five-year-old to bed tonight is a "highest and best" use of your time, something *only* you can do, that will shape your relationship with her for years to come, that has special emotional resonance, and thus gives you energy and motivation for other things. Conversely, you may decide that helping your colleague with that tricky project, or agreeing to host your family's holiday celebration this year, doesn't meet more than a few of the five criteria—and is thus something to avoid or limit spending your time on.

> 66 Years ago one of my own mentors told me 'Our calendars don't show us what we want to do, but who we want to be.' As a working dad, I really think about how I'm using my time. Am I getting done what I need to at work? Building in patterns of rest? Celebration? Togetherness with my kids?
>
> If you're not making decisions about your own time, then your boss, and colleagues, and kids' soccer coach are."
>
> —*Steve, educator and pastor, father of four*

The working-parent time crunch: Are you feeling it?

When the simultaneous time demands of your job and of parenting begin to get out of hand, it can affect your behaviors, decision-making, relationships, and personal mojo. Do you find yourself doing any of the following?

- Repeatedly recreating your to-do list in a new format; making lists of your lists; or adding easily or already-completed items onto a list so you can immediately cross them off
- Berating yourself at the end of each day for not finishing everything on your task list, or commanding yourself to *just pick up the pace* to get more done
- Hurrying the kids through day-to-day routines like bath time or dinner, even when those activities could normally be relaxing and connective
- Secretly hoping for small-scale personal and professional disasters (a dramatic but nonserious health issue, terrible weather, a cancelled client meeting, technology meltdown) that might give you the excuse to turn off, even if only briefly
- Cutting back on any activity that has deep meaning for you, or that comes with real personal benefit—a spiritual practice, exercise, or time alone with your partner—so you can "fit it all in"
- Beginning to feel that the *only* way to get real relief from the time pressures you're under is through radical change—like quitting your job, upending your chosen lifestyle, or moving to a different area

If so, then take it as an important sign that it's time to step back, reconsider, and try some new approaches.

Carefully work the steps found in this chapter. Then, take a look at chapter 21 for further advice on handling difficult working-parent feelings, including being overwhelmed, as well as at chapter 17, on how to secure and enjoy more time off. And if the time demands of working parenthood are affecting your overall wellness or outlook, talk to a qualified counselor or your regular healthcare provider about what's going on.

> ❝ I've always been very engaged with my career, and involved with my community, very service-oriented—and always enjoyed creative, crafty projects. With two kids, I can't do everything I want to all the time. But I can volunteer in different ways—like working on an email campaign instead of showing up in person. And I've come up with a little life hack where I start working on my children's Valentine's and birthday party decorations in November. I want to feel like I'm achieving, while still giving and contributing, and still keeping myself and what I like to do front and center, still me."
>
> —*Erin, diversity and inclusion VP, mother of two*

To qualify as a true priority, not every item has to pass questions 1 through 5 with a resounding yes—and you'll inevitably find that certain items will move onto and fall off of your list at different times and for special reasons. Organizing your team's annual off-site may be a drag, for example, but if a senior person asked you to do it, and the entire team were watching, you might decide that it belongs at the top of your task list, at least for now. Even while raising the priority-setting bar, use your subjective judgment.

Now that you've test-driven the process, try applying it more broadly—to the wider spectrum of your responsibilities and to-dos. To be efficient about it, and to keep yourself both honest and organized, use the Sample Workparent Priority Setter (table 10-1).

In this particular sample, and to illustrate just how you can use the priority setter in the context of your demanding, complex, working-parent life, let's imagine that you're a regional salesperson for a technology company and parent to eight-year-old twin girls. There's pressure to build out client relationships in your territory, but your real goal is to be promoted to regional leader, a job that will simultaneously allow you to do more of what you love—mentoring, developing people, building a team—and keep you on a more regular schedule as the girls enter those critical preteen years.

In this case, meeting your sales targets would clearly be important. Without success in this area, there's no hope for advancement or future for you at the company. But to get ahead, two other things will

TABLE 10-1

Sample Workparent Priority Setter

Item	Priority?	Task or activity	Is it something that…				
			Represents my highest and best use?	Only I can do?	Will be important/ beneficial five years out?	Carries special meaning?	Benefits/ sustains other parts of my life?
1	Yes	Meeting quarterly sales quota	✓	✓	✓		✓
2	Yes	Connecting with the Canadian office	✓	✓	✓		✓
3	Yes	Leading mentoring program	✓	✓	✓	✓	✓
4	Yes	Dinner with partner	✓		✓	✓	✓
5	Yes	Coaching girls' swim team			✓	✓	✓
6	Yes	Gardening and lawn care				✓	✓
7	No	Exceeding sales quota; striving to become Salesperson of the Year		✓			
8	No	Triathlon competition		✓			✓
9	No	School drop-off/pickup			✓	✓	
10	No	Expense reports		✓			
11	No	Housework/cooking					
12	No	School volunteerism					

also be critical for you: establishing good rapport with the Canadian office and making the new-salesperson mentoring program you set up successful (the first for political reasons and the second as a way of demonstrating your people-management potential). Each of these items meets only four of our five criteria, but they easily earn priority status.

Now let's look at item number 4, dinner with your partner. This is the only activity that, hands down, meets all five criteria, so it's obviously a priority. But what about items 5 and 6—coaching the swim team and handling lawn care? Those seem like a radical departure from your other top-rank activities—and they are. But you love swimming, and coaching the girls' team is a great way to "show up" for them when you're working so much—not to mention sharpen your team-building skills. And lawn care happens to be your Point of Control, as discussed in chapter 4: the simple, small thing that gives you a disproportionate sense of energy and well-being amid the day-to-day workparenting frenzy. It may hit only two of the five criteria, but lawn care, you're keeping.

What *doesn't* make the cut includes above-and-beyond sales performance, which isn't needed for the career path you're shooting for; triathlons, which you enjoyed but have decided to give up in favor of shorter workouts in your basement gym; school drop-off and pickup, which got deprioritized as soon as the kids were old enough to take the bus; and admin tasks like expense reports, which have to be done but aren't highest and best priorities. In this fictionalized example, you're still a busy working parent, but you now have a simple, easy-to-remember priority mantra: *sell-connect-mentor, dinner-swim-lawn.* If you're doing those six things, you'll be on a good working-parent path.

Of course, this is an example, and no working parent really gets off after only twelve activities—our lives are much more complex and multifaceted than that. But the *approach* works, and you can now confidently use the priority setter yourself: feeding each of your time commitments through the five-question mill, and being ruthless in your judgment about whether it lands in top-priority territory, and thus deserves more of your attention and focus, or outside it, and should be allocated less.

Don't worry if deprioritizing things feels awkward at first, or if you don't have perfect, clear answers to each of the five questions. And if you want to amend the tracker to include other questions, or to "tier" your priorities, do so—whatever works best. Just be sure that at every phase of working parenthood you're nudging yourself toward a clearer and narrower view on what's really worth your time.

The Calendar Audit: A Way to Win Time Back

Once you've got a solid, refined list of your priorities, you can start *operationalizing* them—making sure that "what's most important" matches your day-to-day actions, and that you're being as mindful and deliberate as possible about where all of your working-parent time and sweat equity are really going. For this, you're going to use a simple hack we'll call the Calendar Audit. To do an audit from start to finish, all you'll need is fifteen to twenty minutes, your calendar and your to-do list in front of you, and a physical or electronic red pen.

Start by glancing over your appointments and tasks for the past week and—marker in hand—circling the commitments and to-dos that, in light of your real priorities, you could feasibly have put off, done in less time, delegated, automated, or said no to. As you work, be ruthless—and look for themes. Don't be afraid to observe when and what you could be doing a bit better (remember, there's no judging, and this exercise is just for *you*). Maybe you have a hard time declining volunteer requests from the kids' school, you're spending more time than you really have to grocery shopping, or someone else in the office could help put the patient billing information into the system.

Once you've finished that look back, marked up your calendar, and taken a few minutes to think about the bigger picture, look *forward*, applying the same thinking and approach to the week ahead—this time, with an action orientation. If you don't *have* to be at an upcoming meeting, for example, decide to bow out and free up the hour; if you're supposed to get back to the school on whether or not you'll volunteer again next week, resolve to say no; and if you're buying the same household products each week, set up regular delivery. Even if at the beginning of the audit your docket looks packed with code-red

How to say no more easily

Getting and keeping a good grip on your working-parent priorities and schedule is going to mean saying no—*a lot*. To avoid feeling lazy, guilty, or sheepish when you do, try:

- **Changing your default answer.** Stifle that knee-jerk "Yes, I will"; make "No" and "Let me think about that and come back to you" your new, go-to responses.
- **Reminding yourself that you're in a zero-sum game.** There are only twenty-four hours in a day, so saying yes to this request means having to say no to something else. Do you *really* want to push something off your to-do list just to take this on?
- **Letting yourself get a little indignant.** Would you ask someone else to spend his or her time this way? Is the person making this request truly honoring your time? Don't get too worked up—just enough that your no feels well justified.
- **Imagining what your response would be if your child (or boss, or partner, or favorite mentor, or company's main investor, etc.) were standing next to you.** Would he or she readily agree that this is a good use of your time?

To make your *nos* definitive, without being harsh or hostile:

- **Provide context.** "I wish I could agree to be class parent this year, but I'm under pressure while our company reorganizes, and unable to do what the school needs."
- **Offer an alternative resource or pathway.** "I won't be at work that day, but one of my colleagues would be happy to help."
- **Create a "no, until" sequence.** "Try doing it by yourself first, and if it doesn't work, Daddy will take a look."

The more you say no over time, the more it will become second nature—and the more you'll be able to focus away from other people's agendas and task lists and onto your own.

tasks, by applying a keen and critical eye here, you should be able to eliminate a few and identify some new "found time." If you've ever decluttered your closet or garage, you know this process already, and how satisfying it is.

Exactly how much of your time you can win back through this exercise will depend on your personal circumstances, but whatever those

> " Push yourself to figure out how the job could be done just as well in 80 percent of the time. Figure out what to cut. For a lot of people, that's going places. You can spend hours getting to meetings, getting home. Even before the pandemic, I was always telling people to skip the trips and do video calls instead. They say, 'But it's not the same as an in-person meeting.' Learn how to talk into the camera! Otherwise you're going to be spending a lot more time on the job and away from your kids."
>
> —*Béla, CEO, father of two*

are, try to set yourself a target of 5 percent. Even though you're a busy workparent, 5 percent is a realistic amount. You're never going to be able to divest yourself of 25 percent of what you're currently doing or audit your way to whole free days or weeks, but by making the kinds of small cuts we're discussing, 5 percent is eminently possible. And while it doesn't sound like much, it is. In a standard forty-hour workweek, 5 percent gives you back two hours to do the morning school run, or exercise. In the fifty-two weeks of a year, it gives you an extra two-week vacation—or twelve more work days to spend on that business plan. It's a small change that creates a noticeable, meaningful sense of "give" in your calendar, moving you from *all-out frantic* to merely *extremely busy*. At the same time, it stays well under the noticeability threshold: even in the most pressured, roll-up-the-sleeves work environments, it's unlikely that your boss will ever say, "Gee, we'd love to promote you, but we notice you're doing only 96.2 percent as much as you did before." Besides, your boss is most likely using some version of the Calendar Audit strategy for himself, and thinks of it as *leadership* or *efficiency*.

From a practical perspective, a Calendar Audit can create some much needed slack in your calendar and shorten your to-do list. Strategically, it lets you see, quickly and practically, if you're backing up your priorities with your time and actions, or if you're "spending" those resources on things that matter less. Emotionally, it gives you a sense of agency: you've moved out of that overwhelmed-and-helpless place and are instead being proactive and taking charge. And the

Time tech

In the past few years there's been a huge proliferation in the number and range of technological products—apps, software, sites, plug-ins, gizmos—designed to help you make better use of your time. To determine which such products are right for you:

- **Start by zeroing in on your biggest time-related pain points.** In other words, focus on what you need the most help *with*, whether that's:
  - **Scheduling, coordination, and integration,** like when attempting to manage two careers and three separate school calendars without dropping any balls.
  - **Logistics planning and streamlining,** such as figuring out how to make the carpool route come together without dozens of weekly phone calls.
  - **Reality checking and accountability,** to prevent procrastination or wasteful habits (like checking your email twelve times an hour), and/or to ensure that you're following through on important commitments (like getting in ten thousand steps per day).
  - **Limit setting,** which helps you "cap" time spent on specific projects, tasks, or activities.
- **Find a specific system designed to address those pain points.** Google Calendar will go a long way toward helping with busy-family coordination, but it may not help much with carpooling. For that, you may want to get all the families on the route to use a dedicated app. And to keep you honest about how much time you're spending online, you can install special time trackers on your phone, tablet, and laptop. In other words, find a solution that meets the precise need.
- **Think how easy or hard it will be to use on a regular basis.** If you're already strapped for time, a system that requires multistep inputs and constant monitoring won't help.
- **Just try it.** There is no one "best" method or product, and you won't know if a specific tool works for your life, career, and family until you give it a go.
- **Use it consistently.** Time management isn't a "one and done" job, it's a habit. To get any real traction from any tech tool, you need to keep on using it.

> " You have to manage your own calendar toward time with your family—not to other people's preferences. Maybe you send out a weekly update, and it's detailed and nicely formatted and everyone loves receiving it. That's great, but if it takes you an hour to put together and a one-liner would work just as well, that's what you should be doing instead. Ask yourself: Is this juice worth the squeeze?"
>
> —*Andrea, regulatory relations leader, mother of five*

> " We focus on the time we get with our daughter, but not in units. We're not clocking it, thinking, 'How can I get another thirty minutes?' It's about understanding, relating to each other, appreciating her, making sure the time we do have together is precious."
>
> —*Shawn, lighting designer, father of one*

personal insights that come out of the audit ("I say yes too often"; "I can be a perfectionist") help you make more-conscious judgments about your time and your commitments for the future. Best of all, the Calendar Audit process is surprisingly quick and easy—and the more often you do it, the more benefit it brings. Think about setting aside a quarter of an hour every Friday morning for this process, or some other time when you're in a reflective mood and have comparatively more mental energy. Gradually, the process will become ingrained and automatic, and help create a sense of control over your busy days.

Containment: What, When, and How

Alright, you've prioritized, and pruned off some of your to-dos. But hang on here: let's circle back to that Workparent Priority Setter for a moment. In our example, what becomes of the cooking, housework, and volunteerism? And in *your* real, day-to-day life, what becomes of all the other activities you don't enjoy, or that you consider low-priority,

Social media

Amid the stresses and strains of career and children, it's perfectly OK to want a little entertainment, connection, and escapism, too— and those things can be good for you. But as you're considering what to prioritize and what to avoid, what to spend less time on or contain, don't forget to set some rules for yourself around social-media usage. Consider spending no more than twenty minutes per day on your favorite platform, and only after the kids go to bed, or give yourself a set amount of time to scroll through your feeds each weekend. *And then stick to the plan.* If you find yourself distracted in meetings, using social media as an emotional salve, or focusing away from the kids to "like" somebody else's vacation photos, it's time to pull back—or deactivate that account.

but that still need to get done? How do you handle your taxes, your work inbox, the kids' endless laundry, the dentist? Even if they're not priorities, those things don't just disappear.

For these items, try using a strategy of *containment*. If you've ever taken an exam in a difficult subject and had the satisfaction of throwing your pen down just as the proctor says "time's up," or if there's a room in your house you keep tidy save for a single drawer crammed with a jumble of household supplies you don't like looking at, then you're well familiar and practiced with the containment strategy already. Containment simply means "placing something within clear and defined limits." You draw a box, and keep necessary but less enjoyable things firmly inside.

If you're fortunate to have an extra little bit of disposable income, you can certainly use it to help contain some of your working-parent to-dos: you can hire a tax preparer or a housekeeper, for example, to limit the amount of time spent on personal accounting or tidying. But most of us aren't long on cash, and anyway, many of the less enjoyable, less high-priority to-dos we face aren't delegable. You can't send anyone else to the dentist on your behalf or ask someone else to respond to personal messages. Containment is therefore usually a matter of personal timing.

To put *containment* into practice, try looking ahead on your calendar for the coming week, finding a few short time blocks free, and marking them as "catch-up time" or "life admin." When each block comes, use it to do nothing but the tasks you've been avoiding or haven't gotten around to: returning those emails, folding that laundry, running those errands, etc.—taking no breaks, fielding no distractions, and working as fast as you can, using *getting this off my plate* as your guiding goal. Feel free to rope in others: If the house is a mess, set your phone alarm for ten minutes and have the kids join you in speed-round cleanup until it rings. Or gather the project team in the breakout room for a dedicated thirty-minute crash-revision of the big presentation. Or go larger scale and set aside half a Saturday every other month to do nothing but handle items you'd rather contain: getting the car serviced, cleaning out your office files, and so on.

Whichever specific approach you take, it's likely that you won't finish all of the work that's on your list. You'll probably only make a dent—but for most containment activities and in working-parent world, a dent is good enough. Use this strategy regularly, and you'll have the satisfaction of getting through what you need to, without those things taking over your calendar or, more crucially, your mind.

Time and Busyness as Part of Your Professional Brand

If you feel a little overcommitted, tired, or frazzled, that's completely normal. Like every other working parent, you've got a lot on your plate. But to be seen as, and to actually *be*, an effective leader—whatever your line of work—means coming across as if you have control over your time. Appearing *anxious, frantic, hounded, exhausted,* and *curt* won't play well with a promotions committee, with your boss's boss, or during an interview. On the other hand, being seen as *active, calm, deliberate, focused, efficient,* and *energized* redounds to your credit, and can draw your colleagues toward you.

Talking about time with the kids

Timing may control our adult lives, but it's incomprehensible to very small children. A toddler easily confuses days with weeks and hours with minutes. But even a preschooler can understand sequence: "We'll leave for the park in ten minutes" won't resonate, but "We'll leave for the park when we're done cleaning up these toys" likely will. In these early years, rely on *before, after,* and *as soon as* whenever talking about schedules and next steps, and peg those phrases to well-understood daily activities—*before bedtime, after your bath.*

Around age five, the game begins to change: the kids can understand basic time measurements more. And to thrive in school, they'll need to. So get ahold of an easy-to-read clock and an old-fashioned, wind-up kitchen timer, and encourage your child to use them. Ask your child if it's 7:15 yet, and thus time to start getting dressed for school.

As they continue to develop, encourage your kids to respect your time—and their own. If everyone knows when the school bus comes, and if you have clocks in visible places throughout the house, your child is more likely to be on time for the bus and you're less likely to have to resort to such nagging as, "Aren't you ready yet? Hurry up!"

At every phase, from toddlerhood through the teenage years, remember that what your child wants more from you than anything else is your time and attention. Even when you're busy, try to use statements like:

- "It's Saturday, and we have the *whole day* to play together!"
- "Don't be scared—Daddy will be with you *the entire time.*"
- "I watched *every single second* you were on stage, and thought the class play was wonderful."

To send the right professional signals without overthinking how best to do so, or feeling like you're an actor playing a role, consider:

- Sharing your calendar. Let your colleagues see and understand how you're using your time—and how confident you are in that. Let them peer at your schedule and think, "He's busy, but he's got his act together."

> ❝ There's a lot of 'hurry up' in this business, but there's also a lot of 'hurry up and wait.' Over time, I've gotten a lot more assertive with my editors about what really needs to get done and by when, because I get two hours with my daughter each evening, and I don't want to miss that window. I'll tell my colleagues, 'If this story isn't running tonight, I'll look at it again tomorrow.' That kind of conversation doesn't come naturally for me, but there's usually very little pushback. I've also gotten better at setting boundaries for myself; telling myself, *this is done*—or at least, done for now."
>
> —*Melissa, journalist, mother of one*

- Using an impossible-to-ignore visual. Keep a whiteboard up in your workspace, with a list of key projects by deadline and status. If you're working remotely, hang this up in the background wherever you do your videoconferencing. Add detail and updates, and never let the information become obviously outdated or too spare. Your message: *I've got a lot on my plate, and I'm in demand, but I'm on it.*

- Having a "time investment" elevator speech. If you can answer the question "How's it going?" with a crisp, upbeat "We're almost finished reconfiguring the curriculum for the September launch—it's busy, but great to see it all coming together," it will speak much better of you than a rapidly recited task list or commenting about how "there's so much to do in the next three weeks!"

- Minding your adjectives. When a colleague asks how your day has been, be wary of responding with words like *overwhelming*, *endless*, *too much*, or *crazy*. Of course it feels that way, and it is, but those aren't the messages you want to send about yourself, or your relationship with whoever's asking the question. Think about using balanced terms like *active*, *engaged*, *productive*, or *busy* instead.

- Setting "priority percentages"—and sharing them with your boss. Figure out how you're spending your total work time, and ask your boss if he agrees that 50 percent devoted to product development, 30 percent to regulatory reporting, and 20 percent to recruitment sounds right (fill in the blanks with your own specifics). Not only will these time-priority conversations let you sound thoughtful, judicious, and aligned with your boss's interests, they will also allow you to recalibrate as needed—and avoid surprises at your performance review later on.

Making Your Working-Parent Calendar Work Even Better

It cannot be said loudly or often enough: **having a single, shared, visible, usable, all-in-one calendar is critical to making the moving parts of your working-parent life come together effectively**. You want to be able to see job commitments next to school breaks, dentist's visits, vacations, work trips, caregiver time off, and anything else that may affect the efficient running of your complete workparent system—and see it all quickly, without confusion or fuss. Whether you've already set up a working-parent calendar that feels like it's doing the job, or you're just now facing that task, here are the guidelines for making it all as easy and as useful as possible—and for keeping it that way over time.

- Do it your way. Your family calendar should reflect how you think about time, what your work and home obligations really are, and how you personally operate day to day. A "good" workparent calendar is one that enables easy coordination and swift retrieval: it lets you sidestep conflicts and timing gaffes, and lets you put your hands on the right information quickly. How and if you color-code or label things is just a matter of personal choice.

- Keep it simple. Beware of setting up a system that takes more time to manage than it gives you back. While it may be tempting to adopt the newest, most complicated technology, or a twelve-shade color-coding system, avoid those things if a more basic, streamlined version works for you and your family.

- Treat the calendar as sacred. A calendar only works if you actively use it and add to it. Make a plan to review it weekly, both on your own and with other family members and/or your caregiver. Consider having a dedicated time to look over the coming week, especially when there are changes to the regular schedule or special events looming.

- Grant access more broadly. Before kids, you could keep your calendar private. Now, your partner, your caregiver, your child's Third Parents, and maybe even a trusted colleague at the office should have access (even if "read only"). Sharing the calendar is the most powerful way to bring your Village together, to distribute responsibilities, and to make sure everyone knows what needs to happen and when. If the idea of allowing a caregiver to see your full calendar freaks you out a little, remember that that person already has total access to the thing that's most precious in the world to you: your child.

- Adapt the system, based on age. When your first child is a baby, the Google Calendar that only the adults can see is just fine. But school-age kids should be in on the act of keeping themselves on track and on schedule. Even if they're not fully computer literate yet, they can develop good time-management skills. Print out the weekly schedule and post it in the kitchen, flagging that playdate on Thursday, or reminding the kids that it's their job to remember to bring their instruments in for band practice.

- Avoid recreating it. Many stressed-out workparents, keen to make the calendar feel more "real" and visible and to get various

> I block my work calendar every day starting at 5:15. Unless there's an emergency, that's parenting time."
> —Nicole, management consultant, mother of three

Time for nothing

When you're so crazy-busy, any blank time in your schedule can both look and feel like a waste. But protecting some white space for important "do nothing" activities like *downtime, think time, transitions, regrouping,* and *catch-up* can bring enormous benefits—professional, practical, and personal. If you can mull over what you want to say right before that big meeting, you'll sound smarter and more on point when it starts.

To protect your Nothing Time, put it on your calendar, just like any other commitment; keep the fifteen-minute slots before big meetings blank, or block out the slice of time you need to get your act together after daycare drop-off and before each working day starts. If you work in an environment that values constant busyness and/or if your colleagues can see your calendar, use a professional-sounding label ("prep time" or "team coordination" sound active and work-like, while being suitably vague). The point is to keep a little slack in your system; you'll figure out the right way to protect it.

members of the family on board with it, will do things like handwrite a version up on a big whiteboard in the kitchen, in addition to keeping the online version. While this is a good instinct, it's a terrible technique, because now you've essentially committed yourself to maintaining two calendars instead of one. If you do want to focus the family on the week's schedule, print it out and display it, or better yet, print, display, and discuss it.

The Real Meaning of "Balance"

Before you became a parent, your days were busy, but they unspooled in a relatively linear way—you knew what was important, you dug in where you needed to, and you moved on. Now you feel as if you're constantly lurching from one priority to the next, lunging from the work sphere to home and back again, diving to catch any spinning plates at risk of falling, spending most of your time listing far to one side, and afraid of falling down yourself.

> ❝ Creating great public spaces like museums and libraries—it's our profession, but it's also our joy. My wife (who's also my business partner) and I used to be in the office in the evenings and on the weekends. When a big project proposal was due, we loved the thrill of getting it out the door just before the midnight deadline. And there was a lot of creative time, not directly correlated to progressing a project . . . time to lean back in your chair and just think, or see what other design projects were happening out there, or to talk to a colleague.
>
> We've had to become a lot less loose with our time now. Every day, we face a deadline: our son's pickup. We call it quits each day at the same time, and we're much more structured about how we work. We try to get ahead of big deadlines. The new goal is 'no drama.'"
>
> —*Lyn, architect, father of one*

And this, as strange and nonintuitive as it is, is working-parent *balance*: not some state of perfect, graceful equilibrium; not some elegantly described concept in a corporate work/life brochure; not some blissful-sounding but unachievable schedule that lets you do precisely the same thing, at the same time, each day—but the ability to go deep on what's important, where you need to, and when you need to, and then deliberately correct in the other direction.

11

Money

Affording Working Parenthood—Now, and Longer Term

Unless you're a lottery winner or the majority shareholder of some wildly successful startup, working parenthood is going to—or already has—put a major crimp in your budget, and its costs are going to keep hitting you in several different ways. Parental leave may cause a short-term dip in your income. Good-quality childcare can come with a hefty price tag . . . and that's *on top* of all of the regular costs of childrearing (the baby food, the clothes, the bigger apartment, and so on). Working fewer hours to spend more time with the kids can also lead to lower pay.

And even if you pride yourself on being particularly money-savvy and are lucky enough to have a solid, stable income, you're still going to have to wrestle with difficult working-parent money questions, large and small: Should you take that higher-paying job, even though it means more time away from home? Is that after-school program really worth it? Can you afford any help at home, with so many other bills to pay? Of course, there are the emotional costs, too: when you're working all-out every single day to provide for your family but keep finding yourself short on cash or lost in a maze of numbers, it's demoralizing and disconcerting.

We can't magically add a bunch of zeros onto the end of the current number in your bank account. We *can* help you maximize the resources you *do* have—and cut a path through that mess of bills and feelings and toward a place of greater working-parent financial insights, capability, and calm. To put together your own best child-plus-career money system, the very first step is to understand what's coming.

The Three Financial Phases of Working Parenthood

The whole eighteen-year timeline of working parenthood seems to have the same financial headline: *Major Cash Outflow*. But peer in closer, and you'll see that working-parent-related money pressures vary meaningfully from one phase of your child's life to the next. If you're aware of those differences, you can prepare for them, make better in-the-moment money decisions, and avoid common and costly mistakes.

Economic Phase One begins the moment you learn that you're expecting your first child and ends the day he starts regular care. It's a sort of financial honeymoon; you get to experience the joys of parenthood without having to bear the brunt of ongoing, month-to-month workparent costs. It's also time to get a jump on what's coming—to think in detail through your working-parent budget; get smart and file for any corporate or government working-parent benefits, like childcare tax credits or subsidized backup care; start building some extra financial cushion, if possible; and get confident on ways to handle the various money challenges ahead. If you're in Phase One now, try "budgeting as if," depositing the estimated costs of daycare, backup

> ❝ I spent a lot of time looking at my finances, and I got a lot of gear used. I realized it wasn't the baby that was expensive, or the gear; it was primarily the care. When you're looking at the cost of care, focus on the length. Think, 'When will this end?' and plan for that expense. And also, let go of any guilt around whatever else you're spending, or can't buy. Kids grow up in all kinds of situations, and they're fine, in fact they thrive, as long as their basic needs are fully met."
>
> —*Kayla, academic program director, mother of one*

> " If I could go back in time, I would have tried to save more. I'm a
> born, bred, and buttered city dweller, but living here is expensive,
> particularly as a single mom.
>
> When my son was born a friend gifted me a year's worth of free legal
> advice. I was able to get a will set up, and life insurance. And instead
> of a baby registry, I asked friends for contributions toward childcare.
> Having that security felt so good."
>
> —*Rachel, event producer, mother of one*

care, and so forth each month into a dedicated Workparent Reserve
bank account that you can tap into as needed later. Then, when the
baby actually arrives or daycare starts, you'll already be accustomed to
workparent spending, have some small bit of financial wiggle room,
and have a feeling of *I'm on this and I get it* self-assurance.

Economic Phase Two starts on that first day of care and lasts until
each of your children is enrolled in school full-time. Let's not mince
words: this may be the toughest financial patch of your life. You're most
likely still earlier-on in your career, your earnings haven't yet peaked,
and you may be paying off student or car debt or trying to save for a
house when—*wham!*—suddenly you're also hit with the costs of care
for one or more children. During this period you may find yourself
panicked about the possibility of completely going off the financial
rails—or having to take drastic action (taking on a second or third job,
selling the house, accepting help you normally wouldn't, etc.) to avoid
that derailment. You may also:

- Go into economic siege mode, shutting off any and all other
  spending that could make working parenthood more feasible in
  the short term

- Develop "what the heck, we're hemorrhaging cash anyway"
  habits

- Decide to leave your career entirely because it just feels too
  expensive to work

- Lose sight of the longer term, fall into a "we're never going to get anywhere financially" mindset, and become overwhelmed and depressed

Don't make those mistakes, though, because the key thing to bear in mind about Phase Two is that *it ends.* In **Economic Phase Three**, which starts on the day your child begins school, you get to trade in full time daycare costs for after-school-program fees—which, financially speaking, is like getting a huge raise. Then, by the early teenage years, care costs should largely or completely disappear, which will feel like yet another bump in your income. Note that while expenses go down during Phase Three, they're usually much lumpier: when school is out for the summer, for example, and your child needs daily care, your working-parent outlay will spike. Beware also that the money choices you do face during this phase may have an uncomfortable, "my future versus the kids' future" quality to them. Just as retirement planning and mortgage pay-down start becoming more important, you'll start feeling more pressure to invest in the kids' extracurricular activities, and to save for their longer-term education.

With that high-level, no-holds-barred view of how your working-parent financial story is likely to unfold, how do you feel? If you're swal-

Setting the tone

You started picking up your own money feelings and habits from the adults around you early on in your life. Now, your child is taking her money cues from *you:* watching your body language when, after a long day on the job, you sit down to pay the bills; gauging your reaction when she asks for that new toy; observing how you check, or don't check, the price of each item that goes in your basket at the super-market; taking in how you talk about your role as a working parent.

Be aware of the messages you're sending—both deliberate and inadvertent—about earning and spending money, and about the trade-offs needed to make your working-family budget come together. Make sure those messages align with how you want your child to think and feel (Safe? Frugal? Comfortable? In charge?) about money now, and as an adult and working parent one day herself.

lowing hard and thinking, *whoa, there's some tough, lean years ahead*, you're not alone. Again, the critical thing to take away here is that you're in a changing game—and with a better understanding of how the financial demands of working parenthood will shift over time, you'll be in a better position to start putting together your very own plan to meet them.

Where Do You Stand?

Once you've gazed down the financial road, it's time to confront your personal financial truth: to get a full-frontal, nonretouched view of your current money situation; to calculate your Total Cost of Working Parenthood (which we'll do in table 11-1); and to figure out what you need to do to make those two things come together. That may sound painful, but don't cringe. There's no review-every-receipt process ahead, or evaluation and finger-pointing about past choices; what we're doing is focusing on the resources you *do* have and how to make the most of them. As we work, we're going to leave negative feelings to the side, focus in on the line items most important to you as a working mother or father, and determine some real and useful next steps—and we're going to move along quickly. In fact, these next two sections should take you no more than about ninety minutes. All you'll need to complete them, and to become more on-it and empowered in terms of your working-parent finances, is some peace and quiet, a computer or tablet, access to your personal financial records, and the willingness to look at your money situation with fresh and unbiased eyes. Ready? Then let's dive in.

Our first task is to understand what you're earning and what you're spending in the normal course of business. If you already keep detailed financial records in one central place, like on a spreadsheet or in a personal-finance app, by all means, work from there. If not, no problem: just grab your most recent annual tax filing and pull up your last month's bank statement and credit-card bill. (The beauty of the more-cards/less-cash economy is that our financial institutions now do most of our personal financial record-keeping for us.)

With that information in front of you, you should be able to fill in the first two full columns in the Working-Parent Financial Dashboard (table 11-1). These portions of the dashboard let you understand, in

TABLE 11-1

The Working-Parent Financial Dashboard

Income	Regular Expenses	Working-Parent Costs

Income

Annual:

+	Salary or hourly wages	$ _____
+	Tips, overtime, bonuses, and commissions	$ _____
+	Any other income (investment income, annuities, help from family, cash benefits, etc.)	$ _____
=	Total annual income	$ _____
−	Total annual taxes	$ _____
=	Total annual income, after tax	$ _____

Regular Expenses

Monthly:

+	Housing	$ _____
+	Food	$ _____
+	Education	$ _____
+	Clothing	$ _____
+	Transportation	$ _____
+	Utilities and insurance	$ _____
+	Phone, internet, and data	$ _____
+	Health, medical, and wellness	$ _____
+	Debt payments (student loans, car loans, etc.)	$ _____
+	Retirement savings	$ _____

Working-Parent Costs

Monthly:

DIRECT COSTS

+	Daycare center or babysitter fees	$ _____
+	Ancillary childcare costs (overtime, late pickup, babysitter food allowance, etc.)	$ _____
+	Backup care	$ _____
+	After-school programs	$ _____
+	Summer care and programs (effective monthly cost)	$ _____
+	Off-hours or fill-in sitters	$ _____

INDIRECT COSTS

+	Reduced hours, lost tips, overtime not worked, salary cut due to four-day week, etc.	$ _____

Months per year 12

A = Total Monthly Income $_____

+ Other savings (emergency fund, college, other) $_____
+ Discretionary spending (entertainment, travel, etc.) $_____

B = Total Monthly Expenses $_____

ADDITIONAL EXPENSES

+ Household help, laundry service, extra commuting costs, etc., connected to working parenthood $_____

ANY WORKING-PARENT-SPECIFIC BENEFITS

− Corporate benefits (daycare or subsidies) $_____
− Tax benefits (any child tax credits, use of pretax dollars for childcare, etc.) $_____

C = Total Cost of Working Parenthood $_____

Total Working-Parent Budget Surplus or Shortfall: (A minus B minus C) $_____

The quarterly review

To stay on top of your working-parent situation as it changes over time, think about scheduling an every-three-months financial review. Those quarterly check-ins will be just enough to let you feel, and stay, in full control of working-parent money matters, without undue time and hassle.

Keep these sessions brief, and during each one, repeat the financial dashboard exercise (see table 11-1), but with an eye toward any recent trends or upcoming changes. Have there been any new or unusual expenses? Will the switch to full-time school, and the savings that that brings in daycare costs, mean you can put more into your retirement accounts? How much will day camp or another care alternative cost this coming summer, when the kids are out of school? Be sure to leave each session with specific, actionable next steps: if that includes setting aside money for day camp and increasing your retirement contributions, both of those items go straight onto your Monday-morning to-do list.

one quick glance, what you're earning each month and what you're spending, before any items specific to working parenthood are factored in. Feel free to customize the dashboard to meet your particular financial picture, and don't worry if you're not able to calculate every number down to the penny or if you have to use a little guesstimation. This is a decision-making tool, not an accounting exam.

Now let's focus on that third column: the one labeled Working-Parent Costs. Here, we're going to calculate the total monthly expenses specifically attributable to the fact that you're combining children and career. We'll look at direct, visible costs—like childcare—and also at indirect or hidden costs, like the overtime pay you're missing because you need to be home by 6:00. Do your best to fill in each item, even if you have to approximate. Be honest and thorough.

With all three columns completed, take a step back and—without touching your pen or keyboard or doing any more math—look at the whole, and ask yourself:

- Is there anything here that surprises me? Am I spending more or less than I imagined in any one category?

- Is my money spent in a way that honors what I see as, and say is, important? Should I reallocate where some of my cash is going, even if I spend the same overall amount?

- Roughly how much of a "workparent raise" will I get when the economic phase I'm in right now ends? In other words, how much more will I be earning (in overtime, commissions, and so forth), and how much less will I be spending (on care, backup sitters, etc.), as my kids grow up?

There are no right, wrong, or necessarily even precise answers to these questions. And in fact, they're not ones you'll likely be able to answer neatly or straightaway. In nudging yourself to think through them, however, you'll develop a *complete* sense of your working-parent finances: what real choices you're making, what's working and what isn't, how your money is matching your life and values, and how your financial picture will change in the near term. You'll come to understand where you are today—and the important directions you need to move in.

Your Workparent Budget

We've been getting the lay of the budgetary land from ten thousand feet up, but now it's time to swoop down to ground level. Go back to the line item at the very bottom of the dashboard, your Total Working-Parent Budget Surplus or Shortfall. Calculate it by subtracting your total monthly expenses and total monthly cost of working parenthood from your total monthly take-home pay (Box A minus Box B minus

> " It's a catch-22 with shift work. You can do a lot of overtime, but the more you earn, the less you're at home. I have to ask myself, 'What is the bigger paycheck *for?*' We just put an addition on the house, but the boys won't be five and three forever. It's not an exact science; we're constantly trying to balance it. I'll work a bunch of OT until my wife just kind of looks at me—and then I know to pull back."
>
> —*Mike, police officer, father of two*

One trick for make cutting back a little easier

Of course you want to be budget conscious—but the time spent hovering on whether or not to spring for that new cell phone, and on feeling guilty about the cash you drop on lattes, is much better used thinking about other, bigger things: like career advancement, your own well-being, or the kids' education.

To save money *and* keep yourself out of the rabbit hole of financial overthinking, try making categorical cuts: simple, specific, one-and-done decisions about when and where to curb your outflow. If you have a longtime personal policy of *never* buying clothes unless they're on sale, or *only* buying used cars, then you're already using this strategy effectively. Now just apply it to your working-parent budget: for example, you may decide that no matter how busy you are, your family will never eat out on weeknights, or that you'll only allow the kids to do one fee-based extracurricular activity per semester. The key words here are *never* and *only*. Using them turns vague fiscal intentions ("spend less on eating out," "don't go overboard on the kids' activities") into fiscal rules—ones that protect you from overspending *and* from having to expend time, thought, and emotion wading through hundreds of one-off money decisions.

Box C). If this number is negative, think of it as a hole: you're going to have to earn more money, use your savings, borrow, or cut your expenses to plug it. If it's positive—if you have a budget surplus—think of it as a wallet with money inside you can choose to save, spend, or use in a way that helps make working parenthood easier.

Now, with that macro view of your finances, and with awareness of the precise amount of your surplus or shortfall, you're ready to make any needed financial decisions. If you were surprised by how much you were spending on entertainment, or by how little you were investing in health and wellness, for example, you can reallocate. If you're running a surplus, you might decide that it's OK to hire a regular Saturday-night sitter, after all. If your daycare costs are creating a shortfall, you can grit your teeth and go back line by line over your expenses and figure out where else to cut.

Two items worth spending on

Even if money is tight, don't ignore two financial safety nets important for every working parent: disability insurance and life insurance. Even if you're young and healthy today, you could—as terrible as it is to think about—face a health problem or have an accident at any time. If you do, and if that means you're no longer able to work to support your family, the financial impact could be devastating. Imagine your family budget—the same mortgage, childcare expenses, and car payments, the same hopes and dreams for your kids—but without you, and without the money you're earning now to make it all happen.

Whether you're an expectant parent or have teenagers, don't give these items short shrift. Set aside time to understand any coverage your employer offers. Look at what your options are, what they cost, what payouts would amount to in the event of illness or injury, how that money would be combined with any government-paid disability benefits—and most important, figure out how to enroll. If you don't yet have a life-insurance policy, set a timeline for getting one in place. You may be able to get a low-cost policy through work, or may need to do more research and go through an independent agent or broker.

Ideally, your family will never need either of these protections—but in the event they do, the money you invested in them will be the best you ever spent.

If you are in shortfall territory, this part of the budgeting process won't be any fun. In fact, it may be downright scary. You may realize that working-parent expenses are going to force you to stop saving, or spend all your savings, or move back in with your own parents, none of which you want to do. You may roll your eyes and think, *why did I ever even start this budgeting exercise if it was going to point me to such painful realities?* But the realities were there all along: what you're doing now—rightly and responsibly—is confronting and managing them. You're driving the same car, but can now see the dashboard, which lets you set your financial direction and create the very best life you can for the kids. And crucially, you're *forecasting*—looking out the car's windshield and at your money situation today and what it will look like down the road.

Putting it all together: Devin's story

" We were living in adult Never Never Land. We rented an apartment downtown, in a new building with a pool. I would spend my tips on whatever I wanted. We had student loans and credit-card debt. Then my wife brought up the idea of having a baby.

I'm very pragmatic, and I remembered seeing that personal-finance TV show with the segment where viewers call in and ask, 'Can I afford it?' We went to a financial adviser, who looked at everything we had and owed and told us, 'On paper, right now, no, you can't afford to become parents.' Then he pointed out that no one really can—it's such a huge expense, and there's never really a right time to take it on.

When we were expecting, we made a really careful budget. We changed our lives, drastically. We moved in with my wife's mom for a year, and paid down our debts. We got ourselves to the zero-dollar mark—a total financial clean slate. We gave up our city-kid lives permanently and bought a condo in a much cheaper area. I changed how I earn my living, too, moving to a new salon where the environment is less fierce, where there's a happy clientele and it's OK to have a family. I'm still doing my thing and love this profession. I just figured out how to make the earnings part match up better with being a dad.

I had always assumed that you had to be in perfect financial standing *before* having a child. It's not easy, but you can get your act together while you're on this journey."

—*Devin, hairdresser, father of one*

Common Workparent Money Dilemmas, and How to Think Through Them

No matter how carefully calibrated our budgets, as working moms and dads we *all* find ourselves grappling with tough, seemingly unresolvable money questions. Each one you face will be completely personal and unique: to your career, your family, your income, your feelings. Most of them, however, will be variations on the Big Four Workparent Money Dilemmas. Let's explore each one.

Guilt-spending

You've been traveling for work all week, so you stop by the airport gift shop before your flight home to buy your five-year-old son a T-shirt. Or with both you and your partner working in superintense jobs and missing so many family dinners, you decide to make each of the kids' birthday parties serious extravaganzas.

In other words, you're *guilt-spending*.

Guilt-spending is a trap that nearly all working parents, regardless of wealth or income, fall into at some point. It resembles spoiling, with the critical difference that it comes from a well-intentioned and deeply sincere place. You love your children completely, and you're determined to prove that love—to the kids, to other people, and to yourself—even when your job keeps you away.

The problem with guilt-spending is that it creates a "race to the bottom" for both parent and child. For a very brief period after you spend the money, your child is happy (*look—a new T-shirt!*) and your sense of guilt is eased. Then those good feelings dissipate, and the cycle starts again. And this time, it's worse: you feel just as crummy and anxious as you did before, but your bank account is lower, and your child has been conditioned to expect—even demand—expensive things she doesn't need.

As you reach for your wallet to pay for treats, gifts, and "stretch" items, ask yourself: Who is this purchase really benefitting, and why am I really making it? Then think about other, less money-based ways of showing your love. Send your five-year-old a postcard (small children love to receive mail); host a small, relaxed birthday celebration in the backyard—and spend every minute focused on your child, rather than on the hordes of guests. Your time and attention are more valuable to your child than anything you buy them.

How am I supposed to prioritize my spending, when every item (daycare, retirement savings, my mortgage, those college-prep classes, etc.) is so critically important?

The current, conventional-wisdom answer to this question, borrowed from the language of airplane safety videos, is to "put your own oxygen mask on first"—meaning, pay attention to and prioritize your own personal financial needs ahead of your kids'. That's certainly a vivid image, and the message on financial self-care is well taken. Yet it's very general guidance, and thus hard to use in the day-to-day. And let's get real: as a devoted mother or father, you're *never* going to skimp on your children's fundamental needs to cover your own. So let's stay out of the realm of metaphors and get much more honest and specific.

One simple but usable way to think about your workparent financial priorities is to categorize them, and then give those categories names, an order by rank, and percentages, as demonstrated in table 11-2. In this table, major items from your working-parent budget have been put into suggested groups, and those groups into a suggested sequence, with *must-do/must-have* type expenses up at the top and *if you've got the extra*

TABLE 11-2

A Guide for Making Working-Parent Financial Decisions

Priority	Key components	Allocated percentage of my budget
1. Short-term security	• Safe and adequate childcare • Housing • Food • Transportation • Emergency-reserve savings	*What (realistic) percentage of your take-home pay should be spent on each category?*
2. Long-term security	• Insurance • Debt repayment • Retirement savings	
3. Investment in the future	• Ongoing professional education, certifications, and networking • College savings • Contributions to any other investment portfolio	
4. Lifestyle, interests, and fun	• Sports, activities, and hobbies • Vacations/travel • Charitable donations • Clubs and memberships • Larger home, newer car, more clothes, etc.	

money items at the bottom. Each category prompts you to think through a rough, *How much of my money should be going toward this?* percentage allocation.

The first category in this stack is—no surprise—the kids' immediate welfare and safety. Next comes the family's financial security, both today and into the post-parenting years. With these more basic and pressing needs covered, investment-spending on the future becomes possible: you can put money toward your kids' education, toward your own professional advancement, and into other assets that will put you on a stronger economic and personal footing over time. With any money left over, you can (here and there) spend on what makes you happy—whether that's a new car or piano lessons for the kids. When you're facing tough trade-offs or forced to prioritize a specific expense, you now have a basic framework for doing so—a way to sanity-check your thinking and make sure you're generally making sensible and consistent financial decisions.

Note that this is a *sample, suggested* framework—one you'll want to make your own, and adjust over time. You might live in a very high-housing-cost area for right now, and need to devote much more of your budget to Category 1; or you might decide that, come hell or high water, you're going to pay the kids' educational expenses, moving that commitment up in rank from where we have it, in Category 3. Try marking this table up with your own additions and tweaks; you know what's most important, and you'll rejigger accordingly. Then, the next time you're confronted with a tough money decision, pull the framework back out and use it to challenge, and validate, your own thinking. If you find yourself stretching to pay for Category 1 items, but spending on Category 3 and 4, or putting too much money into Category 2 and none into 3, you'll know that it's time to rebalance.

What if working doesn't put me ahead financially? I hate the thought of just handing my paycheck over to a sitter.

Nobody wants to be on a financial treadmill, particularly when the reward for hopping off is getting to spend more time with the child you love. That said, before you make what seems at first blush like a completely sensible and responsible decision, try taking a wider-lens view.

Maybe today you *are* spending 100 percent of your take-home pay, and then some, on childcare. But if you keep working, your earnings are likely to go *up* over time. Maybe you'll get a promotion, a raise, or a new gig that pays more . . . and don't forget, as soon as you exit Economic Phase Two, the costs of childcare will go way *down*. Very soon, the equation will change, and the moment it does, it will make tons of dollars-and-cents sense to work. And if you do stay in the professional game, you'll be building up other important assets, like your résumé, your experience, your network, and your retirement-plan balance. On the other hand, if you decide to bow out of the workforce, it may be hard to get back in; you may have to take a significant pay cut when you do. And if your partner happens to lose his or her job during your career break, it may lead to serious financial strain.

There's nothing wrong with a short-term detour off the professional highway, and taking one can come with some wonderful benefits. But if you're rushing into a quit-my-job decision based *only* on the arithmetic of your current cash flow, take the time to really think things through. Staying on that treadmill may be both a good insurance policy and a wise investment.

For specific advice on how to plan and take a career sabbatical with confidence and with a clear way "back in," refer to chapter 17, "Time Off."

Can I take a more flexible job, even if it comes with lower pay?

The decision to "go flex" hangs on a number of different factors, including your career ambitions, your family situation, and what line of work you're in. In chapter 15, we'll unpack all of your flexibility options, and how, when, and why to access and use them. From a purely financial perspective, though, taking lower pay in exchange for more control over your workload and schedule is fine, as long as four key conditions are met:

1. There's no major Category 1 or 2 financial impact to your family as a result of the switch—i.e., working a little less doesn't compromise your top-line financial priorities

2. You've determined that there's no way to get the flexibility you're seeking in your current job, or in another one that offers the same level of pay

3. You don't let yourself get taken advantage of, for example by accepting a three-day-per-week pay package but really working four

4. The door swings both ways—in other words, you could relatively quickly and easily reach your prior earning level

In such cases, you should feel comfortable with the flexibility-versus-income trade-off. If you do so, though, go back and rework your dashboard, keeping a realistic eye on any needed budgeting changes.

Is it OK to spend money on products and services that make working parenthood a little easier to handle? I feel guilty when I do.

If you were raised in a family with finite resources or you're used to a do-more-with-less professional environment (as nearly all of us were, and are), then spending money on "luxury" items like taxis, a housecleaner, that bulk-laundry service, food takeout, next-day delivery of household supplies, or a special kitchen gizmo that steams and zaps any fruit or vegetable into baby-ready puree may—even if it helps bridge the chasm between your professional and personal responsibilities—feel strange, self-indulgent, even wrong.

Of course you can't hand over money you don't have, and you're not going to make dumb, self-defeating decisions like skimping on childcare just to avoid doing laundry. But let's go back to a big, fundamental point we covered at the very beginning of this book: working parenthood has only gotten harder in the past fifteen years—*and nothing and no one has stepped into the fray to help individual mothers and fathers make it happen.* If you're pulling long hours on the job and have the $50 to spend, using that laundry service isn't a luxury—it's just plain prudent. If your great-grandma who lived through the Great

Depression saw what you're going through as a working parent today, she'd tell you to spend that money.

To get yourself a little more comfortable with the "outsource where possible" approach, and at the same time to keep a nice tight grip on your financial steering wheel, go back to your working-parent budget, look at your discretionary spending and your surplus or shortfall, figure out how many working-parent dollars per month you can dedicate to make-it-easier products and services, and then hold yourself to it. If you find $75 per month in *making workparenting easier* dollars, then you spend all $75, every single month, confidently and guilt-free.

Making Money Matters Logistically Easier

Having a clear, realistic working-parent budget is important, but so is simplifying and streamlining the actual block-and-tackle operations of your financial life. When you're this busy, you never want to spend what could have been a relaxed evening with the kids hunched over a spreadsheet and a stack of bills, or to find yourself without any cash on hand to pay the emergency sitter. Happily, whatever your finances look like, you can probably cut down on money-management logistics—and on the time and effort you put into them. A few good approaches:

- Consolidate. If you've got multiple checking, savings, investment, or retirement accounts, consider merging them and maintaining just one of each. The more accounts you have, the harder it is to understand your true financial picture, and getting so many different statements each month creates clutter and distraction. If you've moved jobs or changed family structure within the past five years, there's a high likelihood you're hanging on to some legacy accounts. Go as streamlined and simple as you can.

- Automate. Put all your regular monthly expenses—including the daycare bill, your daughter's violin lessons, and the money you've committed to setting aside toward college savings—onto a direct-debit plan or autopay. Avoiding those repeat manual transactions will save you significant time. Next, activate the "account alert" features your bank and your credit-card company offer. With automated updates, you won't have to log in as often to check your spending or balances.

- Go completely electronic. If you're still receiving paper statements or bills, or if you've handwritten more than a couple of checks over the past year, it's an opportunity to streamline. Opening paper statements and then feeding them into

Is it time to consult an expert?

Many of your working-parent financial questions—if and how to claim parental tax credits, set up college savings accounts, use pretax dollars for qualified childcare expenses, and so on—can be answered quickly and for free via your organization's intranet or HR team or by scanning the personal-finance educational materials and tip sheets published online by most of the major banks and brokerage firms.

That said, if you have complex finances, if your taxes are time-consuming to prepare, if you own your own business, or if you're working through a financial life transition (such as divorcing, vesting in a stock plan, or receiving an inheritance), then enlisting the services of an experienced professional adviser or money manager may make sense. That person can help explain technical tax issues, help you create a plan for retirement savings, or help you see around some of the important financial corners up ahead—which can translate into both more time with your kids and more money to invest where it really matters. Be aware, however, that the quality of the "expert" advice out there varies widely, and that money-management services may come with varying fees. You may also find yourself pushed into certain decisions, accounts, or investments that yield your adviser a tidy commission but aren't to your own benefit.

If you do decide to work with a financial adviser of any kind, make sure to do thorough research on the adviser's background and qualifications, and on specific services offered. Ask any candidate point-blank how much experience he or she has in advising working-parent families. If you do retain professional help, remain an informed consumer and be sure to make your own money decisions. Your buck always stops with *you*.

a shredder is a complete waste of your valuable time (not to mention no good for the environment). Log in to each of your accounts and authorize e-notification. Ensure that you have a cashless system worked out with the Village, also—an app that lets you pay the sitter electronically, for example.

- **Stash cash where you'll need it.** Even in our superefficient, cashless world, you'll still need it. Always keep small amounts of money in small denominations in the kitchen, at the office, in the diaper bag, in the car—and you'll always be ready to tip the pizza-delivery guy on the night you don't have time to make the kids dinner.

- **Ensure all caregivers have access.** If you've hired an in-home caregiver, you'll need to make sure that she always has enough money on hand to cover day-to-day expenses (gas, food shopping, outings with the kids) as well as any emergencies (that sudden taxi to the pediatrician's, getting the pharmacy to deliver the prescription). One smart way to do so is by giving her a refillable debit card: you'll be able to add money to it at the touch of a button, from anywhere, as needed (during a meeting; from an airport, during a layover), and because you control the account, you'll easily be able to monitor any spending. Likewise, and for your own peace of mind, you'll want to make sure that your child's Third Parents and any emergency care providers have adequate money, too. Provide each of them with a similar debit card, tuck some cash into your child's emergency backup bag, or both.

Real Parents, Real Returns

When you hand over hard-earned money, you want to *get* something for it, whether that's new clothes, a holiday, an apartment, a share of stock, or an education—something that satisfies a need, that gives you pleasure, that you can hold on to, or that helps you move *forward* in some way. But now, as a working parent, it may feel as if you're shelling out huge amounts just to run very quickly in place. Paying that daycare bill means that you can go to work and earn money to pay the daycare bill . . . and then get up tomorrow to do it all over again.

Yet the money you're spending now to fit family and career together isn't wasted, and it doesn't disappear. When your kids are safe and well taken care of, it frees you up, both practically and mentally, to deliver your best at work. As you achieve, and as your career progresses, you become better able to provide for your family, both today and in the future. The money you're spending now is a powerful long-term investment.

PART THREE

Success—on Your Own Terms

Accomplishing What You Want, in the Way You Want—at Work and at Home

n the first sections of this book we looked at how you could make the Big Transition to working parenthood and set up an effective workparent operating system. Now let's talk about *you*: your ambitions, where you want to take your career, what it will take to get there, and what that might look and feel like along the way. We'll cover promotions and job changes and all of the other events and decisions that normally get tucked into the manila folder marked career success, but with our eyes firmly on the issues, questions, and apprehensions most central for you as a workparent: *Does part-time work actually work? How do I talk to my manager, and that interviewer, about my ambition and my care needs? Can I take on more, without sacrificing time with the kids? Is striking out on my own the answer? Will I ever get any time off?*

With the tools and perspectives you'll gain here in part 3, you'll be able to move your thinking *and* your career forward, and in the direction you want.

12

Getting Ahead

Everything You Want to Know About Moving Up Professionally While Parenting—but May Be Hesitant to Ask

O f *course* you've always wanted to move up. What a no-brainer! But now, with children, professional matters have become more complex, and more personal, and your career goals may have shifted, and it may feel riskier to put your cards down on the table and talk about things honestly—with anyone. As a result, the critical career-next-steps conversations you need to have may not be happening, or happening only inside your own head, or not leading to answers or action.

Of course, you can choose to stay on that path—or we can take a different one together, and have the professional-advancement dialogue you need safely and confidentially, right here and now. As soon as we confront your workparent career questions head-on, and get the worries, fears, and assumptions that may be coloring your thinking out in the open, we can work through them all in a thoughtful, calm way.

Let's start with the most fundamental question—and continue our conversation from there.

Do I even *want* to move up? Shouldn't my priorities be more centered at home now, and on the kids?

The hidden worries, common fears, and ingrained assumptions that may be shaping your thinking:

- *If I'm spending so much time and mental energy on my career, it's evidence that I'm not devoted enough to my children.*

- *I can have a big career or be a good parent, but I can't do both; nobody can.*

- *The people around me will judge, reject, or laugh at me if I try to "have it all."*

Let's start by unpacking that dangerous concept of *should*. In chapter 1, we reviewed your Workparent Template: the aggregate experiences, impressions, and bits of advice that have shaped your view of working parenthood, and of what a working parent is and does. Now—and every time you catch the word *should* wending its sneaky way back into your thinking about being a working parent—pull your template notes back out and take a good look at them.

It's very possible that you genuinely *don't* want to pursue that big new job opportunity. Maybe you're enjoying the phase the kids are in now, or maybe—to your surprise—becoming a parent tamped down your professional ambitions a little. You might love your particular role, or this time in your career, and find that career happiness makes you a better parent. On the other hand, maybe you're just as ambitious as ever, but you've gotten the impression that you "should" be focusing more on the kids or making certain career-restraining decisions because that's what your own parents did, or your colleagues do, or because of how you've seen parenthood portrayed on TV. As you think the "do I or don't I want this" question through, try to be as conscious as you can about what you *actually* want, versus what outside influences have led you to think you're supposed to want. This is your own life, not anyone else's, and if you're managing toward *should*s you're giving up way too much control.

Different parents, different feelings about ambition

❝ I didn't realize how well suited I was to this job until we had kids. I used to have more of a 'gig' mindset, but when I upped my game and started working the way I do now, it was a revelation. I'm more productive when I'm busy. I love having a full bucket, meeting people, being the face of each property. It's not that I write down specific goals or targets each year: I just have a visual, and I put my head down and work until I get there. It's a big, busy life, and it's so nice to know that when I turn the key in the door at the end of the day, I'll see the kids, and have that reset."

—*Brian, real estate agent, father of two*

❝ I leave the house at 7:00 a.m., and I'm not back till 9:30 p.m. I do the store's merchandising, HR, the employee training, whatever needs to be done. Most of the time, I'm standing. It's a long, hard day, but I do it for my kids. They, and their education, come first. Since preschool, we've been talking to them about college. Whatever it takes to make the kids successful—that's my mission."

—*Jennifer, retail store manager, mother of three*

❝ Before kids, I had it in my head to move up. But being in the senior executive service means late nights, unexpected travel. I have to be able to pick my kids up from daycare—and I want to be able to go on vacation without my laptop. I'm still ambitious. You don't ever fully quiet that voice. It's deferred, not gone."

—*Anne Marie, government contracting officer, mother of two*

❝ You'll still have good ambition, but it may not be the exact same kind of burning ambition. It might not be as much about that next rung on the ladder anymore. Roll with it."

—*João, management consultant, father of two*

If you genuinely want to advance professionally but are nursing apprehensions about what will happen if you do, try making a list of all the positives and advantages that would come with the move. That bigger job might bring a bigger paycheck, or a team to help you get all the work done, or much more leeway in determining your schedule.

How does the decision look with those upsides in mind, as well as any potential risks?

Next, get out and talk to other people in your field who have walked this same path and are a few steps farther ahead. How have they combined children and career? Did advancement turn their lives into disaster zones—did their families fall apart, did their careers derail, or did they find themselves heaped with societal scorn for accepting promotions while parenting? Maybe they *did* have difficult experiences you could learn from. More likely, though, their stories will help soothe your anxieties and help provide some solid, practical direction on how to go about taking on more.

But the kids are so little (or just starting school, or getting bigger and need me in additional ways). Is now the right time to put my foot on the accelerator?

Hidden worries, common fears, ingrained assumptions:

- *This is a critical time in my kids' lives, and if I'm not really there for them, they may suffer from it/perform poorly at school/have social or developmental issues/feel unloved/end up on a psychiatrist's couch.*

- *There are fundamentally right and wrong times for focusing on my career.*

- *If I'm thinking about wanting more right now, it shows that I am a selfish person.*

Let's put a different spin on the question: When *will* it be the right time for you to think about taking on more? While your kids are little, they need huge amounts of physical and emotional caretaking. Then they start school and need you to help guide them as they begin to make their own way in the world, both academically and socially. Then they're teenagers, and it's critical for you to be "on them" in terms of safety and helping figure out their own passage toward adulthood. In other words, your kids need you at every phase, and all the time. Before they become fully self-sufficient adults there's not likely to be a point at which you can heave a huge sigh of relief and refocus single-

> " I hustled to get this business going. I started blogging, took small jobs, invested my own money to get my website up. I wanted to do TV, and after getting a lot of doors slammed in my face, started getting spots on national shows. Some days, I'd be up and working at 4:30 a.m. My career was taking off like a rocket ship. When we moved across the country, I made a choice *not* to work like that—for now. I changed my business model so I could make a good living, still focus on the creative, *and* be a hands-on parent.
>
> Life isn't linear, and neither is career. This is a chapter: one in which I'm prioritizing both family and work. Not everybody would agree with that, but if you're going to live the life you want to, you can't care what other people think."
>
> —*Lorri, interior designer, mother of two*

mindedly on your career. If you do wait for that moment to come, you could be waiting for a very long time. It may be helpful to think about timing in terms of opportunities, preferences, and supports (*Do I want this? Would I be foolish to overlook this terrific opportunity? Do I have the right kind of care in place to make this happen?*) rather than in terms of hitting some objectively "correct" window.

As you consider what the right timing is, though, do yourself a favor and think as holistically and practically as possible. For example, if your child is grappling with significant problems at school, or if in addition to workparenting you're also shouldering the burden of eldercare, perhaps your best move *isn't* to take the huge promotion or to relocate for that new job right now. If you're very nervous about your new childcare arrangement, maybe it *does* make sense to wait a few months and ensure that things are on a good track before taking on that stretch assignment. Be ambitious, but realistic: take your challenges a few at a time. You can always revisit your decision six months from now and decide on a different approach. You're smart, and committed to your work, and you'll find plenty of good opportunities.

As for any feelings of guilt or supposed selfishness: try displacing those by focusing on your sense of responsibility instead. You're working to support your family, and it's your job to do the very best you can in order to fulfill that goal. You're not thinking about moving up *despite* the kids, but *for* them.

Let's say I do want a promotion, a bigger role, or a better job elsewhere. As a busy workparent, how do I position myself and advocate for it?

Hidden worries, common fears, ingrained assumptions:

- *Workparenting has already stretched me paper-thin, emotionally. What if I raise my hand but this doesn't work out? Disappointment is the last thing I need.*

- *Since becoming a working parent, I just haven't been working or performing the way I used to. It would be ridiculous to think of myself as a candidate for advancement.*

- *Time is precious, and if I need to spend massive amounts of it on extra work, politics, networking, etc., for the sole purpose of getting ahead, that isn't going to be feasible.*

- *I don't want to look desperate, or like an idiot, when I ask for more.*

- *If I'm meant to get ahead, it will happen. I don't need to take an active role.*

When you became a working mother or father, chances are you also became so preoccupied, busy, and tired that your attention to career hygiene fell by the wayside. *Career hygiene* consists of all those things you do to keep your overall professional reputation and future in good form. It includes critical activities like networking, honing your technical skills, staying current on industry news and events, remaining visible to the powers that be, appropriate self-promotion, and raising your hand for unique assignments that can get you further into the career spotlight. It also includes smaller, more tactical items: keeping your LinkedIn profile fresh, having your "key wins and accomplishments" speech ready for when you bump into your boss's boss in the elevator, and so forth. Technically, none of those things has anything whatsoever to do with being a parent—but if you're not doing them *because* you're a parent, you're creating some real career headwinds for yourself and may be inadvertently stepping out of contention for that next big gig. If and when you decide to "go for it" careerwise, you'll want to move back into the front seat, so to speak, on all of these activities. Do an honest assessment, just for yourself: Hand on heart, how much opportunistic networking have you done since the baby was born? When's the last time you spoke to a professional recruiter? What about the monthly departmental after-work drinks events— have you been going to those? Have you given your career, and not just your work, adequate care and feeding? If not, you'll want to ease back into doing so.

If you're in a more acute career-management moment, like interviewing for a new role or pushing your boss for that big promotion, there's something else you'll want to do, which is to create a Third-Person Sell—essentially, a concise pitch about who you are as a professional, why the organization can't live without you, and why you deserve to be in a more senior seat. The Third-Person Sell is a means of pulling together the most compelling aspects of your skills and performance and "packaging" them in a way that feels comfortable and genuine to you, that will resonate with the relevant decision-maker, and that—most important—is easily repeatable. When the CEO of your organization turns to your boss and says, "tell me about [him or her]," your Sell is the two next sentences you want to come out of your boss's mouth. It's the senior-leader-resonant version of your professional story.

If you don't have your Sell ready (and few people do), let's go ahead and create it. To start, ask yourself, *How do I want to be known,*

> " This job is intense, and part of it involves being connected and visible, out in the field. But I can get all that networking done during the workday. I'll do calls from the office, spend fifteen minutes on LinkedIn, get down to London and back in one day—and still make it to pickup."
>
> —*Kayla, academic program director, mother of one*

professionally? Get into character a little: imagine you're the head honcho making the hire-or-promote decision (in this case, on yourself). What's *really* important to the organization's success, and why is this person—you—the man or woman particularly equipped to accomplish it? You're a flinty senior leader, and you've got many other candidates to consider. Why is this candidate uniquely qualified? If this person is hired, or advanced, what will he or she likely achieve? General personal qualities like loyalty or hard work are nice-to-haves, but not as impressive as three or four specific sales points that tie straight to the organization's goals. Can this person (you!) generate revenue, offer technical expertise, apply a rare skill, find new efficiencies, lead complex projects, forge new relationships, build a team?

If you need some step-by-step structure for creating your Sell, try using the worksheet in table 12-1. In the first two lines of the worksheet, you'll find sample "sales points" as a model for your own. The first is for a consumer-products executive shooting for promotion. The second is for a restaurant employee who's interested in moving into a manager role.

When you're done with your line-by-line work, try blending together the various points you've come up with in a sentence or two. Maybe you're *uniquely positioned to help this company grow in new markets, given your successful sales record,* or maybe you *combine the ability to deliver unique, creative designs while building team morale.* It's who you are . . . succeeding.

>   I wanted to do interesting, meaningful work *and* show up to chaperone my kids' school field trips. Since the kids were born I've taken a series of jobs that let me do that. That's meant a lot of conversations, and I've seen what really works.
>
>   I don't talk about my résumé, past titles, grades. I talk about what it is I actually *do*, and do well. I tell prospective employers: 'I start things that are new, I grow things that are small, and I fix things that are broken.' If they need those skills, they hire me."
>
> —*Ilana, nonprofit and political consultant, mother of two*

TABLE 12-1

Developing Your Third-Person Sell

	What drives this organization's success?	How you've contributed to it	Your "special sauce" for doing so	What you can achieve in the coming year	Impact to the organization
1.	Product innovation—bringing new items to market	Launched new brand offshoot last year	Unusually good at getting complex projects together; an effective bridge between R&D and marketing teams	Could find new ways to capitalize on existing/core products	Would allow us to reach new customer demographics; sales increase; make us look more relevant in changing market
2.	Filling seats in the restaurant; making sure we have a reliable, happy clientele	Four years of service here; routinely deal with extremely demanding/difficult customers	• Anticipating diners' needs; making them feel taken care of • Good relationships with other staff members	• Train new staff • Get more current customers to use our special events and catering services • Continue serving customers during busiest times	Differentiate ourselves from competing restaurants in the area; be known for an experience that goes beyond the food
3.					

This "branding" process may be a little cringe-inducing. It's awkward if not downright weird to imagine yourself being discussed by other professionals, and it's usually none too easy to toot your own horn in such a direct, sales-y way. On the other side of that discomfort, though, lies efficient, effective self-advocacy and a wonderfully increased sense of confidence. If you can speak about your career and achievements like this, your Sell is much more likely to resonate with the people it needs to. As you look over your completed table and refine your Sell statement, it will be a powerful reminder of why you *do* deserve the big job, and why—whether right now, or very soon— you'll be able to get it.

What if *because* I'm a working parent people don't see me as a candidate for bigger and better things? How do I handle that kind of pushback, and cope with skeptics and naysayers?

Hidden worries, common fears, ingrained assumptions:

- *This industry/profession/organization/management team isn't too family-friendly; there won't be tons of support for the idea of a working parent in a big-dog seat.*

- *The powers that be may ask me to make compromises I don't want to— like giving up flexibility—in exchange for an expanded role.*

- *Getting tough questions or pushback from the higher-ups is a sign that this promotion isn't going to happen.*

- *That one negative comment represents the views and attitudes of everyone in this organization/industry.*

The world is what the world is, and as a working parent, you may well face two distinct and very real types of professional bias.

The first is flat-out, straight-up bias: the company deliberately doesn't hire a lot of working parents, or you were told you were passed over for promotion because you just had a baby. That kind of nastiness and discrimination is plain wrong, but it does exist, and if you encounter it, you have two potential paths ahead. You can either challenge it—by

lodging a complaint, taking legal action, going public about your experiences, and so on—or you can choose to move on, and find a role in an
organization with more-supportive leaders and colleagues.

The more common, and more insidious, form of bias is what we'll
call *benign bias*. It comes from well-intentioned managers, colleagues,
and members of your professional network who assume that, because
you are now a parent, you need special accommodation or treatment—
that you may be a great professional but need to be handled with
kid gloves. Your manager may just assume that you don't want to be
put on that plum, career-making project because it will require extra
hours, for example, or that you're not up for overtime anymore. Or
other members of your team may make small talk with you *only* about
parenting or baby issues instead of about organizational moves or
interesting breakthroughs over in R&D. These colleagues likely all
mean well. They're trying to be sensitive, relieve pressure, signal support, or meet you where you live. If you're gunning for advancement,
however, their efforts may hold you back, and you will likely have to
gently and preemptively redirect them.

In table 12-2, you'll find examples of benign bias, how they might
affect you, and what you might say to address them.

In each case, as totally annoying as the comments and the sentiments
behind them might be, they are—in a backdoor, roundabout way—
intended in a positive spirit, and railing at them doesn't help. What *does*
help is to correct the other person's misperceptions directly, but in a
gentle, pleasant way that acknowledges the speaker's good intent. After
a few similar nudges, he or she should get the picture.

Bottom line: whenever you sense a lack of support for working parents, don't get flustered. Just think very carefully about what you want
to *do* about it.

What if I want more, but I'm already at full capacity?

Hidden worries, common fears, ingrained assumptions:

- *More? Are you kidding? I'm already on the brink. There's no way
  I can put more onto my plate right now without completely losing it.*

TABLE 12-2

Overcoming Benign Bias

Situation	Your potential, natural reaction	What to say
Upon announcing you're expecting your second child, your manager immediately assures you that you would be eligible for flex time upon your return from leave.	*Flex time? Are you for real? Last week we were talking about promotion, and now you're shoving me onto the Parent Track?*	"I'm so grateful you're attuned to what I might be going through as a parent. That said, please know that it's my intention to continue working just as I always have. If I do need flexibility, I'll definitely come back to you. Otherwise, assume that I'm focused on delivering great work, and on all the same goals and outcomes we've discussed in the past."
One of your mentors advises you against taking on a new, high-visibility project right now because it may be "too much."	*Aren't you supposed to be in my corner here? And why does everyone assume that parenthood changed my capabilities somehow? My whole career has been about handling "too much."*	"It is a lot, but I'm excited to take it on. Here are my thoughts on how we can get started . . ."
A senior manager begins each monthly departmental meeting by asking you "how the baby is."	*Why don't they just make me wear a big scarlet P on my chest, for Parent?*	"The baby's great! Regarding the progress we've made out at the construction site . . ."
Your boss's boss asks if you're interested in promotion, given the twins' arrival.	*I had children—not a personality transplant! Of course I'm still interested in promotion, otherwise why would I still be dealing with people like you, and totally crushing it every day at work?*	"I trust you to be the judge of my talent and capabilities. Please trust me to be the judge of my ambition and desire to take on more. Just so we're both clear: I'm still interested in moving ahead."

- *Taking on more increases the risk that I fail, or underperform.*

- *Bigger job = more work = longer hours.*

Good question—and here's the simple, truthful answer: if you want to take on *more*, then you're going to have to give something *up*.

If you tested positive for Do-It-Myselfism, per the assessment at the beginning of chapter 9, the idea of giving anything up might rub you the wrong way or feel completely impossible. Remember, though, that you're only one person, that there are only twenty-four hours in a day. No matter how committed and hardworking you are, there's a limit to how much you can take on, at home, at work, and certainly in combination. You can't keep cramming more bulky sweaters into a suitcase that's already full—either you won't be able to close it, or you'll break the zipper trying. The *only* way forward is to make some careful choices about what to take out: to decide what and how to unpack. Think about the successful, senior people you know in your profession, or organization. There are certain tasks and projects those people just don't do, or get too close to, whether that's writing their own marketing reports or getting to the grocery store. They've smartly realized that getting ahead is less about *buckling down* on an endlessly expanding to-do list and more about *letting go* of responsibilities. As you take this next critical step up, what do *you* plan to let go of, or at least loosen your grip on?

Try using table 12-3 as an organizational means of nudging yourself to come up with good, specific answers. Think through the various tasks and responsibilities you're on the hook for, both in your professional and personal life, and about how you handle each one: whether that's 1) taking total, top-to-bottom responsibility for the task yourself,

TABLE 12-3

What Will I Hold On To—and What Should I Let Go Of?

1.	2.	3.
Own it *Do it all myself*	**Delegate it** *. . . but keep tabs*	**Hand it off** *and don't look back*
• _____	• _____	• _____
• _____	• _____	• _____
• _____	• _____	• _____
• _____	• _____	• _____

2) delegating it to someone else but keeping tabs on it, or 3) completely passing it off. Go broad. Think about specific work projects, the mentoring of junior colleagues, the housework, the kids' school assignments—all the various things you've got on your docket. Try making a list of four or five items that fit each category.

Now, with your sample lists down on paper, stress-test them a little: Which one or two items from column 1 could reasonably be shifted over to column 2, and then which things in column 2 could be transferred to column 3? Now that you're getting ready to take on a bigger role, maybe instead of fully owning certain household or childcare tasks you could get (or even pay) a few Villagers to help, or someone else could draft and send that weekly update email you write to your department heads. Sure, there will be things you don't want to delegate, or get rid of, but your overall goal here is to *shift things right*—on a one-off basis and transactionally for now, and then on a repeat basis and as a habit over time. As you do so, you create capacity. The less you own and have to oversee, the more new and important work you can take on.

What if this goes in the wrong direction? What if I *do* get the bigger role, but it pulls me away from the kids, or makes it impossible to be the mom or dad I want to be . . . and I find myself miserable and stuck?

Hidden worries, common fears, ingrained assumptions:

- *Moving up means ceding additional control over my choices, priorities, and time.*

- *If I do make a commitment, there's no backing out. I won't be able to change my mind or adjust things later.*

Catastrophize here for a minute. Yes, you read that right: go ahead and play through the many and profound ways the new role or opportunity you're considering could go completely, terribly awry. Watch the career-horror movie! Nudge the plot along using a new technique: If/Then. Play things out to the final frame—and you'll find that it's not as scary as you thought.

> "   When I came back from my first leave I took my first manager position. It was a big step, and I wanted to prove myself. So I worked, a *lot*—staying late every day, not taking vacation for a year, responding to emails at 3:00 a.m. I got to a point of burnout, and where I wasn't bringing the best of myself home to my husband and baby.
>
> I realized I had to get strict about my work hours, and booking time off. I sent a message to the team explaining—and it was very well received. After you take the big job, you can recalibrate a little, if you need to."
>
> —*Tracy, nurse manager, mother of two*

Here's an example. Say you're thinking about signing up for a job at a new, high-growth firm. The job comes with a significant increase in salary—but you're apprehensive about what might be longer hours, and about your new boss, who doesn't have kids and may be unsympathetic to your family needs. Using If/Then, you'd work the scenario through as follows:

If I take this offer, then I might have to work longer hours, and

If I work longer hours, then that means all of my salary will be spent on sitters anyway and I'll still miss evenings with the kids, and

If that happens, then I'll be in the same place financially as in my old job, but also miserable, and a neglectful parent, and feel horrible and wrong, and

If that happens, and my new boss turns out to be a total jerk who doesn't allow me any flexibility, then . . .

You get the idea. Keep playing the drama out and pushing your fears to their very edges. And then, most important, keep right on going:

. . . and if I'm totally miserable and my kids are failing in school because they never see me and my boss is a terrible person who refuses my request for flexibility, then I'll decide to get a new job, and if I do decide to make a switch, then at least I'll already have a higher salary to use in my

negotiations, and if I do get a great new offer, then I'll be sure my new boss agrees on my hours before taking it . . . and so on.

By imagining your absolute worst-case scenario, you strip away much of its power over you. You also get to see the much more realistic final ending: that yes, there may be real risk in the new role, but that if things become completely untenable you'll chalk it all up to experience and find something different, and better. Staying trapped forever in the horrible-job dungeon is possible, but unlikely. As we've seen throughout the book, working parenthood is about constant recalibration. Beyond actually having a child, very few workparent decisions are ever permanent, or final. And anyway: in this drama, you're actor, writer, and director. If you need to change the plot and start shooting new scenes, you will.

Honestly, I don't really want "more"—I'm happy hanging out at this level, or even cutting back my work responsibilities a little. Is that even possible?

Hidden worries, common fears, ingrained assumptions:

- *Being a professional is like being a shark: you have to swim forward or die. If I'm not on a constant upward trajectory, I can kiss my career goodbye.*

- *There's no way to ask for less. Nobody around me has any real flexibility.*

There are certain professions, and organizations, with clear and explicit up-or-out policies and practices. You may be given *x* number of years to get to the next title level, or to build out your own business or client base. And for you as a working mother or father, that's scary: just as you're looking to pump the professional brakes a bit, time keeps whizzing by and the pressure keeps ratcheting up. All that said, you've got options.

Even in very rigid up-or-out organizations, you can often find a "career detour" of some kind. Maybe you could move into a staff role temporarily or get assigned to a special project for a defined amount

> ❝ You have more control and ability than you think you do to flatten out your career progression. After my kids were born, and my son was diagnosed with cerebral palsy, I spent five years not working, or working on a reduced schedule, before coming back full-time.
>
> If you're thinking about stepping back temporarily but feeling conflicted, ask yourself: Do I have a hero narrative going on? Try to figure out how much of that is internal and external to you."
>
> —*Lisa, executive search firm partner, mother of two*

of time. You may also be able to strike a specific deal with your employer: negotiating for extra time on the career clock in exchange for different responsibilities or reduced pay. Most up-or-out organizations suffer from high attrition among working parents (and increasingly, the negative brand image that goes along with that attrition) and thus may be willing to get creative with you to find a solution. If not—and as much as you might not want to hear this—you may need to seek work in an organization that offers different career paths, or change your type of employment, for example, by becoming a contractor or consultant instead of a full-time employee. Agreed, there may be drawbacks to any of those alternatives, but if you really and truly are staring anxiously down the barrel of an up-or-out career, it's important to know that there *are* other routes.

If you do want to pump the brakes in a high-octane field, and don't know a lot of other people who have, you may be feeling a little lonely. It's never easy to sense that you're somehow outside the professional mainstream or the "only" person not interested in being put up for VP this year. If that's the case, it's time to do some research. Start making some discreet inquiries with the other working parents you know in your field about mothers and fathers who have taken an at-my-own-pace approach to their careers. Also try pulling up the career profiles or bios of prominent people in your sector. Most careers, even blockbuster ones, involve some zigzagging through both the fast lane and the slow lane, and it can be reassuring to see that even the stars in your field have done such zigging and zagging.

> ❝ My son changed the trajectory of my life *and* my career. Growing up, I didn't have a lot of 'what are you going to do with your career?' conversations. When I found out I was going to be a parent I was still in school and waiting tables. All of a sudden, I was thinking about my professional life: not just how I was going to earn, but leave a legacy. That mindset helped me go out on my own and start this firm, and grow it, despite the crazy fourteen-hour days. It will be eight years ago, this May."
>
> —*TJ, marketing and branding firm founder, mother of one*

If what you're seeking is not just more of your career status quo but an actual *reduction* in your hours or responsibilities, or a way to work differently and get more time with the kids, keep on reading to chapter 15, which will explain exactly how to get that flexibility you're looking for.

Then and Now

A lot can change when you become a parent: your levels of ambition, your overall feelings about your work, the kinds of sacrifices you're willing to make to get ahead in your career, how you make the decision to stay or go in any particular job. What *doesn't* change—ever—are the fundamentals of a good career. As a parent, you're still trying to earn a good living, you still want to do your highest and best work, and you still want to have a job you enjoy, day to day. And you still need to use all the same career-management tools to get there. It's important to know yourself, to take your current family circumstances into account—but never sell yourself short, or neglect to give your career the care and feeding it deserves.

13

Transitions

Workparenting While Changing—or Between—Roles

Maybe you've got a dream-job prospect dangling right in front of you, or you've been thinking about making a bigger switch, into a new field or function that will let you spend more time with the kids. Or maybe you need more change like you need a hole in the head, but because of other pressures at home or at work it's time to find a new gig. Whatever the specifics: you're in, or about to be in, professional transition.

In this chapter, we'll walk through what you need to know, do, and remain alert to throughout times of professional change when also raising kids. We'll cover the special tactics and tools that will help you pivot, as well as address the concerns and feelings it's natural to have as you do so.

Before we get tactical, though, let's start by answering one core, critical question . . .

Is This *Particular* Transition Worth It?

If you're out of work, need the money, and just received a terrific offer, then your next step is clear: you should take the job. Most of the time, though, deciding to make a particular career move is a more ambiguous, complex, and emotionally fraught process, and the prospect of

No time for career management?

If the combined demands of your current job and of parenting have you feeling so underwater, timewise, that you can't even imagine taking steps toward a needed transition, then—to put it bluntly—you need to shift your perspective. The kids will *never* stop needing you, your current organization will *never* cut you a break, the Time-Management Fairy will *never* wave her magic wand and grant you extra hours to spend dusting up your résumé, networking, or on interviews. As long as you continue to deliver for your current boss and organization, they're unlikely to care too much about what it's costing you personally. Fortunately or unfortunately, it's on *you* to be the captain of your own career.

Where to start? Try setting aside some small chunk of your weekly calendar for pure career-management or job-search activities. Maybe you take thirty minutes every Tuesday night to fluff up your CV, draft a few emails to headhunters, or research roles that interest you. However small that chunk of time is, it has the powerful effect of turning career management into a *habit*—and creates momentum toward something new.

change, while exciting, may bring any number of thorny work-plus-family questions. As you consider a new role, you may wonder if the extra money is really worth it, if you should say yes despite the longer commute, or if you might later regret not going after this opportunity. Unfortunately, as you tussle with those questions, and no matter how experienced and career-savvy you are, you become vulnerable to two common career-decision traps, two kinds of thinking that can lead you to subpar or inauthentic choices and onto a bad professional path.

The first is *Blinders Thinking,* or the tendency to overemphasize and overfocus on specific details of a potential role or career move, while neglecting others or failing to take a complete view. Of *course* the commute is important: you don't want to sit in stop-and-start traffic for two hours a day when you could be home with the kids, or at work, doing something productive and making an impact. But the commute is just one factor here. What about the ability to work remotely a few days a week, or your new boss's expectations about your availability on the weekend?

Is this a role that requires you to work with clients or colleagues several time zones away, or with greater or lesser additional administrative responsibilities than you've had in the past? All of those things will affect the hours you work, and what you can accomplish, and your time with the kids, too, and they all deserve to be considered as pieces of this full puzzle. Or take a financial example: maybe the new role is unattractive because it actually comes with a *lower* base salary—but the overtime or bonus potential is much greater, and the new employer kicks into your self-funded pension, so the money's better overall. You want to make sure you're keeping a panoramic view, and making good, holistic decisions.

The second trap is what we'll call the *No-Emotion Error*, or the tendency to force yourself to consider your decision in a professional-to-the-point-of-clinical way, denying or suppressing your natural feelings or instincts. You may keep refocusing yourself on the salary or stock options available in a new job, while ignoring the uncomfortable, non-family-friendly sense you got around your prospective new manager; dupe yourself into thinking that the big new title or impressive business card will make up for the fact that you have zero enthusiasm for the new company's products or mission; or find yourself putting work-from-home flexibility into the "Pro/take the job" column, when you're actually an extrovert and would rather be around your coworkers anyway. There are many components to any career decision, some of them hard/objective/factual, and some of them much softer and

> For nine years I was at a big teaching hospital. We regularly treated the sickest of the sick. I learned a *lot*, but it was very demanding work, and the commute was over an hour.
>
> Before my daughter was born I applied to a hospital much closer to home. It's the same job, and pay, but the cases aren't always quite as complicated, and I can work overnight, from 7:00 p.m. to 7:00 a.m. three nights a week. It lets me get home quickly to take care of my daughter when my husband goes off to work, and my parents are just a mile down the street. It was a good move for our family."
>
> —*Dawn, respiratory therapist, mother of one*

more personal. You'd be wrong to ignore the hard factors, of course, but if you make the mistake of ignoring the softer ones, you're setting yourself up for some lousy career moves.

Table 13-1, "The Workparent Job and Career-Change Decision Framework," is your tool for avoiding both of these traps—and for fully considering and making your very best career choices. The framework will prompt you to think holistically, practically, and authentically through any career move, *as a working parent.*

Start by reading the table over quickly, in one gulp, to get a sense of it. Then—and preferably when you have some time away from the crush of your day-to-day work and family responsibilities—go back carefully, row by row, taking your time and pushing yourself to respond to each line item. If the questions feel probing or you find yourself a bit uncomfortable as you do this exercise, it's a sign that you're doing it correctly. You're at the center of this operation, this is a big-league decision, and as you stand here at the crossroads and stress-test your thinking and assumptions, the wind is going to pick up and things may feel a little breezy. You do *not* have to work through table 13-1 in one sitting. In fact, it's better if you approach your career thinking in an unhurried, iterative way. When you're done working it over, we'll look at your reactions, and at the decision itself again as a whole.

Alright now: you've put the prospective change through the "is it really worth it" gauntlet. You've cut through much of the decision-making noise, homed in on the facts and your own gut feelings, and

> ❝ I came back from leave to a four-day-per-week schedule—and three months later, switched jobs. It was a big change: a promotion, more responsibility—and a regular five-day schedule. In retrospect, it was a bit mad to do that, particularly as a single parent. It was difficult not having that extra day, and difficult to build out a new department. But I knew that kind of opportunity wouldn't come around again—and I wanted to provide my son the best life possible."
>
> —*Christelle, head of contracts, mother of one*

TABLE 13-1

The Workparent Job and Career-Change Decision Framework

Factors to consider	Key questions to ask yourself
	Go slowly through each question, pushing yourself to come up with your most honest and unvarnished response.
Prompt for this particular change	• Why am I considering this transition? For professional or parenting reasons? Why *now*? • Is this a push or a pull? Am I *fleeing the bad* or *moving toward the good*? • Could I possibly get what I'm seeking in my current career, or role? Hand on heart, have I tried? • Will the issues and challenges I want to leave behind follow me into the new role? • What are the consequences of staying put? What about giving it three or six more months to see how things pan out?
Function/role	• How well does this new opportunity map to what I actually want to *do*, and am good at doing, day to day? • On a percentage basis, how much more of my time would be spent doing my preferred function or activity in this new role, versus the job I'm in currently? • What's the headache-to-glory ratio in this new gig? What undesirable activities would I need to handle?
Trajectory	• How would this new role improve my skills? Professional credibility? Visibility? Marketability? Expertise? Confidence? Network? Professional stature? Day-to-day happiness? • How would I describe this decision, and new role, fifteen years from now? How will my kids look at my decision to pursue this, when they're old enough to do so?
Boss and colleagues	• Who will I be reporting to and working with—directly, on a "dotted line" basis, or in effect? • Are these people I can learn from? Work easily with? Act like peers to? Be open about my workparent needs with? • Am I likely to have friction with these people? Will that strain detract from the energy/emotion I bring to parenting?
Money	• What's my economic hit or upside here? Is it short-term or long-term? Certain or uncertain? Do I really need that money (e.g., for a better daycare option), or am I in "maximizing mode"? • What are the hidden or implicit costs/upsides—e.g., worse family benefits; higher earnings power in the future?

(*continued*)

TABLE 13-1 (continued)

Factors to consider	Key questions to ask yourself
Time	• Does this new prospect mean more or less time with the kids, overall?
	• How would my calendar/schedule be configured differently day to day? Week to week? By project?
	• During my off hours, would I have to be connected to work? Available to work? Or would I be completely disconnected?
	• How will this new role fit into my kids' next stage of development? If I'm moving to get more time with the baby, what about when she's in preschool?
Control/ flexibility	• To what extent would I get to call the shots on my daily schedule? Projects and workflow? Timeline for advancement?
	• If my child is sick or the parent-teacher conference is happening, how will I need to handle it in this new environment?
Fit to work-parent responsibilities	• How well does this new role let me [be present for the first year of my son's life/get involved with the school/take care of a child with severe allergies/etc.]?
	• Am I avoiding this new opportunity *because* of parenting? Am I listening to other people's, or to society's, *should*s as I consider whether or not to pursue it? Do I have any sense that seizing this new opportunity *makes me a better parent* or *isn't something that mothers or fathers normally do*?
Will this one change lead to others?	• Consider what other specific factors may be at play as you seek to make this change work. Will you have to go back to school? Create a new budget? Move houses or cities? Find a new care arrangement? Set up a new arrangement with your partner?
Fears	• What are the risks associated with this move, or new job? For me, my career, the kids?
	• Which of those risks is well-founded, versus based on my natural apprehensions about transition and change?
	• What would happen if I did make this move and it went pear-shaped? Could I recover? How?
Loss	• What am I leaving behind if I make this move? Will I have to: – Give up doing the school run? – Abandon my hopes for making VP at this company? – Relinquish a part of my professional identity? – Put aside a sense of personal or moral mission I've always attached to my work? – Walk away from my team and/or colleagues who have meant a lot to me?
	• Do those potential losses outweigh the benefits this change might bring me or my family?
	• If I don't hit this bid now, will I get another, similar opportunity later?

assessed whether this new role or opportunity is actually *better*, versus merely *new and different*. Having done all that, where do you stand?

If you're still uncertain, or the framework left you with some unexpected questions you need to chew on, simply give it some more time. Stick with the process and keep batting around your ideas and feelings until you see the general "yes" or "no" trend line. If you think it will help, try working over table 13-1 with a trusted friend, mentor, or other supporter who can nudge you a little, call you on the mat where needed, and help resolve particular concerns. If, however, you now have an overall, generalized feeling that *this transition is necessary*, or *not worth it*, or *a good choice*, you should be well assured that you're right. The framework makes certain you've given this choice full thought and from every workparent angle. You can now move forward, and with confidence.

IWAP: Interviewing While a Parent

You've decided to go for it. You're going to pursue something new. But now you find yourself on the horns of new dilemmas. Should you tell prospective employers that you've got kids? What's the best way to negotiate a certain schedule or type of flexibility in a new role? How do you respond if you get "parent pushback" in an interview? Is looking for a job while expecting a complete nonstarter? What if you're on the cusp of accepting a new job, and having working-parent cold feet?

Good questions, all—and fortunately, much more easily answerable and manageable than you think. Let's get each one sorted.

Should I tell prospective employers I'm a parent?

Think of this choice as less of an *if* and more of a *when*. If you time things correctly, revealing that you're a parent won't work against you, or feel like such a huge deal. To understand why that is, it helps to get a little insight into how recruitment processes play out—typically in three distinct, sequential phases.

- During Phase 1 of any hiring or selection process, the prospective employer is simply trying to understand if you're sufficiently

The chance to forge a new brand

Once you've established a certain reputation, or "brand," within your organization, it's almost impossible to shake. If people have come to see you as timid, or snappish, or always willing to handle scut work, for example, they may keep on seeing you that way even years after you become more assertive, or sweeter, or selective in the projects you agree to take on. And unfortunately, that "brand persistence" phenomenon can become a particular problem for working parents. If you've always been perceived as the *long hours* type, for example, your boss and colleagues may assume that still holds true now, even if you're parenting three kids under five.

That's why job and career changes are such golden opportunities: they offer you the chance to recast yourself as a professional, and to change how you act and how you're thought of. Maybe at your old organization no one had any qualms about dumping work on you last-minute because you were so accommodating. But nobody in the new organization knows you that way at all. You can adopt and project a new persona, and "teach" your new colleagues to treat you in a different way.

Before starting a new job, think carefully as to how you want to be seen, and how you want your colleagues to relate to you. What five to seven adjectives capture the New Workparenting Brand of You—and how will that brand make life better for you both as a professional and as a parent? Now's the time to set new boundaries around your work hours, advocate for or avoid certain projects, and be known for what you want to be known for—not for who you were before kids.

credentialed, realistically capable, and might be a decent cultural fit. Interviews will likely be few and short, and may be on the phone or by videoconference, as the organization determines—in its own time-efficient way—if you're worthy of a closer look. It's like a first date: you want it to go well, and if it does, it will lead to a second.

- In Phase 2, the real meat-and-potatoes work of assessment happens. Throughout what may be a slew of follow-on interviews, you'll be pushed to discuss more about your past experiences, to demonstrate your plan for success in the new role, and to establish good rapport with a variety of your would-be colleagues. In old-fashioned romantic terms, you're going steady: testing the relationship out and seeing if you're compatible.

- Phase 3 is the period during which you and the organization or hiring manager get down to brass tacks and determine the possibility and details of a long-term commitment: you discuss role terms, compensation, get an offer letter, and if all goes well, accept.

If you make a big deal about being a parent during Phase 1—before building up the employer's confidence in your general suitability for the job, and before establishing mutual interest—the information will likely just be a distraction. You certainly don't have to *hide* the fact that you have kids, but it's unlikely to help both parties move toward where you want to go, which is Phase 2. On the other hand, if you wait until Phase 3 to mention your desired three-day-per-week schedule, it may come across as a surprise, or awkward—or even as if you've been concealing something, acting in mild bad faith. During Phase 2, however, particularly its later stages, the door is open. You've already established something of a relationship with your prospective employer and coworkers, they're clearly interested in you as a candidate, and they're trying to sell you the opportunity as well as to judge you for it. At this point, the revelation that you have a couple of young kids will seem like a natural part of the get-to-know-you process—as appropriate information-sharing.

> " At school, during the recruiting process, I was very conscious about choosing a firm and about where I wanted to work. But at the same time, I was conflicted: I kept wondering if it was a mistake to let family status drive my decision.
>
> It turned out that this was the only firm where my being a mom even came up in conversation! It wasn't even an issue. That made a huge impact on me, and why I felt comfortable making my decision."
>
> —*Zainab, lawyer, mother of two*

If you're anxious about mentioning your family status, try raising the issue in a casual way, or by the by: for example, ask one of your interviewers about the family photo you see in the background during your videoconferencing interview, let drop that you have toddlers also, and then see where the conversation goes. If you prefer to take a more direct approach, that's fine too. When asked if you have any questions about the role, say something like, "It sounds like a terrific position, and as discussed, I think I could make a great impact in it. As a working parent, I would want to make certain that we're both aligned as to how that impact could be achieved. I usually work a solid eight-hour day, take a break to do bath and bedtime with the kids, and then log on for a few hours in the evening . . ." or similar. Keep things simple, factual, unapologetic, nondramatic. Chances are that either strategy will lead to more conversation, to needed openness, and ultimately to the information and assurances you're looking for. If it doesn't, that's too bad—but better to know up front.

What's the best way to advocate for a certain schedule, type of flexibility, etc., when interviewing for a new role?

As in any negotiation, a good way to *get* something is to *give*. Let's say you're negotiating an offer and want a two-day-per-week work-from-home arrangement as part of your package. Simply throwing that demand down on the table in a "this is what I want" way won't feel as collaborative, or be as effective, as graciously saying something like, "that flexibility will make accepting this offer a no-brainer, and will allow me to be as productive as possible over the long term." In other words, let your counterparty feel like you're *both* making a smart choice and getting a good deal.

If you do have a specific ask, make it directly and unambiguously. Your interviewers aren't mind readers, and it's better for everyone if you're clear about what you're looking for. While it's fine to be firm in your requests, having too many family-related nonnegotiables, or coming across as rigid or entitled, or negotiating down to the last dime and detail, will use up personal goodwill, fast. If these are going to be your new colleagues, you want to start out on a positive foot. Make your ask in a concise way, and remain pleasant.

For more guidance on flexible work, and how to negotiate for it, be sure to review the information in chapter 15.

What do I do if I get "parent pushback" in an interview?

If an interviewer asks you if you're really committed to your career, given the kids; or inquires about your plans to expand your family; or pushes on the details of how much parental leave you took; or asks any other mildly offensive to downright discriminatory question, simply respond, "If you're asking me if there's any reason why I couldn't do this job effectively, the answer is 'no.'" It's not worth getting into a *how dare you!* frame of mind or a *but this is bias!* wrestling match with someone you barely know, and you're not likely to want to work for this organization anyway. Without stooping to the interviewer's level you can send a clear message that he or she has crossed the line.

If you find yourself seething in the aftermath of an interaction like this, take some solace in the fact that this organization likely has or will develop an unpleasant reputation as an employer, and will have trouble hiring and retaining talent. Then move on, and go get yourself a terrific offer from an organization aware of which century we're living in.

Can I look for a job while expecting?

In a word: *yes*. The idea that it's somehow taboo or a fool's errand to put yourself out there as a candidate while planning or expecting a family is outdated, off base, and likely self-imposed. Try thinking about it objectively, and from the hiring managers' side: They've certainly seen, and worked with, other parents before, and the fact that an adult member of the workforce is actually procreating is unlikely to shock them. Remember, too, that recruiters and hiring organizations are working in their own best interests in looking for terrific talent, and if they have to wait another few months to get what they want—pushing

> ❝ My inclination was to *not* interview while pregnant. It felt like, this isn't what I'm supposed to be doing. I had to sit there and tell myself over and over, 'My pregnancy does not make me less qualified for this position. It has nothing to do with my abilities.'
>
> I ended up finding this role while I was on leave. I was very open with everyone I interviewed with. At the beginning of phone calls I would tell them, 'The baby may cry in the background.' Throughout the search, I kept expecting negative responses—but I never got them.
>
> Looking back, the only mistake I think I made was showing up to one interview visibly pregnant without giving the company a heads-up. That can dominate people's first impression of you—and become a distraction."
>
> —*Laura, chief marketing officer, mother of two*

the start date out by three extra months while you take parental leave, for example—then they probably will. Anyway, ask yourself: In the event that you *do* interview while expecting, and one of your interviewers reacts with the astonishment, horror, disgust, scorn, laughter, or icy disinterest you're worried about, is that really a person or organization you want to work for? Think of this process as a litmus test: if the manager or organization can't handle expectant parents, they shouldn't be handling parents—or your career and future—at all.

If you do interview while expecting, however, be ready to set the tone and own the narrative. Share the news in a straightforward, nondramatic way; address the special timing or logistics your situation requires; gently dismiss any concerns or questions; and above all, express confidence. A statement like, "I'm expecting my second child in March, which means I'll be ready to start back at work in July. I'm excited about this opportunity, and would look forward to joining your team then . . ." is honest and authentic, and also sends a clear and powerful message to your would-be employer.

What if I'm about to take the offer—but am getting cold feet?

Let's fully acknowledge those nerves, and put them into context. As a parent, you're hardwired for hypervigilance. Think back to those

first few nights of parenting, when you kept checking and recheck-
ing if the baby was breathing. In the macro sense, that instinct to
hover and protect helps make certain that what you're doing is really
right for the kids. As you make a big decision, these I-can't-get-it-
out-of-my-mind, last-minute jitters are your brain's, and body's, and
psyche's, way of making sure you're paying attention and choosing
wisely. (If you felt completely zen and blasé right now, *that* would be a
problem.) Tell yourself: *these cold feet will help me make a careful, honest
decision.*

If you do want additional reassurance while sitting on an open job
offer, it's fine to get it. Simply ask to speak with the hiring manager, or
your prospective boss, and have a direct, peer-to-peer conversation:
"I'm thrilled to have this offer, would love to come work with you, and
am confident I'd add value to this organization. Before we make it official, though, I want to be clear. My career is important to me—but
as a parent, so are my kids. I'll be able to deliver on everything we
discussed in our interviews, but I won't be [staying late at work for no
reason/willing to travel every week/skipping every single one of my
kids' school performances/going out for drinks every week with the
team/etc.]. I'm confident I can handle my personal needs while doing
terrific work for you, but if you have any hesitation about what I just
said, let's discuss it now." In this last-exit-off-the-freeway conversation,
you send a strong, preemptive signal about your workparenting approach and set the tone for future work-plus-family-related conversations. Your boss can speak now, or forever hold his or her peace—and
you both know exactly what you're getting into.

How to Tell if an Employer Is
Working-Parent Friendly

As you go through any job search or interview process, you'll find
yourself wondering: *Is this an environment that supports working parents?
Do I really want to hang my professional hat here, as a mom or dad completely
devoted to my kids?* To answer those questions, you have a number of
information sources at your disposal. Here they are, in rough ascend-
ing order of usefulness and reliability.

- The company website. Table stakes—nothing more. If there isn't some kind of statement about "work/life balance" or how the organization "wants employees to lead full lives" or how there's a working-parent employee network group— *something*—then take it as a red flag.

- Awards and recognitions. If any major website or magazine has cited the organization you're thinking about working for on its annual list of "best companies for working parents" (or similar), that's a nice, encouraging sign, although far from a definitive one. Typically, the organizations included on those lists have to jump through major hoops to apply for the honor, and the ones that do are usually either 1) the most media- and PR-savvy or 2) the most panicked about a negative reputation among working-parent talent. Most typically, they're both. In general, the criteria used for judging those lists are also heavily weighted toward leave, postpartum, and other female-friendly, early-childhood-type benefits, which may not be helpful to you if you're male, the parent of older children, etc. Take citations like this into account, but take them with a big old grain of salt.

- "Employer-review" websites. These crowdsourced sites, like the awards and recognitions mentioned above, will likely provide some color and context, but should never be your only source of information. Many organizations deliberately massage their profiles on those sites (by giving employees incentives to write in positive comments, for example), and many disgruntled current or past employees use the sites as outlets for complaints and bitterness. Thus, for any given organization, you often see a strange "barbelling" of opinion as to the organization's treatment of working moms and dads. Again, read up, but don't use this information to come to a firm opinion.

- The benefits literature. As soon as you get an offer, ask to see the organization's full benefits summary or employee handbook. What's provided in terms of parental leave? Flexibility? Particular programs or assistance for families with older kids?

Are those benefits offered to *all* employees? Have they been updated and upgraded in the past few years? How so? What you're looking for here is 1) if the organization is market-standard in its offerings, 2) if it's evolving with the times, and 3) if it appears to be making a holistic, creative effort to reduce the overall headwinds faced by working parents.

- **Senior leadership.** How many of the folks running the organization have kids? How many are in two-career couples? Do they mention their families in their official bios, or have they at public events or in past media interviews? Do they serve on the boards of working-parent-relevant nonprofits? Are they involved in working-parent-related programs at the organization? This kind of research is *far* from precise, but it may help you develop an overall sense as to whether or not the people running the joint are "with it" and attuned to working-parent issues.

- **Your own discreet observations.** Do your interviewers have family photos at their desks? Do they mention family responsibilities? Activities outside the office? What's your gut feeling as to how "normalized" working parenthood is in this organization? How comfortable are people acknowledging their lives outside? These observations are powerful barometers of day-to-day working-parent experience.

- **Conversations with current and past employees.** Just as you background- and reference-checked your childcare provider, you should do so with the prospective employer. Questions to think about asking:

  - On a scale of 1 to 10, how workparent-friendly is this organization?

  - Do mothers and fathers here have a different experience? (You want to assess if the workparent friendliness is genuine and inclusive.)

  - What is it like to return from leave? Manage a sick child's care?

- How bureaucratic or rigid is the place in terms of flex-work arrangements? Does a flex-work arrangement require filling out a gazillion forms in triplicate, or are you treated as a mature and contributing adult, permitted to make your own decisions?

- How were parents treated and communicated with throughout the 2020 pandemic? Would you describe management's response to the difficulties working parents faced during that time as forthcoming, supportive, solutions-focused, helpful? If not, why?

As we learned during your search for childcare, the past is the best way to predict the future.

• Direct questions. If any aspect of working-parent life is particularly important to you, and you're not getting the answers or context you need to make a good career decision, then *ask*. If that feels awkward, then play things forward and think how awkward it's going to be as a full-time employee, and finding the answer out for yourself.

Explaining It to the Kids (or Choosing Not To)

You've accepted the role, or left your job, or committed to going back to school. As you consider how to share news of that change with the kids, make your watchwords *calm*, *upbeat*, and *age-appropriate*. Your

> While I was planning to go out on my own, I needed to be very careful about what I said around the girls. We call my youngest one the Village Crier—she always knows what's going on and loves announcing her news to everyone she meets. I couldn't have my kids telling my colleagues at my old firm 'Mommy's planning to leave soon and start her own company!' It felt strange, because we're always very open and communicative with the kids, but I needed to keep things under wraps until the formal announcement."
>
> —*Adrianne, financial adviser, mother of three*

goal is to be honest and forthcoming, without discomforting or frightening the children in any way.

For a toddler, you may not choose to make an announcement at all, or you may decide to put the news in very tangible terms, like "Daddy goes to work in a new building now." For school-aged children, you may want to use more details, and/or mark any positive, celebratory aspect of the new job or other transition with a special family meal or outing. Be aware, however, that your eight-year-old son may have natural questions or apprehensions about what's happening, about other attendant changes baked into your transition, and about exactly what this means for *him*. If you pick up on any shred of uncertainty or confusion, go out of your way to provide some extra, and extraspecific, assurances, by saying something like *Mom has a new job, but I'll still be home at the same time to help with your math homework, every day*, or by taking him in for a visit to the new office. For a teenager, consider sharing more of your transitional *whys* and the new job's points of interest. If you've just landed a better-paying new role at a new firm, for example, think about mentioning the upside ("I'll be able to spend more of my time on the tasks I enjoy most"; "this new role will let me save more money for your education"), as well as explaining the organization's mission, products, services, or research; showing your daughter its website; and so on. Big picture: whatever your kids' ages, and whatever your professional situation, you want to role-model the healthy, positive ways you're engaging with the world of work—and the ways they will, too, one day.

In certain circumstances, of course, you may very sensibly decide *not* to tell the kids what's going on, or not to share your true feelings about it. If your organization's financial troubles led to layoffs, and you find yourself panicky and without a job, that's not detail your first-grader is going to be able to healthily process, or do anything about—or that your teenage son necessarily needs to be presented with just before taking his end-of-semester exams. In those situations, downplaying the information, or presenting it in a self-determined way ("I left the company, and I'm going to take my time finding a new job"), may be better. If your child expresses concern about the transition, immediately draw a boundary between your own adult concerns

Involving teachers and caregivers

As we've examined in previous chapters, your child's teachers and caregivers are front-line players on Team Working Parent. They're essential allies and supporters both to you and to your child, and that support is never more important than during periods of uncertainty or transition.

Whether an internal company transfer prompts changes to your schedule, you're stressed out at starting a brand-new job, or you're looking for work and feeling anxious about it, *consider telling your child's school and care providers what's going on.* No matter how discreet you've been about your job or career change, your child has almost certainly picked up on tensions related to it, and there's real risk of him or her becoming confused or worried. With the right context, however, teachers and caregivers can provide the reassurance, continuity, and special attention your child might need. For example, if your son is concerned or upset that your new job is—for the first few weeks, anyway—requiring longer hours, a clued-in teacher can help set his mind to rest that the situation is normal and temporary.

If you feel any shyness or hesitation about sharing details of your situation with teachers, administrators, babysitters, daycare workers, and so forth: don't. They have zero motivation or power to judge you; they're all adults, and have seen this situation before; they've devoted their careers to helping children, and will be happy to do so now; and as always, they'll be appreciative of your open, honest communication.

and what your child's are: "Yes, I will be looking for new work. But that's Mommy's job to think about. Your job is to keep your room tidy and get ready for Friday's math test. Should we go over the long-division problems again?" However you decide to handle this, don't let it leave you feeling dishonest or conflicted in any way. Think of it like this: you've always done an excellent job in protecting your child, and in letting him or her *be* a child, and you're simply doing the same thing now.

If you do anticipate a long period on the bench, try to keep your routines and mood consistent, both from the kids' perspective and

Spending "in between" time with the children

If you're between roles, and find yourself with plenty of spare time on your hands but worry that spending more-than-usual amounts of it with the kids will somehow "spoil" them or set up unrealistic expectations you can't live up to later: relax. Try looking at these precious weeks or months as a unique window of opportunity. Think of them as a time to connect with the kids and to parent (at least, temporarily) in a different way—and one that can benefit the entire family over the longer term. Do school drop-off every single morning and *really* get to know your child's friends, teachers, and schoolyard dynamic so you've got the full perspective even after you're back at work. Tackle that activity or project the kids would love you to, but that you haven't had time for, whether that's building the model Lego tower or reading all seven hundred pages of the next Harry Potter novel aloud. If your child struggles with a particular life skill—and what kid doesn't?—now's the time to offer your patient, gentle support. Use these weeks to help your kindergartener learn to tie her shoes, for example, or help the twins get over their fear of water by spending some unpressured, unhurried afternoons together at the community pool. This time isn't any more "spoiling" or "expectations setting" than a typical vacation would be, and no children have ever suffered from getting a little extra attention from their loving mom or dad.

from your own. Get up when you normally would, sit down at your desk or leave the house at "work time," keep some delineation between your workweeks and weekends, and generally send the same signals you always have as a hardworking parent.

How You Might Be Feeling as You Make the Switch

Throughout your working-parent transition, or while you're in between roles, you may feel:

- Guilt, remorse, or anger in relation to your past role. *I gave them eight years of my life and worked my tail off through both parental leaves, and now they lay me off?*

- Sadness or loss at what you're leaving behind. *Sure, I'm going to a flexible role—but I'll never work at a company with that much market share again.*

- Anxiety around the timeline for finding a new position. *If I don't find a new job by summer, hiring will slow down—and the kids will be on break, and I'll be more distracted, and it will be hopeless to be out there looking.*

- Worry or fear about the financial implications of the transition. *This new entrepreneurial venture could take off, and ensure us a secure future—or blow up, and I'll be back at square one.*

- Tension about starting a new job. *How will I get my arms around all the new client accounts—while still "being there" for the kids?*

- Joy at leaving behind a subpar situation, or vindictive glee at having been able to "stick it" to a difficult boss or colleagues by quitting. *Got a problem with my leaving at 6:30 to go home and see my children? Well, buddy, that's your problem—because now I'm leaving for good!*

- Like you're in an identity crisis, major or minor. *If I'm not providing for my family, what am I? What kind of mother switches jobs like this—my job is to create stability!*

Most likely, you'll experience a powerful, seesawing combination—e.g., you may find yourself moving from glee to fear to joy to tension to relief and back again, in very short order. Since you're a parent, the pressures and expectations you'd normally feel around garden-variety career issues (money, hours worked, etc.) become much higher, and thus the emotional path you walk during any change of role is usually rockier. Expect to be in a heightened emotional state for a while, regardless of your particular situation.

If that state persists, or becomes a distraction to your work, job search, or parenting, you'll need to find healthy ways to take things down a notch. Prioritize rest and exercise, connect with your work-parent mentors, talk with a therapist or counselor if you need to. Above all, remind yourself that while transitional periods are tricky,

> I switched roles internally and relocated to a regional office due to personal reasons. It was a good move, but it also meant a new living arrangement, giving up the nanny we had employed for years, putting the kids in a new daycare (which then didn't work out), and my wife—she's an art director and graphic designer—needing to change roles as well. We were thrown several curveballs right after moving, all in a row. Transition begets change; one change can easily lead to two additional unexpected ones . . . or more. If you're going to make a big move, I would level set your own expectations and realize that feeling settled may take a year or longer. But also recognize that all this transitional craziness and the push/pull of work and family—it's for the good, and it's just a season of life you're in."
>
> —*Basil, P&L director, father of two*

they have one important characteristic: they *end*. Pretty soon you'll be settled again, and have found your new workparent normal.

Always a Working Parent

When you welcomed your first child, you took on a new identity as a working parent: a person every inch as committed and capable on the job as before, yet now also 100 percent devoted to your role as mother or father.

No matter the shifts in your life or career, that identity is unassailable. It doesn't change as your child grows, and it is never tarnished by your needing to move jobs or careers, or even by your experiencing a prolonged stretch between gigs. Nothing and no one can ever take away the essence of who you are: a hard worker, a contributor, and completely in love with your family.

14

When You're the Boss

The Scoop on Combining Work and Family
as an Entrepreneur, a Freelancer, a Family- or
Small-Business Owner, While on Commission
or Self-Employed

Each parent walks his or her own path. Each entrepreneur is on a unique journey. And thus no two self-employed work-parents, or parent-entrepreneurs, have identical experiences. Even if you and your next-door neighbor are both in the same field, both freelancing, and both have ten-year-olds, you'll still make different choices, lead your families in different ways, and feel differently about your work.

On the flip side, *all* workparent entrepreneurs face some important commonalities. Raising kids while working outside of a standard employer/paycheck job inherently comes with certain realities, pressures, and, yes, upsides also. Whether you're an entrepreneur thinking about expanding your family or a parent mulling over going out on your own, it's a smart idea to know precisely what those are—to know what you're getting into. Why drive with a blindfold on when you could have a nice clear view of the road up ahead?

In this chapter, you'll get that real-deal view. You'll hear the important truths on entrepreneurial workparenting straight from the source: from a diverse group of moms and dads who are *there*, and who will tell us what they wish they had known earlier on. After hearing their best, unvarnished advice, you'll have the chance to ask yourself some challenging questions—ones that will help you improve your entrepreneurial plans and confidence.

TRUTH: There's never a perfect time to become a workparent entrepreneur.

You'll have to decide if and when to make the move—without praise or permission.

In prior chapters, we've confronted the fact that there's no ideal or "correct" time to expand your family, take on more at work, or move jobs, and the same holds true here. If you're looking for the Golden Window of Opportunity to become a working-parent entrepreneur, you're going to be looking for a long time. Carefully weigh the pros and cons, and then make your own call. And be confident in your choice, because you don't need, and probably won't get, a lot of encouragement.

> "Although I was working for a well-known company and already had a successful client practice, I wanted to start my own firm. But with three little kids, I was always too busy. I finally came to the realization that, just like with my decision to have children, there was never going to be a perfect time when everything eased up and became less constrictive and the stars aligned. *I* had to draw the line in the sand and make the leap."
> —*Adrianne, financial adviser, mother of three*

> "I started this company with my husband when I was twenty-five and we were dating. A lot of people told me that was a terrible idea. Seven years later we had our first child, and I spent a big chunk of my thirties pregnant and taking care of my boys when they were infants and toddlers, all while growing this business. I got a lot of unsolicited advice on that, too, mostly from people who hadn't been through the same situation firsthand. People

will throw a *lot* of comments at you, but the right way to go is in trusting your instincts."
—*Jessica, videogame company founder and CEO, mother of three*

TRUTH: Your business model matters.

It's not just about having that marketable skill or great idea. You need a revenue plan—one that takes parenting into account.

As basic as it sounds: know how you'll make money, and don't assume that because you're self-employed, your situation will be workparent-friendly. Be honest with yourself about how much time you want with the kids, and carefully manage your income stream and cost structures to let you do so.

> "I love this work, but the very nature of it is that if you're not sitting across from a client, you're not earning money. Cutting back your hours to spend more time at home means cutting back your income. So I've always worked five days a week, and half-days on Saturdays, and then do my admin and catch-up in the evenings. That's a stress. Looking back, I wish I had thought a bit more about other business lines, or been a little more entrepreneurial in my thinking. Last year I took on a partner as a way to create another source of income, and that's worked well."
> —*Kerry-Lee, speech pathologist, mother of two*

> "Thank God for social media. With that, blogging and doing online videos—clients started coming to me. That meant I could focus my time on the creative work I actually wanted to be doing and got paid for, instead of on business development. If you're a parent, and want to start a new venture, don't lead from the question, 'What am I good at?' Ask yourself, 'Who's hiring me?'"
> —*Lorri, interior designer, mother of two*

> "I've fluctuated between business models based in part on my son's needs. When he was born I was working as a private chef, but then I started a meal-delivery business that I ran out of my

home when he was little. He would be in his car seat as I drove all around town, delivering meals. Now he's in school, and it feels a little easier—I have the mental space to think about next steps, and the new business I want to build."

—*Gretchen, chef and entrepreneur, mother of one*

"Singing brings me the most joy, but singing jobs aren't always the most lucrative. It's not that getting rich is so important, but I do want to give my kids half the life my parents gave me. My husband suggested I try out real estate, and I went into it kicking and screaming. Now I'm one of the top producers in the state. He has a 'portfolio career' also: he runs a barbershop, and is an inventor, and does real estate videography. Earning money in multiple ways gives us security. And because some of them are passive ways, we still get good time with the kids."

—*Aundi, singer, real estate agent, and entrepreneur, mother of two*

TRUTH: Systems and infrastructure are essential.

Without them, you'll spend a lot more time away from the kids.

Being your own boss can bring tremendous freedom, flexibility, and focus on big-picture issues. It also brings responsibility for handling all the underlying operations: IT, tax reporting . . . all the infrastructure you may have taken for granted when working for someone else or inside a larger organization. Unless you're realistic, creative, and disciplined about those demands, they can become overwhelming.

"Getting good systems in place, collecting and really organizing all the information you and your team need—that's not a nicety. When you're organized, you're efficient. When you're efficient, you can get good work done even when, like a lot of parents, you're exhausted. If I can call up important information in two seconds rather than fifteen minutes, that's time I've just gotten back to spend with my girls. Learn how to really *work* on your phone as much as you can, too, so that you can get things done on the go, and are less boxed in."

—*Brian, real estate agent, father of two*

"When I started this company, I was young, single, and worked ninety hours a week. Work consumed me, and that was OK. When I had my first child, I jumped right back in—I was the CEO, and it was all I knew. But my willingness to spend every single minute working changed, and I didn't want to work my family into a hole. Fortunately, we had already spent eighteen months taking this company to the next level: getting a functional website up and running, our automated booking system in place, the back-end-payments stuff sorted out. Without those things, being a parent and entrepreneur would have been *very* hard. You don't want to be in the thick of it, dealing with those business nuts and bolts, when you've got a three-month-old."
—*Lindsay, childcare agency founder, mother of two*

TRUTH: "Watch the pennies."

As a working-parent entrepreneur, you'll want to redouble your attentions on costs and spending.

When you work for a bigger organization, the budget may be tight, but it's still *the company's money*, not yours. When you work for yourself, that distinction usually melts away: your personal and work finances can become inextricably linked. That means taking an extrathoughtful approach, both to spending money and to saving it.

"Be on your game and watch those pennies, because nobody else is going to do it for you. I was going over a courier's bill today and saw a $500 error. There are many small businesses—and busy parents—that don't catch things like that because they're consumed with putting money in the register. It's easy to focus on the business operations but ignore your accountant, particularly when it sounds like he or she is speaking Latin! But it pays to watch the small stuff, and be aware of your financial infrastructure. Two years ago I finally looked at the interest charges on my floor samples, and noticed they were upwards of *x* thousand a month. Naturally my immediate thought was: How great it would be to have that money for other things—to grow my business, for the kids? It took two years, but now I own every appliance on display."

—Vito, home-appliance store owner, father of three

"It's worth it to me to pay people to help with the real-estate work—to do a lot of the running around with clients. Early on I would never have given a commission away to another agent, but I realized that *some* part of a deal is better than none. Go ahead and pay for help, because letting go of that money can help you make more, and let you take better care of the kids."

—Aundi, singer, real estate agent, and entrepreneur, mother of two

TRUTH: Grow at the right pace.

And be deliberate and decisive as to what that is.

The whole "he or she started a company and sold it two years later for zillions" story is compelling. Who doesn't want that kind of quick success, or cash? As a parent, though, you may find rapid growth working against you, leading to excess time away from home, and to strain or burnout. Set your growth intentions, and stick to them.

"A big reason running this company works for us is that we've never been sucked into the trap of 'you're not a unicorn, therefore you're useless' thinking, or made it our goal to sit on a yacht. We've grown at a nice steady percentage each year. When the boys were little we alternated taking four-day weeks, and spending that extra time at home. We've been in business for twenty years now, and through some up and very down cycles. I think what's worked for our family reality has actually made this business stronger and more sustainable."

—Jessica, videogame company founder and CEO, mother of three

TRUTH: Family-friendly benefits aren't exclusive to big companies.

You may be able to (re)create some of them on your own.

That corporate backup care plan, the lactation room, the working-parents network—they're all great perks. But those perks don't have to be career-deciding if you can find or build similar supports at an entrepreneurial company or working for yourself.

> "This is a startup, based overseas, and I'm the first local employee here—so in charge of everything, including benefits. At first I had a mental barrier about that. I'm not an HR expert, and I had worked for bigger companies before where all that stuff is set up for you. I felt like I didn't know what I was doing—but putting the working-parent programs I wanted and needed in place wasn't nearly as hard as I thought. For backup care, I found an on-demand nanny service with a low annual subscription and reasonable per-day fees. I pitched that to the founders and they approved—why wouldn't they? Now if one of my kids has a fever at 11:00 p.m., I can book a next-morning sitter through their app. That's taken away a lot of anxiety and pressure, and it was a good lesson: in a startup, don't expect or ask for parenting support—offer to make things happen."
>
> —*Laura, chief marketing officer, mother of two*

TRUTH: "Flexibility" may take on a new and different meaning, require an all-new approach, or prove elusive.

In fact, you may have to work even more.

Entrepreneurship is not—repeat, *not*—the Land of Milk and Honey when it comes to time- and stress-management. When you're the boss, you're accountable, and when you're accountable, you typically have to put in a lot of sweat equity. Yes, there may be an upside, but think through the specifics of how an entrepreneurial career would affect you, and your family situation.

> "Flexibility used to mean being in the office a certain number of days per week. Now, it's about working on the run. While I'm in the car waiting for the kids to come out of school, I'll be on the phone trying to coordinate furniture deliveries. And work goes in waves: there are times I'm hustling like crazy toward a big deadline, and then a lull after. It's that ebb and flow that makes

this work so well and lets me spend concentrated time with the kids."
—*Lorri, interior designer, mother of two*

"I'm much busier than I was before, but I see these first few months as an investment period. When you start your own firm, you recommit yourself to your clients in a big way for sticking with you. You *have* to overdeliver."
—*Adrianne, financial adviser, mother of three*

"I have days when I'd love to 'punch in and punch out' and get more time with the kids, but I can't. The big-retailer albatross looms over me every day. Running a mom-and-pop operation comes home with you, too. There's a lot of pressure to stay relevant."
—*Vito, home-appliance store owner, father of three*

TRUTH: Good news! You get to set the boundaries.

Bad news: that may be very hard to do.

At a bigger organization, or when you're working for someone else, the "on" and "off" switches are more clearly marked. Now they may be hazier, dynamic, or harder to find, and you'll have to set them without guidance, precedent, or anyone else's express approval.

"We try to live one life, not two, which is why we wanted our own firm to begin with. And we've consolidated our lives in many ways: our apartment, office, and son's school are all within a few blocks of each other, which both saves time and gives us a sense of place. Naturally, there's a lot of connection and bleed-through between home and work.

At the same time, we find it's healthy to have some separation . . . we don't always want to talk things out while we're in the office, or bring work home with us, because our son is smart and he knows when we're stressed out, and there's risk of

stressing him out too. We try to leave work issues at
the door."
—*Lyn, architect, father of one*

"Being a freelancer sounds great, but your entire life is self-
guided. There's no boss. The deadline might be three months
away. There's nothing on your calendar but 'work.'

When Daddy can't go to a dance recital because I'm in re-
hearsals in another city, it's easy for the kids to understand. But
when I need to draw boundaries when I'm home, and around,
and there isn't that visible boss, it's harder."
—*Eric, stage director, father of two*

"Since Day One, I've incorporated my children into my work as
much as possible. I kept a porta-crib next to my desk. I brought
my daughter to the court building with me when she was three
weeks old. In the elevator other lawyers peered at the baby sling
I was wearing over my gowns and asked, 'What's *in* there?' I even
appeared in front of judges wearing the sling to argue my cases.

My kids are teenagers now, and there's plenty they can do
around the office. I just brought my fifteen-year-old with me
to an international conference, and she was the only kid there.
She learned a ton from that trip, recorded my presentation
on her 'fancy' phone and I think the other attorneys found it
refreshing."
—*Véronique, law firm founder, mother of four*

TRUTH: Taking time off may be tough.

Or it might carry some very real consequences.

It's hard to be "off" when you're the one bottom-line accountable or
there's no paid leave, but you can try taking different *kinds* of breaks
than the ones you're used to.

"When you're not an employee, you have all the flexibility you
want. You could take years of parental leave, or one minute,

and get paid nothing or a lot. The sky's the limit, which can sometimes make things a little scary, but always exciting."
—*Brian, real estate agent, father of two*

"When my first child was born, I decided to take four months' leave—and lost many of my clients. This is relationship- and trust-based work, and it took six full months to build the practice back up. So when I had my daughter, I didn't take any leave. The stress of reestablishing myself outweighed the stress of bringing the baby to work along with me. I arranged my appointments so I could spend time with her in between."
—*Kerry-Lee, speech pathologist, mother of two*

TRUTH: Entrepreneurship and parenting can mirror each other.

. . . both practically and emotionally.

Both are all-consuming, particularly at the start.

"Our first child was this office. At the beginning, it needed us like a baby would: all the time. Now it's a little more independent."
—*Lyn, architect, father of one*

"A startup is sort of like an infant: it's fragile. You always have anxiety that something's going wrong. Even if the baby's asleep, you're worrying. It's hard to explain that feeling unless you've been there."
—*Eduardo, online retail company cofounder, father of one*

TRUTH: You'll need your family and Village to help raise this child, too.

Be realistic about the support you need and creative in how you get it.

The more help you can get, the better. Look back to the 8-C method we covered in chapter 9, and use the same approach here, thinking out-of-the-box but systematically about who can lend a hand.

"There's the clinical work, and then everything that goes into
running the practice: the office, billing, scheduling. We have a
terrific staff, and my sister—we founded the practice together,
and she's a working mom also—and I brought our dad in as
unofficial CFO. He's helped get the financial part together,
and train our team."

—*Elizabeth, physician, mother of three*

"We sell wholesale to natural-food stores, but most of our sales are
direct-to-consumer through a market in the city. The margins
are better there—and it's also where my brother and his wife live.
He's a teacher, so he's off for the summer, when we're busiest. If
someone calls out sick, he's always willing to pitch in. We brought
our business to our family."

—*Lindsey, farmer, mother of two*

**TRUTH: Working for yourself gives you the power to create a
new and better Workparent Template.**

In forging your own path, you get to be part of the Solution.

"One of the reasons I wanted to start a company was that I
couldn't find models for having a kick-ass career and being a
present, engaged parent. All I saw were trade-offs. So I decided
to build it myself."

—*Jessica, videogame company founder and CEO, mother of three*

"Everyone in the office knows my son. I bring him in all the time.
In my old job, that would have been impossible.

I was only the second person to take parental leave here,
but we make it mandatory. We want to make sure there's
equality, and that people take the time they need with their
families."

—*Eduardo, online retail company cofounder, father of one*

Now, Back to You

Alright, so your eyes are wider open now in terms of the always-there, unavoidable realities of entrepreneurial workparenting, both good and bad. Any vague thoughts or idealization has been replaced with a more specific, grounded view, and perhaps some of your worries and fears have been soothed a little as well. But now you're facing a new question: How do the realities we've covered apply to *your* life, career ambitions, skills, preferences, and family? The challenge questions in table 14-1 will help you figure that out. Whether you've just begun toying with the idea of becoming an entrepreneur-parent or have been at it for years, these questions will help you reflect on how to make this professional pathway best come together for *you*.

Pretend you're discussing your answers with a supportive friend, or mentor—someone who won't snap at you, or laugh, or judge, but

TABLE 14-1

Challenge Questions for the Entrepreneurial Workparent

- Why become (or stay) a workparent entrepreneur? Why now? What's pushing me forward—and holding me back? How, and how much, have I been influenced by outside factors and voices?

- What's my plan B? If business dries up, or I decide that I don't want to work independently any more, what then?

- What percentage of my time is/will be spent on fee-paying work, business development, and infrastructure? Am I comfortable with that balance? If not, what can I do to change it?

- What's my "highest and best use" in terms of building my business or practice, and how do I keep myself in that "highest and best" frame?

- Is my entrepreneurial bucket leaking time, money, energy, or other resources, and if so, how do I plug that hole?

- How will family changes (the arrival of a second child, my partner changing jobs, the start of school, etc.) change my experience of being an entrepreneur, and vice versa?

- How is my Village set up to support me? What other help do I need?

- When and how much will I be "all work," "all parent," or a combination of the two?

- What's my end goal? What do I want to have be my entrepreneurial workparent *legacy* (e.g., having built a sustainable business, earning x amount of money, having been available to my kids each afternoon, a combination)?

who won't take your first glib-and-easy response as a final one, either. Imagine that person nudging you a bit—challenging you to be as truthful and unguarded as possible. Certainly, if you want to have this conversation with an actual, real-life partner, you can, but you can also use the "imaginary mentor" technique here as a safe, effective means of thinking things through iteratively on your own. Either way, the goal is to gain greater clarity on what working independently and entrepreneurially means within the context of your own life— and what decisions and actions you may want to take as a result.

As you work through each question and pressure-test each of your own responses, you may come to some specific, personal insights: that you'll need to change how you handle your business's IT needs, for example, or that you don't want to go freelance until after the twins are in school. You may also have the feeling that you're swirling, or that you don't have perfect answers to *any* of these questions. However disconcerting, *that's just fine*. Remember: an entrepreneur is simply someone who organizes and directs a business, taking on the responsibility and risks for doing so. As an entrepreneurial workparent, you don't have to be able to see the future, or have pat, perfect answers to every possible question, or have your whole life neatly tied up and topped with a bow. You simply have to be willing to organize and direct your career and family life, and to take on responsibility for doing so. In thinking through the challenge questions, that's precisely what you've just done.

Now, whether you're already working long hours at a startup, are just thinking about hanging out your own shingle, or have decided not to go the entrepreneurial route after all, keep right on reading, because in the next three chapters, we'll look at additional, powerful ways to bring together your unique career and your life with the people at home.

15

Flexibility

When, Why, and How to Make Use of
Alternative Schedules, Remote Work,
and Other Special Arrangements

You know you want it. Even the word—*flexibility*—has a delicious, aspirational ring. It lets you imagine a better, healthier
version of your own life: one in which you're doing well professionally *and* spending enough time with the kids *and* enjoying more
personal downtime *and* feeling more even-keeled and all because you
have a little more say over how much you work, where, and when.

Back in capital-R Reality, though, you may not be certain of just
what flexibility really means, or what kind or how much you need,
how to go about getting it, how to really make it work, or what impact
it might have on your career longer term. And the various flexible
work arrangements ("FWAs") you've seen other people using might
not be at all feasible or helpful for *you*. So sure, you *want* flexibility—
almost all of us do. But in terms of plotting your way forward, you
may feel a little uncertain or stuck.

Let's fix that: let's clear up any confusion, get you the practical
information you need, and get you moving in a good direction. To
jump-start your thinking and sense of possibility, we'll begin by looking at the spectrum of flex-work options—and then carefully zoom in
on which one(s) could fit you best. Then we'll go over the important

how-tos for getting your boss on board, making flexibility work day-to-day and longer term, and preserving your career options and capital along the way.

Possible Arrangements, What They Offer—and What to Be Cautious About

Whatever your line of work, and however broad your network, it's likely that you've seen only a few *types* of flexible work, and seen those types used only by certain people or in a narrow fashion. Maybe it's common for recent moms (but not dads) in your workplace to opt for three-day workweeks when they come back from parental leave, or you have friends in the tech industry who've been told that post-Covid-19 they can work remotely forever, or friends from school have managed to get formal, contracted FWA arrangements in place through their employers' HR departments. That's great; those arrangements may serve as terrific models. But if you think of them as the *only possible* models, you're cheating yourself. You're foreclosing on differentiated, custom solutions that could work, or work better, for your specific career and family—and conversely, putting yourself at risk of reaching for an off-the-rack arrangement that turns out to be a terrible fit. And if those options feel too far removed from your own career or circumstances, you can easily get discouraged: you might glumly think, *Yeah, it's fine that other people can work remotely, but my job means showing up.*

Don't forget: vacation

Before you commit to—or even start toying with the idea of using— an FWA, be certain that you're taking, or have a plan to take, every paid day off possible. To reach for flex work without using your full vacation allotment makes no sense: it's the equivalent of putting an addition on your house when you're not using the space you already have. It's a much smarter move to max out every possible existing, built-in flex option you can before pursuing another.

Before you rush into any standard-issue FWA or conclude that flexibility is a no-go, you owe it to yourself to step back and get a sense of the full range and breadth of flex-work strategies. It's possible that gazing across that whole wide vista may not change your mind or plan of action one bit. But it may give you brand-new and actionable ideas, and at the very least, you'll have the satisfaction of knowing you've approached the "flex question" thoughtfully and thoroughly as a proactive working parent.

Table 15-1, "Flexibility Options at a Glance," lets you get that sweeping view quickly. It defines and illustrates flex-work options by general category and lays out the unique benefits and possible drawbacks of each. Take the next few minutes to scan the table, keeping an open mind: try to quell that internal naysayer voice telling you *that would never work for an architect/senior vice president/nursing mother, nobody in my organization has ever done that,* or *the guys on the team would make fun of me just for asking.* You don't have to use each of these options, or any of them. The important thing you're doing here is becoming a savvy, informed consumer.

What's Going to Work for You?

As you reviewed the at-a-glance table and got smart on the range and variety of possible FWAs, it may have confirmed your initial gut sense that a job-sharing arrangement, or *not* working from home, or any other one particular option, is the right way forward. If you're confident, convinced, and ready to try to turn your specific FWA idea into reality, skip ahead to the next section on advocating for it. If, however, you're wavering between a few types or aren't sure how to narrow the overall field down, let's run through the key questions and factors that will help you figure things out. It cannot be stated strongly enough: *while there's no one "right" or permanent approach to flexibility, there is an overall best approach for you, right now*—and now, we'll determine what that is.

Begin by considering what specific problem you're trying to solve for. The more you can zoom in on your workparent pain points, the better you can select an FWA that helps relieve them. For example:

TABLE 15-1

Flexibility Options at a Glance

Type	Description	Example(s)	Key benefits: this approach lets you . . .	Challenges—and things to be cautious about
Change your hours				
Shifted hours	You keep your overall hours and professional commitments consistent but do your work at different times.	Instead of being on the job from 8:00 a.m. until 6:00 p.m. daily, from Monday through Friday, you: • Arrive at the office at 6:30 a.m.—and leave by 4:30 p.m., <u>OR</u> • Work a 10-hour overnight shift, and have your days free, <u>OR</u> • Clock 10 hours of work each weekend—and leave earlier on the weekdays, • Etc.	• Keep your pay, benefits, career capital, network, and overall role intact • Manage to the hard stop of daycare-center hours or other caregiving arrangements • Optimize a difficult commute (e.g., lets you beat rush hour, or make the 5:00 p.m. express train)	• Potential perception that you're working less • Schedule may be rougher on you, personally—for example, 6:00 a.m. wake-ups may move to 4:30 a.m. • Early arrivals or later departures at work may require a special or hybrid childcare arrangement
Reduced hours (or "part-time" work)	You and your employer agree on a specific decrease in the overall amount of work you'll do—and the hours you'll spend doing it.	Instead of working 10 hours per day, you: • Work 7, <u>OR</u> • Instead of working 5 days per week, you work 3, <u>OR</u> • Instead of being required to deliver 2,000 client-billable hours per year, you agree to deliver 1,400.	• "Scale down" your job effectively • Enjoy more-dedicated, intensive stretches of time at home, or on child-related activities (e.g., school volunteerism)	• Reduced pay • May affect perceptions about your long-term ambitions • Significant danger that you end up working more than you're being paid for • Risk of being "out of the loop" or passed over for good opportunities at work • May be harder to find childcare that matches your particular working hours

Compressed schedule

You keep your overall hours and professional commitments consistent, but do your work in condensed time periods, with longer breaks in between.

Instead of working 10 hours per day, 5 days per week, you:
- Work 12.5 hours per day, 4 days per week, OR
- Pull double shifts every Monday, and take Thursdays off, OR
- Instead of seeing patients every day, you "stack" all of your appointments on 10 marathon-length days each month,
- Etc.

- Keep your pay, benefits, work status, and overall role intact
- Enjoy more-dedicated, intensive stretches of time at home, or on child-related activities

- Personal wear and tear from working extralong, intense days
- Colleagues may be confused about your schedule—and commitment
- Hours may prompt the need for special or hybrid childcare arrangement

Change your location

Remote work

You keep the same job and same hours—but do your work, at least some of the time, outside of your regular workplace. The alternative location may be your home, a branch office, or elsewhere.

Instead of working 5 days per week in the office, you work from home:
- On Fridays, OR
- On any day you don't have in-person meetings, OR
- 2 days per month, OR
- All the time.

- Avoid time spent commuting and/or on low-value "face time" or "watercooler conversation" type activities
- Stay physically closer to your child

- Risk of perception that you're working less
- Pressure to find your professional and parenting boundaries (you're always at work . . . and at home)
- May be hard to replicate your ideal work setup at home or elsewhere (adequate work space, needed technology, etc.)
- Lower levels of communication with colleagues

(continued)

TABLE 15-1 (continued)

Type	Description	Example(s)	Key benefits: this approach lets you . . .	Challenges—and things to be cautious about
Change the structure of the job				
Job sharing	You work at a regular full-time job—but *split* that job with a trusted colleague. That split may be 50-50, or be a "job partition"—in which one or the other of you takes the lead on certain duties or projects, or has a clear specialization.	Instead of working 5 days per week, you work 2.5, handing off your work to your job-share partner, who then works the next 2.5 days—thus the two of you together fill one full-time role.	• Stay "in the game" professionally while significantly increasing the amount of time you can spend at home with your child • Make a clean break from work: no checking email, no getting dragged back into calls on days off—your job-share partner handles it all • Hold a senior, leadership, or management role that wouldn't be possible to do part-time	• Hours worked may not let you qualify for benefits, retirement plan, etc. • Need to have incredible trust and communication with your job-share partner • Handoffs are key: need to pass the ball back and forth weekly and in a thorough, thoughtful way
Consulting	Instead of working in a full-time employee capacity, you become a contract worker—paid by the hour or project.	Instead of getting a biweekly paycheck and committing 50 hours per week to your employer (plus evenings, weekends, etc.), you work as requested, as needed, and as negotiated.	• Have a greater degree of control over when and how much you work; allows you to say no more easily • Easier to set and maintain boundaries; no "face time" pressure—if you're not getting paid for it, you don't work	• You become ineligible for benefits, paid sick leave, paid vacation, retirement plan, etc. • Organization may cut back on, or end, your arrangement at any time—with no severance payment to help cushion the blow

Project-by-project, or "situational," flexibility	You remain a regular full-time employee OR move to a consulting arrangement. Either way, you take work in "waves"—alternating from periods of long hours and intense work focus to periods of much lighter commitment.	Stay in the working game, while getting more time at home Instead of working 50 hours per week, you: • Work 80 during the weeks before major deliverables are due—and then cut back to 35 or less when they aren't, OR • You work intensively 10 months per year, during your industry's regular busy season, but spend slower summer months home with the kids.	• Will likely have to make this arrangement happen organically, as you go, and on a constantly negotiated basis—rather than by way of an agreed, long-term contract with your employer • Even with a supportive boss and organization, may be impossible to plan ahead for the "hard weeks" versus the easier ones

Change yourself—or how you do things

Self-directed flexibility	You work the same job, hours, and location—but you take small "bites" of flexibility where and when you can and want to.	You work 50 hours per week, but routinely: • Completely shut off after 7:00 p.m., even though the messages keep coming, AND/OR • Leave for the school play when you need to, AND/OR • If you've worked late one night, decide to start work a little later the next day, AND/OR • Use the Split Day strategy covered in chapter 4, AND/OR • Actually use all of your personal days, • Etc.	Keep your pay, benefits, work status, and overall role 100% intact—all while getting just enough "give" in your work and schedule that you can be the parent you want • Combine the approach with other flexible arrangements • Requires constant personal decision-making and recalibration • Sense of personal anxiety that comes from making independent, under-the-radar decisions • May prompt confusion or negative perceptions among colleagues ("Why is he not working at 1:30 p.m. on a Tuesday?")

Different parents, different career demands, different FWAs

" It's a wonderful thing about shift work that you can organize your hours to suit your family. One of my more senior colleagues set up her schedule to work Sundays, and then Mondays and Tuesdays overnight. She earned the same salary, but her family never missed her—they hardly even knew she was gone."

—*Tracy, nurse manager, mother of two*

" Flex hours really help. I get in by 7:00 and leave at 3:00. That lets me get home and spend time with the kids before they're tired. My son is on a competitive soccer team, and we don't have to race to get him to games or practice. I can be there when they're getting their homework done."

—*Malcolm, industrial psychologist, father of two*

" In operations, you have to be willing to work emergencies, and to be available on weekends and holidays. When there's a snowstorm, you work rotations until it's over. That means you have to be flexible in your own thinking, and how you balance your schedule, and life. I'm off every Tuesday. That's a 9:00-to-5:00 day for other people, but it's a family day for me."

—*Kelly Ann, airport operations, mother of one*

" Don't close any doors: try out different approaches before dismissing them as impossible. You'll figure things out. At first I tried having one full day off, but in a client-services business that can be tough, so I shifted to two half-days. When I came back from my first leave six years ago I didn't necessarily see myself as a partner here, but I was willing to experiment, and make adjustments, until I found what worked for me."

—*Nicole, management consultant, mother of three*

let's say that you work in a physical office, and that the first six months of working parenthood has gone well, but you desperately wish you were able to be present for the dinner-bath-bed ritual with the baby. In that case, a one-day-per-week remote-work approach might provide some small amount of relief—you'd get to do dinner and bath on that particular night of the week—but a shifted schedule that gets you home at 5:00 p.m. each day would *really* solve your problem. On the other hand, if you're superinvolved with the kids' school but commuting ninety minutes each way to work, a remote-working setup could be just the ticket: it would immediately hand you back precious hours each week to attend PTA meetings and do drop-offs. Think of yourself as a "flexibility doctor," prescribing the precise FWA medicine that will heal a specific condition.

As you mull over the best treatment, be pragmatic, and don't forget to take into account:

- **Your type of work.** If you're a restaurant employee, an airline pilot, a factory worker, or a critical-care nurse, you've got to show up to work in person. But you may have other kinds of leeway, like being able to work Saturdays and have Mondays at home with the kids.

- **The full costs to you.** Reduced hours mean a reduced income, which may be a complete nonstarter (unless, of course, that loss is offset by lower care costs).

- **The full costs to your employer.** That job-sharing arrangement may be just what you're looking for, but tricky to get approved if it means your company has to pay for two full employee-insurance plans instead of one.

- **Your home, and how long it takes to get there.** If you live in a tiny city-center apartment two blocks from the office, remote work might be more burden than blessing. Through some clever self-directed flexibility, though, you might get extra time at home.

- **Your family structure, care arrangement, and Village.** If you're toying with the idea of shifted hours, for example, think through who will take over caregiving responsibility during those very early mornings, late nights, or weekends—your partner, paid caregivers, a grandparent?

- **Your own psychology.** Remote work can be a huge benefit—unless, of course, you're a type A, always-on sort of person, who has difficulty backing away from work and going into parent mode, or you're the sort who easily moves into parent mode and then finds the intrusion of work into your home life depressing, and so on.

As you sift and sort all these various factors, you should be able to eliminate options quickly, and the best all-around choice should start coming into view. If it doesn't, or if you're still torn, try getting creative: think about how you might combine strategies, using them in very small bites, or how you might add your own twist to a standard option. Also try speaking to other working parents who have used the FWAs you're considering: their perspective can be invaluable in clarifying your own.

Advocating for It

Once you've settled on the FWA that will work best for you, your next step is getting any approvals needed, getting your boss on board, and getting everything cleared for FWA takeoff.

If you're seeking a more formal arrangement and you work in a large organization where FWAs are common, this is likely to be a fairly straightforward process. Chances are, there's a set of guidelines for putting your flex setup in place or even a sample contract to use for making the request. Once you know the drill, sit down with your manager to talk about your "ask," making it clear you're doing so within approved organizational bounds. Be gracious, positive, and appreciative, but know that if you're in good standing (e.g., haven't been issued any kind of performance warning), chances are decent you'll get the green light.

Enlisting your partner and caregivers

Your boss is an essential partner in making any FWA work—but you also need the support and understanding of the "bosses" in the home sphere: your partner, family, and caregivers. Play it forward: if your partner thinks *working from home* means *available to handle errands and home-repair projects*, or if your mother-in-law sees your second-shift evenings as good times to pop by for a visit, there's going to be a lot of friction.

Before your FWA begins, have a direct conversation about your new schedule and approach with each key member of your at-home Village—just as you may already have done with your boss and colleagues. To help make things clear and to reinforce the idea that this is a real, official, no-joke arrangement, put your timetable on a piece of paper, with "work time" and "nonwork time" clearly marked off. Explain to your spouse/partner/family what you'll need in order to make the arrangement successful—whether that's to be left alone while in your home office, to have their help in doing daycare pickup, or to have dedicated use of the home laptop on Thursdays. Be direct, and refer—nicely—to consequences: "A condensed workweek will give me a lot more time with Mateo, which is a benefit for our whole family. If I can't make it work, though, I'll need to go back to the old way." Be sure to offer a preemptive thank-you as well: flexibility may mean leaning on their time and patience in new ways, and feeling needed and appreciated will motivate them to help.

If you're planning to use self-directed or informal flexibility, or seeking a very small-scale accommodation (e.g., leaving two hours early and only on Wednesdays), try having a this-is-no-big-deal, FYI-type conversation with your manager: "Chris, my plan is simply to duck out for doctor's appointments and other kid-related reasons where needed, making up the work later in the day. I'll keep the team posted, always be reachable on cell—but my hunch is that no one, including you, will notice." If you're seen as diligent and reliable, your manager is unlikely to squawk at this.

If, however, you work in an environment that's less flex-friendly, or if there's no formal policy or other official "permissioning" of flex

When negotiating reduced hours

Be sure to specify what responsibilities, projects, clients, etc., you'll be handing off in order to make your arrangement work. In other words, answer the question: To move from a fifty- to a thirty-five-hour week, what will I *stop* doing?

If you neglect this step, you set yourself up for some major potential strain and frustration. You may find yourself getting paid for only thirty-five hours, while really continuing to work fifty—or you may find yourself in a desperate race to somehow compress fifty good hours of work into that tighter time frame. Neither of those outcomes is desirable or feasible. Be thoughtful, be realistic—and get ahead of the problem now.

work, or if you're making a big ask (like moving from five days per week to two), or if you're the first person in your organization to seek an FWA, then you're probably going to need to go into sell mode.

As you enter those conversations with your manager or with HR, you'll ensure the best possible outcomes by:

Emphasizing that . . .	By saying something like . . .
You plan to use the arrangement responsibly.	"Of course, it's on me to ensure that my work gets done and in a timely way."
There will be minimal if any impact on the team and business as a result.	"Yes, there would be a change in the hours I work—but not in project ownership or in our team's overall staffing."
The FWA creates benefits for your boss and organization, not just for you.	"This kind of flexibility will let me continue practicing law, and let you keep a trained patent attorney at the firm long-term. It may be useful in our recruitment efforts also—other current and aspiring parents will take note."

Emphasizing that . . .	By saying something like . . .
The details are incidental—and on your shoulders.	"I may need to make some small upgrades to my IT setup at home, but that's on me and easy to do."

If you sense discomfort, or get real pushback:

Tell your boss that . . .	Using phrases like . . .
You understand that this is an only-if-it-really-works situation.	"We could try this for two months, and if it doesn't work, either of us could pull the plug."
There appears to be clear precedent.	"It does feel like a big leap, yes—but several of our [colleagues in Department X, at competitor organizations, etc.] have done this successfully already, so it does appear to be possible, even within our field."
	"It is an unusual approach. But the wheels stayed on the bus when many of our colleagues had to adapt their hours/location during the pandemic, so I'm certain I could make this work."
You're in no rush.	"I know it's a lot to process, and I'm not pushing for an answer today. Please take time to think it through, and then we can regroup."

Throughout any conversation, and at every phase of the negotiation—and as hard as it may be to do so—remember to:

- Avoid getting dramatic or shrill

- Stay away from hostage-taking; *do this for me or I quit* is an option you should use only once, only at the tail end of an otherwise failed negotiation, and only if you're prepared to follow through (e.g., to take another job offer)

- Stay in a respectful, friendly, collaborative frame—it's just likely to be more effective

If you don't get what you want, or find yourself getting hot under the collar at any point, remember, you're an employee—not an indentured servant. Your boss and your organization make their choices, and you're free to make your own.

Making It Work, Day to Day

The gold standard of working flexibly is that nobody, including you, really notices. Maybe you're remote and living in a different time zone, but because you're in such regular touch with your colleagues, your physical location feels irrelevant. Or you've compressed your schedule, but because you're producing as much wonderful creative work as ever, your clients are barely if at all aware of the shift. There's no need to keep the fact that you're working flexibly a secret, but what should be most noticeable about you is your competence, impact, and potential, not the niggling bureaucratic details of your FWA.

Used consistently, these five approaches will help you win that gold:

- Paying ruthless attention to nuts-and-bolts operations. If you're working from home, that means ensuring you have 100-percent-reliable high-speed remote access and the ability to print documents in both your regular and home offices—and that you can do so just as quickly, and in high-quality color, and in the weird sizes and formats used for client presentations, and that you can set your phone so it rings straight through from your work line. If you're job sharing, it means taking ample notes on each to-do and going above and beyond to ensure a smooth and successful weekly handoff to your job-sharing partner. And so on. Your goal is to completely eliminate all dropped balls, delays, and operational snafus that might result from your FWA.

On and off

An FWA may actually *worsen* the nagging feeling that you can never turn work, or your work self, completely off. Boundaries become increasingly blurry: working from home means tackling your to-do list in the very environment that should be your refuge, and if you're on a three-day week, you may find yourself glued to your work phone even during that precious time with the kids. Throughout the early aughts and 2010s, we were all encouraged to look at "work/life integration" as the holy grail, but if you don't put guardrails in place that clearly define "when I'm working" and "when I'm not," you risk veering away from the benefits of flexibility, and onto the working-constantly path, and then to burnout, or worse. As you put your FWA in place, think about how to set your own sensible limits: how to keep work and parenting separate, or separate enough, that you can focus on, do well at, and enjoy each of them one at a time. De-integrate a little: think of setting deliberate barriers as being part of Flexibility 2.0.

That may be as basic as paying attention to your physical environment and setup. For example, create a clearly defined work space or "work signals": you may think of yourself as being "at work" *only* when sitting in the blue desk chair in your home office, or when wearing shoes. Or it may involve setting firm time limits, like working on your laptop each evening but always shutting down promptly at 9:00. A small ritual may also work: try playing a certain song or repeating a consistent phrase each day as you transition from work into parenting or the reverse, as a means of effectively self-signaling that *I'm done here, I can let this go temporarily, I can focus on the other.* Do whatever works best for you—but do *something*. Don't let increased flexibility have the reverse effect from what you want.

- Communicating proactively, continuously, and more than you think you "need" to. Whatever flex option you settle on, it's going to mean more time physically away, or adopting a slightly different (at least) schedule than your colleagues. Unfortunately, either of those two things can "read" as reduced effort or engagement. The way to get ahead of those incorrect impressions is by communicating, and often. If working from home, take care to send a few messages or call a few coworkers as soon as you sit down at your desk—not waiting until 10:30 a.m., when you have a question that needs answering. Provide frequent and unsolicited project updates, and circulate your meeting notes without being asked. If you're a manager, provide praise and encouragement to your people on the days you're off. Find small ways to send the message that you're active, in touch, and on it.

- Taking a flexible approach to your flexibility. If you usually don't work Tuesdays, but a new colleague is starting that day and you're essential to his onboarding, think about working that day anyway (or providing a welcome package of information that he can look through and you can discuss on Wednesday morning). If a major deadline looms, be ready to work past your usual earlier stop time. Strike the balance between preserving your own flexibility and sending clear, unambiguous signals that you're results oriented and part of the team.

- Being honest with yourself about your output, work quality, and engagement. If you're working as many hours as ever on your compressed schedule, but not getting quite as much done, or if you find yourself much quieter in meetings you dial into versus those you attend in person, consider how to confront and change those things.

- Seeing your work in terms of relationships as well as outputs. Yes, you may be writing just as much code as before—but you also need to focus on building a good rapport with the user-interface design team and mentoring junior colleagues. It's likely that those connections, as much as your own objective productivity, will drive your longer-term success and engagement.

Sending the Right Career Signals

Whenever you reach for more flexibility—whether that's formally, through a contracted arrangement with your employer, or informally, on a one-off, self-directed basis—you risk being easily misunderstood.

Telling clients and customers

If you need to tell clients, customers, or any other key stakeholders outside of your chain of command about your FWA, do so in the same way you alerted them to your parental leave: directly, matter-of-factly, unapologetically, confidently, and with a solutions focus. For example:

- "I'm not in the clinic Wednesdays, but we can book you in for an appointment any other day that week" or
- "While I won't see you in person—I typically don't work on Fridays—I'll be dialing in for the account update, and we'll have the revised plans back to you by close of business."

For the most part, your clients and customers are busy people, and they're going to be much more focused on the *outcomes* you produce than on obsessively monitoring your physical whereabouts or keeping tabs on your total hours worked. And because many of them are working parents themselves, your flex solution may even prompt a few bonding moments ("You've got a toddler at home? I know what that's like!")—never a bad thing for deepening and cementing any professional relationship.

Colleagues may (wrongly) perceive you as less ambitious, as "stepping off the path," as being "on the parent track," or as less interested in or deserving of juicy, career-making opportunities. They're not being malicious; it's just that without full context, or the ability to read your mind, they're coming to the wrong conclusion.

As at every phase of working parenthood, own your narrative. Make sure you know exactly what message you want to send to your boss, colleagues, and broader career network—and then be sure to convey it in a direct, convincing way. That might mean telling your boss: "Working four days a week has been terrific while I adjust to parenthood, but my long-term goal is still to become account manager, and over the next few years I'll be focused on doing what it takes to get there." Or you might say to colleagues: "Being involved with the kids' sports teams is very important to me, and I allocate the time for it during the week, which means I'm usually picking up slack on weekends." You may even want

> " As a manager, it's easy to fall into the trap of 'I don't need it, but they do.' I feel ownership of the team's experience. I want this to be a place where people can work well *and* attend to what's important to them, so sometimes I feel as if I should be working all the time. But that's not the message I want to send. We're all hardworking and passionate about what we do, and we all deserve that balance."
>
> —*Alexis, artistic director, mother of one*

to include a "context statement" in your FWA contract (if you have one) or annual review: "While working flexibly, my intention is to deliver the same quality and amount of work I always have, and to continue taking on 'stretch' assignments as they become available." Your story is unique, and where and when you'll want to tell it will depend on your FWA, the culture of your organization, how common flex work is in your particular role or position, the amount of challenges or skepticism you face from your boss and colleagues, and so on. Whatever the case, be sure to put flexibility within the context of your efforts, enthusiasm, and long-term commitment.

Taking Stock

A few months into any new FWA, and on an every-three-months basis thereafter, you should take a good hard look at how it's going. Be aware that virtually every organizational flex-work policy, even at the most family-friendly of organizations, contains carve-outs and exceptions allowing formal FWAs to be revoked at any time if performance slips, the demands of the job change, the organization faces headwinds, or there's a reorganization, or simply and very disconcertingly "at manager discretion." Just as jobs can come and go for any reason or none at all, FWAs—both formal and informal—can come and go too. And even if you *are* firing on all cylinders from a performance perspective in an organization that's wildly supportive, that doesn't mean everything's working perfectly or that you can afford to take a "set it and forget it" approach to flex work. A regular review lets you

What if colleagues aren't supportive?

If you've gotten sharp remarks about your FWA from folks in another department, or you sense simmering resentment among your colleagues, don't let it throw you, and don't go marching into HR's offices to complain just yet. Instead, take a much more direct and effective approach: go on a *charm offensive* (definition: "a campaign of flattery and friendliness designed to achieve the support or agreement of others"). In other words, look at those doubters and naysayers as tough customers you can sell, and win over. To do so:

1. Acknowledge and validate their concerns.
   - "It sounds as if you're skeptical that anyone could really serve our clients while working fewer-than-typical hours."
2. Mirror their cynicism a little.
   - "I asked myself the same thing. We both know this job isn't for slackers."
3. Bring them into your operational reality, emphasizing your personal sweat equity.
   - "Fortunately, I can make a 6:00 p.m. departure work by jumping back online each evening as soon as the baby's asleep and working however long I need to."
4. Speak in tough-guy terms, and refer to personal accountability.
   - "Here's the bottom line: if I don't do my part to help our team meet our goals, my career's at risk."
   - "We both know Cynthia will have my head if I don't produce."
5. Make genuine inquiries.
   - "That said, if you have specific concerns or think there are ways I need to be operating differently, I'm happy to hear them."
6. Honor and flatter.
   - "If you have ideas on how I can make this work, I'd appreciate them."
   - "You raised three great kids while working here full-time. There's a lot you could teach me."
   - "I talk to you because you're one of the few people in this organization unafraid to be honest about this stuff."
7. Turn the conversation back to work matters.
   - "But now let's think through the inputs we just got from engineering . . ."

(continued)

If you just don't have the stomach for a charm offensive at this point, that's fine. But be aware that however you *do* react to doubters and skeptics—whether with indignation, optimism, or silence—that reaction becomes part of your professional brand. And if you can nudge those doubters just a teensy bit further toward flex-acceptance, you may make the next working mother or father's experience and life that much easier.

make sure all is working well, that you're fully aligned to expectations, and that there are no hidden issues or concerns.

One useful tool for performing this checkup is the FWA Consideration Grid as shown in table 15-2. The grid prompts you to think both big picture and tactically about what's working and about any needed refinements to your FWA. Crucially, it encourages you to do that thinking from both your own perspective and from your organization's. Try filling out your personal grid following the example provided here. Be honest—this is for your own benefit, and it's a rare FWA that doesn't need a few tweaks over time.

Once you've completed the grid, debrief—quickly—with your manager. No matter how relaxed, honest, and informal your relationship is, it never hurts to show up as a thoughtful, proactive collaborator—one who's "going the extra mile" to make the flexibility you're using work. You may choose to share your grid (in which case, you'll likely score some extra points for organization and diligence), or simply speak to the conclusions and issues the grid exercise highlighted. Whichever route you choose, you can initiate the conversation by saying something like, "As you know, I've been starting and finishing work earlier now for three months. I'm eager to ensure that the flexibility I'm using is 100 percent on a good track—for both of us. My sales numbers are steady, and I don't see any major 'issues' in terms of our work or team. I would like to think ahead to what will work best in February crunch time . . ." Chances are this check-in is brief. Your manager may even cut you off with an "everything's good, no worries" type response. Or

TABLE 15-2

The FWA Consideration Grid

Question	From my perspective	From my organization/ boss's perspective	Needed action(s)
Am I/are we doing what was agreed?	Yes. I've been able to work from home 3 days per week, with certain exceptions, over the past 6 months. Several colleagues have commented that they didn't even know I was on an FWA.	Yes. A key concern was whether or not I would make it to important client meetings if they fell on my "home days." Since beginning the arrangement, I've made it to every single sales pitch— regardless of my preferred schedule.	Discuss plan for February, when most of the team will be doing client check-ins.
Is this arrangement working?	Yes, in that I'm getting the flexibility to spend more wonderful time with my daughter. No, in that I'm often working additional hours.	Yes. The FWA hasn't changed my performance ranking or sales numbers. The organization is getting my best work.	None.
Are there any additional, unexpected, or downstream effects of this arrangement that we need to address or manage?	A few team members have made offhand comments about my "part-time" schedule (even though I'm working full-time).	Several staff members who aren't eligible for flexible work given their job types have heard about my arrangement, and asked their own managers if they can work from home, too.	• Make certain that on my at-home days, I am communicating actively and early on in the day with skeptical colleagues— and otherwise going "above and beyond" to signal my true commitment and engagement. • Alert HR that we have gotten several questions on this.
What's the outlook for this arrangement over the next 6 to 12 months?	Over the next 3 months, fine. When the baby starts walking, I will need to revisit the feasibility of working from my home office/small apartment.	If there's any attrition on the team after year's end, we may have to reallocate responsibilities and workload.	Revisit in December. Consider what an alternative flexibility plan could look like if I needed to cover more accounts.

The Entitlement Trap, and how to steer clear of it

Never take flexibility for granted, or in any way convey that you do. Almost nothing will annoy and alienate your manager and coworkers as quickly and certainly as telegraphing, however inadvertently or subtly, that you see the flexibility you're being extended as a given. The moment you're perceived as acting or feeling *entitled*, your FWA effectively boomerangs on you: instead of being a benefit, it puts a dent in your relationships, reputation, and career.

To keep yourself well clear of landing in the Entitlement Trap, avoid:

- Using language that implies any sense that "I've got this coming." When discussing flex work, never use words like *owed*, *deserve*, *fairness*, *rights*, or *due*.
- Discussing yourself, or working parents in general, as deserving of special privileges. (Remember, your childless coworker who's struggling to care for an aging relative has just as much need for flexibility as you do.)
- Visibly "scorekeeping" your hours worked or your work-from-home days. OK, maybe you *did* come in for an important meeting when you otherwise would have worked remotely. Bummer. But making a stink about it will only come across as petty.
- Expecting colleagues to go to great lengths to accommodate your schedule—for example, by holding certain meetings *only* on days you plan to work. It's on *you*, not your colleagues, to find feasible work-arounds.
- Referring to your ongoing, uphill battle to find work/life balance, despite your preferential arrangement.
- Visibly tying your work status (title, years at the organization, educational attainment, etc.) to flexibility: e.g., saying anything like, "Well of course as a manager, I can decide where and when I work."
- Neglecting to talk with your colleagues about their own families and personal responsibilities. Having young kids is a lot of work—but whether parents or not, and whether using FWAs or not, your coworkers are all facing significant life pressures themselves.

Adapting during the toddler years and beyond

No matter how well your flexible arrangement worked throughout Year One, it may result in some rough sledding when your child becomes a toddler, and then a more vocal, with-it child. Working from home is a completely different game with a mobile, opinionated three-year-old around than it is with a small baby. And if you're on a reduced schedule, you're likely to get a lot of challenging questions as to why you have to go to work today even though you didn't yesterday. Don't waste too much time trying to explain the nuances and rules of your FWA to your small child—it just won't resonate. Instead, think about reaching for some new techniques.

If working remotely:

- Pretend you're leaving for work: dress as usual, grab your work bag, kiss your toddler goodbye—and then sneak back in through the garage door and up the back stairs to your home office. You'll be able to get good work done, and still avoid the commute.
- Have a clear, visible signal—like a large red stop sign you can hang on your office door—signaling when it's OK for your child to come in and when Daddy needs privacy and quiet.
- Make a date: your little one may not be as tempted to burst in on you or demand attention if she knows you'll have lunch together, or go to the park right after.
- Consider working someplace close to, instead of actually inside, your home: the local library, a neighbor's apartment, the coffee shop, a shared work space nearby.

If working reduced or compressed hours, set aside a few minutes each morning and evening to talk about the day's schedule and preview what's happening tomorrow. When your toddler knows that *Today Daddy works late, but tomorrow he's at home*, she's less likely to be upset and confused when you head out the door. To create even more clarity, consider using the "visible schedule" trick we covered in chapter 5.

As you go through these years of rapid change, don't be afraid to reconsider your flexibility arrangement in its totality, and to make any needed adjustments. Maybe remote working was a godsend during that first year of parenthood—but perhaps a Split Day schedule would serve you much better now. As your family and career change and develop, your approach to flexibility will likely need to change too.

you may find yourself in a longer conversation about how February will work. Either way: you've made sure there were no surprises looming, and positioned yourself as a responsible, can-do partner.

Becoming a Builder

It's easy to get lulled into thinking that *flexibility* is passive, or magic— or that it rides on plain old luck. You may see it as something structurally impossible in your particular environment, or that your boss or organization *gives* to you, if you're fortunate, or that you could attain only by developing special insights or superpowers that would let you work differently than you do now. Or it may feel like an elite club, or university: gain admission to Flex-World, life will be great, and you'll be enjoying its special privileges forever. And of course there are some tiny truths there—if you do have a supportive boss, for example, then yes, absolutely and objectively: you're lucky.

Never let your thinking about flexibility turn into longing, or see yourself as a passive flexibility grantee instead of a flexibility *builder*. Reflect back on all of the initially daunting workparent challenges you've surmounted on your own steam thus far. Just as you put together your best possible parental leave; constructed your biggest possible Village; assembled a strong, supportive circle of workparent mentors; and put a good care arrangement in place, you're going to take an active, carpenter-like role here too. You can't and won't get every bit of choice and leeway you want—you're in much too demanding a job and life for that. But using your own self-knowledge, pragmatism, creativity, and hard work, you're going to hammer together the very best flex structure you can.

Mark's story

" When our first daughter was born we lived very close to the city, but even my usual fifteen-minute drive to the office could sometimes take an hour. In a career driven by time and efficiency, that didn't make any sense, and it left me and my wife with only about ten minutes of human conversation together each evening. During those first few months of parenthood, we would take walks around the neighborhood together, pushing the stroller, thinking: 'Is this *it*?' We loved the town where we went to college, and had always said we'd move there after retirement. We said, 'Why not now?' I knew I could do my job remotely—but I wasn't sure how to ask.

I went to see one of my mentors, the guy who had given me my first appellate argument. He's the father of four, and had worked from home one day a week back in the 1980s, before remote work was a thing. His advice was, 'The firm isn't in the business of making people happy. They won't agree unless you really push.' I was still early in my career but I was about to argue my first Supreme Court case, so I had the confidence and naivete to tell my then-bosses, 'This is what I want to do.' They eventually agreed, but only after I had an offer in hand from a competing firm. We sold our house, figuring we would live on the little bit of money we got from the sale when I got fired, which we assumed I would, and we made the move—about two hours away.

At the beginning, I kept going to the office one day a week, getting up at 4:00 a.m. so I could drive in, work a regular day, and be home late in the evening. Now, I go in when I need to—but I've made a big, deliberate, ongoing effort to make things work in a friction-free way both for me and for my colleagues. My home office is away from the living areas, I'm in there from 8:00 a.m. till 6:00 p.m., and the kids know not to bother Dad when I'm working. When one of my clients, or other people at the firm, wants to speak with me, that's when we speak. In a lot of our family-vacation pictures, I'm on the phone with the office. I've tried to be even *more* available than normal—to overcompensate.

I've held on to this arrangement through two job moves, and I can honestly say that I've never heard anyone make a single negative comment. I've worked with clients for years without them even knowing I'm not sitting at a desk in the city. And I've had so much more family time than I would have otherwise.

It's been fifteen years."

—*Mark, appellate lawyer, father of three*

16

Away

Coping with Long Hours and Work Travel

You want to spend good, dedicated time with the kids every day, but sometimes it's just not possible. Maybe you're facing a late night to finish up a sudden and urgent project, or it's busy season and you're working around the clock, or face-to-face meetings are keeping you on the road, or you've just been deployed, or are pulling extra shifts because you need the money—or some combination. Whatever the reason, the result is the same: just as work pressures ratchet up, you have to juggle home and care logistics remotely, you worry about how the separation is affecting the kids . . . and you miss them like absolute crazy. It seems like a no-win situation.

Why not try out some new techniques that might lessen the strain? A few small twists and additions to your usual routines before, during, and after your time apart can make things go a little more smoothly, and keep both you and the kids feeling more comfortable and connected.

Before You Go: Planning and Prep

Getting ready to be away from home for a longer-than-usual stretch typically involves a whole lot of logistics—and some delicate, deep emotions. Here's how, practically and personally, to get ready for departure.

Your workparent Away Planner

You might be a teacher preparing for parent-teacher-conference week and the sixteen-hour days it requires, or have a big client meeting in a distant city, or work in a profession where sudden all-nighters are the norm. Whatever the case, your head is spinning as you struggle to process and tame all the logistical details of being away. You've got extra care arrangements to think of, and perhaps meal planning, and

---

What's the payoff?

Being away from home probably does have a meaningful upside if, for example, you're:
- Putting in extra days and nights at the office or library to cram for those all-important professional licensing exams
- Out on the road hustling new business that will help you get promoted (and that promotion will mean vastly less travel)
- Working all those overtime hours to save for the down payment on a house
- In a field or profession (aviation, healthcare, the military, etc.) where long hours and time away from home are absolute, inescapable realities for anyone who wants to remain employed or get ahead

If one or more of these are the case, your absence has a specific, important benefit, whether financial, professional, or personal. As hard as it is, being away is a *good* thing for the working-parent You of the future.

Be very, very careful about settling into an Away pattern when you can't see a real and clear payoff, though. Regular or prolonged time away from the kids is just too costly, in all possible senses of that word, to keep up longer-term for no good reason—for example, just *because that's how things are done at my particular company, because I used to work this way before I had kids,* or *because my boss expects people to work nutty hours.* Of course there will be many times you'll have to burn the midnight oil—that's inevitable. But remember: the kids are only young once. If there's no payoff, it may be time to think about finding a way to push your career forward while staying closer to home.

---

the babysitter needs to be paid, of course, and there's homework to oversee—and what happens if there's an emergency?

One way to go is simply to tackle each of those details as they occur to you each time you're in prep mode, hoping that you've covered everything while remaining ready to put out the small fires that might flare up due to any neglected detail while you're gone. The other, easier way is to develop your own personalized *Away Planner*: a reusable outline of what will happen while you're not around and a checklist of what you need to do up front in order to make it all work. An Away Planner prevents oversights: it's impossible to forget important to-dos when you have them down on paper. It also facilitates communication between you and the members of your Village who will be covering during your absence; you can stay, quite literally, on the same page in terms of daily care plans, pickups, drop-offs, homework, and so on. When personalized, and done thoughtfully, your planner is also a kind of antianxiety pill, taking the edge off the stress you may be feeling. (While this particular pill will be addictive, it's all-natural and comes with no side effects.)

In table 16-1 you'll find a sample Away Planner, in this case for a workparent who's part of a dual-career family and planning a five-day trip. As you can see, it covers day-to-day blocking and tackling as well as more-personal and emotional issues, like how to stay in touch and how to provide your child extra warmth and reassurance while you're away. Read over this sample and consider how you would tailor it to suit your own family, work demands, care setup, and Village. Feel free to add columns, categories, and checkboxes until it works best for you. When you're done, you'll have an all-in-one, quick-use way of getting ready to go.

Creating counterweights

As you glance over table 16-1 you may find yourself pausing at one particular section: the column labeled "Counterweights." By definition, a counterweight is a balancing force, a stabilizer. It helps compensate for the effect of something pulling in the opposite direction. When you're a workparent and away from home, a counterweight is something that helps offset the impact of your absence—that lets

TABLE 16-1

Sample Workparent Away Planner

- **Travel:** Flight and hotel information in Google Calendar.
- **Communications:** Daily video chat over breakfast. Will try to call at bedtime.
- **Money:** Household cash is on the piano. Sitter has debit card I gave her.
- **Food:** Extra leftovers in freezer. Household cash will cover if need to order in.
- **Village alerted?** Yes—emailed with homeroom teacher. Neighbors know that Phoebe's car will be in the drive.
- **Emergency backups:** Third Parent is aware I'm away and is willing to pitch in as needed.

Day	Core caregiver	Additional caregiver(s)	Drop-off plan	Pickup plan	Evening routine	Other to-dos	Special concerns	My availability	Counterweights
1	Partner	Aunt Phoebe	School bus	School bus	Partner	Show-and-tell: needs to bring special object to present to class	Be sure to ask him how show-and-tell went	Will be on the plane; will call when I land around 6:00 p.m.	Homeroom teacher
2	Partner	Aunt Phoebe	School bus	School bus	Partner	None	Will need extra help to finish math worksheet	Tied up in meetings, will call morning and evening	

#									
3	Aunt Phoebe	None	School bus	Aunt Phoebe	Partner	Math work-sheets due—make sure these are in the backpack	Let Phoebe know household money is on the piano	Doing the client site visit; may be very difficult to reach during the day—if you need me, text	Pizza night with Aunt Phoebe
4	Partner	Weekend sit-ter will work this day until Partner gets home	School bus	Soccer practice; van will drop at home	Aunt Phoebe	Soccer—needs to bring his shin guards and cleats, and don't forget the inhaler!	Pep talk needed; they lost last week's game		
5	Partner		Carpool	Playdate; I will pick up if flight lands on time	Family dinner	None	Ask friend's parents if he can stay for dinner if my flight is late	Traveling	Playdate with Jeremy

> ❝ I travel a hundred days a year for this job. But when I'm home, I work from home quite a bit, and we sit down for dinner every night and breakfast every morning—I'm not rushing toward work. And this firm lets you acknowledge family life, as part of its culture. Whenever I've had to cancel an important meeting because of a family emergency, the first two questions I get are, 'Are you OK?' and 'What can I do?' It's a lot of time away from home, but there's also a lot of advantages."
>
> —*Karen, macro trends expert, mother of two*

the kids feel just a little more comfortable about Mom or Dad being gone for longer than usual. You may choose to use events, activities, or locations as your counterweights, although most often, the offsetting forces you'll be turning to are real live people—family members or other Villagers. Whatever or whoever you settle on, that resource blunts the impact of your being away by providing your child with extra comfort, pleasure, or distraction.

To take a specific example: let's say you're short-staffed at work, it's busy season, and you know you'll be working around the clock this week. Your three-year-old son is extremely apprehensive about your being gone quite so much. Realistically, this won't be his—or, likely, your—happiest several days, but you cleverly think ahead and settle on two effective counterweights: first, a trip to the duck pond near your house, and second, his daycare provider. The duck-pond outing, which a neighbor has kindly agreed to take him on, is something you know he'll look forward to and relish, and those extra hugs and attention from a savvy, trusted caregiver will help him feel better throughout the day. You haven't, and can't, completely cure his feelings of sadness at your absence, but—by arranging a brief excursion and by politely asking a caregiver for a bit of extra support—you've helped ease it.

Note that a counterweight doesn't have to involve any kind of special treat, lavish gift, or rule-breaking, but something simple, that helps stoke positive emotion, and that makes your time away feel a little shorter than it otherwise would. Think what might work as

Not if but when

You may never be able to exert complete control over *how much* and *how often* you're away because of work—but you can do your best to influence *when*.

At the beginning of each year or major work cycle, note which days and weeks are particularly important for you to be closer to, or just more available at, home. Include celebrations, such as the kids' birthdays; transitions, such as the start and end of the school year; and important events, such as family gatherings, the kids' special performances and games, or periods of cultural or religious significance for your family. Give the list a rough prioritization: maybe you'd love to be at your son's first clarinet performance, but it's essential for the family to be together on Greek Easter, for example.

Then start gently advocating—and defending. If your work calendar is accessible to other colleagues, block out the key no-fly dates with a polite note that "my daughter starts first grade this week; please consult me before scheduling." Tell your boss that you're happy to work late and take on the client two time zones away—but you would appreciate staying put on the week of May 5th. Or find a colleague with different personal obligations than yours and agree to cover weekends or work overtime on a mutually beneficial, alternating basis. In other words, plan ahead and *ask* for what you want.

effective counterweights for your child, and see if you can plan one or two out before leaving. Of course, you can always be one of your own counterweights by blocking out special time together for when you return. That shift won't seem so long if your child knows that there's an entire Saturday with Mom, or a trip to the zoo, at the end of it.

Saying goodbye

Your child's normal feelings of sadness that Mom or Dad is going to be away for any period of time are easily compounded through uncertainty—and your own mixed messages. Big, open-ended questions that your kids may have around your departure but may be too young to put into words would include: *Don't you love me and miss me, too? Do you* really *have to go? What will happen to me while you're away?*

When the senior people expect it

Team norms and expectations are difficult things to break, and they're typically set by your group's most senior members—often in a less than working-parent-friendly way. The leaders you work with may see, or even themselves use, endless face time, work benders, or long stretches of professional travel as proof of value within your organization. But it's also very possible they're working less efficiently than they could, and that you can prove your own contributions without selling your soul to the job.

Think carefully about any ways you could still deliver the professional goods without being away from home quite so much. Try landing new clients locally or making sales through VC rather than in person. Speak at industry or trade conferences to generate visibility and new business leads more quickly than you could through multiple single-client visits. Try clustering or smoothing out your overtime hours to ensure a better time-with-the-kids schedule, or think about volunteering to work on a few holidays or other "undesirable" times in exchange for a bit more day-to-day flexibility. With some careful planning and technology on your side, you may be able to generate the same results as any work maniac or road warrior—all while minimizing your time away. When you can point to hard numbers and specific wins that prove your contributions, managers will usually take notice.

When are you coming back? The more preemptive answers you provide, and in a straightforward and positive way, the more secure and calm both you and your child will feel and the easier your leave-taking will be.

Before any Away period, make sure to preview the plan. Tell your child where you're going, when you're returning, and exactly who will be the caregiver while you're gone. Be direct and reassuring: "Mom's going on a work trip for five days, and when you're not in school, either Daddy or Aunt Phoebe will be with you the entire time." If your child is toddler-age or older, post a simplified, age-appropriate version of your planner in the kitchen, or someplace else readily visible. That way, caregivers can help your child "mark off" the time until

> ❝ I've been deployed twelve times. It's what my kids have known their whole lives, since they were infants. We tell them about it directly, but keep things age-appropriate. We'll say, 'Daddy's going on a long business trip'—or a short one. They don't need to know the specifics.
>
> We tried using FaceTime to keep in touch, but when the kids were small, they'd get really upset. It's easier for them if I'm completely gone than some kind of confusing halfway. And I don't play the whole 'who's working hard, whose car is still in the parking lot' game. When I'm home, I put a high premium on being *home*.❞
>
> —*Ashley, military officer, father of three*

you're back: "Look—it's Thursday, which means Aunt Phoebe will be coming to help us with dinner tonight . . . and there's just one more day until Mom comes home!"

As you talk through the plan, and while saying your actual goodbye, be certain to acknowledge and respond to your child's feelings, **without mirroring them**. If your five-year-old gets weepy, hugging her and telling her that "it's OK to be sad" is helpful and healthy, but expressing your own sadness at leaving will only stoke confusion: *If you're so sad*, she'll wonder, *then why are you going?* It also thrusts your child into a difficult, ambiguous position. She may think, *If I keep crying, will Mom decide to stay? If she leaves anyway, does that mean she doesn't care about my feelings?* Be sympathetic but definitive, and anchor your comments in the future: "Mom will be gone for five days, Daddy is here to take care of you, and I can't wait to see you when I get back." That beats a wistful "I wish I didn't have to go, either." Separation, particularly from very young children, will never be easy—but be sure to send the right signals. Your kids take their emotional cues from you.

While You're Gone: Specific and Powerful Ways to Stay, and Feel, in Touch

You miss the kids, and they miss you. To compensate, and to close that physical and emotional gap, your go-to tool will likely be the phone

Homesickness, and how to get through it

The word *homesick* is typically associated with children: hear it, and you may think of a miserable eight-year-old missing home on the first night of summer camp. But adults can miss home, too—and if you're a new working parent, the kids are very small, or you're unused to being away, it's very likely that at some point you'll develop a case of homesickness yourself. If you've ever gotten choked up on the way to the airport, or been trapped at work but found your thoughts wandering to the kids and how great it would be to snuggle them, or just felt allover blue when away, you're certainly not the first.

Chances are those feelings will begin to resolve with a little distraction: landing in a new city or attending to important details before that big deadline forces your focus elsewhere, displacing intense thoughts of *I wish I weren't away*. If you need some additional help, call or message other workparents you trust: their responses should be sympathetic but encouraging (they've all seen this movie themselves). Then remind yourself of your counterweights: yes, you miss your nine-year-old terribly now, but you and she will go bowling—her favorite outing—together this weekend. If the sadness becomes acute, if it's accompanied by any twinge of guilt, or if you find yourself weepy: think "meta" for a moment. *The thing that's making you so upset right now is the exact same thing that makes you a wonderful parent: your total and complete devotion to your children.* You may be away, but homesickness is proof that your heart and mind are in the right place.

or video chat: you'll be tempted to call home several times a day to connect and to see how things are going. Sure, you want to hear the kids, and check in with their caregivers—but you also want to feel present, and more parent-ish, and all-around better about the situation yourself.

Those calls may not go very well, though, or provide either you or the kids much comfort or reassurance. Small children aren't able to engage in adult-style conversations, or to narrate their daily experiences, and older ones may be perfectly capable of doing so but just not want to. Ask a four-year-old or a fourteen-year-old, "How are you?"

> "I'm often away two nights a week, sometimes more. No matter where I am, I always call right before they go to bed—for the songs, the stories. It's wonderful to get to call home and hear, 'Hi Papa!'—and to be there, with them, for that lullaby time."
>
> —*João, management consultant, father of two*

or "How was school?" particularly over the phone, and you may get a monosyllabic answer or silence. And of course, if your child is still a baby or young toddler, it's even harder to connect by calling. So what *will* keep you feeling bonded and closer-by when the demands of your job keep you apart?

- **Tangible reminders.** Make sure that there are small physical reminders of you, and of you and your child together, throughout the house. Display pictures of the two of you where your child can see them, and leave books you like to read together or games you enjoy playing together out within easy reach. If your child is very small, think about giving him one of your belongings as a "comfort object": that favorite T-shirt Dad always wears can make an excellent blankie for a little one to use at naptime. That trick goes both ways: when you're away from home, it can be oddly reassuring to know that you've got one of your son's dinosaur socks in your work bag. In other words: allow yourselves to feel the other's physical presence, even when you're away.

- **Keeping up with your regular routines.** If your bedtime ritual is "song plus story," keep singing and reading, and at the same time of day. Bring one of your child's favorite books along with you and read it over a video call, turning the pages, doing the funny voices, and showing the pictures as you go, and then sing the same song you normally would. Even if you have to read that story during the middle of the night because you're in a different time zone, or have to do so in the middle of the break room during lunch, maintain as much consistency as you can.

- Playing a game, or doing another activity, together. Before you leave, hide a few "I love you" notes or small gifts (a yo-yo, a small piece of candy) around the house, and during each call home provide a new clue that lets your child find one. Or start a game of online chess with your teenager, or have a Ridiculous Faces contest with your middle-schooler via photo message. Whatever the gag is, and no matter how small or silly, it will let you keep *interacting* with your child.

- "Talking" via recorded video. In addition to live/interactive phone calls, record yourself talking to your kids (or singing, or waving, or doing a tour of your hotel room, or showing the scene outside the taxi window, etc.), and then send the clip to them or to their caregiver. Unlike with live, real-time video, they can watch (and rewatch) at their leisure, with zero pressure to immediately respond—and then watch again, if they want to, or send you a message back.

- Sharing where you are and what you're up to. When you're away, your children may feel as if you've fallen into a mysterious hole. You're gone, and they likely have no idea of why, or what you're doing. And unfortunately "we're short-staffed" or "I'm in Birmingham for a meeting" won't resonate with your nine-year-old. So help your children understand a bit better: have their caregiver show them where you are on a map, or send a photo of yourself in the conference room surrounded by papers as you prepare for the big meeting. Provide a window and insight onto what you're doing.

- Following the "when we see x, then y" technique. Have an agreement with your son that today, every time either of you sees someone wearing the color green (or chewing gum, or driving a convertible, etc.), you'll think of the other, and send an imaginary hug or high five. Even when you're not there, you can still stoke positive emotion.

- Eating together. As we explore in chapter 18, "Food and Mealtimes," many of the most powerful connective moments you're likely ever to have with your children are over a meal. So continue having the occasional meal together, even while you're away: prop the iPad in front of you while you're having a quick breakfast at the hotel coffee shop and they're eating their cereal at home. It's just a normal morning together—even if you're five hundred miles away.

- Sending a postcard. In today's world, actual, personalized, hard-copy mail has a retro, novelty appeal, and children love receiving it. Keep stamps in your wallet, ready to go, grab a handful of postcards, and drop the kids a message on each day you're gone—even if in the same city. The metamessage: *I'm thinking of you constantly.*

- Emailing. Open an email address in your child's name—even if she's years away from being able to use a computer—and, every time you think of her, miss her, or see something interesting or unusual while you're away, shoot her a note: "I just got to my hotel. Here's a photo of the view from my window, and I miss you and love you," or "I'm working the overnight shift tonight, honey, and sending you a big hug." That email account

Should the kids come with me?

You may be toying with the idea of bringing your son or daughter along on that work trip—or may have enviously read about the "we'll fly your child and nanny along with you" benefits offered at a few high-end companies. But before you make any plans or start romanticizing this particular type of work/life integration, do a quick reality check. Do you *really* want to lug all the baby gear through the airport or run the risk of needing to make a sudden trip to the pediatrician's in a distant or foreign city? Is staying together worth completely upending your child's regular routine? Can you stay focused and top-of-your-game professionally while sharing a small hotel room with your toddler? Depending on your schedule, your destination, and the ages of your kids, having them join you might work beautifully—but think ahead and be practical.

>   I'll take a piece of the kids' artwork along with me, and send a picture of me holding it in the cockpit, before takeoff. We also play a game where I'll take a super-close-up photo of some object—like a lampshade in my hotel room, or part of the sidewalk—and they'll have to guess what the object is. They know I'm thinking about them, and we're interacting, even when I'm not around.
>
>   If you feel shy about doing that kind of stuff in front of your colleagues, don't. They're all living through the same thing. They get it."
>
> —*Rick, airline pilot, father of three*

may not be opened, or read, for years, but when it is, your child will have ample proof of your feelings and commitment. In the meantime, you'll feel more emotionally connected.

Whatever connection strategies you choose to use, take great care to keep your messages and overall tone warm, upbeat, and *light*. If you're jetlagged, or annoyed at working the double shift because somebody else called out sick, fine—but use your video to make a little joke of it, laughingly pointing out the dark circles under Daddy's eyes instead of moaning that you've gone twenty-two hours without sleep. In the videoconference dinner you're doing from the break room during busy season—when you're feeling ground down and running behind—don't talk about your workload. Ask how the kids' macaroni and cheese is. Keep your connections positive.

Upon Return, and After: Making Your Homecoming Calmer and More Satisfying—for Everyone

You've just finished the marathon work session and arrived back home. The hard part is over now, right?

Well, not quite. Changes in routine are tough on you as an adult and professional, but they're *much* more difficult for children—even when those changes, like your return home, are good ones. As you

walk back through your front door, your children may greet you with
the squeals of joy, full attention, and hugs you're hoping for—or with
confusion, hot-and-cold behavior, demands, hostile questions, a tantrum, or apparent indifference, and from your side any of those responses may feel crushing. Yet a difficult return isn't inevitable: just as
you paid attention to the small-scale mechanics and to the emotional
impact of your departure and time away, you can do the same now on
the way back in, using a few specific maneuvers to make your home-
coming a smoother, more natural-feeling, and happier experience for
everyone.

- **Preannounce your entry.** While bursting through the front
  door with little warning and proclaiming that "Daddy's home!"
  or "Mom's back!" may feel wonderful to you, it probably won't
  to the kids. What you intend as a positive surprise may create
  unintended pressure on older children to respond in a certain
  way (*be thrilled to see me, right this minute!*), and it may startle
  or even frighten little ones. Call en route home and let your
  children—or whoever's taking care of them—know that you'll
  be there shortly. That advance notice offers them the chance to
  get into a good mindset about your return. If you'll be arriving
  home after the kids are asleep, get ahead of that, also: tell your
  six-year-old that you won't see her tonight, but that when she
  wakes up tomorrow morning she should come jump into bed
  with you, or that you'll eat breakfast together. In other words:
  keep your actual, specific point of reentry into the family
  sphere as gentle and as "no surprises" as possible.

- **Talk positively.** OK, maybe the meeting didn't go so well, the
  project is off the rails, you're exhausted, the train was late, traffic terrible, the extra hours a waste of your time. So life goes—
  but your kids can't solve those problems, and those problems
  aren't what they should be focused on when they haven't seen
  you for the past three days. A simple "I'm so glad to be home
  now and to see you" sets a much better tone, and allows better
  connection.

- **Don't force interaction; let them come to you.** Because you've missed the kids like crazy, it's natural to want to race toward them, lavishing them with hugs and expecting their undivided attention. But they may have settled into a routine while you were away, or for the moment their attention may be glued to another person or activity. Maybe your son worked hard all afternoon on that Lego tower, and doesn't want to turn away from it right now, or your teen is still upset over a loss on the sports field. That's not any kind of feedback, or lack of excitement that you're home—they're just in a particular groove. Try sliding into *their* activities, joining *them* in what they're doing and experiencing. Admire the tower and ask how he got the big yellow piece to balance on the top—rather than making yourself the main event.

- **Tie up loose ends in private.** You likely still have a few lingering details to take care of: the update email has to be sent to your boss, your hours logged in the billing system, the team thanked for their hard work, the schedule checked for your next shift. But avoid immediately going into get-it-done mode, sitting down in your home office, or typing on your smartphone screen in front of the kids. Yes, it will feel terrific to close out those annoying, lingering items on your to-do list, but it sends a powerful—if unintentional—message that you're not fully *there*. Finish up what you need to quickly and behind closed doors, or after the kids have gone to bed.

- **Reestablish routines.** No matter how long you've been away, try to get straight back into regular, predictable patterns, both in terms of home and work. Your departure was, at some level, a disruption, and going back to your regular schedule and habits spells a return to normalcy. So sit down to dinner when you usually do, review your eight-year-old's homework, take the dog for his evening walk. Spend some extra time with the kids if you can—do the school run even if it means going into work half an hour later than usual, for example—but don't try

Using time away as time for yourself

It's the dirty little secret known to absolutely everyone but the kids: away time can help you restore, recharge, and reconnect with the noncareer, nonparent You (remember *you*?). If you're staying late at the office anyway, you may be able to walk the longer way home rather than racing home on the subway. On a work trip, you may get a few blessed hours to read a book or watch TV; you have only *yourself* to take care of on that plane; and in the hotel you may even—savor this thought as it washes over you—get a night or two of solid, uninterrupted sleep.

Good for you! When you're working this hard and in the thick of parenting, you don't get a lot of breaks, and you deserve this one. Don't spend any time guiltily wondering if you *should* be more miserable, or wondering if looking forward to that child-free flight makes you a bad parent, because it doesn't. These Away-induced pockets of "me time" are like a few good gulps of a sports drink during an endurance event: they give you a hit of energy and are one small way to increase your overall resilience.

Try to maximize these breaks in whatever way works best for you. Instead of settling for whatever movies are offered on the plane, download several by your favorite director and turn the trip into a film festival. On a night you're already working late, have the sitter stay an extra hour so you can meet a friend. You're not being selfish—you're being smart.

to overcorrect for your absence by hovering, demanding long stretches of one-to-one time, or otherwise throwing the typical family schedule and the kids' expectations even further out of whack. As much as you can, give your kids the gift of predictability.

Showing up, and being there

If you're in a career that requires spending longer stretches away from your child, you may find yourself hovering on that fact—and harboring some guilt. If so, it's time to redefine: to remind yourself what *showing up* and *being there* as a mother or father really means.

Of course you want to connect with your child, in person, and as much as you can—that's critically important, for both of you. But if your family needs the money, you're *showing up* for the kids by working those extra hours. By honoring the treasured bedtime ritual, even when it's over the phone, you can be a *presence* when not actually present. And every time you give your child your total and full attention, wherever both of you are, you're *being there* for her, too. Being physically present or constantly available to your children isn't the sole yardstick of good parenting—your love and commitment are what count.

17

Time Off

Getting, and Getting the Most from,
Breaks in Your Work Routine

Are you getting enough time off? Not half-on/half-off, eyes-on-your-smartphone, doing-the-laundry, supervising-homework kind of off—but really-enjoying-it, relaxed-and-renewed, investing-in-yourself-and-the-family off? *Off* off?

If your answer is no, or if the question prompted any mental protest or self-distancing (*Of course I don't have enough time off. I can't expect much—I'm a working parent. I'll relax when the kids are grown and the mortgage paid. I can't afford to lean back now . . .*), that's not good. Insufficient time off can lead to exhaustion, dissatisfaction, and burnout, which only make the tough task of workparenting even harder.

If you do find yourself in the "too little" category, it's time to think about some action steps. This chapter will help you put together a realistic, personalized plan for getting more: more of the recess time you need and more out of it.

Scaling It Up

If you march into your boss's office right now and demand that he double your annual vacation allowance, the conversation probably won't go well. If you suddenly go on sabbatical and leave your new entrepreneurial endeavor dangling, it may not survive. There are limits to how aggressive you can be in reaching for more time off without real and negative consequences. You can push the needle only so fast and so far. But you *can* nudge it a little—and probably more than you think.

In the next few pages, we'll cover seven different types of time off, starting with the smaller and easier to take and then working our way on up toward the bigger and more challenging. We'll explore how to reach for and use each type of break without chipping any of the paint off your career. We'll also drill down and get a good look at the specific ways each of these time-off opportunities can provide you maximum satisfaction and *oomph*.

As you look this information over, pay particular attention to the time-off techniques and approaches you're not currently using, and consider whether you want to make them part of your working-parent self-management arsenal, and how you might do so. Not all of the approaches here will suit your career, or needs—but some will, and you want to be a clever curator. How *could* you get more time for yourself and with the kids in a gradual, little-risk-of-professional-blowback kind of way? Which tricks here could make your time off feel more rewarding? How could you, gently and gradually, scale up your time off?

When you're finished reading, we'll regroup—and determine your own good path forward.

1. Microcheating

In chapter 4, we explored how, upon return from parental leave, you could get a little more time with the baby via small, unsanctioned, and unpublicized windows of time off: ducking out half an hour earlier now and then so you could get home for your daughter's bath; blocking time on your work calendar for a "meeting" and joining her at the baby music class; taking the occasional personal or sick day to spend as full-time parent; and, if your business trip flight landed at 2:00 p.m., giving yourself permission to head straight home. You learned to think of this approach as situational flexibility—taken in a discreet, low-drama, self-permissioned way.

Even if the kids are much older now, why not continue using this same approach? It worked during your return-from-leave phase, but there's nothing about it that's specific to babies. If you've gotten that flat, dull feeling that comes from working too much and being too far from family, or if you're feeling handcuffed by the endless demands of your job, give this strategy another go: try ending work early this Thursday to do the 4:30 p.m. school pickup, or blocking your calendar for a "meeting" and then getting a workout in. Sure, technically you're using a little bit of subterfuge, but only with the end goal of staying fresh and motivated. Think of microcheating as the personal-time equivalent of filching an extra pen from the workplace supply closet. It's useful to you, but too tiny an offense for others to care about or even notice.

To make your microcheats feel most rewarding, be sure to use them for activities that you don't usually get to do, and—most important—that don't appear on your task list. Logging off of work thirty minutes early to run errands may be productive, but it won't feel as rewarding or as "off" as doing something for yourself, or with one of the kids.

2. Power outages

Sometime in the next few days, try setting aside thirty minutes in which you turn off all devices, ignore your task lists (both personal and professional), and do nothing "productive" at all. Your job is simply to spend time in an activity you truly enjoy, either alone or with your family. It could be reading a novel, eating dinner together, dancing the Hokey Pokey with your toddler, or going on a jog by yourself or with your teenage son. You're a high-powered person in a high-powered career, but for these brief thirty—or sixty, or ninety—minutes, the power is out. If the idea immediately whips up your sense of anxiety (*How can I possibly be out of pocket like that? It's unacceptable! I'll get fired!*), remember that your power will be out only for a very brief period. For thirty minutes, can't work wait?

Unlike with microcheats, power outages involve complete, deliberate, unabashed disconnection. During that window, you're not just away from work or otherwise occupied, but completely and totally *off*. And because you are, you'll find that your stress will decrease and your feeling that *I've done something positive for myself and my family* will go up. You'll also regain a sense of agency, having made an affirmative decision and taken a real break, albeit a brief one, on your own terms.

3. Sabbaths

If you've heard the term *Sabbath* used before, it's almost certainly been in a religious context. Many of the world's faith communities emphasize the tradition of setting aside one day per week to withdraw from the hustle and bustle of daily activity and to rest, focus on the big picture, and spend time with family. Whether in a spiritual, semispiritual, or purely secular sense, why not try doing the same? If your reaction is, *A whole day? No way. I'm too busy. That would never work*, remind yourself that thousands of religiously observant people in extremely demanding jobs follow this practice—and that there's no harm or cost in your trying it out just once.

On an upcoming weekend, alert the rest of the family that you plan to use one specific day as your workparent "day of rest." Leave that day unscheduled, or as underscheduled as you can; put any work you've brought home with you to the side; and let that heap of dirty laundry stay in the hamper. If being completely out of touch with work makes you paranoid, it's fine to check messages—but don't respond to any unless they're truly urgent. Once or twice during the day, try telling yourself, *I am not working today. Today is my designated day off.*

Both that statement and the day itself may feel a little strange. Stepping out of the daily go-go-go frenzy of working-parent activity will feel unfamiliar and disquieting. You may get itchy to do something, to be productive, or you may feel as if you're squandering time. If you

> " I've seen teachers who spend forever working, and that just leads to burnout. I'm busy during the week, and Sundays I do a lot of lesson planning—we're rolling out a new curriculum next year. But I try not to check my email after 6:00 p.m., and I don't work Saturdays."
>
> —Amy, pre-K teacher, mother of one

> " The farm has its own dictates, and we don't get to choose them. In the summer, the days are incredibly long and we don't have a traditional weekend: we're either harvesting or at the market. We've chosen Wednesdays to try not to work, or to try to only do things the kids can do with us."
>
> —*Lindsey, farmer, mother of two*

Staying in—and out—of touch while you're off

If you work in a professional environment where 24-7 responsiveness is the norm, but you really want to enjoy your weekend or that special vacation with the family, here are the communications strategies that can help.

- **Assert control through your out-of-office message.** If your OOO message reads, "I'm currently away, back Monday," all you've done is provide the reader information about your where-abouts. You haven't set limits or boundaries. The reader may feel perfectly within his rights to expect an immediate answer, or one at 8:00 a.m. on Monday. If, however, your OOO reads, "I'm currently out of the office and back next week. I will be checking messages daily, but unless your matter is urgent, I will respond upon my return," then you've taken charge. You've sent a signal that you're responsive and "on it"—but that *you're* the one determining the timing of next steps.

- **Contain your communications.** In chapter 10, "Time," you learned the strategy of *containment*—how to cap the amount of time you spend on activities that are necessary but unrewarding. Try using the same approach here: set a specific, brief amount of time aside each day for checking messages, making phone calls, and so on. When each activity is done, stop. Put the device down, step away from the computer, and permit yourself to be fully present in and to fully enjoy your time away.

- **Create a cost to being reached.** If the folks at work know that they can reach you anytime and easily, and that you'll be unfail-ingly chipper and helpful when they do, then they'll never leave you alone. Why would they? You're making their lives easy. Try making things just a little harder instead. When your colleague

(*continued*)

calls you over the weekend, ask for an update on an unrelated project—or suggest that, since you're already on the phone together, she walk you through the budget numbers in more detail, or that you discuss follow-ups from last week's meeting. Create a mild deterrent: make people think twice before bothering you.
- **Set up a Red Phone.** This is a specific way you can be reached, directly and quickly, in case of true emergency. Let your colleagues know that they should text you if they really need you, or should leave a detailed message with the hotel front desk just in case the big piece of client work starts to completely fall apart. If the Red Phone rings, you're on it. If not, enjoy your holiday.
- **Keep it in perspective.** Yes, work is busy, and yes, it's important to be responsive. But will your organization fall apart, your career end, and the world cease rotating on its axis if you're just briefly out of touch? Probably not.

can resist those feelings until the end of the day, though, you should find yourself significantly refreshed—and the haunting suspicion you had that "if I actually take a break, disaster will ensue" will likely have proved untrue.

If you find that taking a Sabbath provides a wonderful reset but that a weekly cadence just isn't feasible, do it monthly, or even just a few times per year. The point here is to experience, at least occasionally, a full day, fully off—in addition to your regular vacations.

4. The intentional weekend

It hangs out there, just ahead: two days promising blissful respite from the combined intensity of working and parenting. And then it comes, and you find yourself in an exhausting, mad dash of social plans, errands, and other activities that somehow all made their way onto the family calendar, or in improvisation mode, trying to come up with activities that the family can enjoy together. Either way, by Sunday evening you're strangely unsatisfied and completely bushed. Unless, of course, you approach your weekends with more of a deliberate plan.

> " We keep the camping gear in the back of the car, and as soon as
> we start driving, it's an instant mood change—everything falls
> away. We know we're headed to a shared experience that's not about
> school, or work, or daily stress. It's about basics—just us, with a tent, in
> the woods or by a stream. The contrast to our daily lives is so powerful.
> It may be for just a few days, but it's *our* time, and we own it."
>
> —*Astrid, architect, mother of one*

Without the kids

Yes, you're away from the kids a lot because of work, and yes, you
want to maximize the time you spend with them. You're also a real,
three-dimensional, flesh-and-blood, individuated adult with your own
interests, hobbies, friends, and need for relaxation. Not every moment you spend "off" has to be with the kids. Maybe you skip the
bedtime ritual once a week to get to the gym, or plan an annual weekend getaway with your partner, or with friends. Those breaks serve an
important purpose: they give you perspective, remind you of your
you-ness, and help you go the distance as a workparent, longer term.

Instead of allowing weekends to simply *happen*, think about how
they're *serving* you: what you want to get out of them, and take away
from them—and what activities and schedule will help you get those
things. If you want your weekend to feel relaxing, and you want to
spend time together as a family, turn down some of those social plans.
If you want your weekend to be healthy, block out both mornings to
get outside and be active with the kids or to cook a nutritious family
meal together. There's no reason that you have to spend your weekends trapped on a high-speed merry-go-round of activity, or ferrying
your six-year-old to all the birthday parties he was invited to, if the
parties and sugar involved don't fit your plan.

Just like with the Sabbath-day experiment, the intentional-weekend
approach may feel a little uncomfortable at first. The practice of actually

> " I can't control work, but I can control what happens outside of work. I can be 100 percent intentional. After the baby was born, we started structuring our weekends differently. We block out Sundays, and say no to all plans. The three of us will go to the park, the lake. That time is for *us*."
>
> —*Josh, business development manager, father of one*

planning and strategizing your leisure time may feel like a contradiction, or the idea of saying no to an invitation or to your own task list in favor of other, preferred activities, or nothing at all, may feel strange or wrong. That feeling will likely dissolve on the evening of Day 2, when you look back at forty-eight hours well spent.

5. Vacation: how, when, and where

You've been taking vacations since you've been working, and you certainly know how to plan them, and book them, and what kind of vacations you'll enjoy. What you *haven't* had a lot of experience with is planning holidays when you're quite this crazy-busy, or spending them in parent mode, taking care of young children. In order to make workparent vacations happen, and often enough, and in a truly satisfying way, you may need to do a few things differently than you did prekids.

- **Make an annual vacation plan.** When you're managing both career and children, you're busy—busy enough that there's real risk that vacation planning finds a permanent place at the bottom of your to-do list. You may even have the unpleasant experience of looking up halfway through the year and being startled to realize you've taken no, or not nearly enough, time off, don't have any vacations scheduled, and may not even be able to use all the vacation days you have left before they expire. Don't let that happen! Each December, create a rough map of how many days you'll take off over the coming twelve months, and when. If you work in an environment in which you have to jockey for certain days off, be aggressive and get them on that departmental "out of office" calendar early. The specifics (travel arrangements and so on) can be sorted out later. The point now is to be managing, and managing yourself, toward getting every precious day off possible.

- **Hold on tight to your vacation identity, but be willing to tweak your plans.** What you choose to do with your leisure time is core to your sense of self—and as we've explored in several other parts of the book, maintaining your overall sense of self is essential at every phase of working parenthood. If you've always been an "adventure traveler" in your time off from work, you need to remain an adventure traveler now—and you can, as long as you make a few practical concessions. Table 17-1 highlights how to use your time off from work in a way that you'll find truly satisfying, whatever your natural "vacation style" and while accommodating the realities of young kids. Read through these indicative examples, and then imagine what your own authentic, best-self, workparent vacation could look like.

- **Minimize movement.** Most of the stress of workparent vacations is in *getting there*: moving through airports, spending time in the rental car, and otherwise dealing with the logistics of getting from A to B with children and that mountain of child gear in tow. Think about limiting "from here to there" time (only pick destinations accessible by direct flight, for example) and about

> When the kids were little, vacations meant spending most breaks with the grandparents, other relatives. We still do that twice a year. But we also go away on at least one longer trip, and in the summers take a week off to relax, just the four of us, together."
>
> —*Jeff, investor, father of two*

TABLE 17-1

Maintaining Your Vacation Identity and Style—as a Working Parent

Your true vacation identity	Ideal vacation, prekids	Practical ways to adapt as a workparent
Culture hound	Whole days dedicated to wandering great museums and monuments; evenings at the opera or theatre	• An hour or two each morning at the local museum—followed by an hour or two at the children's museum, and then at the nearby playground • An outdoor concert or play, during which the kids can happily move around
Foreign-experience seeker	A trip to a faraway country completely unlike your own, living as close to the native experience as you can	• A trip somewhere your child hasn't been to before, and that's distinctly different from where you live, but that's in the same time zone and less than a four-hour flight away • A rented house or apartment with kitchen and laundry, so that you have a practical "home base" even while soaking up local culture
Beachgoer	A week spent at an oceanfront resort, sipping margaritas and gazing at the palm trees	• A beach resort set up for families, and with swim and sailing lessons for the kids—during which you can relax on the beach
Outdoorsperson	Hiking, hunting, camping, and living completely off the grid in a national park	• A week at a dude ranch, where the kids can learn how to fish and ride horses—but someone else is making the meals
Budget adventurer	A tour around a new country, backpack on, finding lodging in strange places, improvising as you go	• A staycation, spent doing all the things you want to locally but rarely get time for: walks along the riverfront, ethnic restaurants, the zoo

staying put in a single destination while away. That one-week, six-country tour of Europe can wait until the kids are older.

• Consider involving the Village. It used to be that while on vacation, your time was truly your own. Now, vacation means providing 24-7, full-time childcare, which is wonderful in terms of family togetherness but not so helpful if you need more of

> We both work long hours, and we love traveling, because it gives us a real break. I was worried that would change—that we wouldn't have that outlet anymore. In fact, it had been one of my main apprehensions about having a child.
>
> We're just back from our first trip. We went to New Orleans, and my own parents came along as extra pairs of hands. We went to restaurants, we went to the French Quarter—basically everything we wanted to, just with a stroller. You can keep that important part of you, as long as you're aware it won't be *exactly* the same."
>
> —*Jon, physician, father of one*

a break. If you can rope in one or more of your Villagers to your vacation, though, you may be able to get both togetherness and some rest. Consider bringing one of the grandparents along with you for a few days to the beachfront rental house to provide some extra support, or taking a vacation together with another family so that the adults can take turns covering.

• Send it ahead. If your kids are very young, have your regular delivery service drop-ship all the diapers, food, etc., you'll need ahead to your vacation destination. No more schlepping an extra suitcase full of supplies, or spending your precious time off hunting for the drugstore.

• Bring the umbrella stroller. Even if your six-year-old gave up using a stroller a long time ago, if he still physically fits into one of those lightweight, easy-fold ones, bring it anyway. He can use it to take naps on the go, or if he gets tired on that long walk, or in the museum. The stroller can also perform convenient double duty as a "safety space" if he gets overwhelmed in a crowded street, bustling train station, or noisy restaurant, and it easily serves as an extra baggage cart as well.

• Come home a day early. It's counterintuitive, but true: you'll feel as if you've had more time off if you cut your working-parent vacation a tiny bit short. That extra day at home allows

What if my organization offers unlimited vacation?

When an organization switches over to an "unlimited vacation" policy—as more and more are—its employees often take *less* time off than they did before. That may leave economists and HR reps scratching their heads, but as a working parent, of course, you know why: when you're *already* nervous about getting through all the work you need to, *and* you're apprehensive about how your colleagues see you, *and* there's no official sanction for or "nudge" toward time off, you're not going to risk taking much of it.

While you certainly don't be want to be seen as an abuser of an all-you-can-eat vacation policy, you don't want to let it harm you, either. Think of it this way: when there were firm vacation rules in place, the organization was managing you. Now, you need to manage *yourself*. As a sensible, responsible boss, what amount of time will you give yourself? What's standard in the industry? What amount of time do you need to keep up your own good performance? Or to avoid burnout? Think through the problem in the third person—and make your personal time-off decisions from a place of prudence, rather than fear or guilt.

for unpacking, work catch-up, a return to the routine. It lets you step back into your regular working-parent life in a controlled way and on a high note, rather than just off a flight delay and facing a load of laundry.

- Never return without your next vacation lined up. Without having the next family-focused break to look forward to, you might feel, upon returning to work, as if you're surrendering at the gates of a prison, sentenced to serve an indefinite term. Always have your next holiday mapped out, and be able to talk about it with the kids: "In March, we'll spend the whole week together again as a family. It will be so fun, and I can't wait!"

6. Sabbaticals

If you haven't done so already, grab your organization's employee handbook or settle down in front of the intranet site, and check: Are you eligible for a sabbatical? Not many organizations offer sanctioned, longer breaks—but some do, and if yours is one of them, it's good to understand the details even if you have no immediate plans to take one. (In that case, think of it as a back-pocket option.) Typically, sabbatical programs offer a defined amount of time off (say, twelve weeks) to employees in good standing and with a certain number of years of service. They're most prevalent in intense, competitive, long-hours types of organizations—often, professional-service firms—where burnout and attrition tend to run high.

If you desperately need a sabbatical but there's no formal program you can look to, don't despair. There's another longer-break option potentially available to you—one that walks, quacks, and is feathered exactly like a sabbatical: the *unpaid leave of absence*. Unpaid leaves are offered at an organization's, and a manager's, discretion—usually to employees who are facing some sort of nonmedical life crisis, are at serious risk of burnout, or are threatening to bail out of the organization. Such leaves are rarely publicized, but managers and human resources representatives will sometimes offer one as a sort of last-ditch retention move when they're nervous about losing a high performer. If you're truly "on the verge" as a working parent, maybe even on the verge of leaving your job, it may be worth asking about the unpaid-leave alternative. The very worst that can happen is that your employer tells you no.

If you do take a longer break of any kind from your job, retain control of your story. Telling colleagues that you're taking eight weeks of unpaid leave to handle some family matters, and that you look forward to being back, refreshed and ready to go in April, is much better than disappearing and allowing misinformation and rumors to float around. Before you go out, have a deliberate plan for how you'll use the time. How will those eight weeks off help you over the short and long term as a workparent? Collapsing on the couch may be what's needed right now, but it won't help you set yourself up for longer, more viable success. Be prepared, too, for potential "bigger picture" thinking or a change of heart while you're away. With the benefit of perspective that such a long period of time off can bring, you may decide to make larger or more-permanent career moves, like changing roles or organizations.

Corporate returnship programs

Returnships are structured, short-term (typically, twelve- to sixteen-week), paid jobs explicitly designed for men and women who have taken extended breaks from work for family-related reasons. In the past fifteen years, returnship programs (also referred to as "career reentry" programs) have become commonplace within larger corporations and professional-services firms, which see them as a creative, low-risk way to attract skilled, motivated talent—as well as a public-relations-ready way to showcase organizational commitment to diversity and flexible work. Think of a returnship role as you would a student internship: as a résumé-builder, as an extended interview, and as a potential bridge into longer-term work with the particular organization.

So, is a returnship right for you? If you've taken a longer career break for family reasons and are looking for a way "back in" to the professional world, a returnship role may be just the ticket. Returnship programs remove the stigma that can exist from having taken an extended break. Over the course of a few months, you'll get to adjust, or readjust, to working-parent life; refresh your professional skills and confidence; and test-drive a longer-term future with the employer. Because returnship programs typically also include structured onboarding and mentoring components, you get to do all of

7. Career breaks

You've thought about taking a complete career break—leaving your organization, and taking a year or two off—to get some concentrated time with the kids. Yet you've also heard professional horror stories about men and women who have done just that and were never able to find their way back into the professional world, or who did, but in reduced roles and at just a fraction of their previous salaries. Or you've heard breaks discussed in a strange, engineering-esque vocabulary: *off-ramp*, *on-ramp*, career *architecture* or *design*, and so forth. The idea of a career break may be tempting, but it's usually hard to get your arms around it.

Try to step away from the fear and the hype. While it's usually true that it's easier to find a job if you're already in one, and that taking a the above with layers of extra support not provided to other, regular employees.

On the downside: because the returnship idea is so compelling and most corporate programs are so small (even at a huge multinational, there may be only a handful of returnees at any given time), it can be *extremely* difficult to secure a spot. While a returnship is a possibility, it's not a certain option or an on-ramp you can count on. If you do get one, given the short-term nature of the job, pressure is high to perform well and quickly, and even if you do, of course, there's no guarantee of ongoing work when those sixteen weeks are done. You may also need childcare during your returnship—and then need to dismantle or back away from that arrangement when the job is over.

If you *are* interested in a returnship, try to find an organization with a more recently formed program that may not be so bombarded with applications. During the interview process, ask how returnees are supported, how specific assignments are determined, and what specific mentoring or training is available. Also try to find out what percentage of returnees are kept on at the end of the program, and/ or how they've parlayed the experience into full-time work elsewhere. As you do your research, don't forget: returnships are one way, but not the *only* way, back in.

longer break does carry some real risks, it hardly spells the end of your modern-day professional ambitions. In today's world, moves in and out of the workforce are becoming both more frequent and more visible, and they're much more readily accepted than they were even ten years ago. Besides, you're not managing to statistics, or to the careers of *all* professionals, everywhere. You only have to make one career work— yours—and there's no reason you can't swing this as long as you take an eyes-wide-open approach and the correct up-front actions.

Think of the moves outlined next as *career-break preventative care.* They're the maneuvers that will let you take a true and complete career break with minimal hurt or headache. These are the things that, when you do want to get back into the work game, will position you for success and that you'll be incredibly glad to have done.

- Have an endgame in mind, and project-plan your way back from it. If your goal is to return to work "later," it's all too easy to let one year off become two, two become five . . . and then ten. On the other hand, if your goal is *to take eighteen months at home, and return to work when my youngest is in school full-time,* you've got a goal to work toward. You'll be able to enjoy that first full year without worry or guilt, and you'll know to start interviewing around months twelve to fourteen.

- Leave your organization on good terms. One of the easiest ways—if not *the* easiest—to ultimately get back into the work-force will be to return to your past employer. No matter how unpalatable that option looks right now, it's best to keep it open. Even if you're leaving because you feel you've been mistreated in some way, don't be brutally negative in your exit interview, or throw a snit, or toss your manager under the bus when asked why you're leaving. As in any relationship, how you break up is how you'll be remembered.

- While you're out, take care to keep up your relationships with past managers and colleagues. Find a reason to have at least one touch point every quarter with the people you used to work with. That may be lunch, a visit to the workplace, or as small a thing as a text message or social-media exchange. You may even offer to do some part-time consulting work—helping out during busy season, for example—as a means of keeping the lines of communication open, your skills sharp, and your value on display. The point here: *never* let the relationships you worked so hard to establish go completely stale.

- Have, and keep adding to, a "who can hire me" list. Whether or not your past organization is an option, what about the place you worked for before that? What about your past clients? Could they bring you on board? Or old colleagues who've moved on to successful careers elsewhere? Or the other parents at your kids' school, who also work in your field? When you do

Coming back from a career break

" I quit my finance job cold turkey just after the twins—they're seven now—were born. I became a full-time dad.

I had met several people who worked here, and just as the twins were starting preschool, they gave me an opportunity. I said yes, on condition that I could still leave every day in time for the 2:40 p.m. school pickup. It's been four years now, and I've always been part-time. I'm still our girls' primary caregiver. To make that work, I get into the office very early, I'm very focused on being productive in the six or so hours that I'm here, and I'll sometimes have to take calls in the afternoons, around the kids. When clients do hear the girls in the background, it's a good thing: it brings a human element into the relationship.

If you're thinking about putting your career on hold, it's good to know that you can explore new fields; you don't need to have everything so figured out up front. Remember that your skills are applicable in different organizations, different industries. There's a number of people here who, like me, had no prior insurance experience. Because I work part-time, I'm not maximizing my career potential for right now. That's a trade-off, and I'm comfortable with it. That's my biggest advice: be comfortable with your choices."

—*Sujal, central region finance, father of three*

" There was a big layoff during my second maternity leave, so I had no job to go back to. I had really wanted to return to work part-time, but suddenly that wasn't an option. I usually analyze things, but I made the decision to stay home really quickly. Still, it was scary.

During my four years out I thought a *lot* about work. I subscribed to job alerts, kept an eye on the market, looked at a ton of job postings. I saw who was hiring, and for what. When I started my search, I knew what was out there.

I felt like I needed a solid, defensible reason for my time away, so I spent a ton of time crafting cover letters to explain it. But throughout the search, nobody questioned me on it once, or seemed to care. Maybe people don't read cover letters anymore, or maybe they're used to interviewing people who've taken career breaks."

—*Wendy, technology product marketer, mother of two*

start looking for a new role, you want to have an immediate "call list" of ten to fifteen viable options.

- Keep your résumé fresh by volunteering—but only or primarily in ways that feel and look "professional." It's fine to take on the task of organizing the annual bake sale at your kids' school, but—hard facts, here—it's unlikely that any prospective employer will be impressed by this activity (unless, of course, you happen to be interviewing at a bakery). On the other hand, serving in a leadership role with a trade group, taking an adjunct teaching position in your field, writing for an industry publication, taking on occasional project work, doing pro bono consulting for a few relevant startups or nonprofits, or other similar work all speaks well to your professional capabilities and can-do attitude.

- Interview, or rehearse interviewing, well before you want to go back to work. You'll want to be as crisp, convincing, and on message as possible.

- Be able to explain your why, and why now—and keep it snappy. You're going to be asked to explain both your career break and your desire to come back to work, most likely by an interviewer with little interest in your life story. Be able to explain both in two sentences or less, and in an honest, confident way.

Your Time-Off Action Plan

We've thrown a lot of spaghetti at the wall. Now it's time for you to make your "scale up" plan and commit to specific next steps. If the words *commit* and *steps* sound daunting, or like more entries on your already bulging to-do list, bear in mind: *You're doing this to get yourself more well-deserved and wonderful time off! It's for you and for your family, and nobody else.*

Table 17-2 provides you a way to both capture your thoughts on how to get more time and hold your own feet to the fire on following through. There's certainly nothing magic about this table, but what

TABLE 17-2

Sample Time-Off Action Plan

On a scale of 1 to 10, my current time-off satisfaction level is: _____

Six months from now, my goal is to move that to: _____

Core need(s)/What I'm solving for	How I'll scale up my overall time off	Time frame, interim steps, and resources needed
☐ Time off for myself ☐ Dedicated time with the kids ☐ A sense of "off the treadmill" relief ☐ Other	*Insert two or three specific techniques you plan to use for getting more time away from work.*	*If "taking a two-week vacation" is a goal, specify when, what you need to do to plan it, which Villagers might help you, etc.*
	Ways I'll use to make that time more satisfying	**Time frame, interim steps, and resources needed**
	Write in two or three specific techniques you will use to make that time more valuable and restorative.	*If "turning off on Saturdays" is your goal, define what "off" means for you, how your partner might help you resist the temptation to keep checking work messages, how you might start by focusing just on Saturday mornings, and so on.*

will feel like magic is what happens as soon as you start treating your need for R&R as an item worthy of real focus, energy, and attention.

Fill out the template quickly, using simple bullet points. Include just enough detail that when you look back at what you've written three months from now, your commitments are clear. When the three-month mark comes, revisit—and update. Three months later, do it again. Lather, rinse, repeat. From now until the kids are grown, your goal is to keep yourself accountable for getting yourself the time off you—and they—deeply need and deserve, and for loving every minute of it when you do.

Time to Refuel

Imagine that you have to get from one end of a vast desert clear across to the other in a car that is functional but not specially built for the task. The road is long and the heat blazing. The trip will take days or weeks, and you're the only driver—there's no one else ready to take their turn at the wheel. In this hypothetical, what would you naturally do?

Most likely, you'd plan your journey out: mapping how far you could safely drive each day before nodding off, looking ahead for the service stations that could help you in case of mechanical trouble, etc. You'd pull off to the side of the road each time the engine threatened to overheat, and pull into a gas station each time you needed to fill the tank. If staring at the road got to be too much, you'd crank up some good music. You'd unhesitatingly use breaks, downtime, and diversions as ways to compensate for the strains of the journey and ultimately to help *accelerate* it.

As a working parent, you're both that car and driver. To get through this journey well and safely, it's OK—and *right*—for you to do the same.

PART FOUR

Staying Well and Whole

Taking Good Care of Your Family—and Yourself—While You're Hard at Work

Definition: To take care of:

1. To attend to or be heedful of needs and comforts, for oneself or for others

2. To be cautious; to stay safe

3. To cure, preserve, and support

Antonyms: To forget, neglect, or ignore

You're in high workparenting gear. You've got some good moves for handling this phase of the journey, and the next. You've maximized your arsenal of workparent resources, and you're pushing toward career success, however you define it. From the outside looking in, you've got the career-plus-kids thing *down*.

But what about on the inside? How are you doing personally, and how satisfied are you with the ways in which you're nurturing and supporting yourself and your family? For many mothers and fathers, it's this "inside" part of workparenting that feels the most important, and trickiest to get right. Maybe you're forgetting what it's like to have a good, healthy, sit-down family dinner—or are neglecting the need for rest, or ignoring your own feelings. You could have the most brilliant career possible, but may still struggle with this caretaking piece.

So in the next four chapters, we'll deep-dive on sensible, satisfying ways to *take care*: on how to look after your own needs and comforts, on how to preserve and support yourself and the entire family now and in the years ahead. We'll start with the most basic need of all—food—and gradually work our way up the ladder to feelings, and how to cope with them. By the end of this section, you'll be more *together* personally, and more comfortable and confident in your role as caregiver, too.

18

Food and Mealtimes

Getting the Whole Family Nourished—and
Eating Together More Often

It's the glaring irony of working parenthood: you're working so
hard to put food on the table that it's incredibly difficult to get
real, edible food, much less anything appetizing and nutritious,
onto your *actual* table. When you're tired, and have a backlog of emails
to catch up on, and haven't seen the kids since 7:00 a.m., the last thing
you want to do is semi-ignore them to cook food they then may refuse
to eat—assuming you've even got the ingredients. Instead of facing
that same glum scenario every day, you start relying on takeout and
convenience foods, or fixing the kids whatever they're clamoring for.
Or with everything you have to do, you've begun multitasking during
meals, or eating on the go, or eating separately from the kids. Or *all* of
the above, because each of those moves helps you save time and keep
the peace . . . today. You know, though, that as they solidify into habits, these moves don't do your health, wallet, relationships, or sense of
working-parent self any favors.

If the whole issue seems fraught and unfixable, hang in there,
because you're about to see new ways to make this fundamental part
of parenting more feasible. You won't have to grab a spatula or download a bunch of new recipes to get going; you'll just need to be ready

to make some up-front decisions, and to pull from a menu of effective actions in and outside the kitchen.

Setting Your House Rules

A significant proportion of your professional behavior is governed by tried-and-true rules that have become so deeply embedded that you don't even really have to think about them. *Get to work on time. Underpromise and overdeliver. Dress up for interviews. Return phone calls promptly. Try to look smart and alert when the top brass is around.* And so forth. You don't sit around wondering if calling your boss back is the right thing to do—you know it is, and you can redirect the time and mental energy you'd otherwise spend on the matter toward higher-order pursuits (like completing a tough project, or finding a mentor). In IT terms, you've developed a professional *operating system.* Why not create an operating system to help you tame the workparent Food Challenge as well? A simple set of running-in-the-background, don't-have-to-think-about-them guidelines could help you keep everything up and running, nutritionally speaking, and save you a lot of frustration and hassle.

In table 18-1 you'll find a simple format for just such a system—for what we'll call your Workparent Food and Mealtime House Rules. The particular example provided imagines you're part of a dual-

> I've always worked six days a week, but healthy eating is one area that doesn't give. Once a month, we'll do a takeaway, and everything else, we cook. Easy, quick things—veggies, salad. I'll do a slow-cooked meal at the weekend so I can work late Tuesdays without having to think about dinner.
>
> I'll never deny the kids anything. If they want chocolate, that's fine—but they have to try everything on their plate. Picky eating is a power play, but in our family, Mum and Dad are the deciders. We'll tell you what to eat because we love you. It's good for kids to know that authority happens."
>
> —*Kerry-Lee, speech pathologist, mother of two*

TABLE 18-1

Workparent Food and Mealtime House Rules

Always and have-tos	No
• Dinner is at 7:00, at the kitchen table, together, unless one of us is working late or at a school event	• Dinners at the office if that work could be finished later at home
• Breakfast is at the diner every Saturday morning	• Substitute meals—e.g., if you don't like your dinner, there's no cold cereal alternative
• Green vegetable, daily	• Phones at the table
• Milk with every meal	• Drinks with added sugar
• Utensils and napkins	
• You can say that you "dislike" something on your plate only after you've taken two bites of it	
• It's fine to eat whatever's served at the school cafeteria, but you need to tell us, daily, what that was	

Exceptions	Shortcuts
• If either parent has to work past 7:30 p.m., we order in	• Tuesday night=pizza
• Birthday parties. Have all the cake and junk you want.	• Sundays are "fridge buffet," and you can eat whatever you find in there
	• Weeknights, Dad is primary cook, but whoever gets home first makes a salad and turns the oven on
	• If you're running late in the morning, take one of the granola bars in the cabinet

career household with school-aged kids. Read through the table, noting your own reactions and mulling over what you might want your *own* House Rules to be.

Just like your basic professional operating system, your House Rules will never and cannot cover *every* contingency, let you bypass all decisions, or relieve the complete getting-everyone-fed workload. However, as this example illustrates, the Rules—even when kept few and targeted—help lighten your overall practical load, reduce your number of daily decisions, and have the power to quell lingering, lurking self-doubts. If you set a House Rule that *we order pizza on Tuesdays*, it saves you some cook time, prevents you from feeling as if every day is a full-scale food improvisation, and releases you from the anxiety that you're a crummy parent for ordering in again.

What preemptive decisions, like this one, could help you tame the Food Challenge—and let you save precious time and energy to put back into your career, self, or kids? Given the nuances and contours of your own workparent life, what would you strike out in table 18-1, or add? How else might you ease the strain of getting your family healthfully fed, and cap the overall amount of food-related drama and uncertainty? Work through your answers, and then, on a fresh sheet of paper, sketch out your own House Rules, being as honest, specific, and realistic as you can. If you're a vegetarian, or on a tight budget, work that in. If you plan to order dinner five nights out of seven, that's fine, just write it down. There are no judgments here: what you're doing is creating clarity and granting yourself authority and permission—both practical and emotional. You're done playing the role of frantic, guilty chef; you're writing a new personal and family script.

Once you have your Rules sketched out, think about posting copies in your kitchen and dining areas, and walking through them with key Village members, such as your caregivers and Third Parents. If you worry that that's a little controlling or Big Brother–esque, just remember: things are going to be vastly easier and more reassuring for you when you can point to your House Rules when needed. ("That's not how we do things here. I work all day, and I'm only preparing one meal," or "We can't wait to hear about your first band practice! Can you tell the whole family over breakfast at the diner?") Quickly the House Rules will become ingrained, and the Food Challenge will lose its sharpest edges.

As your family grows, and as you advance each time you switch roles, revisit your House Rules and revise them to suit.

Fail-Safe Ways to Make the Overall Logistics Easier

With your House Rules in place, you've already begun to declaw the Food Challenge beast. Now, it's time to tame it even further. Five practical, diverse approaches will give you even more of the upper hand.

Becoming a CPO

If you've always been a great cook or enthusiastic foodie, it may actually—and paradoxically—make the workparent Food Challenge even harder: you'll be haunted by the sense that you should be cooking from scratch for the family *more* or preparing more-complex and -varied meals, and that you're dropping the ball or performing at second-best when you don't.

Instead of acting as family chef, cast yourself in a new role: Chief Procurement Officer. Your job isn't to stand by the stove and turn out impressive, homemade meals every day, but to manage the sourcing, processing, and delivery of good, nutritious food, however it comes— and then sit down with your kids to enjoy it.

1. **Think ahead.** In chapter 10, "Time," we discussed how to set up, or enhance, your workparent calendar, paying close attention to the importance of regular look-aheads. Whatever the forward-planning ritual you've settled on, think about making food and meal planning part of it. If you always use Sunday evenings to prep for the coming week, walk through your food plan alongside your professional deliverables, caregiving plan, and everything else you have going on: *Monday I cook, Tuesday we order in, Wednesday leftovers; I've got early starts, so I'll make the twins breakfast the night before,* and so on. The more you have a jump on what's coming, the less likely you are to be left standing in the kitchen at 7:00 p.m. with low blood sugar and no plan.

2. **Use time and money to save time and money.** Maybe you shop at the prepared-foods section of the grocery store some weeks instead of actually cooking, or maybe you pay up for precleaned, prechopped ingredients that make your job in the kitchen easier. In either scenario you've spent a bit more money, and still had to invest time up front, but the end result is more *overall* time saved, and ultimately cheaper and more satisfying than constant restaurants or takeout.

> *Every week, I make three main meals. On the other nights, we eat leftovers, and once a week, we go out.*
>
> I write out what we're having and need to buy on this paper planner I keep in the kitchen, where we can all see it. Having the plan visible makes it more likely that I'll actually follow it than if I keep it on my phone, and because the kids see it, there's also much less pushback. They know what's coming.
>
> I like going to the grocery store because I like getting the best deals. But if my husband is away or if it's been a particularly busy week at work, I'll have things delivered."
>
> —*Rose, procurement leader, mother of two*

3. **Stock it.** Think of your pantry like a closet: just as it's impossible to get properly dressed without the basic pieces, it's impossible to cook good meals without basic supplies. If you're not sure what those are, search online for "gourmet pantry basics" or "what every healthy (or kosher, spice-loving, diabetic, large-family, etc.) home cook should have on hand," shop the list, and then put staples on regular online reorder. Never get caught one or two items short of a decent meal or having to make extra trips to the store.

4. **ABB.** Always Be Building future capacity. Whenever you cook, double—or better yet, triple—the recipe. If you're out to eat, order an extra serving, take it home, and freeze it. Keep creating extra slack in the system for when you do have to work overtime, or just need a break.

5. **Enlist the kids.** When your kids are very small, you have to be in charge of their entire food universe—the nursing, the bottles, the purees, etc. Ever the conscientious professional and parent, you rise to the occasion, becoming extremely adept at managing it all. Don't let that habit persist, or fall into the trap of thinking that top-to-bottom ownership of food matters is somehow correlated with good parenting. The kids should help, and they can likely do so from a much earlier age than

> ❝ We're pescatarians, so think a lot about meal planning and getting the right nutrients. Getting a good dinner on the table can be time-consuming—so we make our son part of it. He's only two and a half, but he gets up on a stool by the sink and helps me rinse off the vegetables. I'll talk him through it while I cook—'now I'm going to put olive oil into the pan'—and show him how. It's time together, and he loves it, and he'll try all kinds of new foods because he helped make them, and it's expanded his vocabulary like crazy."
>
> —*Adam, program technical manager, father of one*

you would naturally ask. A toddler can put paper napkins on the table before the meal, a six-year-old can toss the salad, your nine-year-old can pack a lunch, and so on. The "help" may not be so helpful, at the start, but you're training your children to be part of the solution.

Trickier Food and Mealtime Matters, and How to Handle Them

Certain parts of the Food Challenge terrain are going to be rockier and harder to navigate than others. Here are the most common rough patches, and special ways of getting through them.

Transitioning to solids; feeding very small children

To get your little one(s) eating well, without feeling as if you have to quit your job to get enough time to do so, try these strategies:

- Decide on a system for buying or making your child's food, and stick to it. Whether you choose to do a weekly run to the farmer's market and blend up everything yourself or your partner buys premade purees from the supermarket, make sure that everyone's clear on the plan for feeding your baby or toddler and that you've worked it into your schedules.

- Keep a food log. Has he had enough rice cereal today? Tried apricots? Gotten the same rash around his mouth every time

Fridgeability

If you've ever confronted a cold, glutinous lump of day-old spaghetti or tried to save the extra salad from yesterday's dinner, then you know: certain foods are delicious when first prepared, but they store poorly. As you make your weekly food plan, think ahead as to what foods will be able to "go the distance"—e.g., what will still be usable and appealing a few days from now, in tomorrow's lunchbox, or in re-heated leftover form. That salad can last a few days if it isn't dressed. Pasta gunks up fast, but a big pot of quinoa cooked on Sunday night will still be fluffy on Thursday and can make an easy, healthy base for any number of different meals. Hard-boiled eggs are good for grab-and-go breakfasts throughout the week. Use "fridgeability" as one of your new culinary criteria and save yourself working-parent time, hassle, and money.

he eats tomato? A consolidated list of everything your child has eaten, and when, lets you, his caregivers, and any other Villagers, answer those questions quickly and stay coordinated on all things nutrition. There's any number of easy-to-use apps for this, or you can keep a small notebook in the diaper bag.

- Stock healthy, age-appropriate, nonperishable foods everywhere you might need them. Keep rice crackers, fruit and vegetable pouches, etc., in your emergency-backup-care bag, at your Third Parents' homes, in the car. Even if care plans change, or you're stuck in traffic on the way home from daycare pickup, you'll avoid hangry-child emergencies.

- Invest in a few rubberized, neck-to-wrist coverall-type bibs for the baby, and keep a full change of clothes for yourself at work. You don't want to change him more than you have to . . . or wear applesauce to the weekly team meeting.

Breakfasts

The start of your day is often frantic, and a difficult time in which to get nutrition right and quickly. A few tips to help:

- Start the morning earlier, or better yet, do the work the night before. Sacrificing sleep or ending a long day with yet another logistical task may feel barbaric, but an extra ten minutes of cushion will help you make breakfast happen. Put the bottle out on the counter, pour the glasses of milk and leave them in the fridge, put the bread next to the toaster, etc.—whatever eases some of that morning rush.

- Have a few standard, quick, no-fail options. These might include instant oatmeal, cold cereal, hard-boiled eggs, or anything else that's easy and that you know your child will eat.

- Plan for grab and go. The bus is coming in ten minutes, or you need to get everyone in the car to drop them off early before an offsite meeting—there are mornings when things run smoothly and mornings when they don't. Stock the pantry with foods

The grocery store as classroom

Even if you're super pinched on time and dislike grocery shopping, be aware that in today's cashless, I-can-get-anything-delivered environment, a trip to the market can serve a vital second purpose: as practical, real-time education. Those food-buying trips can become efficient, in-person opportunities to foster your child's vocabulary, math skills, money awareness, and general can-do-ism—as well as being pleasant time together.

For instance, if your child is age:
- Two: have her say what colors she sees in the produce aisle, and count aloud as you navigate together over to aisle 8
- Five: read price tags, guess how many items you have in the cart, and learn names of new, more unusual food items
- Eight: calculate the total bill, assuming you have fifteen items in your basket and they each cost $3
- Ten: calculate the after-discount prices for sale items
- Fifteen: select all the items needed for a nutritious dinner, if she were cooking and had only x amount of money to spend
If you can double or even triple the benefits of that trip, it will feel like time well used.

Workparenting the picky eater

Everyone has preferences, and within very tight limits, it's fine to honor them: not serving extra broccoli to a child who loathes it, for example. The role of short-order cook, however, is the very last one you should assume given your current workload. It's a terrible use of your time, and worse, it sets up—or reinforces—a nasty precedent that you're some sort of servant to your kids. If that doesn't sound like a problem, then imagine how that dynamic will play out later in childhood, through adolescence, and beyond the realm of the dining table. It's not a pretty picture.

When you are—inevitably—confronted with food pickiness or re-fusals, start by asking yourself if you and your child are really act-ing out some unspoken, non-food-related emotions. After a long day apart from you, your four-year-old may be craving some special, concentrated, just-for-me-type attention. She doesn't know how to articulate that, so she demands that you separate the rice and peas. And you, feeling a little workparent-guilty, may think, *I can be an ideal, attentive mother in this moment if I do that*. Or maybe you're bone-tired after a solid day's work and just not up for fighting about it.

Instead of conceding, think about:

- Other, nonfood ways that you could show specific, immediate affection: ask about an interaction your child had at daycare, sug-gest you play a game together after dinner, or offer to read an extra book together before bed.
- Referring, gently but firmly, back to your House Rules: "Yes, I know carrots aren't your thing, but we have to take two bites of everything that we're served."
- Offering a cheerful, no-hassle, nonoption option: "No problem! If you don't want to eat it now, you can have it for breakfast to-morrow instead."
- Reminding yourself of all the other, more critical things on your to-do list. Is picking the peas out of the rice really a good time investment?
- Diverting to another topic.

Pushing back on pickiness may be unpleasant, initially—but if you stick to your guns, you won't have to live through it often.

that are easy to throw in a backpack or eat on the run: granola bars, fruit, individually wrapped cheeses, and so forth.

- As soon as they're old enough, teach your kids to help themselves. That will give you time to eat and to take care of any last-minute tasks before you get out the door.

Emergency Meals

When you're hungry, tired, and/or running late, and you have no kind of meal ready or planned, it's time to reach for an Emergency Meal. To qualify as such, a particular food or food combination has to be something that 1) you can get on the table in seven minutes or less, 2) the kids will actually eat, 3) is filling, and provides enough *oomph* to get everyone to the next feeding, and 4) is decently healthy.

Your Emergency Meal may be an omelet and salad, a frozen burrito with a piece of fruit, a bag of frozen vegetables cooked in the same water the pasta is and served with sauce from a jar, or something from the

Should you pay up for a prepared-meal delivery service?

Those meal-delivery services and prepared-meal kits you see advertised everywhere may be more expensive than cooking from scratch, but if 1) you have the budget, 2) they help you eat healthier, and 3) they save you time—e.g., if they get you to the table as a family more often, and for longer stretches—then they're no luxury, they're just smart options.

Be a thoughtful consumer, though. In the past few years there's been a huge proliferation of "we make home cooking easy for you!" type companies, each offering its own twist on the concept. Some allow you to pick from preorganized weekly menus and drop all the needed groceries in your garage, others provide boxes of ready-to-heat ingredients required for a single meal, and so on. There's no right or wrong, but be certain that what you've signed up and are paying for eases your real pain point(s). If the service doesn't meaningfully shorten your family's "time to the table," then you may not be getting your money's worth. Be discerning—and shop around.

special stash of frozen leftovers you keep for just this purpose. Whatever that go-to is, be sure to have one. Just like with caregiving plans, you feel more in control when you know you have a quality backup.

Takeout, eating out, and fast food

Let's accept right here and right now that since you're a busy working parent, eating out, takeout, and fast food are all likely to become a regular part of your arsenal. You may not want to turn to them every day, but with a little forward thinking you can keep your nutrition and family dynamic on track even when someone else is doing the cooking.

- **Hold on to your House Rules.** Even in a different physical space, or when the food comes in a cardboard container, you can still apply regular standards, whether that's *milk with the meal, utensils,* or *no complaining.*

Rethinking workday lunches

Whatever your standard work lunch—whether that's a sandwich from the corner deli, leftovers brought from home, something wolfed down in the company canteen, or something whipped up in your own kitchen before you bolt back to your home office—think about what makes sense now given your overall workparent food system. Try to make lunch healthy and convenient, sure—but also make certain that whatever practical solution you come to doesn't shortchange you from a career perspective. Deals are very often brokered, sales made, innovative ideas hatched, and relationships formed over meals. If all of your colleagues use their midday meals for internal networking or outside client connections, and your strategy is to eat solo at your desk, then yes, it will save you time—but you're putting yourself at a significant disadvantage in terms of relationships and visibility. To stay on middle ground, consider setting yourself some kind of reasonable personal quota: join the departmental lunches once a week, ask your boss out to eat once a quarter, use lunch hour as videoconference catch-up time with the colleagues you don't see as often. Be efficient, while thinking "advancement."

> ❝ Our family always has a meal plan, but we reserve the right to change it at the last minute. The other night, we were running late and we realized our favorite local pizza place was having a buy-one, get-one-free special, so we did takeout instead.
>
> No one can do everything perfectly, or the way it's culturally prescribed—all organic and homemade. Would I do drive-through every night? No, but a few nights a week is fine. Think ahead, about what suits the realities of your time, budget, and family—and then give yourself some grace."
>
> —*Steve, educator and pastor, father of four*

- **Take control of the ordering process.** Just because there's a menu doesn't mean everyone has to choose. Consider ordering family style, or multiples of the same dish, to simulate the environment at home.

- **Use the "add healthy" approach.** If you're running late from work and decide to stop at the drive-through on the way home, don't beat yourself up. Sure, it's not your finest culinary moment, but we're dealing in reality here. Serve up the takeout with some carrot sticks, oranges, and glasses of milk and suddenly you've got a meal with vitamins A and C and calcium. Add healthy, lose the guilt.

How to Make Family Meals Happen—and More Often

As every working parent knows, the cuisine itself is only one part of the Food Challenge. Even in the fantasy world where your family employs a full-time professional chef, it would still be hard to get the whole family eating together given your schedules. If the Family Meal is proving hard to pull off, or gathering around the table feels like a historic or near-mythical event (*my grandparents used to have family dinners each night; we ate together during the holidays*), then consider some of these tricks to help make it a more frequent reality.

- **Assign it a higher priority.** It's essential to finish the budget report, get the car repaired, prepare for the big client meeting, make your daughter's school-play costume . . . and on and on and on. Your calendar is crammed, your to-do list is a mile long, and it's all marked *Urgent*. If you're going to make Family Meals happen, you need to give them equal footing.

- **Add it to the calendar.** Block off the times you want to eat with the family. When they're recorded as "official" entries, you're much more likely to honor them.

- **Think beyond dinner.** Chances are when you think "family meal," you imagine a hearty, hot, home-cooked dinner, served nightly and on real china. Yet the reality of workparent scheduling is that the evening isn't always the best time to gather. Consider making your Family Meal breakfast instead, if school and work schedules favor that time slot. The best time for a Family Meal is whenever you can make it happen.

- **Make the food incidental.** Alright, so you'd prefer to sit down over a proper meal prepared in your own kitchen. You can still bond, and connect, and create the ritual of a Family Meal over takeout, though, or at the diner on Saturday mornings, or over microwave pizza. Nutrition is important, but family time is even more so.

> Family dinner is a high priority. When we're around the table, there are no phones, it's just the five of us, and everyone speaks. We'll each talk about the best and worst things that happened to us that day. If one of the girls had an argument with a friend, we talk through it. This way, they'll still be talking to us when they're fourteen.
>
> We also say what we're each thankful for. That started one evening during Covid-19 quarantine when everyone was in a particularly salty mood, and it's amazing how quickly it improves the atmosphere. The kids love it, and will actually argue over who gets to go first."
>
> —*Ashley, military officer, father of three*

- **Label it.** Call it whatever you want—"family dinner," "our family meal," "eating in the dining room," or "sitting down together, all five of us"—but call it *something*, and be consistent. The label sends signals about the meal's meaning and importance, and it makes even the simplest and quickest dinner feel like part of a larger family tradition.

While at the Table: Enjoying Your Time Together

You've procured a meal, you've gotten everyone seated, simultaneously—now what?

- **Keep things light.** For the Family Meal tradition to take hold, time at the table needs to feel like a shelter from the experiences of the day—not a task but a reward. So stay positive: share any good news about weekend plans, for example, or an upcoming visit from Grandma, and start comments with upbeat lead-ins like "The funniest thing happened today," or "You'll never guess who I saw." This isn't the time to interrogate or broach tough subjects, like yesterday's geometry test.

- **Use a conversation starter.** Dinner-party-style chatter and "let me tell you about my day" type recaps don't come naturally to children, and family members of whatever age can experience performance pressure if, as soon as they're at the table, they're expected to be forthcoming, or hold the floor. What can work well and naturally is:

  - A simple fill-in-the-blank-style opener that you're willing to kick off yourself, like "The best [or most unexpected, etc.] thing that happened to me today was . . ." or, "a kind thing I saw someone do this week was . . ."

  - Telling a family story

  - Play a guessing game, like Twenty Questions

  - Asking a lighthearted hypothetical like "If you were [an animal, a flower, etc.], what would you be?"

No comparing: the media

Everything looks so beautiful as you scroll through the foodie pictures. And those cooking competition shows? They're some of the best entertainment around.

What they aren't, however, is workparent reality. Those images took multiple food stylists, a professional photo studio, and a lighting designer to produce, and the calm, smiling host of your favorite cook-off program doesn't have to do his job after ten hours spent working elsewhere and with a low-blood-sugar toddler screaming in an adjacent high chair. You can get wonderful things from the media, and food media in particular: inspiration, new flavors, good quick-prep recipes. But the moment you start using it as a barometer for your own life and kitchen outputs, you're going to feel inadequate. Stay away from the comparison mindset, and use what you see in a positive way: to stoke your own interest in cooking and food . . . and for some easy, low-cost escape and diversion.

- **Be brief.** Children have shorter attention spans than adults do, and good behavior lasts only so long. Fortunately, Family Meals don't need to be long to have impact—it's their regularity and quality that count. When starting your new routine, aim for just fifteen minutes around the table. That timing will naturally lengthen as your kids grow and as the practice of connecting over shared meals becomes an essential, treasured habit.

Food as Part of *Your* Family's Workparent Template

As you read chapter 1, you mapped out your own *Workparent Template*: your collected impressions, assumptions, experiences, and feelings about being a working mom or dad, about what it really means and how it works. Think back to that exercise now—or even look over the notes you jotted down.

Somewhere within that web, you're almost certain to have a few—or more—entries focusing on the Food Challenge. Maybe there's a note on how your own working mom tied on her apron each evening after getting home, or how you had to pack your own school lunches because she was too busy to do so, or how you and your parents sat down to dinner together most nights—or never got to. Time around the table, or its lack, and what food and mealtimes feel like, is a noticeable part of most Workparent Templates. It's like a red thread woven through.

For your own children, it will be too. If you can set sacrosanct Family Meal times, you don't just get to enjoy those half-hour slots—you send a powerful, consistent message that even while you're working hard, family comes first. If you can seem more relaxed and "together" at the grocery store, or when scrambling to get food on the table, it's a way to tell the kids, *working parenthood isn't always easy, but it's possible.* Even on the nights you reach for an Emergency Meal, and then sit down for a few minutes to enjoy it together, you help create a template of strong, calm, capable workparenting for your kids to look to in their own future.

19

Health—Yours and Theirs

Keeping Your Workparent Family Well—and What
to Do When You're Under the Weather

Disclaimer: this chapter isn't going to offer you any medical
advice, or new ways to cure disease, or insights on ensuring
longevity. If you want any of those things, you should speak
with a qualified healthcare practitioner.

If, however, you've turned to this page because the day-to-day challenge of combining children and career is already stretching you thin,
and you need advice and encouragement on how, even in the face
of those pressures, to handle the extrastressful periods when your
kids—or you yourself—aren't in top form, keep right on reading.

Since you've got plenty to worry about, we're going to keep things
simple. For each zone of your working-parent life, we'll flag the name
of the game: the single overall approach that's most helpful when one
of your team is unwell. Then we'll look at specific tactical moves for
getting ahead of and easing the strain until everyone's feeling better.

At Home

The name of the game: prevention and preparation

You, the kids, and their caregiver(s) are all human, which means that
no matter how current you are with your doctor's visits, how robust

What to be ready for

Chances are your kids will go through each of the health challenges listed below at some point, because these challenges are 1) extremely common, and 2) impossible to completely avoid or prevent. Each one has the power to disrupt your regular care arrangement or your child's school schedule, thus wreaking havoc on *your* work and schedule—not to mention on your sleep, to-do list, and emotions. And of course, they'll often crop up during your workday, when you're facing a deadline or traveling, or at some other professionally inconvenient moment.

Here's what you, your medicine cabinet, your caregiving backup plans, and your Village will likely need to handle:

- Colds, viruses, flu, and flu-like illnesses
- Coughs and croup
- Fevers (whether or not accompanied by a cold, virus, or infection)
- Infections, including respiratory, throat, and ear
- Cuts, scrapes, burns, and bruises
- Breaks, fractures, sprains, and strains
- Skin conditions, including rashes, hives, and blisters
- Tummy trouble: stomach upset, motion sickness, vomiting, diarrhea
- Allergies, both food-related and environmental
- Conjunctivitis, also known as "pink eye"
- Head lice

your immune system, and how healthy you eat, each of you is going to get ill and/or injured at some point. It's inevitable; it *will* happen. That said, there are things you can do up front that might make the experience less frequent, and easier to handle when it does occur.

Your first health-related order of workparent business is to remain assertive on illness and injury prevention. It's normal for small children to get seven or eight colds and/or bugs per year. If you can reduce that number, or prevent your preschooler from passing whatever virus he's caught at daycare onto the rest of the family, it's a win: you've just avoided days of disrupted care arrangements, interrupted

> " I bring my work computer home every single night even if I have no intention of using it. That way, if one of the kids suddenly gets sick, I'm ready to work remotely."
>
> —*Sarah, acceleration-capital fund COO and senior director, strategic analysis, mother of two*

sleep, and extra stress. Having lived through Covid-19, you know all the important preventative measures, but let's recap quickly anyway.

Keep the family religious about handwashing, particularly when entering the house and before mealtimes, when germs are most likely to travel from mouths, noses, and hands to other people and surfaces. Keep antiseptic wipes or gel in your own work bag, the diaper bag, and the kids' school backpacks, and make it a habit to use the wipes or gel regularly, especially during transition times, like daycare pickup. To prevent germs and any foodborne nastiness from lingering in the house, clean frequently used surfaces, like doorknobs, laptops, and your kitchen counters, thoroughly and regularly with an antiseptic spray. Be sure to regularly sterilize the children's toys as well (easy to do: just run them through the dishwasher on the high-heat setting), particularly after hosting playdates. To make life easy, consider a family color-coding system to help keep bugs from spreading; accidental sharing of cups, utensils, towels, and toothbrushes is much less likely if your five-year-old son knows that all of *his* are green, his sister's yellow, yours red, and so on.

To prevent common injuries, be sure to have your house completely childproofed, and be certain to review and update those precautions regularly throughout the early-childhood years. A gate at the top of the stairs may once have been your chief concern, to keep your toddler from falling and sustaining bruises and breaks, but if he's now a curious, mischievous six-year-old, it's essential to have a lock on the medicine cabinet and to keep matches, hazardous cleaning materials, and the like out of sight and reach. If all of this sounds paranoid, or overly clinical, think of it this way: you're simply using the same sensible, shown-to-work containment techniques that good healthcare facilities do. They easily become habits, they're not overly time-consuming,

Taking care of *you*

Five of the biggest drivers of your own long-term wellness—nutrition, exercise, rest, relaxation, and positive social connections—are likely to get short shrift, or get completely thrown out the window, when you become a working parent. But remember: you're playing a long game here, and you're in a much better position to foster your family's overall health when you've adequately looked after your own. Make certain to pay attention to, and allocate enough time for, the things that will keep you at the top of your workparenting game—by keeping you healthy and whole.

When you are sick (whether or not the kids are too), draw down as much as you reasonably can on your Village resources. Try to get extra caregiving or help at home so that you can rest and recover. If there are shortcuts or other aids, use them. It's not going to hurt your five-year-old to have an "iPad day," and it may let you get back on your feet more quickly. Don't try to be a hero, or see these periods as tests of workparenting strength or endurance. The sooner you can heal, and get better, the better off you'll be, both at home and at work.

and each ounce of this type of prevention can be worth a pound of cure (or several, if you're working fifty hours a week).

Speaking of cures, do yourself a favor and get as ready as you possibly can for those illnesses and injuries when they do, inevitably, happen: stock the family medicine cabinet *now*. Virtually all seasoned workparents have a story about the time they had to trudge through a rainstorm to the pharmacy at 3:00 a.m. because they ran out of acetaminophen while their kid was spiking a fever—and while those stories may seem heroic or even humorous in retrospect, you don't ever want or need to do the same. Instead, go to your local discount drugstore once a year, for a major haul. Get a fresh first aid kit, as well as ample fever and pain reducers, bandages and antiseptic ointment, antiallergy medicine, the special rehydration fluid to give your small child after the stomach bug, and so on—in other words, everything you're likely to need for at-home treatment of common health concerns. As you shop, think *illness supplies* as much as *medicines*: when that stomach bug does hit (which, unfortunately, it will), you'll need a lot of extra paper towels in addition to that rehydration liquid. And that special precision thermometer that works by gently rolling across the forehead? That thing will be a godsend when you need to take your sick child's temperature while he's sleeping and you've got an 8:00 a.m. start at work the next day. This buying spree won't be cheap, but ultimately it will be much less pricy, in all senses of that word, than having to make a last-minute late-night trip to the pharmacy with a sick child in the backseat, or than having to leave work early to get what you could have had in the house already. When you've sourced all of your special sick-day supplies, put them in a lockable plastic bin and keep it someplace easy for caregivers to access but out of the way of small prying hands, like under the bed or on a higher closet shelf. You'll rest easier knowing that whatever comes, you're ready.

Consider pharmacy matters also. To save yourself time, money, and trouble, and to smooth out the logistical path ahead, you should put all regularly used medications on mail-order autorefill. Then, do some research on which drugstores near your house (and your workplace, and your health provider's office, and your Third Parents' houses, etc.) have pharmacy counters that stay open late, that offer twenty-four-hour service, or that better yet deliver—and include their phone numbers and address information on your family's Emergency Contacts Sheet, which should be prominently posted in your house as well as provided to regular and any backup caregivers. When you're in mad-dash mode to get those needed antibiotics for your daughter's ear infection, you don't want to be Googling "late night pharmacy" or leaving it to other caregivers to hunt for the number.

To create your own sickness-ready, workparent-appropriate Emergency Contacts Sheet, use the template provided in table 19-2, at the very end of this chapter.

At the Doctor's Office

The name of the game: accessibility

Healthcare helps you only *if you can get to it*—and when you're a crazy-busy working mom or dad without the extra hours to spare sitting

Telemedicine

Telemedicine simply means connecting to healthcare providers and resources via modern telecommunications technology: "visiting" a doctor about that sore throat via video call, for example, rather than heading to your regular practitioner's office or the local urgent-care center to have it checked out in person. Think of it as the modern-day, digitally supported version of a house call.

Key things to consider if you're wondering if a telemedicine appointment is right for you:

- Many or most of the old-school-style touch points you have with your regular healthcare provider come via phone or message anyway. So realistically, telemedicine is unlikely to be fundamentally different than some of the care experience you're already used to.

- Whether you're on the line with your regular doctor or a one-off provider, a telemedicine appointment will feel—and be—remarkably similar to a standard in-person visit. The physician will ask about your symptoms and health history, take a look at the problem (for example, by examining your throat, via video), and then provide advice on relieving it. In fact, the only real difference you'll notice is likely to come as a pleasant surprise: because you're connecting via videoconference, the doctor will probably make direct eye contact and provide you his or her full attention the entire time—no turning away from you to type on the computer, no being interrupted by other patient calls.

- All of the care providers you connect with via a telemedicine service will be just as licensed, credentialed, and experienced as any you find at your local ER or drop-in urgent-care center. And in fact, many are working parents who've chosen to become telemedicine providers as a way to gain some career flexibility and more-controlled hours—so in addition to being all-around good healthcare practitioners, they may know *exactly* what you're dealing with.

If you're ready to start using telemedicine as one part of your healthcare arsenal, either for yourself or your child, check out what services may already be available to you through your regular provider or plan. Telemedicine certainly had a "moment" during the Covid-19 crisis, but for various reasons you may or may not want to begin or continue seeing your healthcare providers this way now. Do your research and think it through.

in a waiting room, "getting to it" is the crux of your problem. What-ever phase of workparenting you're currently in, whether you just welcomed a newborn or have teenage kids, it's best if you can get the healthcare your family needs quickly, and without hassle, improvisa-tion, or drama.

If you are on the hunt for a new care provider, whether for the kids or yourself, look for the following; each item on this list signals that the physician or practice will be all-around more workparent friendly.

- A larger, or at least multiphysician, practice. While the old-school, sole-practitioner model may be enticing (More indi-vidual attention! Medicine the way it used to be!), for you as a working parent it can lead to a lot of headache. If your physi-cian isn't available when you need her, you may be bounced to a covering doctor you've never met, in an office you've never been to—which isn't what you want when your child is sick. Look for a clear and reassuring on-call coverage plan, and an easy-to-access nursing and/or physician-assistant staff with the time to help you address basic health concerns like colds, feed-ing issues, and teething.

- Affiliation with a major, well-regarded hospital system. With luck, no member of the family will ever need emergency, inpa-tient, or specialized care, but in case one does, you'll want your primary doctor to be able to make all needed referrals quickly and to oversee your family member's complete experience and treatment. The last thing any working parent needs is to spend hours hunting for referrals or trying to navigate a major medi-cal experience without a knowledgeable guide.

- Early-morning, evening, and weekend appointments, both for urgent issues and for standard checkups and well-child visits. You want to be able to see the doctor outside of your *own* regular business hours—e.g., to take your ill child in for the strep-throat swab before work, and to not miss important on-the-job obligations to make it to that annual checkup.

- A prompt, courteous, can-do office staff and customer-service functions powered by modern technology. You want to ensure that's it's easy and efficient to book regular appointments, request school and camp forms, and retrieve basic medical records. Also inquire about the ability to correspond with the staff electronically. If the *only* way to reach the provider is by phone, and/or if the office is still conducting business via fax machine—which, somewhat incredibly, many still are—you may be better off elsewhere.

- A satisfying answer to the question, "What happens if my child is sick, I can't make the appointment, and someone else brings her instead?" Annual well-child visits normally require a parent's presence, but realistically, many other appointments may be handled by a caregiver or Third Parent. Ideally, the provider is comfortable and used to doing them with working parents dialed in via phone or videoconference—and will immediately reassure you that that's the case. If the response you get has any whiff of surprise or judgment to it, move on.

For urgent and off-hours care, have a family plan on where to go, and when: e.g., which hospital emergency room to head to in case of serious issues, and which local urgent-care drop-in center to use. Note that not all ERs or urgent-care centers will see or specialize in pediatric patients, so do the appropriate research ahead of time. If you do ever need these resources—which most parents do, at some point—you'll want to have a good plan ready.

With Your Caregiver(s)

The name of the game: coordination and information-sharing

When your child is sick, caregiving logistics almost always become more complicated. If you use in-home care, your babysitter may need to take your child to the doctor's and loop you in while you're at work.

Knowing the rules—and following them

Be sure to review your daycare center's and/or school's specific policies about sick children, and to understand them in detail. Under
normal circumstances, most will require you to keep your child home
if he displays any outward signs of contagious illness—such as fever,
stomach upset, or persistent cough—and crucially, to keep him home
for *at least* twenty-four hours *after* those symptoms have ceased.
As of this writing, the coronavirus pandemic continues, and most
institutions have changed their policies: adopting "zero tolerance"
approaches, temperature-checking children upon entry, requiring
seventy-two hours at home after the last cold-like symptom has
ceased, and so forth. Be certain you know the drill, and whatever the
guidelines are, follow them carefully. The daycare center and school
have put them in place for good reasons.

A few months before the end of my first parental leave, we put
our son into daycare one day per week so as to expose him to
what we jokingly called Daycare Ebola. For two or three months, all
three of us kept getting sick, and the baby had a constant runny nose.
But by the time I went back to work, he had been exposed. That ramp-
up of care helps the immune system—and of course, it helps the parent
and child adjust to care, too."

—*Tracy, nurse manager, mother of two*

If your child is typically in school or daycare, you may have to switch
over to the backup plans you carefully mapped out for yourself as you
read through chapter 2. Whatever the case, there are suddenly more
and different people involved, handovers to coordinate, and details
to cover—and all at a time when you're likely more tired and stressed
than average, and when it's extra important to monitor and ensure
your child's well-being. It's completely normal to feel overwhelmed
at this point, and for some of the small-but-important details of care
(like who's calling the school to let them know your child won't be in

TABLE 19-1

Sample Sick-Child Care Tracker

Caregiver	Took over at	Health actions	Observations/ notes	To do
Dad	6:30 a.m.— from wakeup	Gave 5 ml baby fever reducer at 6:30. Also used nasal aspirator. Left message with nurse's line at the doctor's.	She woke up with fever of xx degrees and congested. Did not finish breakfast.	When daycare opens at 8:00, call to say we'll be out today.
Backup sitter	8:30 a.m.	Got call back from nurse practitioner, who said symptoms sound normal, but to call back tomorrow if fever persists, or if it goes higher. Recommended steam for cough.	Was cranky, but fever lower by early afternoon. Minimal coughing.	
Grandma	1:00 p.m.	Gave 5 ml fever reducer.	Fever up again. Nap, forty-five minutes. Had difficulty sleeping due to congestion. Uninterested in lunch.	Stop by market on way home: need crackers and juice.
Mom	5:30 p.m.	Did steam to help reduce cough before bed.	Low appetite, did not finish dinner. Fell asleep at 7:00 p.m.	

today, or exactly when the baby had his last dose of medicine) to become confusing, or even slip.

To make conducting this whole orchestra a little easier, think about using a simple sick-child tracking tool like the one in table 19-1. Your tracker lets you pull all of the specially needed caregiving logistics together, ensures that nothing gets lost—and gives you important reassurance that you're on top of things, the way you want to be. It doesn't need to be fancy; a handwritten version is fine. Just post it by the front door, or in the kitchen, and ask each caregiver as they arrive to review it, and to keep it current during their own shift.

Preparing your Village

Getting through the periods when you, your caregiver, and your child are unwell will often mean relying on your Village's members in a new or different way. To get them on board and ready to help:

- **Inform.** Walk close family members, Third Parents, and backup caregivers through your Emergency Contacts Sheet, providing examples of what to do and when and answering any questions. Provide extra hard and soft copies for them to keep.
- **Educate.** As you prepared to become a parent, you may have taken an infant and child first aid and CPR class (offered by a local community center, a school, a healthcare provider's office, or your local chapter of the Red Cross). If not, now's the time, and it's also the time to consider encouraging, and even sponsoring, other Village members to do the same.
- **Have them practice assertive prevention, too.** Make sure Grandpa and the teenage weekend sitter are washing up regularly, too, and that their vaccine profiles match what you're doing for your child.
- **Preview and normalize.** The college-age sitter may not know what to do when your toddler throws up. Your aunt, who watches the baby on Fridays, may be hesitant to bother you at work. Your Villagers are human, they may not be parents themselves, and they're doing the best they can. Provide them some guidance—and needed reassurance.

If caregivers will be responsible for delivering medicines or handling any other special tasks, make sure that you've provided specific, precise instructions—for example, exact dosages, and how the medicine should be administered (e.g., "He should get 5 ml every six hours. You'll have to squirt it into his mouth, using the dropper"). And be sure to leave any specific instructions on how to help your child feel more comfortable and calm as well; if sleeping with a certain blanket is what he likes, or if it's OK to show him a few episodes of his favorite show on the iPad while the fever is still high, be sure your caregivers know.

At School

The name of the game: rehearsal

By the time your child starts full-time school, you're a pro at managing through sick-child situations. You are used to talking to your colleagues about your needs, have made many same-day appointments with your healthcare provider, know what pharmacy stays open late, and all the rest. There's a key difference now, however, which is that your child suddenly has to become a more active and independent participant in the process, and may have to do things that are far outside his regular experience to date. If your six-year-old doesn't feel well, for example, he'll need to tell the teacher, navigate or be taken to the school nurse's office, be seen and assessed by an adult he likely hasn't met before, and rely on that person to alert you to what's going on, which may mean his having to explain how you can be reached during the day. Depending on his symptoms and the school's setup, he may also have to wait for you in an isolation room—which can be disconcerting for a child. It's all a far cry from his experience at daycare, when regular, trusted caregivers spotted when he was sick, provided him comfort and reassurance, and were well versed in how to get in touch.

In order to make the sick-in-school experience less stressful, it can be helpful to simply talk it through ahead of time and do a bit of rehearsal. Reassure your son that feeling under the weather while at school happens to *everybody* at some point, that there's nothing embarrassing about classmates knowing he's feeling ill, and that he's

> I broke my arm a few weeks ago, and needed surgery. The other moms in both of my children's classes were amazing. They helped with drop-off, got the kids to playdates. We have a messaging group, and it was so great to have that efficient, structured forum in which to ask for help."
>
> —*Chelsea, SVP, strategic partnerships, mother of two*

never "bothering" you if he needs to be picked up. Explain when and why it's a good idea to tell a teacher, and if he's shy or apprehensive about it, take the sting away by role-playing the situation a few times. Walk through what may happen next ("the teacher will send you to Mrs. Williams's office, on the second floor, and she'll ask you more questions and may take your temperature") so that it loses any scariness. Make sure that he knows your phone number by heart, and basic directions as to how you can be reached (e.g., "Call my mom at this number, and if she doesn't answer, call my dad at this one . . ."). Of course the school should have all of that information on file, but if the computer system is down, or if a substitute nurse is covering and can't immediately find it, you still want the school to be able to get in touch quickly—and regardless, your son will feel more confident and empowered knowing it. Finally, explain what happens next: "If

Sending your child the right messages

Whether you hear the dreaded phrase "Mommy/Daddy, I don't feel so good!" or see one of its nonverbal equivalents (like that glazed, pale, listless look that kids get when they're coming down with something), you know all too well what's coming next: you're about to enter a multiday, frantic, improvisational rush to cover work responsibilities while taking care of things at home. Even when illness wreaks havoc on your workparent routine, though, don't let that problem become your child's, don't allow her to sense too much of your stress, and don't inadvertently give her the idea that she's somehow at fault or guilty of throwing a wrench into your professional works. She feels crummy already, and any one of those things will only make her feel worse.

Avoid "oh no!" type exclamations and hand-wringing as soon as illness becomes apparent, keep your panic about tomorrow's deadline or important meeting to yourself, and if you need to place that urgent call to your boss or backup caregiver, do it from another room. Make sure you're projecting nothing but steadiness, warmth, and can-do spirit. No matter what's happening at work, and whether your child is well or sick, be the same competent, unconditionally loving mother or father you always are.

you get sick at school, either Mom or Uncle Chris will come get you, as soon as we can. It will take Mom about twenty minutes to drive to your school from work."

Throughout the school years, don't be afraid to make teachers aware of any health concerns. Major, chronic issues like food allergies should be flagged in the school's own records, but if your daughter's just getting over a doozy of a head cold, or suffering from a bout of seasonal allergy, flag it. (With that knowledge, your teacher will be able to understand your daughter's droopiness in math class, or allow her to sit out the running drills during P.E.) As always, see your child's teachers as trusted, critical partners in your child's overall well-being.

At Work

The name of the game: previewing—and being direct and brief

Your child's health needs will at some point inevitably disrupt your work. The daycare will call and tell you that your daughter is sick and has to be picked up, right now; or you'll have to repeatedly knock off early to make your eleven-year-old's orthodontist appointments. When those things happen, even if you have an understanding employer, you'll be thrust into what might feel like an awkward dynamic: you'll have to explain, often suddenly, and often at very inconvenient times, that parenting needs to take precedence over the job.

You could, of course, take each of those conversations as they come, flagging your need in real time—and if you're in a self-managing role, or have a very relaxed work environment, that may be the best way forward. If you work in a more structured or formal environment, though, another strategy is *previewing*: letting your colleagues know that these situations are coming, and how you intend to handle them. In other words, instead of improvising each announcement, hoping it "lands," and anxiously seeking your colleagues' understanding and forbearance, you talk about your needs and plans up-front, using a script like this: "While I've got good backup plans for Ayaan's regular care, there will occasionally be times when he's sick and I'll need to juggle my work around parenting responsibilities. For example, if he becomes ill at daycare, either my partner, a friend or family member, or I will need to pick him up. If I do, I'll let you know immediately, and make up the hours in the day or two following. Of course, I'm sure you've been there yourself! If you have any concerns around my plans to handle this, let me know." Bringing your colleagues into your practical approach and proactive thinking makes you look much more professional—and takes most of the frenzy, drama, and personal stress out of those situations when they do come up.

When the daycare center does call, and you do have to run out on work, attempt to keep your in-the-moment communications honest, brief, and unapologetic. Your boss needs to know that you're leaving, but doesn't need to know how high your daughter's fever is, or that your son has terrible hives, or just puked. And he doesn't need the news that you're leaving right now wrapped inside a babbled, run-on description of how guilty you feel about missing the weekly team meeting, or a monologue about how sorry you are for having personal needs. (Apologizing implies you've done something wrong, which you haven't.) Think of yourself as writing a newspaper headline—or as a confident senior leader making an announcement: "The daycare called. Ayaan's sick, and I need to leave now to pick him up. I'll be back online as soon as I can." It's not a description, or confession—just an FYI.

Putting It All Together: In Your Own Heart and Mind

You're nursing the kids through their colds, have gotten them to the doctor's—and are still managing to get everything you need to done at work. *And* you're tired, *and* worried, *and* perhaps also feeling extraconflicted about parenting and working at the same time. The fact that your child is sick isn't a referendum on your parenting skills, though, it's just a biological reality. And if you feel like you're "at the edge" right now, professionally, physically, or psychologically, it's entirely normal. Periods of illness are *hard*.

When the problem is bigger, or longer term

If your child has special needs, is coping with a chronic condition, or has just received a difficult diagnosis, it may not be your natural instinct to share that news, or any details about what you're going through, with people at work. Between the practical challenge, the emotions you're facing, and a completely understandable desire for privacy, it may seem preferable to keep things under wraps.

As difficult as it is, consider sharing some of what you're going through. Your boss can't be supportive if he doesn't know what you're facing. The HR folks can't help you navigate the thicket of benefits and insurance matters unless they know you need their help. And the other colleagues who have been in similar situations—and many have—can't provide you any advice or fellowship when they're in the dark. Be aware also that in keeping your news to yourself you assume some potential career risk: a pattern of distractedness or absences from work may be misread as noncommitment or underperformance.

That doesn't mean that you have to overshare, or put specific health or developmental matters out in the open. Simply give your manager a heads up that you're dealing with a "health concern," let her know that you're just as committed as ever to your work—and say that you want to discuss a plan for taking care of business, both at work and at home. No matter how "rough and tough" a person your manager may be normally, chances are high she'll be helpful and understanding.

"There's nothing more isolating than getting the news that your child has special needs, and disability can be a conversation stopper. At first I was uncertain about how to bring it up with the people at work. I tried to walk a fine line—to have *just* enough people be aware. Looking back now, I may have overemphasized that. There were a lot of school meetings and therapy appointments and doctor's visits I needed to do, but I've realized that as long as you're delivering, people don't really care.

A lot of organizations have special disability-focused employee-resource groups you can go to for support, HR may be able to help connect you to other parents, and you can always go with word of mouth. Parents in the same situation tend to find—and support—each other."

—*Lisa, executive search firm partner, mother of two*

"Of the thirty sales reps here, I'm the only one with kids. I need to be extra-vigilant about my time management and showing up as 'in it.' One of my kids has special medical needs, although things are changing, and unclear. There's been a lot of doctor's appointments and insurance stuff to deal with, but because it wasn't affecting my work, I didn't talk about it.

I finally went to my manager, without an 'ask'—it was just, 'here's what I want you to be aware of, just in case my needs do change, or I find myself dealing with a specific diagnosis.' Around the same time, I stepped back from a lot of work extracurriculars, and I had to give my colleagues some idea as to why.

I found so much support I didn't expect. My HR contact said, 'you don't have to tell me anything, but here are all the benefits that might be useful.' It never would have occurred to me that any of them were even available! I've found that the more I share, the more I get."

—*Caitlin, account executive, mother of two*

Try to focus on your *own* name of the game right now, which is cutting yourself some slack. It's fine to order in, to relax the kids' screen-time rules, to ask for more help at home, and to miss work for a bit if you have to. You're a working parent, not magical or superhuman. Just focus on making it through this difficult patch, and doing whatever it is that helps you get to the other side.

TABLE 19-2

Sample Workparent All-in-One Emergency Contacts Sheet

Child's name

Age

Medical concerns/allergies

Home address

Home phone

Caregivers (in order of contact preference)					
	Parent 1	Parent 2	Regular caregiver	Third Parent	Other Village contact
Name					
Relationship					
Best way to contact quickly					
Cell phone					
Work contact information					
What to do if out of reach/not responding					
Work switchboard, colleague, or manager info					

School/daycare information	Backup care
School or daycare name	Person, center, or service
Child's primary teacher or caregiver	Direct line
Switchboard number	Address/location
Emergency/administrative office number	

Medical information	
Main healthcare provider Preferred/primary physician Office hours What to do off-hours How to contact nurse's line/other providers in practice	**Dental health provider** Office hours What to do off-hours
Preferred hospital Address/location of pediatric ER Direct phone	**Walk-in urgent-care center** Address/location Phone
Closest pharmacy Closest 24-hour pharmacy Pharmacy delivery	Insurance plan ID number Customer service line

Safety and emergency contacts

General emergency (fire, police, medical)

Local police precinct

Poison Control

(*continued*)

TABLE 19-2 (continued)

Other key Village contacts		
Name	Name	Name
Relationship	Relationship	Relationship
Contact for	Contact for	Contact for
Primary phone	Primary phone	Primary phone
Other contact information	Other contact information	Other contact information

Supplies

Regular medical supplies are kept:

Backup/extra supplies are kept:

Emergency household cash is kept:

20

Energy

Your Workparent Mind and Body, at Rest and in Motion

t the center of this whole working-parent operation is something you may not have been tending to much recently: your own battery. Take a minute now simply to check in with *yourself*—with the brain and physical being that's doing all this work and caregiving. How are you doing? Feeling? What's your energy like? How high—or low—are your reserves? This isn't a test; you're just taking stock. What words best describe your current state?

If ones like *strong, fit, motivated, focused, vigorous,* and *ready* come to mind, you can safely skip this chapter. Whether by dint of luck or habit, you're already in a good place. If, however:

- Your reaction was more of a mixed picture

- The words that floated up were ones like *tired, depleted, foggy, heavy, glum, sluggish,* or *ground down*

- You found yourself thinking longingly back to when you were in better form, prekids

- You can't think of how to turn things around, so in addition to feeling tired and/or out-of-shape, you also feel helpless

- You're secretly wondering if this is the beginning of a long, irreversible slide toward . . .

. . . then STOP! Read these next few pages carefully. They're a menu of workparent-specific, nuts-and-bolts ways to manage your own energy and stamina, both mental and physical, organized by general category or what we'll call *levers of control*.

As you read, put a check next to the specific techniques you want to start using, or using more. Just a few tick marks: that's it. When you're done, we'll wrap those insights into your personal plan to recharge.

Lever 1: Getting More Sleep

There's good reason that sleep deprivation is used as torture. Without enough rest, human beings break down quickly. Your workparenting sleep deficit may be more chronic and cumulative in nature, but it's still corrosive, and makes it *very* hard to deliver everything you want to at work and at home.

To start getting more sleep:

☐ **Believe that it's possible.** That's not a cosmic statement, but a practical one. If you're firmly subscribed to the idea that workparenting means being chronically underslept, and you accept that fact, or if you somehow see exhaustion as a badge of honor—well, then that's what will probably happen. Have faith that you can get more rest, and that you deserve it.

☐ **Practice workparent-style sleep hygiene.** "Sleep hygiene" means all of those small behaviors that help you get a decent

> " We don't talk about specific bedtimes, so the kids aren't really aware that they go to bed earlier than their peers. Before they fall asleep, I spend ten or fifteen minutes with them, lying in bed—just connective, quiet time. Later in the evenings, I have a few hours to get things done, spend time with my husband, relax."
>
> —*Rose, procurement leader, mother of two*

night's shut-eye—limiting caffeine intake, putting your devices away a full hour before bed, keeping your bedroom dark and quiet, and so on. All are important, yet realistically speaking very hard for any parent or busy professional to follow. You can't tell the baby not to make noise, and if you're working a Split Day, as we covered in chapter 4, there's no way you're going to have the luxury of a full device-free hour each evening. Nevertheless, try to develop your own regimen. Maybe you have a "no screens for the fifteen minutes before bed" rule, or drink plenty of coffee until noon, but none after. The core idea here is to manage toward good-quality sleep throughout the day, not just when your head hits the pillow.

☐ **Wind down.** When you and the kids haven't seen each other for ten hours, it's natural to want to pack in some let's-live-a-little activities: exuberant play, listening to music, doing sports in the backyard, roughhousing, watching an episode of that exciting new series—all the things you'd want to do if you didn't have to go to work. That's fine, but it's difficult for children, and adults, to move from boisterous, higher-charge activities straight into bedtime mode: it's too abrupt of a switch. Try using and pacing your evenings as an enjoyable preface to bed. Quieter and less physical activities, lower lighting, and reading will help the whole family taper down from wakefulness to rest. Doing those evening activities in a set order, as a routine, will also act as a cue for sleep.

☐ **Create a shut-off switch.** It's 11:30 p.m., and you still have a gazillion items on your work and family to-do lists. You could easily keep chugging through those to-dos all night or, worse, lie awake mentally reciting, reorganizing, or working them through. That's crazy-making, and there's no big red button, like on a treadmill, allowing you to stop and safely get off. So create one, at least in your own mind: have a *no "productive" activity after 11:00 p.m.* policy, or tell yourself that *as soon as I turn off my desk light [or switch off my laptop, or get into my pajamas, etc.], it's time for me to relax.* Each evening, take a moment to push that mental button, giving yourself explicit permission to stop doing, and worrying: *What isn't done isn't done, and can wait till tomorrow. Now, it's time for me to rest.*

☐ **Be the decider.** What time the kids have to go to sleep, whether or not they're allowed to come into bed with you during the night, when you serve them breakfast in the morning: those are all choices *you* should be making. Telling your five-year-old that bedtime is nonnegotiable, or that he needs to stay in his room, or that there won't be cereal available until 6:00 a.m., doesn't make you harsh or punitive—you're merely defending your night's sleep. If you don't do it, no one else will.

☐ **Sleep-block.** If the kids aren't sleeping well because of age, illness, or any other reason, and you have a partner or fellow caregiver, tackle the night(s) in shifts; for example, you rest from 10:00 p.m. until 3:00 a.m., and are then "on" from 3:00 until 7:00, while your partner does the reverse. You'll still be tired, but that four-to-five-hour block of sleep will be just enough to allow you to stay functional tomorrow, and you won't fall into the 3:00 a.m. whose-turn-is-it arguments or resentment.

☐ **Use 15-3.** If you need to shift the kids' or your own sleep schedules, tackle the change in "fifteen-minutes, every three days" increments. If you want to start your days earlier, for example, get up at 6:15 instead of your usual 6:30 on Monday, and then on Thursday, hitch it back to 6:00. The small-step changes will be barely perceptible, and more likely to endure.

☐ **Stop negative sleep-talk.** Telling the kids that they "*have* to go to bed!" or berating yourself that "if I don't fall asleep right now, I'll be a basket case in the morning" only ratchets up the anxiety and makes it that much harder to calm down and drift off. A simple, firm "it's bedtime now," or telling yourself *I'm doing the right thing, being in bed, resting* is better. Gentleness works.

Solutions that aren't

Coffee, sugary snacks, the snooze button, a glass of wine, the remote control: these things work. Each one provides immediate pep or relaxation—a reward, and some *relief*. In small(ish) quantities, they're great workparenting tools, yet their habitual use, or overuse, can actually make the underlying problems of fatigue and stress worse.

Try this: over the next week, go about your regular routine, with a watchful eye on the relaxants and pick-me-ups you naturally turn to when your stress spikes and physical and mental energy dips. For each one, ask yourself: *How is this habit (or substance, or activity) serving me? Should I use more or less of it? Is there something else that would be equally satisfying in the moment, without forcing me to "borrow" from my energy later?* Maybe you decide to cut back from five cups of coffee a day to three. Or not—you decide. The point is simply to become more deliberate and mindful as to how these common, small-scale solutions can truly work *for* you in the short and long term.

Lever 2: Exercise and Movement

Prekids, your exercise habits likely involved some combination of the following: trips to a dedicated gym, hour-long workouts, special clothing, special equipment, scheduled classes or events, objective metrics (the precise number of pounds bench-pressed, your personal best time for the 5K, and the like), a sense of *need to* or *should*, time spent in a group/communal activity or connecting with friends, time spent completely alone, and personal goal-setting and scorekeeping—in the form of pounds lost, miles run, number of classes taken, and so forth.

That was exercise *then*. If you try to graft that approach and those habits onto your life now, you probably won't find yourself exercising much if at all. Be honest: with a toddler at home, are you really going to drive to the gym at the end of your workday, take an hour-long class, miss mealtime together, feel terrific about it all—and do so regularly? Why beat yourself up about "failing" to do that, or not managing to wake up at 4:30 a.m. to do crunches like you keep vowing

The ExcerSnack

You've got favorite snacks—the things you naturally grab when you need a quick hit of energy, a little fuel, a yummy boost. Why not apply the same concept to movement? Have a few easy, two-minute, go-to exercises you can reach for when you feel moody or sluggish and need that little lift. A brisk walk through the office hallway, a few quick stretches done at your desk. You'll have the full meal later—for now, just take a quick bite.

you will, when you're wrangling so much working-parent stress and emotion already? Instead of sticking to the prekids model, change the model—rethink what exercise and fitness mean and how to come at them.

☐ **Set a new purpose.** Maybe you used to want to look good in spandex, or stay at your twenty-five-year-old weight, or complete a triathlon. Those were all fine goals and good reasons to get moving. Now, exercise can serve you in a different way: it will help ensure your health and longevity, it provides the best stress relief going, and it lets you set a self-care example for the kids. To help yourself reset and find new motivation, try filling in the sentence, "movement is important to me at this phase of my life because . . ." or "as a working parent, exercise lets me . . ."

☐ **Take it in small bites.** If your schedule permits that hour-long workout, terrific. If it doesn't, break your movement and exercise up into smaller chunks of time. Check if your gym has any "speed workout" or shorter, high-intensity classes available; do your ten thousand daily steps in five-minute walks spread out throughout the day—on the way to work, during lunch, during a nice relaxing amble around your neighborhood with the stroller in the evening; download a five-minute-workout app onto your phone.

☐ **Be able to access it, and transition into it, quickly.** It may be hard to get to the hiking trails you love that are twenty minutes away, but you can easily put on your running shoes and run around your block. Getting to the gym may be a production, but you can do the stretching routine in your bedroom each morning. In this Golden Age of Streaming Exercise Content, you can work out easily and at any time.

☐ **Find something that feels like a reward.** Maybe you used to be willing to "take the pain," in terms of exercise, but you're taking a lot of pain now, as a working parent, and should make exercise a fun, enjoyable diversion. Try out new activities until you find one that feels more like a break than a burden.

☐ **Make it serve a dual purpose.** Have a walking meeting with a coworker and you've just checked *two* daily activities off your list.

☐ **Have location-by-location options.** What exercise can you do, and access, at home, at work, and in any other important "zones" of your life? Perhaps the park across the street from your house is where you usually run on the weekends, but at work, you sneak in more exercise by taking the stairs. Geography shouldn't hem you in.

☐ **Do it around—or with—the kids.** Of course you want a break from them—you're an individuated adult, and that long run or your spinning class can be sanity-preserving, invaluable "me time," but you also have the option of doing a workout video with your kids playing in the same room, or of cuing up

> ❝ If you're going to go to the gym, do it at the beginning or end of the day, on your commute if you have one. Nobody really knows where you are, and it only takes thirty minutes."
> —*Béla, CEO, father of two*

> 66 I run, but if you hate running, just get out for a walk. It's a technical thing: when you're moving around outside, you're taking in more oxygen, and that helps.
>
> When I'm running I don't think about my daughter, or about work, or what's happening in the world. I focus on the music I'm listening to, or on my breath. I enjoy that time. Exercise doesn't have to be hard."
>
> —*Alexis, artistic director, mother of one*

one of the many "parent and child" versions. Being on Kid Duty doesn't have to hold you back from getting in some movement.

Lever 3: Finding Rituals and Activities That Relax and Recharge You

As important as it is to get your heart rate *up*, you also have to get your stress level *down*. That means finding, and prioritizing, reliable ways to unplug and decompress. If you're like many working parents, the idea of spending time on any activity purely for its soothingness or psychic benefits may feel profoundly selfish (*Shouldn't I be doing something more productive?*); may seem like a hurdle (*Activity? Are you kidding? All I have the energy to do is watch TV*); or may become a priority only when you're completely at the end of your rope.

Pretend, though, that a healthcare provider you trust has just written you a lifesaving prescription, and it's this: *spend at least fifteen minutes per day doing something you perceive as relaxing.* In the context of a busy working-parent life, that might mean reading, meditating, knitting, playing Ping-Pong, driving, talking to a friend, taking a bath—anything at all. What characterizes the activity is that it serves no particular purpose. It has no "goal" per se, and it's usually noncompetitive. You're not trying to *get it done*, you're just enjoying yourself. Make those fifteen minutes an unapologetic part of your daily routine.

On a larger level, you may also choose to stoke up psychologically and mentally by:

The introverted workparent

If you're an introvert accustomed to using "alone time" as a way to recover your energy at the end of long workdays spent within the field, in meetings, or in other social situations, then workparenting will pose a particular challenge. You love your kids to pieces, but the time spent with them will displace much (or all) of the time you'd normally spend solo. You just won't have as much time to regroup in the way you're naturally wired to.

If so, start by simply acknowledging the fact that you *are* an introvert, and there's nothing wrong with your need for a little downtime. Then, focus on small-bite ways you might get *just enough* downtime to make workparenting a little easier. Think about using your commute as reenergizing time (create an "isolation booth" and deter conversation by putting on headphones, even if you're not listening to anything); try to carve out regular weekend time alone; and if it's possible to do so at work, find an empty or unused space to take a daily fifteen-minute "introvert break." If working remotely, leave the house for a walk and some time inside your own head. If your kids are young, make Silence a game: set a timer, and see how long both of you can go without making any noise. As the kids get older, be open with them when Mom or Dad needs ten minutes to recharge. Finally, remind yourself of all the powerful ways in which introversion makes you the *perfect* colleague and parent: a patient listener, a true connector, and capable of giving others your full attention, one-to-one.

- Dedicating time to spiritual practices

- Serving others—whether through volunteering, mentoring, or donation

- Getting social support, whether that's by joining your organization's parents network, or just by ensuring you spend adequate time with good friends

Any of these habits may feel "inefficient" or awkward at first, but as you make a regular investment in them, you'll quickly find a personal energy and bounce-back-ness that you didn't have before.

> ❝ I've tried a million things to figure out what fills me up instead of depleting me. You've got to be authentic—don't force yourself to get up early and work out if you're not a morning person. For me, it's about thinking bigger picture, not starting my day with minutiae."
>
> —*Kendra, marketing project manager, mother of one*

> ❝ I get out of work when there's a lot of traffic, and my commute can take an hour and a half. In the car, I listen to music, but more often I listen to comedy. Did you know Pandora has channels with all these great different comedians? I'm cracking up the whole ride home."
>
> —*Keywanda, senior timekeeper, mother of two*

Creating Your Energy Action Plan

Now that you've read over the various techniques and approaches—and started hatching more of your own—it's time to move things forward.

In the space provided in table 20-1, record your physical and mental starting place, as you described at the beginning of the chapter. Don't edit yourself: just jot whatever words came to mind. Then note which specific techniques and overall lever jumped out at you as you read.

Now, look over what you've written, and in a sentence or two describe what you'll try doing differently over the coming two weeks, in the context of your day-to-day life. If you've got several techniques you want to try, that's great, but start with just one or two (remember: incremental changes). Maybe you'll *stop watching streaming shows past 11:00*, or *take a five-minute walk every day during work*, or maybe you'll smartly combine a few of the new moves here with ones from other chapters—for example, with a few healthier-eating strategies from chapter 18, "Food and Mealtimes." The point here is to commit to *doing*—and to make that commitment small and specific enough

TABLE 20-1

Energy Action Plan

Body and mind check-in	As I pay attention to my body and mind right now, I am . . .
Critical lever	The one general approach that will help me become more energized is . . .
New approaches and techniques	The specific approaches and activities that will be most feasible and powerful for me are . . . 1. _____ 2. _____ 3. _____ 4. _____ 5. _____

that you'll easily be able to follow through. Think of this as the Anti–New Year's Resolution—something so small and nonrevolutionary that you'll have no problem sticking with it. Two weeks is just enough runway to try out your new habits, and to determine if they're giving you the benefits they should.

Fourteen days from now, revisit. Do the check-in exercise again, noting any differences, and then add a few new energy-forward techniques into your repertoire for the next two-week cycle. Keep on in this way, gently layering in new approaches.

Learning to Work Well When Your Battery Is Low

In certain professions—medicine, the military, certain branches of professional services, for example—learning how to work when utterly exhausted is an important and/or explicit part of the training. You don't have to be in those fields to borrow their particular compensatory techniques, though. When you've been up all night with a sick child and have to be "on" and functional the next morning at work:

- **Break it down.** That whole day or massive pile of work may feel impossible to tackle, but if you can focus on just a small piece of it, it won't be so overwhelming. Pick some part of the project or your task list you can make good headway on, or think about tackling just the next thirty minutes. Think *near vision, small goals, short sprints*.

- **Knock out the work with a one-two punch.** The first thing that goes out the window when you're exhausted is your ability to fully "see" your work—and catch mistakes. If, however, you can allow for some time between producing the work and finalizing it, you're more likely to bring the critical and accurate eye it needs. Write the memo in the morning and proofread it in the afternoon, or have that supplier call now but put the purchasing orders in tomorrow.

- **Save the interpersonal issues and judgment calls for later.** Nuance, emotional equilibrium, the ability to read small personal cues, patience: all go out the window when you're overwhelmed and underslept. Deliver the goods you need to, but avoid having that difficult feedback conversation or making decisions related to strategy, hiring, or career issues until you're a little more rested.

- **Draw a line.** Is what you've done good enough—or good enough for now? Then stop! When you're feeling more energized, you can go back to being more of a perfectionist.

- **Enlist a second.** Ask a colleague or team member to eyeball your work: to read over the message you've just drafted and check it for tone, for example, or to play devil's advocate on the argument you're about to make to your boss. You can't lean on your colleagues for backup like this *every* day, but you can certainly ask a favor occasionally, and their help may allow you to avoid a lot of unforced errors.

- Pretend you're an actor, playing a role. You don't have to *be* high-energy and full of optimism and vigor in that meeting, or on that call, or in that interview, or when greeting the kids after getting home—you just have to *seem* like it, temporarily. Think of your professional impact the way a doctor would his or her own bedside manner—as something deliberate, considered, and cultivated. How can you inspire trust and project competence? Take a deep breath, step into character, and "give good professional," or "parent," until the next break.

More You

Even on those days when you feel as if you're running on fumes, you'll probably still be able to get to workparenting baseline: to muddle through at work, or get the kids fed and off to school. What won't

---

Being the bad guy

What do . . .
- Sleep training the baby
- Leaving your partner alone with a sick toddler on a weekend afternoon so you can go jogging
- Not staying as current with your friends on social media, because you're dedicating time to other, more genuinely replenishing activities, and
- Asking your colleague if you can defer making that judgment call until the morning, when you're fresh
. . . all have in common? You, as the villain—that's what!

As you focus on preserving and building your mental and physical reserves, you will sometimes feel selfish, or as if you're letting other people down. When that happens, remind yourself of what's really at stake here: your ability to be a strong, effective workparent over the long term, and to truly be there for the people who matter. If you can get the baby on a good sleep schedule, it lets you be a better mother or father *and* perform better at work, every day. If you can stay healthy and even-keeled through exercise, you can be there more for your partner, and your kids and colleagues.

be so doable is excelling on the job, or truly connecting with your children. When you're shredded, it's just plain harder to be creative, or to make the sale, or to come up with new solutions, or to savor family time. It's also harder to be yourself. When you're personally depleted, all of your uniqueness—your humor, smarts, creativity—takes a hit.

Don't let it. Treat your energy for what it is: a resource, and an asset. Spend it, but tend it—for your career, for the kids, and for *you*.

21

Feelings

Coping with Guilt, Overwhelmed-ness—and Other
Completely Normal Workparent Emotions

Sooner or later, you—just like almost every other working mother and father out there—will face serious stresses as you try to combine career and family, and will go through periods of guilt, apprehension, and self-doubt. If you find yourself . . .

- Drooping at the sight of your seemingly endless to-do list

- Questioning your own choices or competence

- Feeling remorse about having missed that big work meeting or school play

- Hurt and/or angry on the heels of a colleague's (or your mother-in-law's, or a neighbor's) snarky comment about how you're combining career and kids

- Imagining the potential terrible outcomes of your workparenting (emotionally damaged children, a derailed career, etc.)

. . . know first and foremost: you're not alone.

Know also that *you have the power to make yourself feel better.* There *are* effective means of putting yourself onto more stable emotional ground. To get you there—and quickly—we'll start by pinpointing

Is it like this for everyone?

As you build your roster of working-parent mentors, be sure to connect with a few whose Workparent Templates (as discussed in chapter 1) are fundamentally different than your own, and who as a result bring a very different lens to the issue of what working parenthood "should" or "has to" feel like. Try speaking to the moms and dads raised in different cultures, family structures, and eras, or who have had very different professional experiences and ambitions. Chances are, they'll bring a fresh, even eye-opening perspective: describing how things are seen differently in their country of origin, or explaining why, as the child of two high-octane professionals themselves, they perceive workparenting challenges as a source of pride instead of internal conflict. While you can't take on their experiences and past as your own, you can assume some of their views and ideas.

And if you haven't experienced many negative or conflicting emotions yourself: good on you! It's not a sign that something's wrong: you're just well-grounded in working-parent reality. You're one person, doing two roles—without any inherent contradiction or need for apology.

the source of those difficult feelings, and then go through effective ways for you to manage and defuse them.

Where the Difficult Feelings Come From

If you don't know the source of a leak, you can't fix it; you're just left scrambling to deal with the damage. It's better to go right to the source, and for you as a working mom or dad, the source of your tough emotions is usually a *contradiction*: a seemingly unresolvable clash between your very good intentions, beliefs, and values on the one hand and some specific, day-to-day aspect of your working-parent reality on the other.

In table 21-1 you'll find three illustrative examples. These examples may shine a very direct light on these types of contradictions and their effects, but the situations described here are neither unique nor severe.

TABLE 21-1

Where Difficult Feelings Come from—and How They Cascade

Your belief, intention, or personal value . . .	Hits a "trip wire," causing a contradiction, which leads to . . .	Questioning, blaming, and pattern-finding, and then to . . .	Catastrophizing and labeling . . .	And finally to erosion of identity, and a complete emotional dead end.
I am a devoted parent. My kids are the center of my life, and I make it my priority to be there for them.	A major work emergency flares up immediately before the end-of-year school concert, which you're then forced to miss.	If I'm so devoted to my kids, why did I miss the concert? Why couldn't I find a way around this? And I missed the football game last week, too.	My daughter is always going to remember that I missed her concert. All the *other* parents were there. I'm a crummy parent.	*I guess I'm not so devoted, after all.*
This team can be successful under my leadership.	At the work-drinks event celebrating your new leadership role, two more-senior colleagues indicate surprise that you were willing to take on the big job—"while your children are still so small." One asks if you're worried about "being able to put in the extra hours."	Would they ask that of someone who didn't have kids? We've worked together for years—don't they see how committed I am? Why can't they just be supportive?	All my colleagues are judgmental jerks. There's no way for a working parent to succeed in an environment like this.	*I'll do my best . . . but the deck is stacked against me.*
I'm a hard worker, and persistent. I can manage my career and home responsibilities at the same time.	You glance at your coming week's jam-packed calendar—and long to-do list.	Why can't I get through my work faster? I used to be able to check every item off my to-do list, quickly. That time I spent out at dinner with a friend last week was wasted—I should have been more productive. Just another example of how I've handled time badly. It's no wonder I'm so behind.	I'm less effective and efficient than I used to be. If I were [smarter/harder-working], I could figure this out.	*Hard worker? What a joke. I can't even get through one day's tasks, let alone manage my whole life and career.* AND/OR *This is hopeless. I could work forever, and never get ahead.*

Circuit breakers

A circuit breaker is the thing you reach for when tensions are high, emotions are low, and you need a healthy and instantaneous emotional reset. Common circuit breakers include exercise, humor, fellowship and connection with other human beings, mental exercises, deliberate distraction, deep breathing, meditation, prayer, and music. Unlike your Point of Control, which we discussed in chapter 4 and which serves as part of your general emotional-wellness-building routine, your circuit breaker is there for emergencies—when you feel at risk of "losing it."

What's yours? Whether it's watching snippets of your favorite comedy show on YouTube, taking a walk in the park across the street from your workplace, chatting with a colleague or friend, focusing on the photo of your family beach vacation you keep at your desk, or singing a song with your toddler (even if that has to be by phone), be sure to have one—and know it's there for you when you need it.

In fact, they represent very common workparent situations, and you've likely experienced similar yourself. Read through each row, and as you go, note how quickly the initial contradiction "tripwire" can so easily prompt negative emotions, and how easily those emotions can then cascade forward—how quickly the well-meaning, hardworking parent in question (you!) moves from a positive frame of mind and into an emotional funk.

As you can see in these examples—and have likely seen in your own life—the real problem isn't the "trip wire" event. Sure, that's unpleasant: you really wanted to see your daughter sing, and she might be very upset you weren't there. But the real doozy is what comes after: you slide down a greasy slope of questioning and self-criticism and land with a *thud* in a place where you feel out of line with your own deeply held beliefs and values. You end up feeling inauthentic, or like a transgressor, or a fraud. You're not a *good parent* or *a parent who prioritizes your children* anymore, you're *the type of parent who misses concerts*, or worse, *a parent who doesn't care*. The bitter irony, of course, is that in some ways you've become the victim of your own good

> ## Your guilt is not an asset
>
> Working-parent guilt can feel awful—and comfortable and reassuring. *After all*, you may think, *being so conflicted when away from the kids is proof of how much I love them! And if I always feel as though I'm falling down on the job somehow, it just goes to show the impressive extent of my professional commitment.* In other words, however toxic, distracting, and wrenching your guilt is, you may have come to see it as an asset: as evidence or reassurance that your heart is in the right place.
>
> Have you grown to rely on guiltiness as a sort of security blanket? If so, try running an experiment: see if you can go one day without "using" your guilt, taking as much satisfaction in work and in parenting as you can, and refusing to beat yourself up about any conflict between the two. That approach will be uncomfortable at first. Odds are, though, that come the end of the day, you'll have been just as effective at home and at work as you always are—and that you'll be feeling much better without carrying around that heavy emotional baggage.

intentions: if you weren't so devoted to your kids in the first place, you wouldn't be feeling so lousy about not making it to your daughter's performance.

It's no wonder you're so upset! Or that, facing so many emotional contortions, you may be finding it hard to feel positive, proud, true to yourself, and just all-around *good* while workparenting. Now that you understand the cycle, though, you can upend it. You can also try out some new, workparent-specific emotional self-management techniques that will leave you feeling more authentic, whole, and all-around *better*.

Ten Specific Strategies That Work

The following ten emotional self-management techniques can help you stop that cascade effect we just examined, free yourself up when you are caught, and stay on a better emotional plane day to day. Each of these disparate, differentiated approaches is its own jujitsu move:

when you are in a rough spot, or worried that you're heading into one, try one or more out and see if you can disarm or overcome the emotional hijacker. Be bold, and push yourself a little. Give each one a whirl even if it feels a little uncomfortable or awkward. What do you have to lose? Because these are self-management techniques—they're just for you, and play out discreetly inside your own mind and feelings—there's no risk that using any of them comes with consequence or embarrassment; your boss can't yell at you or your colleagues laugh at you for using them. And they require no special resources; they're free. At the very worst, you decide a certain technique isn't for you, and move on to the next. Either way, you've zoomed in more closely on what's really helpful and taken one decisive step forward to feeling better.

1. Restaking. In the examples in table 21-1, we observed how quickly and easily a small trip-wire event can do a number on your own self-perception, making you feel like you're in the wrong. But why let it? You can easily halt the process by reasserting your good, healthy intentions. When you do miss the school concert, tell yourself, *I am a devoted parent, and my children are the center of my life. Because of events out of my control at work, I had to miss this one event. That was disappointing, but it doesn't change my commitment, or who I am. I am a devoted parent.* By restaking, you get to remain in charge of your identity territory.

2. "Really?" Let's say you missed that concert, and have already fallen down the rabbit hole of identity erosion, accusing yourself of being *a crummy parent.* Damage has been done, but it's

> ❝ I'm careful about language. I don't say 'Mommy *has* to go to work,' but 'Mommy *gets* to go.' If I have to work on the weekend, I'll give my daughter some kind of small treat—like screen time. I don't want either of us to see work as a chore that I hate—because I don't."
>
> —*Melissa, journalist, mother of one*

not irreversible. Try pushing back on your feelings, conclusions, and self-assigned labels by asking, "Really?" Are you *really* a bad parent, just because you missed one event? Are the years you've spent nurturing and caring for your child *really* evidence of the great big zero you are as a parent? Is that one missed event *really* part of a larger pattern of negligence and selfishness, as you've been telling yourself? Or in the case of the to-do list: Is the fact that you have a lot on your plate *really* evidence that you're not performing the way you should? Are you *really* a lazy, ineffective person? Of course not! Any of those conclusions are obviously false. When the questions are phrased this way, it cuts through the static, shows how off-base all your negative self-talk is, and puts you firmly back in reality. You're just a busy parent, is all.

3. Remembering your "why." You missed the concert—and dinnertime several times this week, and other family commitments you would have preferred to honor as well. But you didn't miss those things because you didn't care and chose to go out and play tennis or have your nails done. You missed them because of the demands of an urgent situation at work—the work you do to put food on the table and provide a stable home and future for your child. You may have to make tough choices, but you're making them for good, authentic reasons.

> " My job is to help people breathe—through different treatments, or machines, including ventilators. Some patients complain, or get emotional. I always try to comfort them, even if they're treating me in a not-so-nice way.
>
> Work can get so stressful that sometimes I feel as if I'm living a double life. I get home, and I'm so happy to see my husband and daughter. I think, man, this is worth it."
>
> —*Dawn, respiratory therapist, mother of one*

> " Having that Village, that network of supporters—that's what lets you cut down on the guilt. I did my MBA full-time while working full-time. It was intense, but when the kids were having dinner with Grandma and Grandpa, I felt OK."
>
> —*Carrie, private equity investor, mother of two*

4. **Thinking bigger-picture.** Your colleagues' office-party comments stung. How dare they imply that you're putting your own ambitions ahead of your kids! But do the offhand comments of two colleagues after a few gin-and-tonics really mean "the deck is stacked" against you? They're only two out of many colleagues, and they were speaking in an unguarded moment. Maybe they're jealous, or were expecting the promotion themselves. They're certainly no diplomats. And didn't other people at the event say nice, supportive things? Anyway, you don't need anyone else's seal of moral approval in order to manage this team effectively. You've got years of experience and are prepared for success in this role. You *know* you can do this. As you open up the aperture like this, and think more broadly, it puts those snarky comments into a larger context and they lose much of their power.

5. **Avoiding and correcting your saboteurs.** Every working parent has to deal with naysayers and saboteurs: people who, for whatever reason, enjoying pulling you down. In the examples above, it's the two colleagues at the party. Your saboteurs might be colleagues, but they may also be friends or family members. Whatever the case, their poison-dart comments have a unique power to make you feel terrible. Whoever they are, avoid them! Do whatever you can simply to stay out of their way. That means steering clear of them at the office party, or if your saboteur is your mother-in-law, quickly handing her the baby and asking her to do the diaper change every time she looks as if she's about to dole out more criticism. And if you

> I was on a plane once for a work trip, and got to talking to my seatmate, who said, 'I don't know how you do it, working like this and raising kids.' I thought, unless there's something I don't know and your kids are down in the cargo hold, then you and I are doing exactly the same thing.
>
> When you do get backhand comments like that, don't start criticizing yourself. Tune out—just don't listen."
>
> —*Karen, macro trends expert, mother of two*

can't avoid them, *correct* them. Tell the office-party colleagues that you appreciate their concern, but that "I've always considered myself fortunate to have so much support at home, and to be able to do everything I want to at work and with my kids." Like all bullies, working-parent saboteurs get their charge from hurting or controlling other people. As soon as you make it clear that you're neither hurt nor controlled, they'll lose interest and move on—to bully someone else. You'll have your work cut out for you managing your own feelings and emotions. Don't let these freelance emotional abusers make things any harder.

6. **Tomorrow-plus-twenty-years thinking.** As a professional, you have incentives to focus on the intermediate term: you're rewarded for completing that six-month project or meeting your annual revenue targets or working a certain number of shifts per year. But as a working mother or father who's already feeling low, that intermediate time horizon is emotionally treacherous. If you're just back from parental leave, sitting miserably at your desk and missing the baby, it can be crushing to think forward six months. Instead, try thinking very short term and very long term, at the same time. Yes, you do miss the baby terribly right now, but you'll be home to see her in a few hours, and you'll spend time together tomorrow morning—and years from now you know you'll have provided her with a stable

home, and a superb example of tenacity, career commitment, and hard work. Or if you did miss the concert, plan to watch the video of it together with your daughter tonight—and be sure that, as she grows, she's aware of your love and commitment. In other words, acknowledge the reality and depth of your current feelings, identify a point of imminent relief, and then project far *forward*, to the ultimate, positive outcome.

7. Creating an already-done list. You look at your to-do list, and you do feel overwhelmed and behind. It's no wonder: it's long, the incredible amounts of work you're putting in don't seem to make it any shorter—and like every other human being, you're naturally neurologically wired to fixate on incomplete tasks more than finished ones. To-dos produce anxiety, and given all the open items you have both at home and at work, that's *a lot* of anxiety. The effective circuit breaker here is to keep a brief, informal list of *completed* items, from both work and home. Make a habit of writing down finished projects, problems solved, and wins, however small. *Beat our quarterly numbers. Found Sasha a science tutor. Brought in the pharma account. Made it to gym last week. Cooked family dinner Saturday. Had a good meeting with my boss's boss.* Then, at regular intervals, look over this list and remind yourself of how much you've done, produced, and accomplished, in both work and home spheres. Push out some of that constant "to-do" noise with "already-done" confidence, and you'll find yourself calmer and happier—and not thinking of yourself as lazy or negligent anymore.

8. Breaks. There are two things uniquely capable of amplifying and accelerating negative working-parent emotions. Those things are *exhaustion* and *busyness*. If you're feeling low, being tired will make you feel even lower. If you feel guilty, being frantic and frenzied will make that sense of culpability more pronounced. To keep yourself in the best possible frame of working-parent mind, you need breaks: deliberate, set-aside times to rest, regroup, and step away from *doing*—at least

> ❝ Several times a week I'll swim in the morning before hitting my
> computer. I read a lot. I crochet. My life sounds pretty exciting,
> doesn't it? But those practices help me put things into perspective. If
> I fall away from those habits, I feel the effects. If I'm not meeting my
> own needs, then the time I spend with my colleagues, or my family,
> isn't of the same quality. I make self-care a discipline, and that kind of
> discipline gives you freedom."
>
> —*June, chief operating officer, mother of one*

briefly. Every time you're at low tide, feelings-wise, try to take
a break. Even ten minutes of no-work time can help you gain
a little more perspective on those blues. (For practical advice
on how to find time for and get the most of breaks, large and
small, turn to chapter 17, "Time Off.")

9. **Write your story in the third person.** Imagine that you're a
magazine writer assigned to write one of those celebrity puff-
piece articles—in this case, about *you* as a working parent.
Think how, in the language of an upbeat, admiring profile,
you could be described. Give yourself five hundred words or
less. What's most important? The article would surely cover
your long hours, your professional successes, and your good
relationships with colleagues. It would also highlight the huge
lengths to which you go to be there for your kids, every day,
and how much you're juggling and sacrificing to do so. Try actually writing a few sentences worthy of publication. And then
step back and try to see yourself anew. No one's perfect, and
you're not defined by your long to-do list or that missed concert: there's a different story here, and it's one for you to take
pride in.

10. **Displacement and replacement.** Another very effective way to
tamp down difficult feelings is to effectively crowd them out
with better, more positive emotions and activities. It will be
more difficult to hang on to your guilt about missing the school

concert if you focus on the fact that your daughter was picked for the choir: your pride in her musical ability and how hard she worked to prepare for the audition will come to the fore. Likewise, it will be hard to continue lashing yourself about your limited time with your toddler if you spend some of that time doing activities you truly enjoy together. Have you ever felt like a guilty, no-good person or professional underachiever while dancing the Hokey-Pokey with your small child? It's virtually impossible. That doesn't mean denying your feelings—just doing your best to bring the "positive emotion/negative emotion" equation into balance.

. . . And Strategies That Don't

Your working-parent time and energies should be devoted to *what works*: in this case, to the specific techniques that have the most, and most positive, impact on your feelings and overall emotional resilience.

It's also worth taking a few minutes to review the strategies that *won't* work—that you should be wary of, and not waste your time on. These are the habits that lure you in by promising quick fixes, but over time yield nothing, or even lead to further distress. If you've already indulged in any of these: no worries. Most if not all working parents do, and it's just fine to do so in moderate doses or occasionally. Take care, though, to see these habits for what they really are: the snake oils of working-parent well-being.

> Sometimes I'll be at school, enjoying it, having fun—and feel guilty that I'm away from my son. Or I'll be at home, playing with him, and I'll feel guilty because there's forty pages of dense reading to do before tomorrow.
>
> I don't try to shove it away. I allow that feeling to be true, because somehow allowing myself to feel guilty about what I'm *not* doing allows me to enjoy what I *am* doing."
>
> —*Zack, actor and graduate student, father of one*

- Guilt-working. If you're up late at night baking cupcakes for one of your kid's school events (cupcakes you could easily have bought at the local store), or if you just raised your hand to volunteer for the so-so assignment that's going to involve a lot of interaction with a client ten time zones away, you're likely *guilt-working*: overallocating time, energy, and labor to a given task as a means of proving your authenticity and intentions, both to yourself and others. If you make the cupcakes yourself, or are willing to take those late night videoconference calls, it proves how committed you are, "going the extra mile" both at home and at work, right? Actually, it doesn't—and playing martyr and doing more than you're really on the hook for usually only leads to exhaustion and burnout.

- Commiseration. Blowing off emotional steam is healthy, and as we've discussed, it's important to develop good working-parent connections and camaraderie. That colleague who also has a toddler can feel like, and be, a lifeline when workparenting gets you down. The more time you spend in problem-recital mode with that colleague, though, the *worse* your situation may appear, and you waste precious time that could have been much better spent on exploring proactive solutions. If you do need to "get it off your chest" with a fellow workparent or workparent mentor, by all means, do so—but set a firm time limit. Give yourself five minutes to vent—and then go into solutions mode.

- Trapdoor thinking. Yes, it's possible you could win the lottery. And you could drop out of the rat race, move to a cabin in the woods, and not have to worry about your job anymore. But neither is likely, and daydreaming about them is going to be much less effective than trying to improve the situation you're in right now.

- Spoiling your kids—or yourself. Giving the kids candy, or toys, or the keys to the car, or allowing yourself more trips, treats, and retail spending than your budget really allows, gives you a

Workparenting in recovery

If you're a working mother or father who's in recovery, take specific care to keep yourself on a good keel, particularly during the critical early transitions (parental leave, the return to work, and your first year back on the job). You've worked so hard to get where you are right now; the last thing you want is for the new strains and stresses of workparenting to lead to any setbacks.

No matter how firm your recovery may be, consider reconnecting with past resources and supporters—your therapist, group, center, or sponsor—for help in "playing through" workparent pressures and emotions. If you attend regular meetings or appointments, make certain they remain a top priority in your increasingly jam-packed schedule. And take strength in everything you've already accomplished: the honesty, determination, and resilience that have brought you this far are going to help drive your success as a working mom or dad, too.

quick rush, but then you're back at square one—this time, with a smaller bank account, or a kid who expects more candy.

- Other, more destructive habits and behaviors. If you find yourself blowing up at the kids or while at work, withdrawing from family members, or endlessly using social media as a way to self-soothe or find emotional relief, it's time to step back and consider other approaches. And it cannot be said strongly or bluntly enough: if you're indulging in *any* activity that poses danger to you or to others, that has become a significant distraction from work or home responsibilities, or that you want to stop but can't, seek professional support immediately.

Giving Yourself What You Need and Deserve

Does paying concerted attention to your emotional well-being feel self-indulgent, or impossible somehow? Do you find yourself wondering

Expressing your feelings at work

Of course you want to be your authentic self on the job. Be careful, however, of indulging in too much detail or candor about challenging workparent feelings in your workplace. It's fine to tell coworkers, or even clients, that "managing three young kids with this job can be tough" or that yes, you do have to focus on balancing your competing responsibilities. Yet as soon as you start spending significant airtime on those matters, or providing a lot of detail, or describing the psychological effects the experience has on you, or using down-in-the-dumps vocabulary like *struggle, tension, conflict, guilt, overwhelm, shame,* or *hopeless,* you're doing yourself a disservice. Think about it: no one wants a distracted, or completely beaten-down, nurse, or editor, or fireman, or consumer-products marketer, or [fill in the blank, your profession]. Maybe you're being honest, but you risk eroding your professional credibility in being so. Reserve that type of all-cards-on-the-table conversation for trusted mentors, personal supporters, and professional helpers, like a therapist or members of a parenting support group. You have the right to be yourself, and to blow off steam regularly as well—just be mindful of the context.

if feeling like crud is just inevitable, or if it might be better to suppress your feelings—to put them in a box, bury them, and return your focus to the gazillion practical career and parenting tasks you have at hand? You're certainly free to think that, and to take either approach; many working parents do. Before you make that decision, though, consider one more thing.

Think back over the past week, and to the attention you paid to managing and protecting *other* people's emotions during that time. Even if you're the poker-faced type, and expect other people around you to be the same, you probably spent a good amount of time and effort at this. Maybe you spoke to your boss in a manner that let her feel respected; made a point of praising a junior colleague's efforts in order to beef up his self-confidence a little; used the cc line on your email as a way of making other coworkers feel included and up

Elizabeth's story

> I met my best friend on the first day of medical school, and we were inseparable for thirteen years. Throughout our training we ate breakfast together every day. We thought about which specialties we would go into, and who we would marry. Our first kids were born around the same time, and we talked about how to provide great patient care and build our careers while being good moms. Medicine is intense: you have to miss some of those family dinners, the toddler music classes, sports practices. It's easy to feel guilty.
>
> When my friend was thirty-eight, she passed away suddenly, unexpectedly. Her kids were six, four, and one. It was horrible. I missed her so much, and I saw how much her family missed her—how they would give anything to have her back with them for a single day.
>
> All that working-mom guilt I had felt up till then went away—it was completely displaced. I realized how incredibly fortunate and grateful I was: to have a job I loved, to be able to go home and see my kids—how lucky I am to have this full and complicated life. I stopped beating myself up about sometimes getting home late, or not making every single one of my kids' school plays. I don't think about what I've missed, or can't do for my family. I focus on what I *can*.
>
> My gratitude is huge."

—*Elizabeth, physician, mother of three*

to date; held back from criticizing your partner, given how stressful things have been for him or her lately; told your young child, *I know you can do it!*; or patted and rocked your baby. You've helped other people to get into and stay in a good frame of mind, and to experience themselves positively—and you've been successful at it.

Couldn't you give yourself the same?

PART FIVE

Your Family, Your Way

Special Tips—and Extra Encouragement—for Winning at Workparenting in Any Family Structure

W e've reached a turning point. Up until this point in the book, we've focused on what *every* working mother and father needs to do and know—on the inevitabilities and "have tos" of working parenthood. Through your own hard work you've built skills and confidence for meeting them.

In this section, we shift gears and focus in on the realities and challenges you're most likely to face while workparenting in the context of *your particular family structure*. Maybe you're part of a high-octane two-career couple and have a detailed family calendar, but are finding that too many of the commitments on it collide and it's creating confusion and tension between you. Or you're a main breadwinner who works longs hours but still wants to be a loving, connected, present parent. Or you're parenting solo, or as part of an LGBTQIA+ family, or both. Whatever the case, you may feel as if there's a little gap between all-purpose workparenting approaches and your unique life and experiences at home.

In part 5, we'll try to close it: we'll address just what workparenting in the context of your particular family means. With those insights, and the actionable techniques provided, you'll be better able to bring your career and parenting life together more easily, more seamlessly. Less surprise, less strain.

For simplicity's sake, the four chapters that follow (22 through 25) are sliced demographically, covering two-career couples, sole earners, single parents, and LGBTQIA+ workparents, respectively. It's very possible that more than one of these slices applies to you—and that

454 YOUR FAMILY, YOUR WAY

you could therefore benefit by looking over *each* of the chapters relevant to your family situation. If you're a working dad whose husband is on a year-long career sabbatical to take care of your new baby, for example, you'll want to scan the chapters on two-career couplehood, sole earners, and LGBTQIA+ workparenting (22, 23, and 25). If you work full-time and your partner is away on a military deployment, it's a good idea to read up on two-career couplehood *and* single parenthood (22 and 24)—and so on. Browse around to find the right mix. If your personal situation is evolving, or if you're thinking about making changes—like taking a career break, starting a family, or creating a new, blended one—use this part of the book as a preview and to help you make good forward plans.

As you read, be certain to remind yourself of how much hard work you've already done. Even if you only scanned a few short segments earlier in the book, you've already opened yourself up to the rigors of the coaching process, challenged your own thinking, tried out new habits and approaches, and peered through a wider-angle lens on how to handle one of the biggest, hairiest challenges of your adult life. That's *a lot* to take on—and if you're feeling a little tired, don't worry. Think of the following chapters as little vials of energy and insight to drink from while you do all that other hard work. With each drop you take in, you'll feel better able to stay the workparent course. Big impact, little sips: that's what this section of the book is, and it's how you'll become even better able to bring together your career and your life with the people you love.

22

The Two-Career Couple

Managing the Double Balancing Act—Together

There's the big meeting you've got to prepare for, and your partner's on deadline, of course. And one of you has to drive swim-team carpool tomorrow, and that stack of bills won't pay itself, and it's 4:30 p.m. already, and *what are we having for dinner?*

Being part of a two-career workparent couple can feel as if you're caught in a spin cycle of logistics and coordination, and with this much to do and to sync up about, your sense of self and of partnership can shift. Maybe you used to take pride in being on top of things at home and at work but all too often now you're running behind or you're *the person who forgot the groceries*. And that amazing human being you fell head over heels for? That's now the person with whom you manage daycare drop-offs, compare schedules, and argue about the car. Even if you have a rock-solid overall relationship, the two-careers-plus-kids thing can alter its tone, and—ironically, given how much you're both in this—leave each of you feeling a bit lonely.

What follows is a list of seven techniques to help you shape your workparent experience in a deliberate way and feel more *together*, in every sense. Starting with a few bigger-picture approaches, we'll proceed to more-tactical, do-it-anytime moves. While these instructions are written with current working parents in mind, they're equally usable if you're an expectant couple or planning a two-career-couple

Other fixes

The techniques provided in this chapter won't bring you the same juice unless you've already covered what we'll call the working-parent baseline. If you're facing a childcare crisis, it's going to be harder to maximize your workparent partnership. First things first.

If you have broader concerns about your partnership, out beyond the type of advice provided in this chapter—for example, if the two of you find yourselves in regular, pitched conflict, or if daily communications feel fraught—think about seeking the support of a couples counselor or therapist. If your reaction is *No way* or you worry that professional help is simply a precursor to a breakup: rest assured, many busy working (and nonworking) couples, including ones you know and admire, have used similar resources and to powerful effect. To destigmatize this kind of support, think about it in sports terms: your favorite athlete has a coach, a trainer, and a sports psychologist helping her prep for play. You may not be on the field during World Cup, but isn't your career-plus-kids life demanding enough that the two of you deserve someone in your corner, also?

When couples counseling sounds like a good idea but you're not sure where to start, check in with your regular healthcare provider, community center, employee-assistance program, or house of worship, any of which may offer the service directly and/or be able to make local referrals.

workparent future. Work these exercises through in the same mental and emotional frame in which you began your partnership: as two for the road.

1. Why?

Goal:

In this exercise, you'll focus on and crystallize the *benefits* and *upsides* of your family-plus-career structure and create mutual motivation in the process.

When, how, and how long:

Find thirty minutes when neither of you is working, hungry, overtired, etc.—for example, on a weekend afternoon during the baby's nap. While there's no preparation required, be sure to record and store the ideas that come from this conversation.

What to do:

Take turns filling in the following sentences: "Because we both work, we can . . ." and "Ten years from now, the reasons we'll be glad we both worked when the kids were younger are . . ."

Let yourselves riff and volley. Many of your ideas may be emotional or spiritual or feel "virtuous" in nature, and some of what you blurt out may seem narrow, flip, or even selfish. Don't hold back.

When time's up, your list may include items like these:

- Because we're both working, we can:

  - Live in a safe neighborhood

  - Take career risks without undue worry

  - Help your mom out financially

  - Take the kids on a trip abroad each year

  - Tithe to our church

  - Stay in careers we love, even though they're less financially rewarding

  - Be role models for the kids

  - Feel like *me*

  - Not resent you

  - Do work I love (or that has other/special significance to me)

  - Spend meaningful time around smart grown-ups instead of only around our kids, which despite my endless love for them would drive me crazy

- Harvest all the hard work I put in during all those years of school/training
- Ten years from now, we'll be glad that we:
  - Had the chance to keep progressing professionally
  - Didn't ride each other so hard about spending money on sports gear/refurbishing the house/etc.
  - Each of us stayed the [merchandising expert/computer whiz/etc.] that the other one fell in love with
  - Built up our retirement savings

Note that your answers can be both joint and individual. Maybe as a couple you're appreciative of the increased financial security of two incomes, but you're *personally* glad that the extra money lets you buy top-of-the-line fishing equipment.

How to take it forward:

When you're clear on your *whys*, and have a more vivid view of positive future outcomes, two-career workparenting will seem more powerful and natural—more like a first choice, instead of something that requires constant second-guessing. To keep stoking that sense of confidence and purpose, refer back and add to your list on a regular basis (for example, each year around the holidays), during particularly pressured phases of workparenting, or—better yet—both.

> My husband and I met in the military. We're both committed to our careers—and to our children. So we've figured out how to optimize for convenience: we live near work so we have short commutes, we pay for a meal-delivery service. We've figured out ways to be able to work hard while being the parents we want."
>
> —*Katherine, chief of staff to the COO, mother of two*

2. Template Talk

Goal:

To build a more specific, shared vision of how your two-career workparent life together can work, while eliminating stressful, often unspoken conflicts about how it "should."

When, how, and how long:

Set aside at least one quiet, uninterrupted hour and speak in a private place. Agree that during this time, you will *begin* an important dialogue—one of the most important of your workparent partnership—but need not finish it. Through this conversation, you're simply setting a more effective, collaborative frame for future ones.

Explanation:

In chapter 1, we examined your Workparent Template: the collage-like collection of advice, experiences, and observations that have formed your personal view of working parenthood. Your template is individual, and thus unique, and thus inherently different than your partner's. Which is fine: you certainly don't have to be carbon copies of each other to be a happy workparent couple. When your templates bump up against each other, though, it can lead to arguments of a particularly distressing and bewildering type. Why can't your partner just understand that *it's impossible to be a good parent working these kinds of hours*? Why is he or she so completely blind to your keenest anxieties about combining career and children? Why does it always lead to a spat when you suggest ordering in dinner, even though your budget allows it? You've always been such good partners in crime, so why do you now both sense this lurking tension? It may be because of a template difference.

What to do:

- Get out the sketch you did of your Workparent Template back in chapter 1. If you haven't each yet completed the exercise outlined in table 1-1, do so now.

- Take ten minutes, in turn, and walk your partner through your template. Describe those experiences and glimpses of working parenthood—inside your family of origin, among friends and mentors, on social media, and so on—that have shaped your view of what a working parent *is* and *does*.

- Be thorough and honest, and as much as you love each other, don't assume your partner is clairvoyant. He or she may not know that yes, your father was a wonderful provider but that his constant work left you craving his attention . . . or that you've heard colleagues make snide comments about part-time work.

- When each of you is done speaking, have the other gently paraphrase back what he or she has heard. You don't have to recite back every point, just ensure understanding. "So the other parents in the social-media group keep telling you that having a second child will be harder careerwise than the first?"

- As your partner speaks, avoid any urge to editorialize, advise, or "spouse-splain." Comments like "that doesn't surprise me, knowing your father" or "well then maybe you should just get out of corporate law" will bring this process, and any goodwill that comes along with it, to a screeching halt. Instead, ask gentle, open-ended questions: "What was that like?" "How so?" This should be a safe-harbor discussion. If the emotional temperature spikes, take a break.

- When you're done, make up three lists: 1) *how our templates mirror each other*, 2) *where they differ*, and 3) *where one of us has had strong template-shaping experiences and the other hasn't*. Maybe you both work for bosses less open to flexible work

> ## You too?
>
> Is that new colleague, or the person you've just met at the kids' school event, *also* part of a dual-workparent couple? No matter how genuinely curious and well intentioned you mean to be, asking "do you both work?" or "Is your partner at home full-time?" may feel—or come off as—judgy.
>
> A more neutral way to ask the question is to frame it around professional identity or life story instead of around current role. Questions like "Does John have a graphic-design background also?" or "Did the two of you meet at work?" then allow your counterparty to respond, "Yes, and he has his own firm," "No, I'm a paramedic," or "We did meet on the job, but John's decided to become a stay-at-home parent for the next few years," without feeling evaluated.

arrangements; one of you is the child of a happy two-career couple and the other isn't; and one of you has overheard a gazillion conversations about childcare, and the other none at all.

How to take it forward:

Whenever the two of you find yourselves making different assumptions about working parenthood, or in conflict, or unable to see or "get" the other's perspective, tap the brakes and ask yourselves: Are we having a template difference? Try to be considerate of each other's lived realities and perceptions as you work toward a mutual solution.

3. Structured Check-In

Goal:

To reduce the strain, both practical and personal, of covering all the details and logistics of your busy, two-career family.

Explanation:

It's inevitable that day to day, you'll have to deal with a certain amount of "life admin" and ping-pong with your partner about logistics. If, however, you can set aside regular, concentrated time to preemptively coordinate the moving pieces of career, household, and childcare, *and* you have a positive, reliable framework for doing so, it makes things easier.

When, how, and how long:

Shoot to have a Check-In conversation weekly, although you may prefer more often. The precise cadence doesn't matter as much as the regularity. This should be a habit, not an event. For each Check-In conversation, you and your partner will need your calendar(s) and to-do lists in front of you and twenty to twenty-five solid minutes.

What to do:

- Use table 22-1 as a basic outline for the conversation, a jumping-off point. If there are items particular and important to your family but not on this list (home renovation? a job search? pet care?), add them in. Tweak the outline until you agree that it touches on each of your essential, recurring responsibilities and *feels like us*.

- During your Check-In time, work your personalized outline through. As you go, bear in mind that what you're solving for here is that "drowning in immediate logistics" feeling. If bigger-picture issues come up—the decision to change jobs, the need to look at your total financial picture, etc.— acknowledge them but keep on working.

- Repeat each week.

How to take it forward:

Performed regularly, the Check-In should become a straightforward, mutually understood, and mutually affirming routine. You

TABLE 22-1

The Two-Career Workparent-Couple Check-In Outline

Topic/approx. time	What and why	Example(s)
Look back (two minutes)	What has worked well in your two-career workparent operation since your last Check-In? Call out what you're proud of and any special efforts each of you made.	• When you picked Colin up from daycare on Thursday it let me have that important conversation with my boss. • Having those dinners ready to go in the freezer was a big help during a busy few days. • We both really unplugged this weekend and had fun at the park.
Schedule (five minutes)	• Preview your work needs, particularly any travel, changes in shifts or hours, or early starts/later departures. • Flag any out-of-the-usual-routine child-related appointments.	• Tuesday is the department monthly meeting, so I'll need to be at work thirty minutes early. • Our appointment with Susannah's speech therapist got moved back to Friday afternoon, but we can do it remotely.
Care (five minutes)	Is your regular childcare sufficient? Is any extra help needed from the broader Village? Are there any FYIs to or special requests of your caregiver?	• Susannah can do early drop-off at school, so I can get to the Tuesday meeting. • Call Mom to see if she can cover Friday evening.
Transport, food, schoolwork, and household (ten minutes)	Otherwise known as the Four Horsemen of the Workparent Apocalypse. To prevent them from becoming any more time-consuming, focus your conversation on *new needs*, *special events*, and *exceptions*.	• I'll need to take the car Thursday; I'm spending that morning at a supplier site. • Susie will need a bagged lunch for the field trip—no lunch box, it needs to be disposable.
Me/us/the family, together (five minutes)	How will you stay healthy—and build your own resilience—this week? How do you plan to be present for each other? With the kids?	• If I want to get a run in tomorrow morning, can you cover? • Reading with kids thirty minutes before bed. • Date night Friday, if Mom can babysit. • Saturday: the park.

> " We each have things we like to do, that we're good at. We divide all the to-dos, and neither of us wants to give our particular roles up. I focus on our family's finances, on operations. My husband handles groceries and meals. We're a two-person team."
>
> —*Sarah, acceleration-capital fund COO and senior director, strategic analysis, mother of two*

may also wish to do a "bigger-ticket" version on a quarterly or annual basis, focusing on larger, longer-term to-dos like career progression, the kids' overall educational process, or retirement planning.

4. On Call

Goal(s):

Allow each of you to focus on your careers and selves in a more concerted way for sprint-distance stretches of time—and occasionally hit the Off Switch, as needed.

What to do:

Agree on a defined period that one of you will be the "parent in charge." That period may be as short as a few hours, or at the outside, a few weeks long. During this window, the other partner will remain a loving, committed parent, but be permitted to step away from the routine challenges that take up so much workparent time and headspace.

Example:

Three days from now regional management will be visiting your partner's workplace to conduct an annual review. Your partner is, understandably, frantic. Turning to On Call, the two of you agree that for the next seventy-two hours, you're the go-to parent. You'll be the one to do drop-off, get dinner on, review homework, take the call from the school when your child misbehaves on the playground, read bedtime stories, and so forth, picking up all the day-to-day tasks that are normally divvied up between you. Your partner will be able to dive into work without a backward glance at those dishes in the sink and keep plugging as long as needed. Yes, it's a lot for you to handle—but for this short burst of time you can manage it, all while freeing your partner up to "get it done" (and be better positioned to get that promotion he or she deserves). Then, one day next weekend, your partner will switch into On Call mode so that you can exercise, rest, or goof off. Next month, when you're under the gun to make annual quota, your partner will take a few days of On Call. And so on. The value here is in the clarity: you don't have to be fully dual-hatting at every moment.

How to take it forward:

Make "shared duty" your default, reaching for On Call as a special way to cope when one of you is especially busy, in the final stages of a major work project, traveling, ill, dealing with other life issues (such as eldercare), pursuing an important personal project, or in need of a recharge.

> The other night the girls had gone to bed, and my husband asked if I thought he should go back out and finish something he had been working on earlier in the day. I said, 'no—stop.' He'll do the same for me; we're harder on ourselves than on others, and it's important to help each other find those limits. Because we can read each other well, we also know when to do the reverse: to give each other permission to keep working—to complete that one last thing."
>
> —*Lindsey, farmer, mother of two*

5. Joint Activity

Goal:

To spend time relating to each other as life mates instead of purely as joint chief operating officers of your workparent household.

Explanation:

We've all been there: you move heaven and earth to get out for a proper date night and then spend your entire, expensive time at the restaurant reminding each other to call your son's math tutor or talking about the political mess at work. Whatever happened to actually enjoying each other? It's not even romance that's missing, per se. You just wish you could be *yourselves* for a short while without the conversation veering toward potty training, the electrician's estimate, or your boss's difficult personality. You may be together, but you're stuck in gear.

What to do:

This coming week, try to spend thirty minutes together in an activity that's *just* physically or intellectually demanding enough that it doesn't permit you to think about much else. If you both love jogging, or bowling, go for it. If you can make it to one of those evening adult-ed classes at your local community center, great. If

The midweek break

If you're trying to get some quality time together or a minivacation for just the two of you, consider doing so midweek, when your regular childcare is in place and/or school in session. Take Tuesday as a "leisure day" together, or go away for a Wednesday night, and you'll likely have fewer logistics to think through and less disruption to your family routine than if you tried to escape on the weekend.

For more advice on finding and using time off, see chapter 17.

> ❝ There are ways to incorporate the two domains, even when you're both working and busy. My wife's a nurse, and she was on last New Year's Eve. At 11:45 p.m. that evening I piled the kids in the car, we went to the pharmacy, stocked up on snacks and sodas, and then drove down to the hospital to ring in the holiday with her. Both of us have done that—brought our kids to each other during meaningful moments."
>
> —*Steve, educator and pastor, father of four*

you need to stay home, put on some music and get out the checkers set. You choose, but pick something that will let you *displace* the urge to "get it done," and simply be in the moment with your partner instead.

To be clear: you do not need to accomplish anything, make progress, or demonstrate mastery at this chosen activity. In fact, it may be more effective to try out new ones, or engage in those you have no particular talent for. Note that eating a meal, watching TV, attending a concert or lecture, driving, or getting together with friends will all work less well than more-active, hands-on, just-the-two-of-us pursuits.

How to take it forward:

Make Joint Activity a part of your regular routine, taking particular care to do so during phases of transition (job change, arrival of a new child) and higher-than-usual career pressure.

6. Tell Me More

Goal:

To help your partner feel more heard and understood as a working parent—and closer to you.

How long:

Five minutes—or less.

What to do:

The next time your partner expresses frustration, anger, exhaustion, or indignation or is overwhelmed with any aspect of working parenthood, sidestep your instinct to immediately help "solve" the problem. Instead, actively listen.

Example:

Your partner comes home fuming that her boss has dumped more work on her, yet again, and that your son's school didn't mention the science project, due Friday.

As a take-charge, can-do professional, your natural urge might be to say "push back," "maybe it's time to get your résumé together," or "I can help make the model solar system," but start by

"We didn't do it that way!"

Your partner's relatives keep making editorial comments about the fact that you're both pursuing your careers while parenting. Or at the annual school mixer another parent tells you how glad she is to be at home and "fully focused" on the kids. Or one of the old-guard types at the office asks flat-out how your partner feels about both of you working.

Ignore them—or, if you prefer, gently and directly correct them by saying something along the lines of:

- "Of course, [partner's name] and I love our careers so much that, even as dedicated parents, we can't imagine leaving them."
- "It sounds as if you made the right choice for you, which is awesome. Just like you, we've gone with what's best for our family."
- "Like so many couples, we've found that both working and sharing in baby care has worked out very well—and brought us great joy."
- "It's a mutual and happy decision."

Then move on. You can't blame someone else for not having your exact perspective, and the other person's barbed comments may stem from complex feelings about his or her own situation. Save your emotional currency, and spend it elsewhere: at work, on the kids, on each other.

meeting your partner where she is in the moment. She's already feeling lousy—don't let her reach that even-worse place of lousy-alone.

Put down your phone and any other distractions. Ask a few empathic questions, and make a couple of "mirroring" statements: "That's ridiculous. Doesn't he know how hard you're already working?" "Of course you're annoyed, who wouldn't be?" "What happened then?" Make direct eye contact, nod—use your body language to show that *I'm listening, and that this is important.* Give your partner the clear sense that *I'm in there with you.*

How to take it forward:

Practice this we're-in-it-together signaling maneuver regularly, but keep it time-limited. After a few minutes, when things have de-escalated a bit, pivot—together—toward constructive next steps.

7. Public Admiration

Goal:

To bolster your partner's pride and sense of achievement in being part of a dual-career working-parent couple.

What to do:

The next time you're in a group setting (a party, parents' event at the school, or family gathering) praise how your partner is handling things at the four-way intersection of self/parent/career/couple. Making your comments detailed and specific will help the compliment land.

Examples:

- At your annual family holiday dinner, as your partner discusses the big work project just completed, you add, "It was a huge amount of work, but the incredible thing was how [partner's name] was really there for the kids, despite the hours. [He/she] would read them stories and tuck them into bed before heading back to work. [He/she] is such a committed [mom/dad]."

- You're at a neighborhood get-together a few weeks after your return from parental leave, and someone who lives a few doors down asks how the transition is going. You acknowledge that "It hasn't been easy. The new schedule is tight and I miss the baby while I'm at work. But [partner's name] has been incredible—a rock. [He/she] sent me ten messages that first day back, cheering me on. I don't know how I could have done it without [him/her]."

How to take it forward:

If you're not the gushy type, this may feel a little awkward. But the two of you are operating in a world that doesn't (yet) offer workparent families, particularly dual-career ones, much or any positive feedback. It is *essential* to give each other some direct, in-person, can't-deny-it approbation. Doing so publicly also lets you provide other dual-workparent couples, both current and future, a bit of role-modeling and inspiration.

23

Sole or Almost-Sole Earner

Succeeding in Two Places

You're a SASE—a Sole or Almost-Sole Earner. Which means that your partner either is a full-time parent or has a much more flexible and less-well-paid job, and shoulders most of the burden at home. In terms of workparenting, you get off easy . . . in a way. Maybe you don't have to worry about relieving the sitter, fixing the school lunches, or scrambling to coordinate work calendars. But you do face other working-while-parenting pressures, and very real ones. You want to get ahead at work *and* be a good parent, don't you? Some of those tensions and pressures may be obvious, others subtle. Either way, there aren't tons of people with whom you can be open and really get at them—which is exactly what we'll do right now.

In the following pages is a baker's dozen of Key Questions that capture the range of common SASE-workparent concerns, both apparent and unspoken. Each comes with additional drill-down queries to further stimulate your thinking, as well as coaching pointers that will help you move toward any needed action. All together, these prompts ensure that you're approaching workparenting carefully and thoroughly: looking around all the corners, maximizing your impact with job and kids, building confidence as you go. In other words, self-coaching.

You can hold the first iteration of this important conversation solo, in your own head. As you work through the questions, simply jot down your reflections and reactions. The next round, however, needs to happen with your partner, reflecting and incorporating both of your views. Before kicking things off, be aware that while there's some *general* advice provided here, there aren't any prescriptive answers. You'll hear from a few experienced SASE mothers and fathers who will share their own outlook and experiences, but this is *your* life, career, and family. You'll do your own thinking, and that will lead you to the right calls.

Big Picture

Question 1: Why?

Drill-down:

- Why did we select—or adopt—the SASE model?

- What benefits does it bring me, us, the kids, our whole family unit?

Coaching pointer(s): The greater your sense of purpose and upside, the greater your motivation, and the greater speed and confidence with which you can make decisions, large and small. Maybe you're SASE workparenting to accommodate the above-and-beyond demands of your job, or to take better care of a child with special needs, or because you both prefer to "divide and conquer." Maybe you fell into it—and found it works. Whatever the case, be clear.

Question 2: Is it new, or temporary?

Drill-down:

- If so, how do we need to adapt?

Coaching pointer(s): If one of you has decided to stay home, that's more than a job change: it also typically requires changes in care, responsibilities, schedule, budget, communications, and so forth. Be certain you've rebalanced everything you need to.

> ❝ We swapped roles in March of last year. Before, I was at home, and that was a good fit for a long time, but I started to miss the adult interaction and cognitive stimulation. The cost of childcare was definitely a factor in my husband's becoming a full-time parent when I went back to work, but it wasn't the only one.
>
> Because we've both done both roles, we understand each other. I recognize the impact my husband has on my career right now. I appreciate having someone there who can take care of the kids, the laundry, parent-teacher. And I also understand that he's ready to take a break from caregiving when I get home."
>
> —*Caitlin, account executive, mother of two*

Question 3: What's my *identity* in this arrangement?

Drill-down:

- How do I see myself?

- Do I worry about how others see me? Us?

Coaching pointer(s): Are you the proud career warrior/sole breadwinner? Maybe the role feels natural—or strange, or it contradicts the norms of your tribe, however you define it. Try calling out the ways SASE feels *like me, awkward, comfortable, difficult*; the ways SASE *fits expectations of others, contradicts expectations of others.*

Question 4: Is our family going to stick to this model, or change in the future?

Drill-down:

- If "stick to it," are there other factors or events that would lead us to reconsider?

- If "change in the future," what's the time horizon, and what needs to happen between now and then?

Coaching pointer(s): What if you disliked your job, or had another child, or your economic picture suddenly shifted? If your partner plans to be back at work in a year, what's the job-search plan? This kind of "if/then" thinking can help smooth the path ahead.

Question 5: What's our financial plan?

Drill-down:

- Are we saving enough? Do we have a financial cushion?

- What happens if my job/career goes away?

Coaching pointer(s): If things feel steady and stable, that's great—but make sure you're able to weather setbacks and reversals without undue strain or worry. That may involve cutting back.

On the Job

Question 6: Do I have a good board of directors?

Drill-down:

- Do I have a trusted group of people who 1) are career savvy, 2) have my best interests in mind, and 3) are willing to give me no-holds-barred perspective and advice?

Coaching pointer(s): You're carrying an entire family's economics and future, here. Progression, risk-taking, self-advocacy, conflict with the higher-ups, job change: you need some mechanisms and supports to ensure that you're approaching all those things in the right way.

> I was considering a new role—a kind I hadn't done before, and that came with business development pressure. I called up six or eight people I trust, who I see as mentors, and we talked through the decision, and the risks. That helped me check and validate my thinking. It created a buffer."
>
> —*Brant, chief information officer, father of seven*

Question 7: What kind of touch points am I having with the other workparents at my job/organization?

Drill-down:

- How am I harnessing the interpersonal connective magic—the "secret handshake"—of working parenthood?

- How do the other folks at work perceive me as a workparent?

Coaching pointer(s): These days, it's standard to be juggling career and kids. If you don't acknowledge that, or come off as immune to or unthinking about that challenge, it may be harder to form relationships with certain colleagues, or gain the leadership following you want to, or develop the most compelling professional brand. You may be perceived as *clueless* or *unsympathetic*, or worse, be written off as *out of touch* or even *biased*—even if none of those things is actually true.

So: How are you discussing your experience? Are you ignoring it, discounting it, or apologizing? Using words like *fortunate* or *luxury* to describe the fact that you have a partner focused at home? Are you involved with the workplace efforts and activities that other working parents are? When's the last time you had an honest-to-god conversation about working parenthood with a colleague who has a completely different life than you do at home? Are you visibly trying to understand other workparents around you? Help them out? How, while staying authentic, can you relate to other working moms and dads?

At Home with the Kids

Question 8: What message are we sending?

Drill-down:

- When, one day, our children do the Workparent Template exercise in chapter 1, what will they say about our family?

Coaching pointer(s): You don't want it to be a surprise.

> " As soon as I come through the door at home, I try to quickly assess, to read where the energy is. How is everyone, and what's happening? My wife and I don't lock ourselves into roles. Our approach is to support each other—to say, 'I got you.' I've learned to switch work off, get in there, and do what my family needs."
>
> —*Robert, learning specialist, father of three*

Question 9: How am I connecting with my children?

Drill-down:

- Are there any ways to "amp up" the time I do get at home? To feel and be more *there* in the kids' lives?

- On a scale of 1 to 10, how present and engaged do I feel with my kids? How could I push that up a few notches?

Coaching pointer(s): To be a present parent while SASE-workparenting, you'll need to be deliberate. So, how do you:

- Use routines, habits, activities, and rituals to bond with the kids?

- Express love?

- Spend time with each child alone?

- Ensure that the kids feel connected to you?

- Use your "power windows": mornings, evenings, and weekends?

Managing Myself

Question 10: Under what (difficult) circumstances do I prioritize work over my kids? My kids over work?

Drill-down:

- Important meeting versus school concert: Which wins?

Coaching pointer(s): You may make these choices situationally and instinctively, or have special criteria or a "system." The benefits of the latter are that your colleagues and kids can both understand and better anticipate your decisions—and are less likely to be disappointed.

Question 11: What don't or shouldn't I do? What's *not* a good use of my time?

Drill-down:

- I'm supporting our family and 100 percent committed to my children—both of which are huge priorities. What's *not* such a huge priority? What do I ignore/delegate/let drop so I can focus on the Big Stuff?

Coaching pointer(s): Try identifying what work and home tasks you'll *never or rarely* take on. (Attending business conferences? Doing your taxes? Cooking?) Then, think what personal projects or items you'll still engage with, but *minimize* so you can focus more on your career and kids. (Volunteering? Social media?)

Question 12: What do I fear? What am I missing out on?

Drill-down:

- It's fifteen years from now. Regrets: name them.

Coaching pointer(s): Look over the list of common regrets, below: What could you do now to avoid them?

- Financial security was important, but I prioritized it too much/ often.

- Given the support I had at home, maybe I could have tried to "go for it" more, careerwise.

- I kept "rainbow thinking": telling myself I'd spend more time at home after the next raise/promotion/etc.

- The kids often experienced me as gruff, stressed, remote, or preoccupied.

- I was so busy providing and parenting that I didn't spend enough time with my partner.

- The kids and my partner had "their own thing" . . . and I wasn't a part of it.

Question 13: How am I building my own resilience?

Drill-down:

- How do I ensure that I can keep delivering at or above my current pace, at work and home?

Coaching pointer(s): If my battery runs too low, this whole machine stops! How do I prevent that? What personal activities and approaches will help? Exercise, friendships, spiritual practices, vacations? How much time can and should I be devoting to these battery-recharging activities?

24

Single Workparenting

Leading at Work, Leading at Home

You went separate ways from your partner a while ago and have full custody of the kids. Or the split was recent and amicable, and you're sharing parenting responsibilities 50–50. Or you've been widowed, or became a single parent by choice. Whatever your family story, you're earning a living and building your career while taking full charge of your household. And you're far from unique: in the United States alone, there are twelve million other men and women workparenting just like you.

As a single working mom or dad, you deal with *a lot*: more caregiving responsibility, more financial pressures, and so on. And in addition to that "volume challenge," you may have specific apprehensions and questions you're facing, ones that may not get any airtime during your organization's working-parents network meetings, and ones with extra topspin.

Let's talk through the more common ones now, calmly and constructively. No silver bullets, deadlines, or do-it-this-way cram-downs: just conversation, with some new tools and techniques mixed in. You'll see which issues and approaches resonate, and over time, what to do.

My colleagues assume that there's someone else who I can pass parenting responsibilities off to. They don't understand that it's all (or, often all) on me.

You're right: they probably don't. Even if your coworkers are in the thick of workparenting themselves, they see the challenge through the lens of their own family structure and personal circumstances—as part of a dual-career couple, for example, or with *x* level of resources. That's not inconsiderate, or malicious; they just have a different experience than you do. Even if they are aware that you're a sole head of household, they may not know any specifics, like the cadence of your custody arrangement, or grasp the nuances of single versus solo parenting (e.g., if you have a coparent who helps, or are fully on your own), and if and how all those factors shape your life, and approach to work.

So, what to do?

Tools/techniques/approaches: For reasons of personal privacy or organizational culture, you may choose to be discreet, and deal with your colleagues' assumptions on a just-in-time, relevant-facts-only basis: "I can't join in for the 6:00 p.m. meeting, because I need to pick Benjamin up from daycare, but I'll call you to get the update later this evening." Many single workparents opt for this situational, low-volume approach. Why make a big deal out of being a single parent unless you really need to? Alternatively, you may decide to be assertive and

---

66 I'm mindful about my day. I think about it the way I would a rehearsal: blocks of time, what needs focusing on and when. At 4:45 p.m. people start returning every work email I've ever written, but if I have to pick up the kids by 5:30, I've got to put the Off switch into locked position. My tendency used to be to keep family a bit more private—to not talk about the kids at work. Now all my colleagues know when I'm on parent duty. I've found that talking about parenthood creates a bond that's very special—it's as if you're both members of a secret society, because you've got that shared experience."

—*Eric, stage director, father of two*

out-front in your communications—for instance, by blocking your calendar each day and telling each member of your team that, "As a single mother by choice, I'm Ben's only parent. That means that I'll need to log off by 5:45 each day to make it to daycare pickup."

There's no right or wrong, but think carefully about where you want to be on the Single Workparent Openness Continuum, and why, and what it gains you, and what feels most genuine and natural to you. Otherwise, you risk stewing on the issue, and mildly resenting your colleagues. Over time, that low-grade, simmering resentment can become a personal energy sapper and a professional distraction. And with this many important pots on the stove, distraction is the last thing you need.

My manager and colleagues are always referencing my single parenthood. They mean well, but single parenthood isn't the *only* thing that defines me, and I worry about being labeled or pigeonholed.

Of course it isn't: you're a competent, capable professional and three-dimensional individual who happens to be raising a child or children by yourself. And you want to get that across: staying sufficiently open about who you are, and about the practical requirements of caregiving—*without* arriving at a place where your manager and coworkers think of you only or primarily as "a single parent," or get the erroneous notion that you're anything other than a committed, competent professional.

Tools/techniques/approaches: Think about your total workplace communications, and the impressions you leave with your colleagues, as a *ratio*. Let's say you have ten interactions with your manager each week. If four of them have to do with the fact that you're the only one who can handle daycare pickup, then yes, you will be creating a specific (and potentially limiting) impression of yourself. But if only *one* of those touch points includes a reference to single parenting, and the other nine center on everything you're delivering for the team, you'll be presenting a very different picture. In that second scenario, you're in no way hiding your family needs, but keeping the focus square on your capabilities and performance.

In the same vein, but bigger picture, pay a little more attention to what you want your overall professional brand to be: not *how I'm seen* but *how I want to be seen*. What five to seven adjectives would you want your colleagues to use to describe you and your work? You might land on *creative, entrepreneurial, judicious, collaborative, calm, detail-oriented, strategic*—or any other positive traits. Once you've got those five to seven clear, simply add *and a devoted and capable single parent* to that list. As long as you keep that *total* brand in mind, and take care to display each one of those characteristics regularly, you reduce the risk of being labeled or pigeonholed. You can be the *generous, whip-smart, efficient business development executive who's also raising a terrific kid on her own* as opposed to being seen purely as *a single parent*.

Finally, think what other unique characteristics or personal traits you want to bring forward at work, and be known for: What's your personal brand, as distinct from your professional one? Maybe you're a die-hard foodie or football fan or fashion maven who's up on all the trends, or the tech geek who patiently explains the digital world to your less-savvy colleagues. Whatever your thing is, the more you play it up at work, the less you'll be seen uniquely as "the single mom" or "single dad." If your workspace is filled with photos of your daughters, for example, put a few football-match photos up, too.

In other words: think about the complete professional impact you want to steer toward—and then actually do some deliberate, concerted steering.

Workparenting involves one major decision after another . . . and it's tough to make them alone.

Figuring out which daycare to choose . . . or whether or not to take the new job . . . or push back on that difficult coworker . . . or send your eight-year-old to the school with the excellent math program even though it's farther away and complicates your commute . . . it *is* a lot of decisions. And when most of us are in decision-making mode, we crave a wingperson: someone who brings in different views, who

> I don't approach decisions as, 'oh, I'll just do whatever.' I research, think things through, make my best attempt. But I don't have time to interview seventy-four nannies: I get a referral from someone I trust and who's in my neighborhood, get as much information as I can, use my best judgment, trust my intuition and the feelings I get from people and situations, and then *go*. Because my days are tight, I can't waste time on overthinking."
>
> —*Gretchen, chef and entrepreneur, mother of one*

we can gently spar with, who reassures us when it's time to pull the trigger, and who can shoulder some of the responsibility, practical and emotional, for how things turn out later on. Without a partner, you may feel as if you don't have any of those things—that you're making decisions in a workparent vacuum. Nevertheless: the daycare deposit is due.

Tools/techniques/approaches:

- **Reframe it.** Ask yourself: Do all of the workparent couples you know make perfect decisions, every time? Do *only* people with spouses or life partners have the inherent ability to make reasoned choices? Are you clueless, ill-intentioned, inept, or blasé about your career and children—to the point that you can't possibly come to a sensible, well-considered conclusion here? Of course not—each of these ideas is completely preposterous! But in posing these types of silly, exaggerated questions, you can remind yourself of a core fact: that you *are* capable of deciding well, all on your own.

- **Involve others.** Alright, so maybe you're still uncomfortable making this particular choice alone. If that's the case, enlist a few allies. Make it a collective, group process. Think of it in work terms: sure, your boss ultimately calls the shots, but he or she probably spends a lot of time in meetings, mulling over other peoples' recommendations, or running his or her own judgment calls through some kind of committee for approval.

Even the know-it-all people at the very top of an organization do this: if your company is about to acquire another, it has to go to the board of directors for a vote. So follow that lead: get four or five people who know you well, who are smart and honest, and who care about your success and happiness, and get *their* thoughts on the daycare selection.

- Play it through. What's the impact of this decision—how is it likely to turn out? Is there a material impact to the choice you're hovering on, or are you really just picking A versus an equally good B? Maybe the school with the special math curriculum would help your daughter excel—but she's likely to do that anyway in her current school, which has a strong Spanish program and where she's comfortable socially. You're not being cavalier about your choices: just putting them into broader context, and taking away some of the "I could pick the right answer, or the horribly, catastrophically wrong one" binary-decision drama.

- Work with the information you have. Who really knows if that other job will be better? You may make the trade, be glad you did, and then the new organization goes bankrupt within a year. Without a crystal ball, you're going to need to make a whole lot of critical workparent choices without the benefit of perfect foresight or even full current information. And for the record, nobody else, including workparent couples, has those crystal balls, either.

- Give yourself some credit. You spend a lot of time thinking through the right things to do in terms of career and kids. Will each choice you make be golden? Probably not. But the simple, unassailable facts are that your head and heart are in the right place and that you're going to make the very best choices you can. And that, at its essence, is what good workparenting is.

Workparenting is intense—but this is different. I'm carrying the ball 100 percent of the time, and it's wearing on me.

> " It's not easy to do all this as a single parent. And as a small-business owner, if I don't take care of myself, everything shuts down. When you're self-employed, your body, mind, and soul are your investment. I've taught myself how, even if it's just two minutes out of my day, to step back, and have that moment of calm."
>
> —*TJ, marketing and branding firm founder, mother of one*

If we tried to write a top-to-bottom job spec for single workparenting using twenty-five words or less, it would look something like this:

1. Earn a living.

2. Raise your child.

3. Make sure you're personally capable of doing items 1 and 2 sustainably, over time.

Chances are good you're all in on items 1 and 2: you're working hard and spending huge amounts of time and mental energy on the kids. But what about item 3? It's easy to ignore that third piece: to give short shrift to the ways you're ensuring that you can "go the distance" as a professional and parent. Yet you're not a machine, or superhuman—you need to do something to bolster your ability to keep on keeping on. Look back at our job description again: at that sturdy three-legged stool. It's simple, but will stand up over time. Knock that third leg away, though, and this whole single-working-parent thing falls over.

Tools/techniques/approaches: Start practicing—and prioritizing—self-care.

The very term *self-care* may have an uncomfortably New Agey ring to it, or feel hazy and undefined, or you may associate it only with specific domains or activities, like spas, meditation. or yoga. The real definition of workparent self-care, though, is *everything I do to keep my personal battery charged up enough that I can workparent the way I want and need to.* For you, that battery-charging may well involve a spa, but more likely it will involve nutritional habits, sleep, exercise, spiritual practices, time spent solo, time spent with friends, hobbies, dressing a certain way, vacations, an intellectual pursuit, community service—or anything else. Whatever those activities are, they allow you to feel and be more resilient: to be a terrific parent at home, to bring the thunder at work, and then wake up tomorrow and do it all over again.

For your self-care to be most effective—to keep that very real stress of single workparenting from wearing on you—it needs to be all three of the following:

- **Personal:** something that connects you back to your own unique identity, separate and outside of your all-consuming roles as professional and parent

- **Genuine:** an activity or practice that you truly enjoy and find restorative (e.g., not yoga for yoga's sake, or because other people practice it)

- **Regular:** a routine occurrence or habit—as opposed to something you reach for in desperation when you're at the end of your rope

Look forward on your calendar to the next week, and find one or more blocks of time you can spend on self-care. Schedule it, because otherwise—let's not kid ourselves—it will never happen. And be tough: hold yourself accountable for going running, or calling your friend, or watching the movie that makes you laugh. Otherwise, it will be hard to keep doing your single-workparent job over time.

> " I'm the first member of my family in uniformed service, but my mother was a teacher for special-needs kids. She was a single mum also—I'm one of seven. I think about her work ethic, her service and leadership in giving back to her community, and about how loving she is. Her example gives me strength and inspiration."
>
> —*Kylei, firefighter, mother of one*

How can I give my child what he or she needs from me, after all the hours I put in at work?

Imagine that you come home from work tired and in a bad mood, and your son hasn't done his geometry homework. You snap, and give him the what-for.

In a two-parent household, your son can then slink off and go find his other parent, who may be more rested and cheerful, or who can help with the homework, or who can spend time together with your son and talk about the day without yelling. But in your single-parent household, he can't. You're it. The burden of parenting, and of creating the right emotional (and relational, and educational) tone for your son—that's all on you.

Tools/techniques/approaches:

- **Practice your pivots.** Go back to chapter 4, "The First Year," and review the section on making effective transitions between work and parenting. Experiment with various ways to "park" your stress and work concerns and be the Mom or Dad you want to be, on cue.

- **Draw a line around it.** Have an agreement with yourself that dinnertime conversation needs to be free of nagging and have-tos, or that no matter what's happened earlier in the evening, you'll try to keep the half hour before bed relaxing and light. Even if you have barked about the homework, draw a perimeter around that conflict, and step outside of it.

- **Be active.** Engage in activities you both find enjoyable, such as cooking dinner, going for a walk, or playing a game. The activity isn't the point: it's about the pure focus on your child, of *us doing this together.*

- **Call out the positive.** OK, maybe the geometry homework isn't done. But if he waited for you before having dinner, or did his chores, "catch" him doing those things right.

- Think "open." Every child in the history of time has messed up, made bad choices, and bumped into problems he or she didn't know how to solve. What you're striving for is to be the person your child comes to when he's stuck, confused, or in the wrong. So ask instead of judging, and pause before reacting. Be the person your child feels most comfortable talking to.

- Volunteer to do it together. Whether it's doing the geometry homework, cleaning her room, or getting her to brush her teeth, offer to do it alongside. What your child really wants is time with you, together.

How do I build out—and use—my Village with a realistic eye to being a single parent?

In chapter 9, we covered how to build, expand, and manage your Village. As a single parent, though, you'll likely want to build out your Village even further and in different ways, and need a few extra moves for taking full advantage of its resources.

Tools/techniques/approaches:

- Identify and solve for your sharpest pain points, even if they feel "small." Let's say you have to supervise your daughter's homework each night—when you're both tired and hungry for dinner. Sure, it's only a few spelling words and math worksheets, but it corrodes your time together, and your relationship. *I'm her only parent, and we spend the one hour we do get together each day doing long division?* If so, maybe the supervisors at the after-school program could help her get a jump on her assignments, or a grandparent could "drop in" via video call each evening to play math tutor while you cook dinner—or maybe there's a way to get weeknight meals ready-made. If it's causing real strain, try to find a way around it.

- Think about the three-week horizon. Sure, you've got an emergency backup care plan for when you have to work overtime, or the nanny calls out. But what happens if you get ill, and you're physically unable to parent for the next month—or if the nanny suddenly quits, and you're left scrambling to find new care? In those cases, that friendly neighbor or the backup care center you have access to through work may not be able or willing to provide as much cover as you need. If you have a helpful coparent or former partner, you'll be able to muddle through. But if not, you'll need a specific plan: relying on other family members, friends, paid help, or Third Parents. In the crush of your day-to-day responsibilities, the three-week problem may feel too daunting to even contemplate. But getting ahead of it can allow you to stay out of a very difficult situation in the future.

- Be assertive, specific, and regular in asking for the help you need. "Would Sophie be able to sleep at your house after the playdate?" "If you're running to the grocery store, would you mind picking me up some paper towels?" "Could you be my second set of eyes on this message before it goes to the senior leadership committee?" Remember: your Villagers aren't clairvoyant; they can only help when they know what to do.

- Make no an OK answer. If the people you ask workparent favors of always say yes, it's a good indicator that you're underasking—that you could be requesting more. But if you worry about asking for too much, too often: simply offer an out. "Would Sophie be able to sleep at your house after the playdate? If so, great, but I understand if it doesn't work." Your request may be met with a yes or no, but either way, you're certain that you've made the most of your resources.

- Diversify. Don't expect all the help you need to come from one person, or even from a trusted inner circle. Be realistic: Grandma may be willing to help, but she's seventy. Your best friends may be wonderful, but they have their own lives and limitations. Spread your requests out: the broader your Village, the better.

I just worry about being a single parent, and working this hard. Am I making the right choices? Doing OK?

Every working parent has similar doubts and anxieties, and when you're workparenting solo, they can amplify. But think about it this way: if you're *this* focused on combining career and parenting, it's a sign you're doing things right. You're focused on what matters, and you're putting in all the effort you can. Worries and fears are really just your goals and priorities and conscience talking a bit too loudly.

To keep the volume down, speak with a friend or another adult who was raised by a single workparent. Ask that person to describe his or her own mother or father, both as a parent and a professional. Listen as that person talks about their own mom or dad with admiration, respect, and love—and think how, one day, your child will say similar things about you.

25

Proud Workparents

Combining Career and Children as a Member of the LGBTQIA+ Community

J ust like every working parent everywhere, you're going to deal with blowout diapers, a packed schedule, guilt and self-doubt, performance feedback—and you're going to savor each career win, weekend, and end-of-workday reconnection with the kids. LGBTQIA+ workparenting is just that: workparenting. At the same time, this road can come with a few distinct twists, particularly early on. While your own experience will be unique, let's take a look at what those common turns are, in rough workparent-chronological order. We'll also look at how to steer through each one safely and confidently so you can keep your true focus where you want it: on your career, family, and future.

Templating, Role Models, and Mentors

Even if you live in a progressive area and work in an inclusive organization, you may not have had much exposure to successful, satisfied, confident, career-minded-yet-balanced LGBTQIA+ workparents, or perhaps to many LGBTQIA+ workparents at all. Your family of origin, education, and early-career experiences likely didn't offer a host of

> " People will often reach out to me to talk about being a working parent. It's a mix, and from inside and outside the firm, often LGBT—people who are thinking about starting a family, and want some advice, some insight. That kind of mentoring and connection is important. It's not easy as a busy working parent, but I try to talk to each one."
>
> —*João, management consultant, father of two*

examples, and you may or may not easily find them now, among your peers. Which isn't the end of the world: as we've explored throughout this book, you can become the workparent you want to on your own terms.

The risk, though, is that you forge ahead into workparenting without a *yes, that's what I'm shooting for, and I know I can get there!* kind of vision. Combining career and kids is already a tall order, and without a comforting, compelling, empowering template, and/or role models you "see yourself" in, or fully relatable mentors who can advise and encourage you, things may feel a bit harder.

To do: Think about how to expand your LGBTQIA+ Workparent Template now, in real time. How can you find workparents who resonate with you? Inspire you? What can you learn from them? Those role models and mentors may be inside your organization or out. If you don't know where to start:

- See if your organization has a parenting group, and/or a LGBTQIA+ employee network.

- Seek out other LGBTQIA+ parents working in your field, perhaps even at senior levels.

- Ascertain whether there's a local LGBTQIA+ community center near you that offers career and/or family programming.

- Look into professional and trade associations. Many have dedicated LGBTQIA+ subchapters.

- See if there are LGBTQIA+ parent and aspiring-parent "meet-up" groups in your community.

- Make use of social media, where you might find examples of professional, successful LGBTQIA+ folks with kids. (Yes, social media can be a double-edged sword with all the ideal images of a life nobody actually lives. But if you're ever going to look to it for inspiration, why not now?)

- Rely on your existing mentors and sponsors at work. Maybe they don't identify as LGBTQIA+, but if they've reached a certain professional level, they're likely very well networked, and given that they clearly care about you and your success, they may be able to help make some good connections.

We could keep on going here, but you get the point: if you're willing to network persistently and creatively, just as you would when hustling for a new job, you can find LGBTQIA+ workparents who are a little farther down the path—who are top of the game at work and at home, and who can help you "see" your workparenting future.

When you do find those people, don't be shy. A statement like the following will open many doors: "I'm thinking about starting a family, and wondering if you would be willing to speak with me for twenty minutes about your career-plus-parenting experience . . ." Remember: most workparents *want* to help each other. And even if some ignore you, who cares? The conversations that you do have will provide anchoring and confidence—two things every workparent deserves.

Extra notes: While the template-building process is particularly powerful before or at the very start of workparenting, it remains useful all the way through. Whether you're just planning a family, or have an eight-year-old already, keep building that positive, authentic, can-do vision.

The Path-to-Parenthood Timeline

As an LGBTQIA+ parent, and depending on how you're forming your family, you may find yourself *effectively workparenting*—simultaneously managing work and child-related responsibilities and concerns—for quite some time before your child's arrival. Whether you'll be welcoming your child via adoption, or surrogacy, or with the help of reproductive technology, there's the up-front work, decision-making, and costs that go into the process. And then if the surrogate lives far away and you've committed to attending prenatal appointments in person, you'll need x days out of the office to be there . . . and so on. In other words, if the "typical" path-into-workparenting sequence looks like this:

Expectant period	Arrival and leave	The first few months and years
Nervousness and anticipation; a lot to do and prepare		• Transition back from leave • Packed schedule • Caregiving concerns • Practical and emotional challenges, including fear of judgment from manager/colleagues • High costs/money outflow – – – – – – – – – – – – – – – – ➤

. . . yours may look more like this:

Expectant period	Arrival and leave	The first few months and years
• Packed schedule • Practical and emotional challenges, including fear of judgment from manager/colleagues • High costs/money outflow – – – – – – – – – – – – –		• Transition back • Caregiving concerns • New practical and emotional challenges – – – – – – – – – ➤ – – – – – – – – – ➤

And this can be stressful. *All those days for the appointments, right before our annual deadlines. And* then *twelve weeks for parental leave? Nobody takes that kind of time!* If you're one of few LGBTQIA+ parents in your organization, or if you don't yet have a good array of workparent mentors to guide you, these up-front pressures and attendant anxieties may loom even larger.

To do: Talk yourself up—and down. Try getting a little indignant: becoming a parent is a wonderful thing, and you're not going to allow any professional pressures to chisel away at your joy, are you? Besides, you've worked hard for this organization, you've been supportive of other colleagues with varying family needs, and you're not the type of person to let work projects drop. So sure, time away from work can be stressful, and maybe you feel unusually preoccupied when you are on the job, and your bank balance is lower than you want. Welcome to workparenting! But is there any reason you should be taking an awkward or apologetic stance here? No. Other workparents cover off on their family and professional commitments, and you're covering off on yours. This is your family—and your priority.

Then—crucially—flip the timing coin over and gaze at the other side, which is this: any additional time between the decision to start your family and the child's actual arrival is, from a pure-play workparenting perspective, a huge plus. It's extra runway to get ready for what's ahead. You can fully examine your template, talk to other working parents about their various care arrangements, consider various scheduling options, cut back on other expenses, build out your Village, get more comfortable talking about parenthood at work, and attend to all the other to-dos we covered in earlier chapters. If you need to make any big move, like a job change, you'll have more time to properly attend to it. You'll get to step into working parenthood well prepared, and with your intentions set.

Extra notes: For guidance on how to announce that you're expecting— including if it may come as a surprise, or if you're not certain of your child's arrival date—refer back to the section on "announcing the news" in chapter 1.

Benefits and Leave

Let's say you're at an organization that's employee-friendly and well resourced: you're still likely to face a complex maze when it comes to family-related benefits, including parental leave, and that maze may have a distinctly heteronormative bent to it. Maybe the leave policy offers "primary caregivers" additional time away . . . but what if neither of you is carrying the baby? Or what if your partner is, but she's a freelancer without paid leave, and the two of you are both all-in as parents? Or what if the organization is sensitive and accommodating toward new moms who are lactating (offering flexible schedules, lactation rooms, and the like), but doesn't seem to offer any logistical or scheduling "give" to dedicated parents who aren't?

Because the range of individual circumstances, plans, and programs is so broad, and because those plans' fine print is so varied, and because relevant laws and workplace norms are so wide-ranging and dynamic, we can't cover every possible what-if scenario here (that would be its own book). The key point is that you owe it to yourself to get smart, early on; to consider how you may want to advocate for yourself; and to think about how to actually use the benefits and programs available to you.

To do: Start by working through the "Planning Your Leave" section in chapter 3, paying particular attention to any policy differences for men, women, birth mothers, and "primary caregivers," as well as to permitted timing. (Does leave need to be taken directly after the birth/arrival, for example, or can it be taken sequentially to your partner's?) If you can, connect with other LGBTQIA+ parents inside your organization, or in comparable ones, to get their advice and hear their experiences. If you have a partner, be certain you're both doing this research and assessment. You'll also want to perform a side-by-side comparison and combination of your plans, to see how they fit together into a "total family benefit."

If you can't easily find the information you're looking for, or if it's in any way confusing or ambiguous, ask your human resources contact to walk you through things in person. Any HR representative worth their salt should—note the conditional *should*—have full mastery of the details, including how various plans and programs dovetail with any legal requirements or government offerings (for example: in the United States, your Family and Medical Leave Act entitlement), and be able to provide you a lucid, respectful explanation. During that conversation, assume good intent, but—particularly if you work at a newer or smaller organization—do not assume that the person has played through the implications of any particular offering, or the overall family-benefits package, from an LGBTQIA+ perspective. Be ready to push a little: if you bump up against a policy that feels poorly defined or inequitable, try inquiring/explaining why that's so. If your organization has an LGBTQIA+ employee resource group, its leadership will likely be wise to any specific benefits concerns or policy changes.

Extra notes: If you have questions about market standards or your legal rights, or you want to connect with other LGBTQIA+ parents about their experiences, consider consulting a family-law attorney or contacting your local LGBTQIA+ community center; many larger ones have dedicated family-issues advocates who may be able to help.

Boundaryless Questions

As soon as your colleagues learn that you're expecting, chances are high that they'll start asking questions, and a lot of them, and of a jaw-droppingly personal type. Most will be earnest, and well-intentioned. In fact, some colleagues may even ask about the details of how your family was formed as a sort of ham-handed way of signaling their support. That's well and good, but those questions can still feel assaulting. You're at this organization to do your particular job, not to be a one-on-one diversity educator or science tutor. Nevertheless, here you are.

To do: To keep both your personal cool and your professional brand intact, here are options for responding.

- **The direct answer.** Depending on your personality, workplace culture, relationship to the person asking the question, and desire to "fund the future" by normalizing LGBTQIA+ workparenting, you may choose to be forthcoming. Which is fine, but bear in mind that in telling any one colleague, you're effectively telling all, and that the more information you share, the more likely you are to get follow-on questions.

- **The generalized education.** "Good question. What many LGBTQIA+ parents do is . . ." In other words: shield your own personal life while doing a bit of public education.

- **The new-parent-chatter deflection.** "Of course, what [partner's name] and I are really focused on is the baby. Becoming a parent is such a profound and wonderful thing! And wow, the number of choices you have to make to find the right stroller . . ."

- **The flip-around.** When you get that total stunner of a question, gently put it back to the person by very politely saying, "Why are you asking?" The questioner may realize he has crossed the line, and stammer or slink away. Or he may confess that he just doesn't know a lot about LGBTQIA+ families, and is curious— that he comes from a positive place. Either way, you've called out the awkwardness, and subtly taken control.

- **The shut-down.** A firm, confident "I don't believe that relates to our work together. But I do believe we have more to do to get ready for Tuesday's presentation . . ." or, "I know you're asking in a positive spirit, but that conversation isn't one I'm going to have in a professional setting . . ." should put an end to things.

LGBTQIA+-Friendly Care

Bias has no place whatsoever in your child's life—or your own. It is essential that the day-to-day care experience be consistently warm, nurturing, honest, and affirming, for your whole family.

To do: Make inclusion one of your key search criteria. Here are various things to look for as you sift through the options.

- **An explicit commitment to diversity.** If touring a daycare center that's part of a larger chain or institution (e.g., an ongoing school, church, community center, etc.), ask or check online if that larger entity has issued a diversity statement. In this day and age, we can all reasonably expect institutions to have a

> " We're completely open and honest: it's one of our guiding princi-
> ples, and we want the people around us to be completely com-
> fortable too. So when we interviewed nannies, we went right in for it:
> 'We're a two-dad family. How do you feel about this?' It was a job re-
> quirement, just like the ability to work certain hours.
>
> The answer you *really* want to hear from a prospective caregiver is,
> 'I know a lot about babies and children, and I can support your family,
> and help make you an effective parent."
>
> —*A.J., venture capitalist, father of one*

stance on inclusion, and to be up front about it. A strong de-
clarative statement doesn't guarantee the center will be right
for you, but it does provide a bit of top-line reassurance that
families of all kinds are welcome—and that staff can be held to
account.

- **Parent composition.** Are there other LGBTQIA+ families
  at the center? Single parents? Blended families? Again, not a
  guarantee—but if parents of all sorts are happily using the center, it's a good sign.

- **Past experience.** Make the issue part of your reference-
  checking process. What other LGBTQIA+ families have used
  the center, and can you speak with a few of them? Has the prospective nanny been unfailingly positive and nonjudgmental
  with past employers?

- **Visual and interpersonal signaling.** You know what to look for
  here: trust your spidey sense. If the nursery library has books
  about different family types, or the walls are decorated with
  pictures of an incredible array of different families, or if the
  babysitter admires your wedding photo during the interview:
  positive. Aloof body language, awkward conversation, hesitation on those reference calls: warning.

- **Direct questioning.** Be blunt! Say to the center director or
  prospective babysitter, "We want to make sure our experience

is a comfortable and positive one, in both directions. We're an LGBTQIA+ family. Will that be an issue?" If you sense any equivocation, move on.

Extra notes: You may not be able to find a care center or caregiver who's worked with LGBTQIA+ families before. That's fine: past experience is helpful, but it's the *approach*, *attitude*, and *willingness* that count. Trust your gut as you determine which care arrangement will be right.

Finding Overall Workparent Community on the Job

As we've discussed throughout this book, the camaraderie and practical advice you can get from other mothers and fathers, particularly within your specific professional environment, is invaluable. Joining a formal parenting affinity network, or informal meet-up, can be both helpful and reassuring. That said, the membership of the "parents" network may be made up mostly or entirely of recent moms, or the network's programming may be focused around (heterosexual) dual-career couples. That is, it may or may not reflect your identity or concerns, or provide the welcome, breadth, or value you want.

To do: If it doesn't, consider:

1. Talking to the network leadership about expanding the frame to include fathers, LGBTQIA+ parents, and so on; or

2. If your organization has a dedicated LGBTQIA+ network, asking if there's any way to "joint venture" with the parents group on events or discussions; or

3. Talking to HR or your diversity & inclusion head about numbers 1 and 2, and how to make employee resource groups more inclusive; or

4. Starting your own informal subgroup, even if it's as simple as opening a messaging channel; or

5. Joining an LGBTQIA+ parents group *outside* the company or institution you work for as a way of broadening your network.

> ❝ A lot of our friends don't have kids, and there's no model for queer parenting. We joined a local queer-parents listserv that has a lot of other families enrolled. And our son's daycare is a collective, run by a group of very involved—and competent—working parents. I can drop him off at 8:00 and do pickup at 6:00, and run into other families doing the same. Being able to connect, and get referrals and ideas, and have that community is so important."
>
> —*Tracy, creative producer, parent of two*

In other words, do not be dissuaded—or afraid to take an entre-preneurial approach. There are a lot of other parents interested in getting together and sharing notes.

The Need to Divide and Conquer

It's a powerful thing to be in a partnership free of gender assumptions and culturally assigned roles, but if you don't have a basic agreement on who's supposed to do daycare pickup or dinner prep, or pay the sitter, or be up with your sick child the night before you both work double shifts, you're going to spend a lot of time in improv mode—which can be confusing, and generate tension between you, and become an additional strain for the entire family.

To do: If you're part of a busy dual-career LGBTQIA+ workparent couple, be sure to spend dedicated, thoughtful time working through the nuts and bolts of managing child-related responsibilities on top of your jobs. While the beauty is that you're unconstrained by *shoulds*, you do still need the *who*, *what*, *how*, and *whens*. That doesn't require an elaborate treaty, but whatever system you come to should be 1) something you both understand and are comfortable with, 2) realis-tic, given your work, finances, etc., 3) reflective of the values of your partnership, and 4) regularly updated and adapted to meet the needs of growing children and advancing careers.

Extra notes: To make the weekly division of labor easier, and a positive part of your partnership, use the Check-In tool outlined in chapter 22.

Owning Your Narrative

Read the following two scenarios. Does either ring a bell?

- You're a lesbian just back from maternity leave—dead set on getting promoted this year and looking to get on that next big project. But your colleagues keep asking you "how the baby is" . . . and if you want to go part-time.

- You're a gay dad whose wonderful six-year-old has just been diagnosed with a learning difference. Because your husband works crazy hours, and you take the lead on the kids' health and education concerns, you've had to be off work several times recently for all the related appointments. You've started picking up some snark from colleagues—and your manager made a recent comment about "focus."

In some sense both scenarios are workparent-typical: in the absence of better information, and based generally around their views of parenting, your colleagues have come to their own conclusion about your professionalism, priorities, way of working, and desire to get ahead. In these cases, though—or in others you may well face—those assumptions are further complicated by the intersection of gender stereotypes and LGBTQIA+ parenting—by "what moms want" or the "fact" that many dads have (female) partners at home to handle things. That may not be right, or fair—but the promotion committee looms, and you have your boss to deal with, today.

To do: Make your workparenting approach clear. Don't let your colleagues come to their own conclusions: tell them what to think! That means talking about career goals, schedules, outside responsibilities, and the ways you're meeting them without dropping the ball at work— and perhaps talking about how your family works. In the first case:

- "I'm delighted to be back from leave—and focused on earning my next promotion. While we're both very engaged mothers, Bettina's schedule allows more flexibility, so I'll be billing the same hours as I usually do. I understand there's an interesting new project opportunity with the California client . . ."

Remember, tell the story: Priorities, commitment, enthusiasm, next steps.

Creating Allies

You know the ones: those colleagues who aren't opposed to LGBTQIA+ workparenting, exactly . . . but aren't explicit supporters, either. Maybe the body language you get from them is awkward, or the senior vice president in your department didn't offer much in the way of congratulations when you announced that you were expecting, or the startup parents group somehow forgot to include you on the invitation. It's frustrating and wrong. And it's not on you to reeducate anyone or to co-opt everyone at your workplace.

To do: If you want to soften those people up, or for career reasons want to improve your rapport, simply hold up the Professional Mirror.

Every single working person, from the mail room all the way to the CEO suite, has particular ways they want to be seen professionally—part of a closely-held work identity, for which they may or may not get much regular or external validation. Each person differs, but for the most part, we all see ourselves as *hardworking, intelligent, expert, important to the organization, good with people, generous, moral,* and *a mentor.* We have workparenting-specific professional identities too: most busy mothers and fathers want to see themselves as *committed, going above and beyond, balanced,* and so forth.

If you're dealing with a difficult or an unsupportive person and can manage to reflect one or more of those "identity stakes" back at them—in other words, if you can allow them to see and experience themselves in the way they wish to be seen and experienced—it usually softens them up, often considerably. So:

- With the senior vice president: "Jonathan, don't be surprised if I come back to you and ask for advice on how to balance this whole working-parent thing. Even with three kids, you clearly have it all together. And with a team of twenty, you've no doubt mentored a lot of people through this before . . ."

- With the head of the parenting group: "Do you mind adding my name to the distribution? You're clearly the expert working parent around here, and I know you've killed yourself to put next week's session together. There's so much I could learn from it . . ."

In other words: hold up that Mirror, and let them like what they see. If the senior vice president knows that he's going to feel validated when he speaks with you, he'll want to speak with you more often.

Extra notes: If you're recoiling as you read this, or thinking, *how political! How disingenuous!* Well, yes: it is "political," or manipulative, in a way. But people maneuver and play politics at work all the time, and often for not-so-good reasons. Why shouldn't you do the same, as an LGBTQIA+ workparent? Particularly given that this concerted approach is in the service of greater goods: your comfort at work, your positive, genuine connection to other colleagues who are also combining career and kids—and some small erosion of the barriers that can exist for proud workparents.

Paving the Road Ahead

The LGBTQIA+ workparenting movement is happening in real time. Whatever your experience so far, you can use it to help smooth and guide the way for other workparents to follow.

To do: Speak with prospective LGBTQIA+ workparents one-on-one—be a model and mentor. Offer to be one of the presenters on the "return from parental leave" panel that your workplace-parenting employee resource group puts on, and share your personal experience. At your organization's next recruiting event, talk with potential employees about your experiences as an LGBTQIA+ leader, and parent. Tell the daycare director that you stand ready to help welcome new families. Be visible, and set an example. Think of what help, advice, and support you would have liked, and could have used at the beginning of your journey—and then provide it to others.

A New Template, All Our Own

You've reached the end of *Workparent*—and maybe of your working-parent journey. And if you've taken nothing else away from this book, I hope you've taken away this:

Becoming a successful and satisfied working parent is fundamentally tough *and* it is fundamentally possible. With the right information and insights, surrounded by other working parents who understand and support you, filled with a sense of purpose, and trusting in your own good instincts, you can do this. You can earn a living and build your career while being a wonderful mother or father—and you can remain yourself in the process.

As your coach, I've pushed you to take this core message on board as you try out new behaviors and ways of thinking. In each chapter, I asked you to *consider, reflect, play through,* and *imagine* how various aspects of your professional life, parenting, and relationships (including your relationship with yourself) could work differently and better. My essential goal has been to expand your sense of possibility and confidence about combining career and children—to stretch the Workparent Template you started with out across a larger, more flexible frame. Now, in that same vein, let's do one final task together.

I want you to take a good deep breath and *imagine* many years forward, to when your child—the one whose arrival may have prompted you to pick up this book in the first place—is an independent adult with a career. Let that movie play for a minute. Allow yourself to savor the thought of your child all grown up, working hard, contributing his or her particular talents out there in the world, still young but at the very top of the game.

Then, and as much of a leap as this will be, imagine even further forward, to the happy day when that same child calls to tell you that they're expecting a child of their own. Play that moment through in your mind. Think how you'll receive the news: with joy, of course, and mild disbelief. (*Wait, what? I'm going to be a grandparent?!*)

Imagine, though, that what you don't feel is any concern. You're not worried at all about how becoming a parent will affect your child's career, or sense of self. You have zero fears about his or her ability to be a parent, live a healthy and full life, and do good work all at the same time. This kid grew up with the benefit of your example, after all—and since earliest childhood saw how authentic, self-assured workparenting is done. And if you made mistakes or had moments of self-doubt along the way, so what? Working parenthood is so normalized and accepted now, so celebrated. Your child will have many role models to learn from and peers to turn to for advice. And there won't be any stress around announcing the news at work, or negotiating leave, or finding care, or paying for it, or creating a workable schedule, because in the years since you had to do all those things yourself, the world changed. These days there's plenty of support—practical, personal, and professional—for any mother or father who needs it. Finding daycare is straightforward; in even the most intense workplaces no one bats an eye when a colleague has to spend a few hours on family obligations; and it's unimaginable that anybody would question your child's loyalty or commitment to work just because they have kids.

You and your fellow workparents saw to that. Because of your firm intentions, and the day-in, day-out example you set, and because of how you brought the topic of family needs right out into the open throughout society and in every workplace, things are different now. You created a whole new template in which *anyone* can become a successful and satisfied working parent—in which every person who wants to can join together what Sigmund Freud called the very "cornerstones of our humanness": love and work.

Imagine *that*.

Can you imagine anything better?

The Workparent Leader

This book focuses on the tools and mindset you yourself need to thrive as an individual working mother or father. But what if you want to help *other* workparents succeed? In this section, we'll look at specific, actionable ways to become a Workparent Leader: to set a better, more productive course for your organization, your working-parents network, and your team and colleagues, when it comes to combining children and career, both bigger-picture and day-to-day.

Depending on your organization's status quo, this may feel like bold stuff, but all of it's achievable, actionable. You won't need a big budget or team or special permission to get moving and have impact. We'll start at the top—with what more-seasoned and -senior leaders can do—and work our way down to the grassroots level where workparenting really happens.

Becoming a More Workparent-Friendly Organization

As a senior leader, or if you're running your own organization, you may feel in a bit of a bind. It may feel impossible to support working parents without distracting from, or even setting the business back in some way. Yet every organization, regardless of resources, can become more workparent-friendly by relying on the following moves. They're powerful, low-cost, low-drama, easy to implement—and they *work*.

Look to the facts

Before launching *any* support programs or special strategies for working parents, gather the relevant data: Where do parents sit within the organization? What are their attrition patterns? What insights can you gather from annual performance reviews or culture-survey data or simply from informal conversations? The answers, which should be the basis of your working-parent approach, may surprise you. Perhaps there's actually very low attrition immediately following parental leave, but a concerning, previously unseen pattern of departures twelve to eighteen months afterward, or perhaps some polling will reveal that the moms around you feel well supported but not the dads. If so, you may think about holding preemptive manager and HR check-ins six to nine months following parental leave, using the time to problem-solve work/life issues and discuss a range of career paths—or you may decide to sponsor a dedicated working-dads group. In other words, just as you would in any other work project, target the *actual* pain point, as opposed to the perceived or assumed one.

Define the demographic

Many organizations concentrate their working-parent efforts on newer biological mothers. To be 100 percent, crystal clear here: expectant and new moms are a vitally important group, and absolutely need and deserve your organization's support. But if *all* your programming centers on things like phaseback programs and lactation facilities, then you're addressing the "working-parent problem" too narrowly. Workparenting is an eighteen-year job, and it is done by both dads and moms, biological and adoptive, gay and straight, and in all kinds of family structures. Aligning your organization's programs accordingly—for example, by offering parental leave, and phaseback, *and* encouraging *all* employees to use existing personal days for family-care needs—helps target the issue in its broader-spectrum reality, and it sends a more inclusive, talent-focused message.

Focus the specific resources you *do* have on key transition points

As in any relay race, working parenthood depends on the ability to successfully navigate transition points—the hand-offs, the turns. Coming back from leave, welcoming a second or third child, or accepting a change in role or schedule are just a few of the transition points that can derail or strain the most competent working parent. That's why concentrating benefits and programming on these critical points can yield significant return on investment. Make sure that peer-to-peer parent-mentoring program you just launched scoops up all the parents back from their *second* parental leave, for example—or make certain that your new-manager training program covers how to take on time-consuming people-management responsibilities when you're also busy at home. If you can ease those pivots, you can keep your workparent employees more focused and engaged in the moment, and over the long haul.

Become a market maker

Leverage your organization's existing infrastructure to connect working parents and to make some of the practical aspects of parenting easier. Put up an intranet page, open a messaging channel, or even just mount a bulletin board in the cafeteria, allowing any employees to trade tips and leads on childcare or to pass hand-me-down baby and child gear on to their colleagues. You'll have just created a more collaborative culture *and* allowed employees to spend less time worrying about and solving practical parenting problems.

Acknowledge and foster peer-to-peer learning

When working parents need advice or motivation, they turn to the real experts: their respected colleagues and mentors, people they trust who understand the politics and culture inside the organization. Providing basic guidance, even simple talking points, to these internal "peer coaches" enables them to deliver the right messages when it matters.

Prepare managers to lead the charge

An employee's day-to-day experience—and desire to remain in the organization—is shaped by his or her direct manager, not by company policies or what's included in the employee handbook. So equip your frontline managers, particularly new ones, to connect with and get the best from working-parent talent, without huge efforts or time. Lay out general guidelines as to how managers should handle parental leaves and requests for flexibility (ongoing or situational), educate them on the benefits and programs available for working-parent team members, and encourage them to convey their support for employees' lives outside of work.

Advertise resources already in place—and destigmatize their use

Many corporations already have significant employee resources in place—employee-assistance programs, counseling benefits, human resources staffers trained in coaching and employee support. Yet most employees don't know such benefits exist, don't know how to access them, or are certain that access comes with professional or personal consequence (cost, judgments from peers, resulting embarrassment, etc.). Smart companies make existing benefits visible and accessible to all. Don't just *offer* resources—help your people easily reach them.

Talk about it from the top

The coronavirus pandemic cast a new and glaring spotlight on the challenges of working parenthood—just as those challenges ratcheted up enormously. Yet what many working mothers and father heard from their organizations' seniormost leaders throughout that period was . . . silence. The crisis was complex, and leaders were busy, in many cases trying to ensure that the organization remained viable. Nobody had ill intent. But in that silence, many working parents heard an unintentional message that "we don't see, or care, what you're going through."

Just as your organization likely has carefully considered, consistent messages on its commitment to clients, on diversity, on environmental impact, and so forth, it should have a clear message to working parents as well. And you should use that message in your communications with employees: include it in the annual benefits materials and reiterate it when addressing employees at the quarterly town hall. And then use it externally, too: post it on your website and talk about it at recruiting events. You don't have to promise working parents the world, but it's in your organization's best interests to acknowledge their challenges and contributions, and to show that you're awake and aware of the problem. Don't be the company or leader who "doesn't care."

Setting Up a Working-Parents Network in Your Community or Organization

As we explored right off in chapter 1, working-parent employee networks (also called "affinity networks" or "employee-resource groups"; ERGs, for short) are one powerful vehicle for helping working parents to feel connected, supported, and empowered throughout their entire working-parent journey. The good news is that in recent years, these groups have proliferated. In fact, it's increasingly unusual for any established organization *not* to have some kind of working-parent employee hub.

The bad news is that if you're steering that group yourself, or trying to get one off the ground, you probably have the disconcerting feeling of working without a playbook. What's the best way to get started? Gain traction? Provide real value? The specific answers will be unique to your organization, but these overall guidelines can only help turn your fledgling working-parents network or ERG into a real asset—one that benefits individual members as well as your community or organization as a whole.

Build up from what works

Don't spend time intuiting and hypothesizing what the network should do; *scale up what's already working*. Every organization—whether that's a company, a church, a campus, or a community center—has an existing working-parent network: organic and unseen, perhaps, but functional.

Maybe there's an email chain through which new parents swap gently used baby gear, or a few people with reputations as "on top of it" parents have ended up mentoring and informally coaching a disproportionate number of the fellow parents around them. In identifying these kinds of under-the-radar influences and peer-to-peer relationships, you'll discover a lot about what prospective members want and need, how those needs can be met, and who can help meet them. It helps you build an agenda you know will work, because it already has. Now try making that email chain an organized distribution, available to all working moms and dads throughout the company, or rope in one of those de facto expert parents as the featured speaker at a network event. Think of yourself, and the group, as an *amplifier*.

Be assertively inclusive

Working parents come in all packages. They're male, female, biological, adoptive, gay, straight, from every conceivable background, and from all parts and levels of the organization or community. As network lead, it's your job to make sure that every single one of those parents gets the message, LOUD AND CLEAR, that "You are welcome here. This is for *you*." Start by ensuring that the group's leadership is demonstrably diverse; prospective members will want to "see themselves" in the network's composition. Make sure also to keep communications demographically neutral: in emails, for example, specify that "this group/seminar is open to *every* interested working parent at [organization/community name]." And don't be afraid to get personal: tell that single, adoptive dad that the door is open, and that you'd love to have him join you at the group's next meeting. Remember: the broader and deeper your network is, the more durable it will be. If you're concerned about aligning the group's work to specific parenting concerns—like lactation, or fatherhood, or parenting teenagers—that's fine; you can always organize special-interest events and subgroups.

Align it to your organization or community's mission and DNA

At one leading law firm, the working-parent affinity network features seminars on how to navigate legal issues important to new parents, like drafting a will. At a leading US cancer-treatment and -research center, the working-parents ERG was founded with a mission "to improve conditions for the working parent"—just as the mission of the center itself is to improve conditions for everyone affected by cancer. In these organizations, the working-parent groups feel like natural and essential outgrowths of core operations. They're easy for working parents to align themselves to and—just as important—for senior stakeholders to get on board with.

Keep your figureheads relatable

In an effort to generate maximum visibility and "street cred" for a new network, you may have enlisted a working mother or father at the very top of the organization to serve as the public face of the effort, or to speak at an early event. But if that person makes an enormous amount of money, doesn't spend much time with new parents, has a large in-office team, and/or openly discusses the copious amount of help he or she has at home, that person is going to be hard for mothers and fathers in general, and particularly ones without those resources or advantages, to identify with. Try tapping a broader pool of sponsors and speakers, ones who can address the day-to-day challenges most of your fellow parents are living. If you are fortunate enough to have the advantage of a C-suite or celebrity supporter, help sensitize him or her to what's *really* on other parents' minds: finding good daycare, being able to work flexibly when their children are sick, figuring out how to save for the future, and so on.

Have a curriculum—one that puts parents in control

At the network's outset, and at the beginning of each year following, have a clear view of what you want members to learn—and be able to do for themselves. Whether it's to "better manage time," "find greater flexibility," or any other key working-parent skill, organize your events and programming around teaching it. Without that narrative thread, the network's activities risk becoming disjointed and having less stickiness; you may end up with a grab bag of events and messages, each of which may have seemed like a good idea at the time, but which together don't provide the punch of a more curated, tapered effort.

Use "friends of" as your faculty

The best way to create a rich and relevant curriculum on a limited budget? Use resources on hand. Have a member with a finance background lead a seminar on tax-law changes that affect working parents, or on how to set up a college savings account. Ask someone who works in IT to do a session on "the best apps and tech hacks for parents and caregivers." Or host a panel of recently-returned-from-leave parents to talk about the experience with expectant moms and dads. Scope the range and depth of expertise around you and bring it to bear for your membership. Cheap, easy, effective.

Stay in the Solutions Frame

Working parenthood can be overwhelming, and it's a natural tendency for working mothers and fathers to connect over—and take comfort in—comparing (copious) notes about challenges and pain points: exhaustion, difficulties with their kids' schools, long to-do lists, lack of flexibility. But as network lead, you need to help move people *forward*: to help them find the ways to cope, to effectively manage through what they're facing, and to feel more empowered and positive while doing it. In other words, your job is to keep the network events, dialogue, and members in the Solutions Frame. Do so by focusing group discussions—whether in person or online—around approaches, hacks, and fixes. Start a network email thread on "best advice for back-to-school season," or organize a group discussion on "effective ways to talk to your boss about flexibility." You'll be unearthing specific, actionable advice that helps fellow parents find new ways to handle common challenges.

Use it to help shine light on other resources and benefits

It may be HR's job to provide and manage your organization's benefits offerings—parental leave, flexibility programs, family healthcare plans, and the like—but the network can help keep those benefits accessible and top-of-mind. Lucky enough to have corporate backup daycare? Organize a tour of the center your company has contracted with: have parents meet the care providers, help them with the enrollment paperwork, and walk them through what the drop-off process looks like. Educate, disseminate, inform.

Keep all events on "working-parent time"

Make gatherings short, and if possible, hold them outside of the morning and evening working-parent crunch times; the thirty-minute brown-bag lunch or the group video call held after the kids go to bed can be your most powerful formats. And *always* distribute summary notes to those who couldn't make it or had to leave early. (Remember, the network is about working parents giving each other a hand.)

Be bold

Maybe your organization has few working parents and you're breaking entirely new ground in forming this group. Who cares? It doesn't matter if you're not the most senior or experienced professional or parent. You're doing something deeply important here, which benefits the entire organization. Don't be afraid to be entrepreneurial, to step up, and to forge connections with colleagues and community members you wouldn't otherwise. Mothers and fathers trying to combine children and career need to feel both in control and supported— and with some advance planning and the right approach, you can create a group that will help get them there.

Managing Workparents, Day to Day

As a manager, *you* cast the long shadow. *You* have more impact on your people's experiences than anything else. So how to make that impact a positive one for working parents? Whether you work inside an organization that's wildly supportive of family responsibilities or one that has had a mixed record, here are a few critical ways to keep working moms and dads productive, motivated—and on your team for the longer term.

Set a visible example

No program or policy will ever be as effective in supporting and motivating working parents as the day-in, day-out examples of leaders who are balancing professional commitments and family. If you keep current photos of your children at your desk, or visible in the background on videoconferences; visibly flex your schedule once in a while for your child's school play or sports game; and with a sympathetic, laughing roll of the eyes occasionally refer to the evening of homework-checking you face—all while projecting an upbeat, can-do attitude about work— it sends a powerful message: *I'm combining career and family, and you can, too.* In other words, make certain you're modeling and permissioning the behavior and feelings you want to see in others. If you don't have kids, the same approach still works: just display and talk about whatever's important to you personally, whether that's time with your nieces, marathon training, or gourmet cookery.

Make vacation nonnegotiable

Has every single one of your people taken his or her allotted vacation in the past year? Does anyone have significant accumulated rollover days? Who—and why? How many of them are working parents, or have other significant outside responsibilities? Type A professionals working in high-performance organizations often, even in the absence of direct pressure to do so, voluntarily bypass holidays and time off. Among working parents, this practice is particularly dangerous, as it easily leads to burnout, family issues, performance decline, attrition, or all of the above. Figure out appropriate ways to signal to your employees that it's time to take a break, and remember that having your people use their *existing* benefits is easier and more powerful than adding any special or additional "work/life" programs—and *much* easier than recruiting new talent.

Get (a little more) personal

You may tend to shy away from anything other than completely professional conversations for fear of being inappropriate. And many employees, particularly if working in a pressured environment, may hesitate to discuss personal issues with their manager for fear of seeming unambitious or unfocused. Unfortunately, what starts out as well-intentioned on both sides quickly results in a managerial stalemate:

because there's no open dialogue, no coaching or mentoring is possible. You can, however, open the door to genuine discussions on work-parenting issues in an appropriate, constructive way. To do so, simply pose neutral, open-ended questions. For example, at performance-review time, ask, "Are there any other career concerns you want to discuss that I may not be aware of?" This signals that you're open to a conversation. Or on Monday morning, ask, "How were the kids this weekend?" This normalizes discussion of family within your team environment. An employee who can raise difficult issues with you and who feels whole and authentic at work is less likely to look for other professional options.

Categorize your communications

Mitigate work/life strain and an "always on" culture by categorizing your communications, particularly the ones you send outside regular business hours. Consider attaching a priority headline to each message: "Not urgent," "For Monday," "FYI Only," "Need Response Today." These simple labels let employees easily sort through what needs to be done ASAP and what can wait until after the recital, or the weekend. It lets them relax, and focus on what's important outside of work—with no dent to your team's productivity.

See the calendar from a parent's perspective

The 8:00 a.m. meetings and after-work drinks you may feel are essential to the team's performance and morale are likely to do a number on any working parent, for whom morning and evening care-transition times are the most complicated and stressful. Consider using the Core Day strategy instead: set a portion of each workday (for example, 9:30 a.m. to 4:00 p.m.) as nonnegotiable, "I expect you to be at work and productive" hours, with any meetings or obligations outside of that scheduled only on an as-needed basis. For team-building events, vary your times: hold after-work drinks one month, a team lunch the next, the all-hands videoconference in the early morning this time and later in the evening (after bedtimes) the next.

Have a parental-leave game plan

Don't wait for an employee to announce he or she is expecting before you come up with a supportive response—know what you'll say, and rehearse it. And while that employee is out on leave, don't just hope he or she will be coming back—or assume that the details of when and how you'll communicate during the employee's absence will sort themselves out. As with any other important managerial matter: have a plan.

RESEARCH NOTE: LEARNING FROM WORKING PARENTS

Workparent is based on the expertise I developed over many years in human capital roles; my extensive work as an executive coach; my own lived experience as a working parent, confronting the same issues and challenges that you and other workparents do; and, importantly, on the insights, advice, encouragement, and example of a great many fellow working mothers and fathers. Over the past decade I've had the privilege of connecting with and listening to thousands, and the inspiring view I've taken away from all those interactions as to what working parenthood *is*, *means*, and *can be* is exactly what I've tried to capture in this book.

Those interactions came about in a great many different ways. I've spoken with workparents inside and at the fringes of my own personal and professional networks; spent time one-on-one with hundreds of coaching clients; received messages full of advice, ideas, and feedback from readers of my *Harvard Business Review* articles; discussed "what works" with attendees of my in-person and online workshops (and during the online ones, seen a treasure trove of questions, stories, and tips pop up in the chat and Q&A boxes); and collected material from the many working parents who've gotten in touch through the Workparent website. I've also reached out directly to working mothers and fathers who've taken public or leadership stances on the issue—as heads of their organizations' working-parent ERGs, for example—as well as worked with and through corporations, civic and charitable organizations, and grassroots community groups to find even more parents willing to share observations, advice, and encouragement. Three important "red threads" ran through this research and advice gathering (a process, I will add, that continued throughout the work-parenting crisis triggered by the Covid-19 pandemic, and that I'm still actively engaged in today).

The first red thread was what social scientists call an *ethnographic* approach. That means that my goal was to understand the real, lived, and individual experience of working parenthood from each partic-ular workparent's perspective—situationally, in context, and without judgment. To do so, I turned to the inquiry skills and interviewing tactics I'd honed throughout my time in the human capital field and as a longtime business writer specializing in personal leadership nar-rative. I kept my questions few and open ended, and began most con-versations by asking some version of "Tell me about yourself, your work, and your family." My most common follow-ups included "How so?" "Tell me more," "What's that like?" "What's your best advice on . . . ?" and "What works?"

Which brings me to the second red thread, which early on in my business career I was taught to think of as a *bias to action*. In other words, I wanted to understand what working parents actually *do* to bridge their professional and personal commitments . . . that you and I can do also. What were these parents' moves, habits, life hacks? What effective, *That-could-work-for-me-too!* techniques had these vet-eran workparents used and honed over time? When I stepped into the workparent field, those were the specific grains I was looking to harvest.

The third red thread was *breadth*—of experience, circumstances, and perspective. As I've said multiple times and in many ways throughout this book, workparents come in all packages, and there's an enormous amount we can learn from each other precisely because of those differences. I therefore deliberately spoke to parents with different backgrounds, beliefs, ambitions, and life situations and in different regions, fields, job types, family structures, and phases of parenting. It was a wonderfully nonlinear, iterative process: if I heard *x* piece of time-management advice from the mother of a tod-dler who had a formal flexible work arrangement, for example, I then spoke to fathers, traditional schedule holders, shift workers, and parents of older children to see what their time-management techniques were. In my view, there were no right or wrong answers, but this three-dimensional, nonjudgmental, compare-and-contrast, sift-and-sort process allowed me to push the boundaries of acknowledged working-parent approaches and develop a more complete, detailed and options-rich picture.

Throughout these pages, you'll see direct quotes from many working mothers and fathers who generously agreed to be interviewed for this book and to be cited here. Their voices are their own; I changed wording only with their explicit permission and for purposes of brevity and clarity. For privacy reasons, several asked me to change small personal details, including their names or number of children. Note that because I used the specific job identifier each parent preferred, there is some variation in their type: general function and role terms like "physician" or "chef" appear, as do descriptive labels like "co-founder," compound titles (such as ". . . and entrepreneur"), and specific organizational titles like "project leader" or "VP."

While the sheer amount of time I've spent talking to working parents is unique, the methods I've described here aren't. I encourage you to take this approach and adapt it for yourself in the way most comfortable and feasible for you. In just a few minutes at a time and with some good questions at the ready, you can connect with workparents both similar and very different from you and pick up new tools throughout your workparent experience—and feel supported and motivated as you do.

INDEX

ACKNOWLEDGMENTS

Over the past five years, while imagining, researching, and writing *Workparent*, I was fortunate to receive help, advice, support, and encouragement from many people and organizations. If I named them all here, I'm afraid the list would be longer than this book itself, but I am deeply grateful to each and every one. I offer special thanks to:

- My friends Richard Linder and Seneca Mudd, who sensed potential in my idea for a complete, inclusive how-to book for working parents and pushed me to spend that weekend at the whiteboard, mapping *Workparent* out.

- My agent at Writers House, Lisa DiMona, who since our very first phone call believed in this book and who has been a brilliant publishing-world guide, adviser, and supporter every step of the way, from concept to final manuscript. Also at Writers House, Nora Long and Lauren Carsley provided wonderful assistance throughout the writing and publishing process.

- Melinda Merino, for keeping me in the *Harvard Business Review* fold, for giving me the opportunity to write about working mothers and fathers for HBR.org, and then for greenlighting *Workparent*. Melinda, thank you so very much for your sponsorship, support, and belief in this idea.

- The incredibly talented editorial, creative, production, and publicity staff at Harvard Business Review Press, including

Julie Devoll, Lindsey Dietrich, Stephani Finks, Kelsey Gripenstraw, Alexandra Kephart, Amy Poftak, Jon Shipley, Felicia Sinusas, Jennifer Waring, and Alicyn Zall. I also send heartfelt thanks to the many other wonderful team members at HBR who I've had the privilege of working with on various other working-parent-related publications.

- Lydia Yadi and the team at Penguin Business. Lydia, the thoughtful questions you asked at the very beginning of the writing process fundamentally shaped *Workparent*. Your encouragement helped keep me motivated and on task (even while workparenting amid the pandemic!) and your keen observations and edits helped make this book both better and more inclusive. I am in your debt. Thank you.

- The countless hardworking parents who so thoughtfully shared their experiences and insights with me both before and during the writing of this book—and continue to do so today.

- The many and varied organizations that, throughout the course of my research, graciously connected me with individual employees, contacts, and affiliates willing to "talk working parent." I send particular thanks to: Bain & Company, Harvard Law Couples and Families Association, Kimberly-Clark, London Fire Brigade, National Young Farmers Coalition, On Site Opera, Oscar Health, Inc., The Port Authority of New York and New Jersey, and The Riverside Company.

- My editor at the Press, Kevin Evers. Kevin, I'm not certain what to say here, because no matter what I write you'll only edit the sentence so that it's three times better than the original, and then I'll not only have to change what I've written but begrudgingly admit that you were right *again*. So I'll just say this: I couldn't ask for a better boss. This book wouldn't have happened without your perseverance, feedback, good humor, high standards, and unbelievable editorial eye, not to mention your own working-dad insights and commitment. Thank you.

- Each of the working moms and dads who, over the course of my own life, I've had the opportunity to observe, listen to, and take advice and inspiration from: the family members, teachers, mentors, colleagues, clients, and friends who helped shape my own workparent template.

- Finally, and most importantly, to my home team: L, P, and M, the awesomest fellow workparent and two kids I can imagine. You're why I workparent—and, despite the pressures and stresses that it can bring, why I love it and feel lucky to do so. Thank you for the endless patience you've shown and the support you've given while Mom's been writing this book. *Je vous aime.*